HISTORY OF THE COMMUNIST PARTY
OF THE SOVIET UNION
(*Bolsheviks*)

HISTORY

OF THE

COMMUNIST PARTY

OF THE

SOVIET UNION

(BOLSHEVIKS)

Short Course

EDITED BY A COMMISSION OF THE
CENTRAL COMMITTEE OF THE C.P.S.U.(B.)

AUTHORIZED BY THE CENTRAL COMMITTEE
OF THE C.P.S.U.(B.)

INTERNATIONAL PUBLISHERS, NEW YORK

ISBN10: 0-7178-0788-6   ISBN13: 978-0-7178-0788-8

Printed in the U. S. A.

This Printing 2020

Cover image from the oil painting, "The Bolshevik" by Boris Kustodiev, 1920

CONTENTS

Chapter Three

THE MENSHEVIKS AND THE BOLSHEVIKS IN THE PERIOD OF THE RUSSO-JAPANESE WAR AND THE FIRST RUSSIAN REVOLUTION

(1904-1907)

Chapter Four

Chapter Five

Chapter Six

Chapter Seven

THE BOLSHEVIK PARTY IN THE PERIOD OF PREPARATION AND REALIZATION OF THE OCTOBER SOCIALIST REVOLUTION
(April 1917-1918)

Chapter Eight

THE BOLSHEVIK PARTY IN THE PERIOD OF FOREIGN MILITARY INTERVENTION AND CIVIL WAR
(1918-1920)

Chapter Nine

THE BOLSHEVIK PARTY IN THE PERIOD OF TRANSITION TO THE PEACEFUL WORK OF ECONOMIC RESTORATION
(1921-1925)

Chapter Ten

THE BOLSHEVIK PARTY IN THE STRUGGLE FOR THE SOCIALIST INDUSTRIALIZATION OF THE COUNTRY

(1926-1929)

Chapter Eleven

THE BOLSHEVIK PARTY IN THE STRUGGLE FOR THE COLLECTIVIZATION OF AGRICULTURE

(1930-1934)

Chapter Twelve

THE BOLSHEVIK PARTY IN THE STRUGGLE TO COMPLETE THE
BUILDING OF THE SOCIALIST SOCIETY. INTRODUCTION
OF THE NEW CONSTITUTION

(1935-1937)

HISTORY OF THE COMMUNIST PARTY
OF THE SOVIET UNION
(*Bolsheviks*)

INTRODUCTION

The Communist Party of the Soviet Union (Bolsheviks) has traversed a long and glorious road, leading from the first tiny Marxist circles and groups that appeared in Russia in the eighties of the past century to the great Party of the Bolsheviks, which now directs the first Socialist State of Workers and Peasants in the world.

The C.P.S.U.(B.) grew up on the basis of the working-class movement in pre-revolutionary Russia; it sprang from the Marxist circles and groups which had established connection with the working-class movement and imparted to it a Socialist consciousness. The C.P.S.U.(B.) has always been guided by the revolutionary teachings of Marxism-Leninism. In the new conditions of the era of imperialism, imperialist wars and proletarian revolutions, its leaders further developed the teachings of Marx and Engels and raised them to a new level.

The C.P.S.U.(B.) grew and gained strength in a fight over fundamental principles waged against the petty-bourgeois parties within the working-class movement—the Socialist-Revolutionaries (and earlier still, against their predecessors, the Narodniks), the Mensheviks, Anarchists and bourgeois nationalists of all shades—and, within the Party itself, against the Menshevik, opportunist trends—the Trotskyites, Bukharinites, nationalist deviators and other anti-Leninist groups.

The C.P.S.U.(B.) gained strength and became tempered in the revolutionary struggle against all enemies of the working class and of all working people—against landlords, capitalists, kulaks, wreckers, spies, against all the hirelings of the surrounding capitalist states.

The history of the C.P.S.U.(B.) is the history of three revolutions: the bourgeois-democratic revolution of 1905, the bourgeois-democratic revolution of February 1917, and the Socialist revolution of October 1917.

The history of the C.P.S.U.(B.) is the history of the overthrow of tsardom, of the overthrow of the power of the landlords and capitalists; it is the history of the rout of the armed foreign intervention during the Civil War; it is the history of the building of the Soviet state and of Socialist society in our country.

The study of the history of the C.P.S.U.(B.) enriches us with the experience of the fight for Socialism waged by the workers and peasants of our country.

The study of the history of the C.P.S.U.(B.), the history of the struggle of our Party against all enemies of Marxism-Leninism, against all enemies of the working people, helps us to *master Bolshevism* and sharpens our political vigilance.

The study of the heroic history of the Bolshevik Party arms us with a knowledge of the laws of social development and of the political struggle, with a knowledge of the motive forces of revolution.

The study of the history of the C.P.S.U.(B.) strengthens our certainty of the ultimate victory of the great cause of the Party of Lenin-Stalin, the victory of Communism throughout the world.

This book sets forth briefly the history of the Communist Party of the Soviet Union (Bolsheviks).

CHAPTER ONE

THE STRUGGLE FOR THE CREATION OF A SOCIAL-DEMOCRATIC LABOUR PARTY IN RUSSIA
(1883-1901)

1. ABOLITION OF SERFDOM AND THE DEVELOPMENT OF INDUS-
TRIAL CAPITALISM IN RUSSIA. RISE OF THE MODERN IN-
DUSTRIAL PROLETARIAT. FIRST STEPS OF THE WORKING-CLASS
MOVEMENT

Tsarist Russia entered the path of capitalist development later than other countries. Prior to the sixties of the past century there were very few mills and factories in Russia. Manorial estates based on serfdom constituted the prevailing form of economy. There could be no real development of industry under serfdom. The involuntary labour of the serfs in agriculture was of low productivity. The whole course of economic development made the abolition of serfdom imperative. In 1861, the tsarist government, weakened by defeat in the Crimean War, and frightened by the peasant revolts against the landlords, was compelled to abolish serfdom.

But even after serfdom had been abolished the landlords continued to oppress the peasants. In the process of "emancipation" they robbed the peasants by inclosing, cutting off, considerable portions of the land previously used by the peasants. These cut-off portions of land were called by the peasants *otrezki* (cuts). The peasants were compelled to pay about 2,000,000,000 rubles to the landlords as the redemption price for their "emancipation."

After serfdom had been abolished the peasants were obliged to rent land from the landlords on most onerous terms. In addition to paying money rent, the peasants were often compelled by the landlord to cultivate without remuneration a definite portion of his land with their own implements and horses. This was called *otrabotki* or *barshchina* (labour rent, corvée). In most cases the peasants were obliged to pay the landlords rent in kind in the amount of one-half of their harvests. This was known as *ispolu* (half and half system).

Thus the situation remained almost the same as it had been under serfdom, the only difference being that the peasant was now personally free, could not be bought and sold like a chattel.

The landlords bled the backward peasant farms white by various methods of extortion (rent, fines). Owing to the oppression of the landlords the bulk of the peasantry were unable to improve their farms. Hence the extreme backwardness of agriculture in pre-revolutionary Russia, which led to frequent crop failures and famines.

The survivals of serfdom, crushing taxation and the redemption payments to the landlords, which not infrequently exceeded the income of the peasant household, ruined the peasants, reduced them to pauperism and forced them to quit their villages in search of a livelihood. They went to work in the mills and factories. This was a source of cheap labour power for the manufacturers.

Over the workers and peasants stood a veritable army of sheriffs, deputy sheriffs, gendarmes, constables, rural police, who protected the tsar, the capitalists and the landlords from the toiling and exploited people. Corporal punishment existed right up to 1903. Although serfdom had been abolished the peasants were flogged for the slightest offence and for the non-payment of taxes. Workers were manhandled by the police and the Cossacks, especially during strikes, when the workers downed tools because their lives had been made intolerable by the manufacturers. Under the tsars the workers and peasants had no political rights whatever. The tsarist autocracy was the worst enemy of the people.

Tsarist Russia was a prison of nations. The numerous non-Russian nationalities were entirely devoid of rights and were subjected to constant insult and humiliation of every kind. The tsarist government taught the Russian population to look down upon the native peoples of the national regions as an inferior race, officially referred to them as *inorodtsi* (aliens), and fostered contempt and hatred of them. The tsarist government deliberately fanned national discord, instigated one nation against another, engineered Jewish pogroms and, in Transcaucasia, incited Tatars and Armenians to massacre each other.

Nearly all, if not all, government posts in the national regions were held by Russian officials. All business in government institutions and in the courts was conducted in the Russian language. It was forbidden to publish newspapers and books in the languages of the non-Russian nationalities or to teach in the schools in the native tongue. The tsarist government strove to extinguish every spark of national culture and pursued a policy of forcible "Russification." Tsardom was a hangman and torturer of the non-Russian peoples.

After the abolition of serfdom, the development of industrial capitalism in Russia proceeded at a fairly rapid pace in spite of the fact that it was still hampered by survivals of serfdom. During the twenty-five years, 1865-90, the number of workers employed in large mills and factories and on the railways increased from 706,000 to 1,433,000, or more than doubled.

Large-scale capitalist industry in Russia began to develop even more rapidly in the nineties. By the end of that decade the number of workers employed in the large mills and factories, in the mining industry and on the railways amounted in the fifty European provinces of Russia alone to 2,207,000, and in the whole of Russia to 2,792,000 persons.

This was a modern industrial proletariat, radically different from the workers employed in the factories of the period of serfdom and from the workers in small, handicraft and other kinds of industry, both because of the spirit of solidarity prevailing among the workers in big capitalist enterprises and because of their militant revolutionary qualities.

The industrial boom of the nineties was chiefly due to intensive railroad construction. During the course of the decade (1890-1900) over 21,000 versts of new railway line were laid. The railways created a big demand for metal (for rails, locomotives and cars), and also for increasing quantities of fuel—coal and oil. This led to the development of the metal and fuel industries.

In pre-revolutionary Russia, as in all capitalist countries, periods of industrial boom alternated with industrial crises, stagnation, which severely affected the working class and condemned hundreds of thousands of workers to unemployment and poverty.

Although the development of capitalism in Russia proceeded fairly rapidly after the abolition of serfdom, nevertheless, in economic development Russia lagged considerably behind other capitalist countries. The vast majority of the population was still engaged in agriculture. In his celebrated work, *The Development of Capitalism in Russia*, Lenin cited significant figures from the general census of the population of 1897 which showed that about five-sixths of the total population were engaged in agriculture, and only one-sixth in large and small industry, trade, on the railways and waterways, in building work, lumbering, and so on.

This shows that although capitalism was developing in Russia, she was still an agrarian, economically backward country, a petty-bourgeois country, that is, a country in which low-productive individual peasant farming based on small ownership still predominated.

Capitalism was developing not only in the towns but also in the countryside. The peasantry, the most numerous class in pre-revolutionary Russia, was undergoing a process of disintegration, of cleavage.

From among the more well-to-do peasants there was emerging an upper layer of kulaks, the rural bourgeoisie, while on the other hand many peasants were being ruined, and the number of poor peasants, rural proletarians and semi-proletarians, was on the increase. As to the middle peasants, their number decreased from year to year.

In 1903 there were about ten million peasant households in Russia. In his pamphlet entitled *To the Village Poor*, Lenin calculated that of this total not less than three and a half million households consisted of peasants *possessing no horses*. These were the poorest peasants who usually sowed only a small part of their land, leased the rest to the kulaks, and themselves left to seek other sources of livelihood. The position of these peasants came nearest to that of the proletariat. Lenin called them rural proletarians or semi-proletarians.

On the other hand, one and a half million rich, kulak households (out of a total of ten million peasant households) concentrated in their hands half the total sown area of the peasants. This peasant bourgeoisie was growing rich by grinding down the poor and middle peasantry and profiting from the toil of agricultural labourers, and was developing into rural capitalists.

The working class of Russia began to awaken already in the seventies, and especially in the eighties, and started a struggle against the capitalists. Exceedingly hard was the lot of the workers in tsarist Russia. In the eighties the working day in the mills and factories was not less than 12½ hours, and in the textile industry reached 14 to 15 hours. The exploitation of female and child labour was widely resorted to. Children worked the same hours as adults, but, like the women, received a much smaller wage. Wages were inordinately low. The majority of the workers were paid seven or eight rubles per month. The most highly paid workers in the metal works and foundries received no more than 35 rubles per month. There were no regulations for the protection of labour, with the result that workers were maimed and killed in large numbers. Workers were not insured, and all medical services had to be paid for. Housing conditions were appalling. In the factory-owned barracks, workers were crowded as many as 10 or 12 to a small "cell." In paying wages, the manufacturers often cheated the workers, compelled them to make their purchases in the factory-owned shops at exorbitant prices, and mulcted them by means of fines.

The workers began to take a common stand and present joint demands to the factory owners for the improvement of their intolerable conditions. They would down tools and go on strike. The earlier strikes in the seventies and eighties were usually provoked by excessive fines, cheating and swindling of the workers over wages, and reductions in the rates of pay.

In the earlier strikes, the workers, driven to despair, would sometimes smash machinery, break factory windows and wreck factory-owned shops and factory offices.

The more advanced workers began to realize that if they were to be successful in their struggle against the capitalists, they needed organization. Workers' unions began to arise.

In 1875 the South Russian Workers' Union was formed in Odessa. This first workers' organization lasted eight or nine months and was then smashed by the tsarist government.

In 1878 the Northern Union of Russian Workers was formed in St. Petersburg, headed by Khalturin, a carpenter, and Obnorsky, a fitter. The program of the Union stated that its aims and objects were similar to those of the Social-Democratic labour parties of the West. The ultimate aim of the Union was to bring about a Socialist revolution—"the overthrow of the existing political and economic system, as an extremely unjust system." Obnorsky, one of the founders of the Union, had lived abroad for some time and had there acquainted himself with the activities of the Marxist Social-Democratic parties and of the First International, which was directed by Marx. This circumstance left its impress on the program of the Northern Union of Russian Workers. The immediate aim of the Union was to win political liberty and political rights for the people (freedom of speech, press, assembly, etc.). The immediate demands also included a reduction of the working day.

The membership of the Union reached 200, and it had about as many sympathizers. It began to take part in workers' strikes, to lead them. The tsarist government smashed this workers' Union too.

But the working-class movement continued to grow, spreading from district to district. The eighties were marked by a large number of strikes. In the space of five years (1881-86) there were as many as 48 strikes involving 80,000 workers.

An exceptional part in the history of the revolutionary movement was played by the big strike that broke out at the Morozov mill in Orekhovo-Zuyevo in 1885.

About 8,000 workers were employed at this mill. Working conditions grew worse from day to day: there were five wage cuts between 1882 and 1884, and in the latter year rates were reduced by 25 per cent at one blow. In addition, Morozov, the manufacturer, tormented the workers with fines. It was revealed at the trial which followed the strike that of every ruble earned by the workers, from 30 to 50 kopeks went into the pocket of the manufacturer in the form of fines. The workers could not stand this robbery any longer and in January 1885 went out on strike. The strike had been organized beforehand. It was led by a politically advanced worker, Pyotr Moiseyenko, who had been a member of the Northern Union of Russian Workers and already had some revolutionary experience. On the eve of the strike Moiseyenko and others of the more class-conscious weavers drew up a number of demands for presentation to the mill owners; they were endorsed at a secret meeting of the workers. The chief demand was the abolition of the rapacious fines.

This strike was suppressed by armed force. Over 600 workers were arrested and scores of them committed for trial.

Similar strikes broke out in the mills of Ivanovo-Voznesensk in 1885.

In the following year the tsarist government was compelled by its fear of the growth of the working-class movement to promulgate a law on fines which provided that the proceeds from fines were not to go into the pockets of the manufacturers but were to be used for the needs of the workers themselves.

The Morozov and other strikes taught the workers that a great deal could be gained by organized struggle. The working-class movement began to produce capable leaders and organizers who staunchly championed the interests of the working class.

At the same time, on the basis of the growth of the working-class movement and under the influence of the working-class movement of Western Europe, the first Marxist organizations began to arise in Russia.

2. NARODISM (POPULISM) AND MARXISM IN RUSSIA. PLEKHANOV AND HIS "EMANCIPATION OF LABOUR" GROUP. PLEKHANOV'S FIGHT AGAINST NARODISM. SPREAD OF MARXISM IN RUSSIA

Prior to the appearance of the Marxist groups revolutionary work in Russia was carried on by the Narodniks (Populists), who were opponents of Marxism.

The first Russian Marxist group arose in 1883. This was the "Emancipation of Labour" group formed by G. V. Plekhanov abroad, in Geneva, where he had been obliged to take refuge from the persecution of the tsarist government for his revolutionary activities.

Previously Plekhanov had himself been a Narodnik. But having studied Marxism while abroad, he broke with Narodism and became an outstanding propagandist of Marxism.

The "Emancipation of Labour" group did a great deal to disseminate Marxism in Russia. They translated works of Marx and Engels into Russian—*The Communist Manifesto, Wage-Labour and Capital, Socialism, Utopian and Scientific*, etc.—had them printed abroad and circulated them secretly in Russia. Plekhanov, Zasulich, Axelrod and other members of this group also wrote a number of works explaining the teachings of Marx and Engels, the ideas of *scientific Socialism*.

Marx and Engels, the great teachers of the proletariat, were the first to explain that, contrary to the opinion of the utopian Socialists, Socialism was not the invention of dreamers (utopians), but the inevitable outcome of the development of modern capitalist society. They showed that the capitalist system would fall, just as serfdom had fallen, and that capitalism was creating its own gravediggers in the person of the proletariat. They showed that only the class struggle of the proletariat, only the victory of the proletariat over the bourgeoisie, would rid humanity of capitalism and exploitation.

Marx and Engels taught the proletariat to be conscious of its own strength, to be conscious of its class interests and to unite for a determined struggle against the bourgeoisie. Marx and Engels discovered the laws of development of capitalist society and proved scientifically that the development of capitalist society, and the class struggle going on within it, must inevitably lead to the fall of capitalism, to the victory of the proletariat, to the *dictatorship of the proletariat*.

Marx and Engels taught that it was impossible to get rid of the power of capital and to convert capitalist property into public property by peaceful means, and that the working class could achieve this only by revolutionary violence against the bourgeoisie, by *a proletarian revolution*, by establishing its own political rule—the dictatorship of the proletariat —which must crush the resistance of the exploiters and create a new, classless, Communist society.

Marx and Engels taught that the industrial proletariat is the most revolutionary and therefore the most advanced class in capitalist society, and that only a class like the proletariat could rally around itself all the forces discontented with capitalism and lead them in the storming of capitalism. But in order to vanquish the old world and create a new, classless society, the proletariat must have its own working-class party, which Marx and Engels called the Communist Party.

It was to the dissemination of the views of Marx and Engels that the first Russian Marxist group, Plekhanov's "Emancipation of Labour" group, devoted itself.

The "Emancipation of Labour" group raised the banner of Marxism in the Russian press abroad at a time when no Social-Democratic movement in Russia yet existed.   It was first necessary to prepare the theoretical, ideological ground for such a movement.   The chief ideological obstacle to the spread of Marxism and of the Social-Democratic movement was the Narodnik views which at that time prevailed among the advanced workers and the revolutionary-minded intelligentsia.

As capitalism developed in Russia the working class became a powerful and advanced force that was capable of waging an organized revolutionary struggle.   But the leading role of the working class was not understood by the Narodniks.   The Russian Narodniks erroneously held that the principal revolutionary force was not the working class, but the peasantry, and that the rule of the tsar and the landlords could be overthrown by means of peasant revolts alone.   The Narodniks did not know the working class and did not realize that the peasants alone were incapable of vanquishing tsardom and the landlords without an alliance with the working class and without its guidance.   The Narodniks did not understand that the working class was the most revolutionary and the most advanced class of society.

The Narodniks first endeavoured to rouse the peasants for a struggle against the tsarist government.   With this purpose in view, young revolutionary intellectuals donned peasant garb and flocked to the countryside—"to the people," as it used to be called.   Hence the term "Narodnik," from the word *narod*, the people.   But they found no backing among the peasantry, for they did not have a proper knowledge or understanding of the peasants either.   The majority of them were arrested by the police.   Thereupon the Narodniks decided to continue the struggle against the tsarist autocracy single-handed, without the people, and this led to even more serious mistakes.

A secret Narodnik society known as "Narodnaya Volya" ("People's Will") began to plot the assassination of the tsar.   On March 1, 1881, members of the "Narodnaya Volya" succeeded in killing Tsar Alexander II with a bomb.   But the people did not benefit from this in any way.   The assassination of individuals could not bring about the overthrow of the tsarist autocracy or the abolition of the landlord class.   The assassinated tsar was replaced by another, Alexander III, under whom the conditions of the workers and peasants became still worse.

The method of combating tsardom chosen by the Narodniks, namely, by the assassination of individuals, by individual terrorism, was wrong and detrimental to the revolution.   The policy of individual terrorism was based on the erroneous Narodnik theory of active "heroes" and a passive "mob," which awaited exploits from the "heroes."   This false theory maintained that it is only outstanding individuals who make history, while the masses, the people, the class, the "mob," as the Narodnik writers contemptuously called them, are incapable of conscious, organized activity and can only blindly follow the "heroes." For this reason the Narodniks abandoned mass revolutionary work among the peasantry and the working class and changed to individual terrorism. They induced one of the most prominent revolutionaries of the time, Stepan Khalturin, to give up his work of organizing a revolutionary workers' union and to devote himself entirely to terrorism.

By these assassinations of individual representatives of the class of exploiters, assassinations that were of no benefit to the revolution, the Narodniks diverted the attention of the working people from the struggle against that class as a whole. They hampered the development of the revolutionary initiative and activity of the working class and the peasantry.

The Narodniks prevented the working class from understanding its leading role in the revolution and retarded the creation of an independent party of the working class.

Although the Narodniks' secret organization had been smashed by the tsarist government, Narodnik views continued to persist for a long time among the revolutionary-minded intelligentsia. The surviving Narodniks stubbornly resisted the spread of Marxism in Russia and hampered the organization of the working class.

Marxism in Russia could therefore grow and gain strength only by combating Narodism.

The "Emancipation of Labour" group launched a fight against the erroneous views of the Narodniks and showed how greatly their views and methods of struggle were prejudicing the working-class movement.

In his writings directed against the Narodniks, Plekhanov showed that their views had nothing in common with scientific Socialism, even though they called themselves Socialists.

Plekhanov was the first to give a Marxist criticism of the erroneous views of the Narodniks. Delivering well-aimed blows at the Narodnik views, Plekhanov at the same time developed a brilliant defence of the Marxist views.

What were the major errors of the Narodniks which Plekhanov hammered at with such destructive effect?

First, the Narodniks asserted that capitalism was something "accidental" in Russia, that it would not develop, and that therefore the proletariat would not grow and develop either.

Secondly, the Narodniks did not regard the working class as the foremost class in the revolution. They dreamed of attaining Socialism without the proletariat. They considered that the principal revolutionary force was the peasantry—led by the intelligentsia—and the peasant commune, which they regarded as the embryo and foundation of Socialism.

Thirdly, the Narodniks' view of the whole course of human history was erroneous and harmful. They neither knew nor understood the laws of the economic and political development of society. In this respect they were quite backward. According to them, history was made not by classes, and not by the struggle of classes, but by outstanding individuals—"heroes"—who were blindly followed by the masses, the "mob," the people, the classes.

In combating and exposing the Narodniks Plekhanov wrote a number of Marxist works which were instrumental in rearing and educating the Marxists in Russia. Such works of his as *Socialism and the Political Struggle, Our Differences, On the Development of the Monistic View of History* cleared the way for the victory of Marxism in Russia.

In his works Plekhanov expounded the basic principles of Marxism. Of particular importance was his *On the Development of the Monistic View of History*, published in 1895. Lenin said that this book served to "rear a whole generation of Russian Marxists." (Lenin, *Collected Works*, Russ. ed., Vol. XIV, p. 347.)

In his writings aimed against the Narodniks, Plekhanov showed that it was absurd to put the question the way the Narodniks did: should capitalism develop in Russia or not? As a matter of fact Russia *had already entered* the path of capitalist development, Plekhanov said, producing facts to prove it, and there was no force that could divert her from this path.

The task of the revolutionaries was not to *arrest* the development of capitalism in Russia—that they could not do anyhow. Their task was to secure the support of the powerful revolutionary force brought into being by the development of capitalism, namely, the working class, to develop its class-consciousness, to organize it, and to help it to create its own working-class party.

Plekhanov also shattered the second major error of the Narodniks, namely, their denial of the role of the proletariat as the vanguard in the revolutionary struggle. The Narodniks looked upon the rise of the proletariat in Russia as something in the nature of a "historical misfortune," and spoke of the "ulcer of proletarianism." Plekhanov, championing the teachings of Marxism, showed that they were fully applicable to Russia and that in spite of the numerical preponderance of the peasantry and the relative numerical weakness of the proletariat, it was on the proletariat and on its growth that the revolutionaries should base their chief hopes.

Why on the proletariat?

Because the proletariat, although it was still numerically small, was a labouring class which was connected with the *most advanced* form of economy, large-scale production, and which for this reason had a great future before it.

Because the proletariat, as a class, was *growing* from year to year, was *developing* politically, easily lent itself to organization owing to the conditions of labour prevailing in large-scale production, and was the most revolutionary class owing to its proletarian status, for it had nothing to lose in the revolution but its chains.

The case was different with the peasantry.

The peasantry (meaning here the individual peasants, each of whom worked for himself—*Ed.*), despite its numerical strength, was a labouring class that was connected with the *most backward* form of economy, small-scale production, owing to which it had not and could not have any great future before it.

Far from growing as a class, the peasantry was splitting up more and more into bourgeois (kulaks) and poor peasants (proletarians and semi-proletarians). Moreover, being scattered, it lent itself less easily than the proletariat to organization, and, consisting of small owners, it joined the revolutionary movement less readily than the proletariat.

The Narodniks maintained that Socialism in Russia would come not through the dictatorship of the proletariat, but through the peasant commune, which they regarded as the embryo and basis of Socialism. But the commune was neither the basis nor the embryo of Socialism, nor could it be, because the commune was dominated by the kulaks—the bloodsuckers who exploited the poor peasants, the agricultural labourers and the economically weaker middle peasants. The formal existence of communal land ownership and the periodical redivision of the land according to the number of mouths in each peasant household did not alter the situation in any way. Those members of the commune used the land who owned draught cattle, implements and seed, that is, the well-to-do middle peasants and kulaks. The peasants who possessed no horses, the poor peasants, the small peasants generally, had to surrender their land to the kulaks and to hire themselves out as agricultural labourers. As a matter of fact, the peasant commune was a convenient means of masking the dominance of the kulaks and an inexpensive instrument in the hands of the tsarist government for the collection of taxes from the peasants on the basis of collective responsibility. That was why tsardom left the peasant commune intact. It was absurd to regard a commune of this character as the embryo or basis of Socialism.

Plekhanov shattered the third major error of the Narodniks as well, namely, that "heroes," outstanding individuals, and their ideas played a prime role in social development, and that the role of the masses, the "mob," the people, classes, was insignificant. Plekhanov accused the Narodniks of *idealism*, and showed that the truth lay not with idealism, but with the *materialism* of Marx and Engels.

Plekhanov expounded and substantiated the view of Marxist materialism. In conformity with Marxist materialism, he showed that in the long run the development of society is determined not by the wishes and ideas of outstanding individuals, but by the development of the material conditions of existence of society, by the changes in the mode of production of the material wealth required for the existence of society, by the changes in the mutual relations of classes in the production of material wealth, by the struggle of classes for place and position in the production and distribution of material wealth. It was not ideas that determined the social and economic status of men, but the social and economic status of men that determined their ideas. Outstanding individuals may become nonentities if their ideas and wishes run counter to the economic development of society, to the needs of the foremost class; and vice versa, outstanding people may really become outstanding individuals if their ideas and wishes correctly express the needs of the economic development of society, the needs of the foremost class.

In answer to the Narodniks' assertion that the masses are nothing but a mob, and that it is heroes who make history and convert the mob into a people, the Marxists affirmed that it is not heroes that make history, but history that makes heroes, and that, consequently, it is not heroes who create a people, but the people who create heroes and move history onward. Heroes, outstanding individuals, may play an important part in the life of society only in so far as they are capable of correctly understanding the conditions of development of society and the ways of changing them for the better. Heroes, outstanding individuals, may become ridiculous and useless failures if they do not correctly understand the conditions of development of society and go counter to the historical needs of society in the conceited belief that they are "makers" of history.

To this category of ill-starred heroes belonged the Narodniks.

Plekhanov's writings and the fight he waged against the Narodniks thoroughly undermined their influence among the revolutionary intelligentsia. But the ideological destruction of Narodism was still far from complete. It was left to Lenin to deal the final blow to Narodism, as an enemy of Marxism.

Soon after the suppression of the "Narodnaya Volya" Party the majority of the Narodniks renounced the revolutionary struggle against the tsarist government and began to preach a policy of reconciliation and agreement with it. In the eighties and nineties the Narodniks began to voice the interests of the kulaks.

The "Emancipation of Labour" group prepared two drafts of a program for a Russian Social-Democratic party (the first in 1884 and the second in 1887). This was a very important preparatory step in the formation of a Marxist Social-Democratic party in Russia.

But at the same time the "Emancipation of Labour" group was guilty of some very serious mistakes. Its first draft program still contained vestiges of the Narodnik views; it countenanced the tactics of individual terrorism. Furthermore, Plekhanov failed to take into account that in the course of the revolution the proletariat could and should lead the peasantry, and that only in an alliance with the peasantry could the proletariat gain the victory over tsardom. Plekhanov further considered that the liberal bourgeoisie was a force that could give support, albeit unstable support, to the revolution; but as to the peasantry, in some of his writings he discounted it entirely, declaring, for instance, that:

"Apart from the bourgeoisie and the proletariat we perceive no social forces in our country in which oppositional or revolutionary combinations might find support." (Plekhanov, *Works*, Russ. ed., Vol. III, p. 119.)

These erroneous views were the germ of Plekhanov's future Menshevik views.

Neither the "Emancipation of Labour" group nor the Marxist circles of that period had yet any practical connections with the working-class movement. It was a period in which the theory of Marxism, the ideas of Marxism, and the principles of the Social-Democratic program were just appearing and gaining a foothold in Russia. In the decade of 1884-94 the Social-Democratic movement still existed in the form of small separate groups and circles which had no connections, or very scant connections, with the mass working-class movement. Like an infant still unborn but already developing in its mother's womb, the Social-Democratic movement, as Lenin wrote, was in the *"process of foetal development."*

The "Emancipation of Labor" group, Lenin said, "only laid the theoretical foundations for the Social-Democratic movement and made the first step towards the working-class movement."

The task of uniting Marxism and the working-class movement in Russia, and of correcting the mistakes of the "Emancipation of Labour" group fell to Lenin.

3. BEGINNING OF LENIN'S REVOLUTIONARY ACTIVITIES. ST. PETERSBURG LEAGUE OF STRUGGLE FOR THE EMANCIPATION OF THE WORKING CLASS

Vladimir Ilyich Ulyanov (Lenin), the founder of Bolshevism, was born in the city of Simbirsk (now Ulyanovsk) in 1870. In 1887 Lenin entered the Kazan University, but was soon arrested and expelled from the university for taking part in the revolutionary student movement. In Kazan Lenin joined a Marxist circle formed by one Fedoseyev. Lenin later removed to Samara and soon afterwards the first Marxist circle in that city was formed with Lenin as the central figure. Already in those days Lenin amazed everyone by his thorough knowledge of Marxism.

At the end of 1893 Lenin removed to St. Petersburg. His very first utterances in the Marxist circles of that city made a deep impression on their members. His extraordinarily profound knowledge of Marx, his ability to apply Marxism to the economic and political situation of Russia at that time, his ardent and unshakable belief in the victory of the workers' cause, and his outstanding talent as an organizer made Lenin the acknowledged leader of the St. Petersburg Marxists.

Lenin enjoyed the warm affection of the politically advanced workers whom he taught in the circles.

"Our lectures," says the worker Babushkin recalling Lenin's teaching activities in the workers' circles, "were of a very lively and interesting character; we were all very pleased with these lectures and constantly admired the wisdom of our lecturer."

In 1895 Lenin united all the Marxist workers' circles in St. Petersburg (there were already about twenty of them) into a single League of Struggle for the Emancipation of the Working Class. He thus prepared the way for the founding of a revolutionary Marxist workers' party.

Lenin put before the League of Struggle the task of forming closer connections with the mass working-class movement and of giving it political leadership. Lenin proposed to pass from the *propaganda* of

Marxism among the few politically advanced workers who gathered in the propaganda circles to political *agitation* among the broad masses of the working class on issues of the day. This turn towards mass agitation was of profound importance for the subsequent development of the working-class movement in Russia.

The nineties were a period of industrial boom. The number of workers was increasing. The working-class movement was gaining strength. In the period of 1895-99, according to incomplete data, not less than 221,000 workers took part in strikes. The working-class movement was becoming an important force in the political life of the country. The course of events was corroborating the view which the Marxists had championed against the Narodniks, namely, that the working class was to play the leading role in the revolutionary movement.

Under Lenin's guidance, the League of Struggle for the Emancipation of the Working Class linked up the struggle of the workers for economic demands—improvement of working conditions, shorter hours and higher wages—with the political struggle against tsardom. The League of Struggle educated the workers politically.

Under Lenin's guidance, the St. Petersburg League of Struggle for the Emancipation of the Working Class was the first body in Russia that began to *unite Socialism with the working-class movement.* When a strike broke out in some factory, the League of Struggle, which through the members of its circles was kept well posted on the state of affairs in the factories, immediately responded by issuing leaflets and Socialist proclamations. These leaflets exposed the oppression of the workers by the manufacturers, explained how the workers should fight for their interests, and set forth the workers' demands. The leaflets told the plain truth about the ulcers of capitalism, the poverty of the workers, their intolerably hard working day of 12 to 14 hours, and their utter lack of rights. They also put forward appropriate political demands. With the collaboration of the worker Babushkin, Lenin at the end of 1894 wrote the first agitational leaflet of this kind and an appeal to the workers of the Semyannikov Works in St. Petersburg who were on strike. In the autumn of 1895 Lenin wrote a leaflet for the men and women strikers of the Thornton Mills. These mills belonged to English owners who were making millions in profits out of them. The working day in these mills exceeded 14 hours, while the wages of a weaver were about 7 rubles per month. The workers won the strike. In a short space of time the League of Struggle printed dozens of such leaflets and appeals to the workers of various factories. Every leaflet greatly helped to stiffen the spirit of the workers. They saw that the Socialists were helping and defending them.

In the summer of 1896 a strike of 30,000 textile workers, led by the League of Struggle, took place in St. Petersburg. The chief demand was for shorter hours. This strike forced the tsarist government to pass, on June 2, 1897, a law limiting the working day to 11½ hours. Prior to this the working day was not limited in any way.

In December 1895 Lenin was arrested by the tsarist government. But even in prison he did not discontinue his revolutionary work. He assisted the League of Struggle with advice and direction and wrote pamphlets and leaflets for it. There he wrote a pamphlet entitled *On Strikes* and a leaflet entitled *To the Tsarist Government,* exposing its savage despotism. There too Lenin drafted a program for the party (he used milk as an invisible ink and wrote between the lines of a book on medicine).

The St. Petersburg League of Struggle gave a powerful impetus to the amalgamation of the workers' circles in other cities and regions of Russia into similar leagues. In the middle of the nineties Marxist organizations arose in Transcaucasia. In 1894 a Workers' Union was formed in Moscow. Towards the end of the nineties a Social-Democratic Union was formed in Siberia. In the nineties Marxist groups arose in Ivanovo-Voznesensk, Yaroslavl and Kostroma and subsequently merged to form the Northern Union of the Social-Democratic Party. In the second half of the nineties Social-Democratic groups and unions were formed in Rostov-on-Don, Ekaterinoslav, Kiev, Nikolayev, Tula, Samara, Kazan, Orekhovo-Zuyevo and other cities.

The importance of the St. Petersburg League of Struggle for the Emancipation of the Working Class consisted in the fact that, as Lenin said, it was the first real *rudiment of a revolutionary party which was backed by the working-class movement.*

Lenin drew on the revolutionary experience of the St. Petersburg League of Struggle in his subsequent work of creating a Marxist Social-Democratic party in Russia.

After the arrest of Lenin and his close associates, the leadership of the St. Petersburg League of Struggle changed considerably. New people appeared who called themselves the "young" and Lenin and his associates the "old fellows." These people pursued an erroneous political line. They declared that the workers should be called upon to wage only an economic struggle against their employers; as for the political struggle, that was the affair of the liberal bourgeoisie, to whom the leadership of the political struggle should be left.

These people came to be called "Economists."

They were the first group of compromisers and opportunists within the ranks of the Marxist organizations in Russia.

4. LENIN'S STRUGGLE AGAINST NARODISM AND "LEGAL MARXISM." LENIN'S IDEA OF AN ALLIANCE OF THE WORKING CLASS AND THE PEASANTRY. FIRST CONGRESS OF THE RUSSIAN SOCIAL-DEMOCRATIC LABOUR PARTY

Although Plekhanov had already in the eighties dealt the chief blow to the Narodnik system of views, at the beginning of the nineties Narodnik views still found sympathy among certain sections of the revolutionary youth. Some of them continued to hold that Russia could avoid the capitalist path of development and that the principal role in the revolution would be played by the peasantry, and not by the working class. The Narodniks that still remained did their utmost to prevent the spread of Marxism in Russia, fought the Marxists and endeavoured to discredit them in every way. Narodism had to be completely *smashed* ideologically if the further spread of Marxism and the creation of a Social-Democratic party were to be assured.

This task was performed by Lenin.

In his book, *What the "Friends of the People" Are and How They Fight Against the Social-Democrats* (1894), Lenin thoroughly exposed the true character of the Narodniks, showing that they were false "friends of the people" actually working against the people.

Essentially, the Narodniks of the nineties had long ago renounced all revolutionary struggle against the tsarist government. The liberal Narodniks preached reconciliation with the tsarist government. "They think," Lenin wrote in reference to the Narodniks of that period, "that if they simply plead with this government nicely enough and humbly enough, it will put everything right." (Lenin, *Selected Works*, Vol. I, p. 413.)*

The Narodniks of the nineties shut their eyes to the condition of the poor peasants, to the class struggle in the countryside, and to the exploitation of the poor peasants by the kulaks, and sang praises to the development of kulak farming. As a matter of fact they voiced the interests of the kulaks.

---

*Quotations from English translations of Lenin and Stalin have been checked with the original and the translations in some cases revised.—*Tr.*

At the same time, the Narodniks in their periodicals baited the Marxists. They deliberately distorted and falsified the views of the Russian Marxists and claimed that the latter desired the ruin of the countryside and wanted "every muzhik to be stewed in the factory kettle." Lenin exposed the falsity of the Narodnik criticism and pointed out that it was not a matter of the "wishes" of the Marxists, but of the fact that capitalism was actually developing in Russia and that this development was inevitably accompanied by a growth of the proletariat. And the proletariat would be the gravedigger of the capitalist system.

Lenin showed that it was the Marxists and not the Narodniks who were the real friends of the people, that it was the Marxists who wanted to throw off the capitalist and landlord yoke, to destroy tsardom.

In his book, *What the "Friends of the People" Are,* Lenin for the first time advanced the idea of a revolutionary alliance of the workers and peasants as the principal means of overthrowing tsardom, the landlords and the bourgeoisie.

In a number of his writings during this period Lenin criticized the methods of political struggle employed by the principal Narodnik group, the "Narodnaya Volya," and later by the successors of the Narodniks, the Socialist-Revolutionaries—especially the tactics of individual terrorism. Lenin considered these tactics harmful to the revolutionary movement, for they substituted the struggle of individual heroes for the struggle of the masses. They signified a lack of confidence in the revolutionary movement of the people.

In the book, *What the "Friends of the People" Are,* Lenin outlined the main tasks of the Russian Marxists. In his opinion, the first duty of the Russian Marxists was to weld the disunited Marxist circles into a united Socialist workers' party. He further pointed out that it would be the working class of Russia, in alliance with the peasantry, that would overthrow the tsarist autocracy, after which the Russian proletariat, in alliance with the labouring and exploited masses, would, along with the proletariat of other countries, take the straight road of open political struggle to the victorious Communist revolution.

Thus, over forty years ago, Lenin correctly pointed out to the working class its path of struggle, defined its role as the foremost revolutionary force in society, and that of the peasantry as the ally of the working class.

The struggle waged by Lenin and his followers against Narodism led to the latter's complete ideological defeat already in the nineties.

Of immense significance, too, was Lenin's struggle against "legal Marxism." It usually happens with big social movements in history that transient "fellow-travelers" fasten on them. The *"legal Marxists,"* as they were called, were such fellow-travelers. Marxism began to spread widely throughout Russia; and so we found bourgeois intellectuals decking themselves out in a Marxist garb. They published their articles in newspapers and periodicals that were legal, that is, allowed by the tsarist government. That is why they came to be called "legal Marxists."

After their own fashion, they too fought Narodism. But they tried to make use of this fight and of the banner of Marxism in order to subordinate and adapt the working-class movement to the interests of bourgeois society, to the interests of the bourgeoisie. They cut out the very core of Marxism, namely, the doctrine of the proletarian revolution and the dictatorship of the proletariat. One prominent legal Marxist, Peter Struve, extolled the bourgeoisie, and instead of calling for a revolutionary struggle against capitalism, urged that "we acknowledge our lack of culture and go to capitalism for schooling."

In the fight against the Narodniks Lenin considered it permissible to come to a temporary agreement with the "legal Marxists" in order to use them against the Narodniks, as, for example, for the joint publication of a collection of articles directed against the Narodniks. At the same time, however, Lenin was unsparing in his criticism of the "legal Marxists" and exposed their liberal bourgeois nature.

Many of these fellow-travelers later became Constitutional-Democrats (the principal party of the Russian bourgeoisie), and during the Civil War out-and-out Whiteguards.

Along with the Leagues of Struggle in St. Petersburg, Moscow, Kiev and other places, Social-Democratic organizations arose also in the western national border regions of Russia. In the nineties the Marxist elements in the Polish nationalist party broke away to form the Social-Democratic Party of Poland and Lithuania. At the end of the nineties Latvian Social-Democratic organizations were formed, and in October 1897 the Jewish General Social-Democratic Union—known as the Bund—was founded in the western provinces of Russia.

In 1898 several of the Leagues of Struggle—those of St. Petersburg, Moscow, Kiev and Ekaterinoslav—together with the Bund made the first attempt to unite and form a Social-Democratic party. For this purpose they summoned the First Congress of the Russian Social-Democratic Labour Party (R.S.D.L.P.), which was held in Minsk in March 1898.

The First Congress of the R.S.D.L.P. was attended by only nine persons. Lenin was not present because at that time he was living in exile in Siberia. The Central Committee of the Party elected at the congress was very soon arrested. The Manifesto published in the name of the congress was in many respects unsatisfactory. It evaded the question of the conquest of political power by the proletariat, it made no mention of the hegemony of the proletariat, and said nothing about the allies of the proletariat in its struggle against tsardom and the bourgeoisie.

In its decisions and in its Manifesto the congress announced the formation of the Russian Social-Democratic Labour Party.

It is this formal act, which played a great revolutionary propagandist role, that constituted the significance of the First Congress of the R.S.D.L.P.

But although the First Congress had been held, in reality no Marxist Social-Democratic Party was as yet formed in Russia. The congress did not succeed in uniting the separate Marxist circles and organizations and welding them together organizationally. There was still no common line of action in the work of the local organizations, nor was there a party program, party rules or a single leading centre.

For this and for a number of other reasons, the ideological confusion in the local organizations began to increase, and this created favourable ground for the growth within the working-class movement of the opportunist trend known as "Economism."

It required several years of intense effort on the part of Lenin and of *Iskra* (*Spark*), the newspaper he founded, before this confusion could be overcome, the opportunist vacillations put an end to, and the way prepared for the formation of the Russian Social-Democratic Labour Party.

5. LENIN'S FIGHT AGAINST "ECONOMISM." APPEARANCE OF LENIN'S NEWSPAPER "ISKRA"

Lenin was not present at the First Congress of the R.S.D.L.P. He was at that time in exile in Siberia, in the village of Shushenskoye, where he had been banished by the tsarist government after a long period of imprisonment in St. Petersburg in connection with the prosecution of the League of Struggle.

But Lenin continued his revolutionary activities even while in exile. There he finished a highly important scientific work, *The Development of Capitalism in Russia,* which completed the ideological destruction of Narodism. There, too, he wrote his well-known pamphlet, *The Tasks of the Russian Social-Democrats.*

Although Lenin was cut off from direct, practical revolutionary work, he nevertheless managed to maintain some connections with those engaged in this work; he carried on a correspondence with them from exile, obtained information from them and gave them advice. At this time Lenin was very much preoccupied with the "Economists." He realized better than anybody else that "Economism" was the main nucleus of compromise and opportunism, and that if "Economism" were to gain the upper hand in the working-class movement, it would undermine the revolutionary movement of the proletariat and lead to the defeat of Marxism.

Lenin therefore started a vigorous attack on the "Economists" as soon as they appeared on the scene.

The "Economists" maintained that the workers should engage only in the economic struggle; as to the political struggle, that should be left to the liberal bourgeoisie, whom the workers should support. In Lenin's eyes this tenet was a desertion of Marxism, a denial of the necessity for an independent political party of the working class, an attempt to convert the working class into a political appendage of the bourgeoisie.

In 1899 a group of "Economists" (Prokopovich, Kuskova and others, who later became Constitutional-Democrats) issued a manifesto in which they opposed revolutionary Marxism, and insisted that the idea of an independent political party of the proletariat and of independent political demands by the working class be renounced. The "Economists" held that the political struggle was a matter for the liberal bourgeoisie, and that as far as the workers were concerned, the economic struggle against the employers was enough for them.

When Lenin acquainted himself with this opportunist document he called a conference of Marxist political exiles living in the vicinity. Seventeen of them met and, headed by Lenin, issued a trenchant protest denouncing the views of the "Economists."

This protest, which was written by Lenin, was circulated among the Marxist organizations all over the country and played an outstanding part in the development of Marxist ideas and of the Marxist party in Russia.

The Russian "Economists" advocated the same views as the opponents of Marxism in the Social-Democratic parties abroad who were known as the Bernsteinites, that is, followers of the opportunist Bernstein.

Lenin's struggle against the "Economists" was therefore at the same time a struggle against opportunism on an international scale.

The fight against "Economism," the fight for the creation of an independent political party of the proletariat, was chiefly waged by *Iskra*, the illegal newspaper founded by Lenin.

At the beginning of 1900, Lenin and other members of the League of Struggle returned from their Siberian exile to Russia. Lenin conceived the idea of founding a big illegal Marxist newspaper on an all-Russian scale. The numerous small Marxist circles and organizations which already existed in Russia were not yet linked up. At a moment when, in the words of Comrade Stalin, "amateurishness and the parochial outlook of the circles were corroding the Party from top to bottom, when ideological confusion was the characteristic feature of the internal life of the Party," the creation of an illegal newspaper on an all-Russian scale was the chief task of the Russian revolutionary Marxists. Only such a newspaper could link up the disunited Marxist organizations and prepare the way for the creation of a real party.

But such a newspaper could not be published in tsarist Russia owing to police persecution. Within a month or two at most the tsar's sleuths would get on its track and smash it. Lenin therefore decided to publish the newspaper abroad. There it was printed on very thin but durable paper and secretly smuggled into Russia. Some of the issues of *Iskra* were reprinted in Russia by secret printing plants in Baku, Kishinev and Siberia.

In the autumn of 1900 Lenin went abroad to make arrangements with the comrades in the "Emancipation of Labour" group for the publication of a political newspaper on an all-Russian scale. The idea had been worked out by Lenin in all its details while he was in exile. On his way back from exile he had held a number of conferences on the subject in Ufa, Pskov, Moscow and St. Petersburg. Everywhere he made arrangements with the comrades about codes for secret correspondence, addresses to which literature could be sent, and so on, and discussed with them plans for the future struggle.

The tsarist government scented a most dangerous enemy in Lenin. Zubatov, an officer of gendarmes in the tsarist *Okhrana,* expressed the opinion in a confidential report that "there is nobody bigger than Ulyanov [Lenin] in the revolution today," in view of which he considered it expedient to have Lenin assassinated.

Abroad, Lenin came to an arrangement with the "Emancipation of Labour" group, namely, with Plekhanov, Axelrod and V. Zasulich, for the publication of *Iskra* under joint auspices. The whole plan of publication from beginning to end had been worked out by Lenin.

The first issue of *Iskra* appeared abroad in December 1900. The title page bore the epigraph: *"The Spark Will Kindle a Flame."* These words were taken from the reply of the Decembrists to the poet Pushkin who had sent greetings to them in their place of exile in Siberia.

And indeed, from the spark (*Iskra*) started by Lenin there subsequently flamed up the great revolutionary conflagration in which the tsarist monarchy of the landed nobility, and the power of the bourgeoisie were reduced to ashes.

BRIEF SUMMARY

The Marxist Social-Democratic Labour Party in Russia was formed in a struggle waged in the first place against Narodism and its views, which were erroneous and harmful to the cause of revolution.

Only by ideologically shattering the views of the Narodniks was it possible to clear the way for a Marxist workers' party in Russia. A decisive blow to Narodism was dealt by Plekhanov and his "Emancipation of Labour" group in the eighties.

Lenin completed the ideological defeat of Narodism and dealt it the final blow in the nineties.

The "Emancipation of Labour" group, founded in 1883, did a great deal for the dissemination of Marxism in Russia; it laid the theoretical foundations for Social-Democracy and took the first step to establish connection with the working-class movement.

With the development of capitalism in Russia the industrial proletariat rapidly grew in numbers. In the middle of the eighties the working class adopted the path of organized struggle, of mass action in the form of organized strikes. But the Marxist circles and groups only carried on propaganda and did not realize the necessity for passing to mass agitation among the working class; they therefore still had no practical connection with the working-class movement and did not lead it.

The St. Petersburg League of Struggle for the Emancipation of the Working Class, which Lenin formed in 1895 and which started mass agitation among the workers and led mass strikes, marked a new stage— the transition to mass agitation among the workers and the union of Marxism with the working-class movement. The St. Petersburg League of Struggle for the Emancipation of the Working Class was the rudiment of a revolutionary proletarian party in Russia. The formation of the St. Petersburg League of Struggle was followed by the formation of Marxist organizations in all the principal industrial centres as well as in the border regions.

In 1898 at the First Congress of the R.S.D.L.P. the first, although unsuccessful, attempt was made to unite the Marxist Social-Democratic organizations into a party. But this congress did not yet create a party:

there was neither a party program nor party rules; there was no single leading centre, and there was scarcely any connection between the separate Marxist circles and groups.

In order to unite and link together the separate Marxist organizations into a single party, Lenin put forward and carried out a plan for the founding of *Iskra*, the first newspaper of the revolutionary Marxists on an all-Russian scale.

The principal opponents to the creation of a single political working-class party at that period were the "Economists." They denied the necessity for such a party. They fostered the disunity and amateurish methods of the separate groups. It was against them that Lenin and the newspaper *Iskra* organized by him directed their blows.

The appearance of the first issues of *Iskra* (1900-01) marked a transition to a new period—a period in which a single Russian Social-Democratic Labour Party was really formed from the disconnected groups and circles.

CHAPTER TWO

FORMATION OF THE RUSSIAN SOCIAL-DEMOCRATIC LABOUR PARTY. APPEARANCE OF THE BOLSHEVIK AND THE MENSHEVIK GROUPS WITHIN THE PARTY

(1901-1904)

1. UPSURGE OF THE REVOLUTIONARY MOVEMENT IN RUSSIA IN 1901-04

The end of the nineteenth century in Europe was marked by an industrial crisis. It soon spread to Russia. During the period of the crisis (1900-03) about 3,000 large and small enterprises were closed down and over 100,000 workers thrown on the streets. The wages of the workers that remained employed were sharply reduced. The insignificant concessions previously wrung from the capitalists as the result of stubborn economic strikes were now withdrawn.

Industrial crisis and unemployment did not halt or weaken the working-class movement. On the contrary, the workers' struggle assumed an increasingly revolutionary character. From economic strikes, the workers passed to political strikes, and finally to demonstrations, put forward political demands for democratic liberties, and raised the slogan, "Down with the tsarist autocracy!"

A May Day strike at the Obukhov munitions plant in St. Petersburg in 1901 resulted in a bloody encounter between the workers and troops. The only weapons the workers could oppose to the armed forces of the tsar were stones and lumps of iron. The stubborn resistance of the workers was broken. This was followed by savage reprisals: about 800 workers were arrested, and many were cast into prison or condemned to penal servitude and exile. But the heroic "Obukhov defence" made a profound impression on the workers of Russia and called forth a wave of sympathy among them.

In March 1902 big strikes and a demonstration of workers took place in Batum, organized by the Batum Social-Democratic Committee. The Batum demonstration stirred up the workers and peasants of Transcaucasia.

In 1902 a big strike broke out in Rostov-on-Don as well. The first to come out were the railwaymen, who were soon joined by the workers of many factories. The strike agitated all the workers. As many as 30,000 would gather at meetings held outside the city limits on several successive days. At these meetings Social-Democratic proclamations were read aloud and speakers addressed the workers. The police and the Cossacks were powerless to disperse these meetings, attended as they were by many thousands. When several workers were killed by the police, a huge procession of working people attended their funeral on the following day. Only by summoning troops from surrounding cities was the tsarist government able to suppress the strike. The struggle of the Rostov workers was led by the Don Committee of the R.S.D.L.P.

The strikes that broke out in 1903 were of even larger dimensions. Mass political strikes took place that year in the south, sweeping Transcaucasia (Baku, Tiflis, Batum) and the large cities of the Ukraine (Odessa, Kiev, Ekaterinoslav). The strikes became increasingly stubborn and better organized. Unlike earlier actions of the working class, the political struggle of the workers was nearly everywhere directed by the Social-Democratic committees.

The working class of Russia was rising to wage a revolutionary struggle against the tsarist regime.

The working-class movement influenced the peasantry. In the spring and summer of 1902 a peasant movement broke out in the Ukraine (Poltava and Kharkov provinces) and in the Volga region. The peasants set fire to landlords' mansions, seized their land, and killed the detested *zemsky nachalniks* (rural prefects) and landlords. Troops were sent to quell the rebellious peasants. Peasants were shot down, hundreds were arrested, and their leaders and organizers were flung into prison, but the revolutionary peasant movement continued to grow.

The revolutionary actions of the workers and peasants indicated that revolution was maturing and drawing near in Russia.

Under the influence of the revolutionary struggle of the workers the opposition movement of the students against the government assumed greater intensity. In retaliation for the student demonstrations and strikes, the government shut down the universities, flung hundreds of students into prison, and finally conceived the idea of sending recalcitrant students into the army as common soldiers. In response, the students of all the universities organized a general strike in the winter of 1901-02. About thirty thousand students were involved in this strike.

The revolutionary movement of the workers and peasants, and

especially the reprisals against the students, induced also the liberal bourgeois and the liberal landlords who sat on what was known as the Zemstovs to bestir themselves and to raise their voices in "protest" against the "excesses" of the tsarist government in repressing their student sons.

The Zemstvo liberals had their stronghold in the Zemstvo boards. These were local government bodies which had charge of purely local affairs affecting the rural population (building of roads, hospitals and schools). The liberal landlords played a fairly prominent part on the Zemstvo boards. They were closely associated with the liberal bourgeois, in fact were almost merged with them, for they themselves were beginning to abandon methods based on survivals of serfdom for capitalist methods of farming on their estates, as being more profitable. Of course, both these groups of liberals supported the tsarist government; but they were opposed to the "excesses" of tsardom, fearing that these "excesses" would only intensify the revolutionary movement. While they feared the "excesses" of tsardom, they feared revolution even more. In protesting against these "excesses," the liberals pursued two aims: first, to "bring the tsar to his senses," and secondly, by donning a mask of "profound dissatisfaction" with tsardom, to gain the confidence of the people, and to get them, or part of them, to break away from the revolution, and thus undermine its strength.

Of course, the Zemstvo liberal movement offered no menace whatever to the existence of tsardom; nevertheless, it served to show that all was not well with the "eternal" pillars of tsardom.

In 1902 the Zemstvo liberal movement led to the formation of the bourgeois "Liberation" group, the nucleus of the future principal party of the bourgeoisie in Russia—the Constitutional-Democratic Party.

Perceiving that the movement of the workers and peasants was sweeping the country in a formidable torrent, the tsarist government did everything it could to stem the revolutionary tide. Armed force was used with increasing frequency to suppress the workers' strikes and demonstrations; the bullet and the knout became the government's usual reply to the actions of the workers and peasants; prisons and places of exile were filled to overflowing.

While tightening up the measures of repression, the tsarist government tried at the same time to resort to other, non-repressive and more "flexible," measures to divert the workers from the revolutionary movement. Attempts were made to create bogus workers' organizations under the ægis of the gendarmes and police. They were dubbed organizations of "police socialism" or Zubatov organizations (after the name of a colonel of gendarmerie, Zubatov, who was the founder of these police-controlled workers' organizations). Through its agents the *Okhrana* tried to get the workers to believe that the tsarist government was itself prepared to assist them in securing the satisfaction of their economic demands. "Why engage in politics, why make a revolution, when the tsar himself is on the side of the workers?"—Zubatov agents would insinuate to the workers. Zubatov organizations were formed in several cities. On the model of these organizations and with the same purposes in view, an organization known as the Assembly of Russian Factory Workers of St. Petersburg was formed in 1904 by a priest by the name of Gapon.

But the attempt of the tsarist *Okhrana* to gain control over the working-class movement failed. The tsarist government proved unable by such measures to cope with the growing working-class movement. The rising revolutionary movement of the working class swept these police-controlled organizations from its path.

2. LENIN'S PLAN FOR THE BUILDING OF A MARXIST PARTY. OP-
PORTUNISM OF THE "ECONOMISTS." "ISKRA'S" FIGHT FOR
LENIN'S PLAN. LENIN'S BOOK "WHAT IS TO BE DONE?" IDEO-
LOGICAL FOUNDATIONS OF THE MARXIST PARTY

Notwithstanding the fact that the First Congress of the Russian Social-Democratic Party had been held in 1898, and that it had announced the formation of the Party, no real party was as yet created. There was no party program or party rules. The Central Committee of the Party elected at the First Congress was arrested and never replaced, for there was nobody to replace it. Worse still, the ideological confusion and lack of organizational cohesion of the Party became even more marked after the First Congress.

While the years 1884-94 were a period of victory over Narodism and of ideological preparation for the formation of a Social-Democratic Party, and the years 1894-98 a period in which an attempt, although unsuccessful, was made to weld the separate Marxist organizations into a Social-Democratic Party, the period immediately following 1898 was one of increased ideological and organizational confusion within the Party. The victory gained by the Marxists over Narodism and the revolutionary actions of the working class, which proved that the Marxists were right, stimulated the sympathy of the revolutionary youth for Marxism. Marxism became the fashion. This resulted in an influx into the

Marxist organizations of throngs of young revolutionary intellectuals, who were weak in theory and inexperienced in political organization, and who had only a vague, and for the most part incorrect, idea of Marxism, derived from the opportunist writings of the "legal Marxists" with which the press was filled. This resulted in the lowering of the theoretical and political standard of the Marxist organizations, in their infection with the "legal Marxist" opportunist tendencies, and in the aggravation of ideological confusion, political vacillation and organizational chaos.

The rising tide of the working-class movement and the obvious proximity of revolution demanded a united and centralized party of the working class which would be capable of leading the revolutionary movement. But the local Party organizations, the local committees, groups and circles were in such a deplorable state, and their organizational disunity and ideological discord so profound, that the task of creating such a party was one of immense difficulty.

The difficulty lay not only in the fact that the Party had to be built under the fire of savage persecution by the tsarist government, which every now and then robbed the organizations of their finest workers whom it condemned to exile, imprisonment and penal servitude, but also in the fact that a large number of the local committees and their members would have nothing to do with anything but their local, petty practical activities, did not realize the harm caused by the absence of organizational and ideological unity in the Party, were accustomed to the disunity and ideological confusion that prevailed within it, and believed that they could get along quite well without a united centralized party.

If a centralized party was to be created, this backwardness, inertia, and narrow outlook of the local bodies had to be overcome.

But this was not all. There was a fairly large group of people within the Party who had their own press—the *Rabochaya Mysl* (*Workers' Thought*) in Russia and *Rabocheye Delo* (*Workers' Cause*) abroad—and who were trying to justify on theoretical grounds the lack of organizational cohesion and the ideological confusion within the Party, frequently even lauding such a state of affairs, and holding that the plan for creating a united and centralized political party of the working class was unnecessary and artificial.

These were the "Economists" and their followers.

Before a united political party of the proletariat could be created, the "Economists" had to be defeated.

It was to this task and to the building of a working-class party that Lenin addressed himself.

How to begin the building of a united party of the working class was a question on which opinions differed. Some thought that the building of the Party should be begun by summoning the Second Congress of the Party, which would unite the local organizations and create the Party. Lenin was opposed to this. He held that before convening a congress it was necessary to make the aims and objects of the Party clear, to ascertain what sort of a party was wanted, to effect an ideological demarcation from the "Economists," to tell the Party honestly and frankly that there existed two different opinions regarding the aims and objects of the Party—the opinion of the "Economists" and the opinion of the revolutionary Social-Democrats—to start a wide campaign in the press in favour of the views of revolutionary Social-Democracy—just as the "Economists" were conducting a campaign in their own press in favour of their own views—and to give the local organizations the opportunity to make a deliberate choice between these two trends. Only after this indispensable preliminary work had been done could a Party Congress be summoned.

Lenin put it plainly:

"Before we can unite, and in order that we may unite, we must first of all draw firm and definite lines of demarcation." (Lenin, *Selected Works*, Vol. II, p. 45.)

Lenin accordingly held that the building of a political party of the working class should be begun by the founding of a militant political newspaper on an all-Russian scale, which would carry on propaganda and agitation in favour of the views of revolutionary Social-Democracy —that the establishment of such a newspaper should be the first step in the building of the Party.

In his well-known article, "Where to Begin?" Lenin outlined a concrete plan for the building of the Party, a plan which was later expanded in his famous work *What Is To Be Done?*

"In our opinion," wrote Lenin in this article, "the starting point of our activities, the first practical step towards creating the organization desired,* finally, the main thread following which we would be able to develop, deepen and expand that organization unswervingly, should be the establishment of a political newspaper on an all-Russian scale. . . . Without it we cannot systematically carry on that all-embracing propaganda and agitation, consistent in principle, which form the chief and constant task of Social-Democrats in general, and the particularly urgent task of the present moment when

---

* That is, the formation of a party.—*Ed.*

interest in politics, in questions of Socialism, has been aroused among the widest sections of the population." (*Ibid.*, p. 19.)

Lenin considered that such a newspaper would serve not only to weld the Party ideologically, but also to unite the local bodies within the Party organizationally. The network of agents and correspondents of the newspaper, representing the local organizations, would provide a skeleton around which the Party could be built up organizationally. For, Lenin said, "a newspaper is not only a collective propagandist and collective agitator, but also a collective organizer."

"This network of agents," writes Lenin in the same article, "will form the skeleton of precisely the organization we need, namely, one that is sufficiently large to embrace the whole country, sufficiently wide and many-sided to effect a strict and detailed division of labour; sufficiently tried and tempered to be able unswervingly to carry on *its own* work under all circumstances, at all 'turns' and in all contingencies; sufficiently flexible to be able to avoid open battle against an enemy of overwhelming strength, when he has concentrated all his forces at one spot, and yet able to take advantage of the awkwardness of this enemy and to attack him whenever and wherever least expected." (*Ibid.*, pp. 21-2.)

Iskra was to be such a newspaper.

And *Iskra* did indeed become such a political newspaper on an all-Russian scale which prepared the way for the ideological and organizational consolidation of the Party.

As to the structure and composition of the Party itself, Lenin considered that it should consist of two parts: a) a close circle of regular cadres of leading Party workers, chiefly professional revolutionaries, that is, Party workers free from all occupation except Party work and possessing the necessary minimum of theoretical knowledge, political experience, organizational practice and the art of combating the tsarist police and of eluding them; and b) a broad network of local Party organizations and a large number of Party members enjoying the sympathy and support of hundreds of thousands of working people.

"I assert," Lenin wrote, "1) that no revolutionary movement can endure without a stable organization of leaders that maintains continuity; 2) that the wider the masses spontaneously drawn into the struggle . . . the more urgent the need of such an organization, and the more solid this organization must be . . . 3) that such an organization must consist chiefly of people professionally engaged in revolutionary activity; 4) that in an autocratic state the more we *confine* the membership of such organization to people who are professionally engaged in revolutionary activity and who have been professionally trained in the art of combating the political police, the more difficult will it be to wipe out such an organization, and 5) the *greater* will be the number of people of the working class and of the other classes of society who will be able to join the movement and perform active work in it." (*Ibid.*, pp. 138-39.)

As to the character of the Party that was being built up and its role in relation to the working class, as well as its aims and objects, Lenin held that the Party should form the vanguard of the working class, that it should be the guiding force of the working-class movement, co-ordinating and directing the class struggle of the proletariat. The ultimate goal of the Party was the overthrow of capitalism and the establishment of Socialism. Its immediate aim was the overthrow of tsardom and the establishment of a democratic order. And inasmuch as the overthrow of capitalism was impossible without the preliminary overthrow of tsardom, the principal task of the Party at the given moment was to rouse the working class and the whole people for a struggle against tsardom, to develop a revolutionary movement of the people against it, and to overthrow it as the first and serious obstacle in the path of Socialism.

"History," Lenin wrote, "has now confronted us with an immediate task which is *the most revolutionary* of all the *immediate* tasks that confront the proletariat of any country. The fulfilment of this task, the destruction of the most powerful bulwark not only of European but also (it may now be said) of Asiatic reaction would make the Russian proletariat the vanguard of the international revolutionary proletariat." (*Ibid.*, p. 50.)

And further:

"We must bear in mind that the struggle with the government for partial demands, the winning of partial concessions, are only petty skirmishes with the enemy, petty encounters on the outposts, whereas the decisive engagement is still to come. Before us, in all its strength, stands the enemy's fortress, which is raining shot and shell upon us and mowing down our best fighters. We must capture this fortress; and we shall capture it if we unite all the forces of the awakening proletariat with all the forces of the Russian revolutionaries into one party, which will attract all that is alive and honest in Russia. And only then will the great prophecy of Pyotr Alexeyev, the Russian worker revolutionary, be fulfilled: 'the muscular arm of the working millions will be lifted, and the yoke of despotism,

guarded by the soldiers' bayonets, will be smashed to atoms!'"
(Lenin, *Collected Works*, Russ. ed., Vol. IV, p. 59.)

Such was Lenin's plan for the creation of a party of the working class in autocratic tsarist Russia.

The "Economists" showed no delay in launching an attack on Lenin's plan.

They asserted that the general political struggle against tsardom was a matter for all classes, but primarily for the bourgeoisie, and that therefore it was of no serious interest to the working class, for the chief interest of the workers lay in the economic struggle against the employers for higher wages, better working conditions, etc. The primary and immediate aim of the Social-Democrats should therefore be not a political struggle against tsardom, and not the overthrow of tsardom, but the organization of the "economic struggle of the workers against the employers and the government." By the economic struggle against the government they meant a struggle for better factory legislation. The "Economists" claimed that in this way it would be possible "to lend the economic struggle itself a political character."

The "Economists" no longer dared openly to contest the need for a political party of the working class. But they considered that it should not be the guiding force of the working-class movement, that it should not interfere in the spontaneous movement of the working class, let alone direct it, but that it should follow in the wake of this movement, study it and draw lessons from it.

The "Economists" furthermore asserted that the role of the conscious element in the working-class movement, the organizing and directing role of Socialist consciousness and Socialist theory, was insignificant, or almost insignificant; that the Social-Democrats should not elevate the minds of the workers to the level of Socialist consciousness, but, on the contrary, should adjust themselves and descend to the level of the average, or even of the more backward sections of the working class, and that the Social-Democrats should not try to impart a Socialist consciousness to the working class, but should wait until the spontaneous movement of the working class arrived of itself at a Socialist consciousness.

As regards Lenin's plan for the organization of the Party, the "Economists" regarded it almost as an act of violence against the spontaneous movement.

In the columns of *Iskra*, and especially in his celebrated work *What Is To Be Done?*, Lenin launched a vehement attack against this opportunist philosophy of the "Economists" and demolished it.

1) Lenin showed that to divert the working class from the general political struggle against tsardom and to confine its task to that of the economic struggle against the employers and the government, while leaving both employers and government intact, meant to condemn the workers to eternal slavery. The economic struggle of the workers against the employers and the government was a trade union struggle for better terms in the sale of their labour power to the capitalists. The workers, however, wanted to fight not only for better terms in the sale of their labour power to the capitalists, but also for the abolition of the capitalist system itself which condemned them to sell their labour power to the capitalists and to suffer exploitation. But the workers could not develop their struggle against capitalism, their struggle for Socialism to the full, as long as the path of the working-class movement was barred by tsardom, that watchdog of capitalism. It was therefore the immediate task of the Party and of the working class to remove tsardom from the path and thus clear the way to Socialism.

2) Lenin showed that to extol the spontaneous process in the working-class movement, to deny that the Party had a leading role to play, to reduce its role to that of a recorder of events, meant to preach *khvostism* (following in the tail), to preach the conversion of the Party into a tail-piece of the spontaneous process, into a passive force of the movement, capable only of contemplating the spontaneous process and allowing events to take their own course. To advocate this meant working for the destruction of the Party, that is, leaving the working class without a party—that is, leaving the working class unarmed. But to leave the working class unarmed when it was faced by such enemies as tsardom, which was armed to the teeth, and the bourgeoisie, which was organized on modern lines and had its own party to direct its struggle against the working class, meant to betray the working class.

3) Lenin showed that to bow in worship of the spontaneous working-class movement and to belittle the importance of consciousness, of Socialist consciousness and Socialist theory, meant, in the first place, to insult the workers, who were drawn to consciousness as to light; in the second place, to lower the value of theory in the eyes of the Party, that is, to depreciate the instrument which helped the Party to understand the present and foresee the future; and, in the third place, it meant to sink completely and irrevocably into the bog of opportunism.

"Without a revolutionary theory," Lenin said, "there can be no revolutionary movement. . . . The role of vanguard can be fulfilled only by a party that is guided by the most advanced theory." (Lenin, *Selected Works*, Vol. II, pp. 47, 48.)

4) Lenin showed that the "Economists" were deceiving the working class when they asserted that a Socialist ideology could arise from the spontaneous movement of the working class, for in reality the Socialist ideology arises not from the spontaneous movement, but from science. By denying the necessity of imparting a Socialist consciousness to the working class, the "Economists" were clearing the way for bourgeois ideology, facilitating its introduction and dissemination among the working class, and, consequently, they were burying the idea of union between the working-class movement and Socialism, thus helping the bourgeoisie.

"*All* worship of the spontaneity of the labour movement," Lenin said, "all belittling of the role of 'the conscious element,' of the role of the party of Social-Democracy, *means, altogether irrespective of whether the belittler likes it or not, strengthening the influence of the bourgeois ideology among the workers.*" (*Ibid.*, p. 61.)
And further:

"The *only* choice is: either the bourgeois or the Socialist ideology. There is no middle course. . . . Hence to belittle the Socialist ideology *in any way, to turn away from it in the slightest degree* means to strengthen the bourgeois ideology." (*Ibid.*, p. 62.)

5) Summing up all these mistakes of the "Economists," Lenin came to the conclusion that they did not want a party of social revolution for the emancipation of the working class from capitalism, but a party of "social reform," which presupposed the preservation of capitalist rule, and that, consequently, the "Economists" were reformists who were betraying the fundamental interests of the proletariat.

6) Lastly, Lenin showed that "Economism" was not an accidental phenomenon in Russia, but that the "Economists" were an instrument of bourgeois influence upon the working class, that they had allies in the West-European Social-Democratic parties in the person of the revisionists, the followers of the opportunist Bernstein. The opportunist trend in Social-Democratic parties was gaining strength in Western Europe; on the plea of "freedom to criticize" Marx, it demanded a "revision" of the Marxist doctrine (hence the term "revisionism"); it demanded renunciation of the revolution, of Socialism and of the dictatorship of the proletariat. Lenin showed that the Russian "Economists" were pursuing a similar policy of renunciation of the revolutionary struggle, of Socialism and of the dictatorship of the proletariat.

Such were the main theoretical principles expounded by Lenin in *What Is To Be Done?*

As a result of the wide circulation of this book, by the time of the

Second Congress of the Russian Social-Democratic Party, that is, within a year after its publication (it appeared in March 1902), nothing but a distasteful memory remained of the ideological stand of "Economism," and to be called an "Economist" was regarded by the majority of the members of the Party as an insult.

It was a complete ideological defeat for "Economism," for the ideology of opportunism, *khvostism* and spontaneity.

But this does not exhaust the significance of Lenin's *What Is To Be Done?*

The historic significance of this celebrated book lies in the fact that in it Lenin:

1) For the first time in the history of Marxist thought, laid bare the ideological roots of opportunism, showing that they principally consisted in worshipping the spontaneous working-class movement and belittling the role of Socialist consciousness in the working-class movement;

2) Brought out the great importance of theory, of consciousness, and of the Party as a revolutionizing and guiding force of the spontaneous working-class movement;

3) Brilliantly substantiated the fundamental Marxist thesis that a Marxist party is a union of the working-class movement with Socialism;

4) Gave a brilliant exposition of the ideological foundations of a Marxist party.

The theoretical theses expounded in *What Is To Be Done?* later became the foundation of the ideology of the Bolshevik Party.

Possessing such a wealth of theory, *Iskra* was able to, and actually did, develop an extensive campaign for Lenin's plan for the building of the Party, for mustering its forces, for calling the Second Party Congress, for revolutionary Social-Democracy, and against the "Economists," revisionists, and opportunists of all kinds.

One of the most important things that *Iskra* did was to draft a program for the Party. The program of a workers' party, as we know, is a brief, scientifically formulated statement of the aims and objects of the struggle of the working class. The program defines both the ultimate goal of the revolutionary movement of the proletariat, and the demands for which the party fights while on the way to the achievement of the ultimate goal. The drafting of a program was therefore a matter of prime importance.

During the drafting of the program serious differences arose on the editorial board of *Iskra* between Lenin, on the one hand, and Plekhanov and other members of the board, on the other. These differences and disputes almost led to a complete rupture between Lenin and Plekhanov. But matters did not come to a head at that time. Lenin secured the inclusion in the draft program of a most important clause on the dictatorship of the proletariat and of a clear statement on the leading role of the working class in the revolution.

It was Lenin, too, who drew up the whole agrarian section of the program. Already at that time Lenin was in favour of the nationalization of the land, but he considered it necessary in the first stage of the struggle to put forward the demand for the return to the peasants of the *otrezki*, that is, those portions of the land which had been cut off the peasants' land by the landlords at the time of "emancipation" of the peasants. Plekhanov was opposed to the demand for the nationalization of the land.

The disputes between Lenin and Plekhanov over the Party program to some extent determined the future differences between the Bolsheviks and the Mensheviks.

3. SECOND CONGRESS OF THE RUSSIAN SOCIAL-DEMOCRATIC LA-
BOUR PARTY. ADOPTION OF PROGRAM AND RULES AND FOR-
MATION OF A SINGLE PARTY. DIFFERENCES AT THE CONGRESS
AND APPEARANCE OF TWO TRENDS WITHIN THE PARTY: THE
BOLSHEVIK AND THE MENSHEVIK

Thus the triumph of Lenin's principles and the successful struggle waged by *Iskra* for Lenin's plan of organization brought about all the principal conditions necessary for the creation of a party, or, as it was said at the time, of a real party. The *Iskra* trend gained the upper hand among the Social-Democratic organizations in Russia. The Second Party Congress could now be summoned.

The Second Congress of the R.S.D.L.P. opened on July 17 (30, New Style), 1903. It was held abroad, in secret. It first met in Brussels, but the Belgian police requested the delegates to leave the country. Thereupon the congress transferred its sittings to London.

Forty-three delegates in all, representing 26 organizations, assembled at the congress. Each committee was entitled to send two delegates, but some of them sent only one. The 43 delegates commanded 51 votes between them.

The chief purpose of the congress was "to create a *real* party on that basis of principles and organization which had been advanced and elaborated by *Iskra*." (Lenin, *Selected Works*, Vol. II, p. 412.)

The composition of the congress was heterogeneous. The avowed

"Economists" were not represented, because of the defeat they had suffered. But they had since disguised their views so artfully that they managed to smuggle several of their delegates into the congress. Moreover, the Bund delegates differed only ostensibly from the "Economists"; in reality they supported the "Economists."

Thus the congress was attended not only by supporters of *Iskra*, but also by its adversaries. Thirty-three of the delegates, that is, the majority, were supporters of *Iskra*. But not all those who considered themselves *Iskra*-ists were real Leninist *Iskra*-ists. The delegates fell into several groups. The supporters of Lenin, or the firm *Iskra*-ists, commanded 24 votes; nine of the *Iskra*-ists followed Martov; these were unstable *Iskra*-ists. Some of the delegates vacillated between *Iskra* and its opponents; they commanded 10 votes and constituted the Centre. The avowed opponents of *Iskra* commanded 8 votes (3 "Economists" and 5 Bundists). A split in the ranks of the *Iskra*-ists would be enough to give the enemies of *Iskra* the upper hand.

It will therefore be seen how complex the situation was at the congress. Lenin expended a great deal of energy to ensure the victory of *Iskra*.

The most important item on the agenda was the adoption of the Party program. The chief point which, during the discussion of the program, aroused the objections of the opportunist section of the congress was the question of the dictatorship of the proletariat. There were a number of other items in the program on which the opportunists did not agree with the revolutionary section of the congress. But they decided to put up the main fight on the question of the dictatorship of the proletariat, on the plea that the programs of a number of foreign Social-Democratic parties contained no clause on the dictatorship of the proletariat, and that therefore the program of the Russian Social-Democratic Party could dispense with it too.

The opportunists also objected to the inclusion in the Party program of demands on the peasant question. These people did not want revolution; they, therefore, fought shy of the ally of the working class—the peasantry—and adopted an unfriendly attitude towards it.

The Bundists and the Polish Social-Democrats objected to the right of nations to self-determination. Lenin had always taught that the working class must combat national oppression. To object to the inclusion of this demand in the program was tantamount to a proposal to renounce proletarian internationalism and to become accomplices in national oppression.

Lenin made short work of all these objections.

The congress adopted the program proposed by *Iskra*.

This program consisted of two parts: a maximum program and a minimum program. The maximum program dealt with the principal aim of the working-class party, namely, the Socialist revolution, the overthrow of the power of the capitalists, and the establishment of the dictatorship of the proletariat. The minimum program dealt with the immediate aims of the Party, aims to be achieved before the overthrow of the capitalist system and the establishment of the dictatorship of the proletariat, namely, the overthrow of the tsarist autocracy, the establishment of a democratic republic, the introduction of an 8-hour working day, the abolition of all survivals of serfdom in the countryside, and the restoration to the peasants of the cut-off lands (*otrezki*) of which they had been deprived by the landlords.

Subsequently, the Bolsheviks replaced the demand for the return of the *otrezki* by the demand for the confiscation of all the landed estates.

The program adopted by the Second Congress was a revolutionary program of the party of the working class.

It remained in force until the Eighth Party Congress, held after the victory of the proletarian revolution, when our Party adopted a new program.

Having adopted the program, the Second Party Congress proceeded to discuss the draft of the Party Rules. Now that the congress had adopted a program and had laid the foundation for the ideological unity of the Party, it had also to adopt Party Rules so as to put an end to amateurishness and the parochial outlook of the circles, to organizational disunity and the absence of strict discipline in the Party.

The adoption of the program had gone through comparatively smoothly, but fierce disputes arose at the congress over the Party Rules. The sharpest differences arose over the formulation of the first paragraph of the rules, dealing with Party membership. Who could be a member of the Party, what was to be the composition of the Party, what was to be the organizational nature of the Party, an organized whole or something amorphous? —such were the questions that arose in connection with the first paragraph of the rules. Two different formulations contested the ground: Lenin's formulation, which was supported by Plekhanov and the firm *Iskra*-ists; and Martov's formulation, which was supported by Axelrod, Zasulich, the unstable *Iskra*-ists, Trotsky, and all the avowed opportunists at the congress.

According to Lenin's formulation, one could be a member of the Party who accepted its program, supported it financially, and belonged to one of its organizations. Martov's formulation, while admitting that acceptance of the program and financial support of the Party were indispensable conditions of Party membership, did not, however, make it a condition that a Party member should belong to one of the Party organizations, maintaining that a Party member need not necessarily belong to a Party organization.

Lenin regarded the Party as an *organized* detachment, whose members cannot just enrol themselves in the Party, but must be admitted into the Party by one of its organizations, and hence must submit to Party discipline. Martov, on the other hand, regarded the Party as something organizationally *amorphous*, whose members enrol themselves in the Party and are therefore not obliged to submit to Party discipline, inasmuch as they do not belong to a Party organization.

Thus, unlike Lenin's formulation, Martov's formulation would throw the door of the Party wide open to unstable non-proletarian elements. On the eve of the bourgeois-democratic revolution there were people among the bourgeois intelligentsia who for a while sympathized with the revolution. From time to time they might even render some small service to the Party. But such people would not join an organization, submit to Party discipline, carry out Party tasks and run the accompanying risks. Yet Martov and the other Mensheviks proposed to regard such people as Party members, and to accord them the right and opportunity to influence Party affairs. They even proposed to grant any striker the right to "enrol" himself in the Party, although non-Socialists, Anarchists and Socialist-Revolutionaries also took part in strikes.

And so it was that instead of a monolithic and militant party with a clearly defined organization, for which Lenin and the Leninists fought at the congress, the Martovites wanted a heterogeneous and loose, amorphous party, which could not be a militant party with firm discipline because of its heterogeneous character, if for no other reason.

The breaking away of the unstable *Iskra*-ists from the firm *Iskra*-ists, their alliance with the Centrists, joined as they were by the avowed opportunists, turned the balance in favour of Martov on this point. By 28 votes to 22, with one abstention, the congress adopted Martov's formulation of the first paragraph of the Rules.

After the split in the ranks of the *Iskra*-ists over the first paragraph of the Rules the struggle at the congress became still more acute. The congress was coming to the last item on the agenda—the elections of the leading institutions of the Party: the editorial board of the central organ of the Party (*Iskra*), and the Central Committee. However, before the elections were reached, certain incidents occurred which changed the alignment of forces.

In connection with the Party Rules, the congress had to deal with the question of the Bund. The Bund laid claim to a special position within the Party. It demanded to be recognized as the sole representative of the Jewish workers in Russia. To comply with this demand would have meant to divide the workers in the Party organizations according to nationality, and to renounce common territorial class organizations of the workers. The congress rejected the system of organization on national lines proposed by the Bund. Thereupon the Bundists quit the congress. Two "Economists" also left the congress when the latter refused to recognize their Foreign League as the representative of the Party abroad.

The departure of these seven opportunists altered the balance of forces at the congress in favour of the Leninists.

From the very outset Lenin focussed his attention on the composition of the central institutions of the Party. He deemed it necessary that the Central Committee should be composed of staunch and consistent revolutionaries. The Martovites strove to secure the predominance of unstable, opportunist elements on the Central Committee. The majority of the congress supported Lenin on this question. The Central Committee that was elected consisted of Lenin's followers.

On Lenin's proposal, Lenin, Plekhanov and Martov were elected to the editorial board of *Iskra*. Martov had demanded the election of all the six former members of the *Iskra* editorial board, the majority of whom were Martov's followers. This demand was rejected by the majority of the congress. The three proposed by Lenin were elected. Martov thereupon announced that he would not join the editorial board of the central organ.

Thus, by its vote on the central institutions of the Party, the congress sealed the defeat of Martov's followers and the victory of Lenin's followers.

From that time on, Lenin's followers, who received the majority of votes in the elections at the congress, have been called Bolsheviks (from *bolshinstvo*, majority), and Lenin's opponents, who received the minority of votes, have been called Mensheviks (from *menshinstvo*, minority).

Summing up the work of the Second Congress, the following conclusions may be drawn:

1) The congress sealed the victory of Marxism over "Economism," over open opportunism.

2) The congress adopted a Program and Rules, created the Social-Democratic Party, and thus built the framework of a single party.

3) The congress revealed the existence of grave differences over questions of organization which divided the Party into two sections, the

Bolsheviks and the Mensheviks, of whom the former championed the organizational principles of revolutionary Social-Democracy, while the latter sank into the bog of organizational looseness and of opportunism.

4) The congress showed that the place of the old opportunists, the "Economists," who had already been defeated by the Party, was being taken by new opportunists, the Mensheviks.

5) The congress did not prove equal to its task in matters of organization, showed vacillation, and at times even gave the preponderance to the Mensheviks; and although it corrected its position towards the end, it was nevertheless unable to expose the opportunism of the Mensheviks on matters of organization and to isolate them in the Party, or even to put such a task before the Party.

This latter circumstance proved one of the main reasons why the struggle between the Bolsheviks and the Mensheviks, far from subsiding after the congress, became even more acute.

4. SPLITTING ACTIVITIES OF THE MENSHEVIK LEADERS AND SHARPENING OF THE STRUGGLE WITHIN THE PARTY AFTER THE SECOND CONGRESS. OPPORTUNISM OF THE MENSHEVIKS. LENIN'S BOOK "ONE STEP FORWARD, TWO STEPS BACK." ORGANIZATIONAL PRINCIPLES OF THE MARXIST PARTY

After the Second Congress the struggle within the Party became even more acute. The Mensheviks did their utmost to frustrate the decisions of the Second Congress and to seize the central institutions of the Party. They demanded that their representatives be included in the editorial board of *Iskra* and in the Central Committee in such numbers as would give them a majority on the editorial board and parity with the Bolsheviks on the Central Committee. As this ran directly counter to the decisions of the Second Congress, the Bolsheviks rejected the Menshevik's demand. Thereupon the Mensheviks, secretly from the Party, created their own anti-Party factional organization, headed by Martov, Trotsky and Axelrod, and, as Martov wrote, "broke into revolt against Leninism." The methods they adopted for combating the Party were, as Lenin expressed it, "to disorganize the whole Party work, damage the cause, and hamper all and everything." They entrenched themselves in the Foreign League of Russian Social-Democrats, nine-tenths of whom were émigré intellectuals isolated from the work in Russia, and from this position they opened fire on the Party, on Lenin and the Leninists.

The Mensheviks received considerable help from Plekhanov. At the Second Congress Plekhanov sided with Lenin. But after the Second Congress he allowed the Mensheviks to intimidate him with threats of a split. He decided to "make peace" with the Mensheviks at all costs. It was the deadweight of his earlier opportunist mistakes that dragged Plekhanov down to the Mensheviks. From an advocate of reconciliation with the opportunist Mensheviks he soon became a Menshevik himself. Plekhanov demanded that all the former Menshevik editors of the *Iskra* who had been rejected by the congress be included in the editorial board. Lenin, of course, could not agree to this and resigned from the *Iskra* editorial board in order to entrench himself in the Central Committee of the Party and to strike at the opportunists from this position. Acting by himself, and in defiance of the will of the congress, Plekhanov co-opted the former Menshevik editors to the editorial board of *Iskra.* From that moment on, beginning with the 52nd issue of *Iskra,* the Mensheviks converted it into their own organ and began to propagate their opportunist views in its columns.

Ever since then Lenin's Bolshevik *Iskra* has been known in the Party as the *old Iskra,* and the Menshevik, opportunist *Iskra* as the *new Iskra.*

When it passed into the hands of the Mensheviks, *Iskra* became a weapon in the fight against Lenin and the Bolsheviks, and an organ for the propaganda of Menshevik opportunism, primarily on questions of organization. Joining forces with the "Economists" and the Bundists, the Mensheviks started a campaign in the columns of *Iskra,* as they said, against Leninism. Plekhanov could not stick to his position as an advocate of conciliation, and soon he too joined the campaign. This was bound to happen by the very logic of things: whoever insists on a conciliatory attitude towards opportunists is bound to sink to opportunism himself. There began to flow from the columns of the new *Iskra,* as from a cornucopia, articles and statements claiming that the Party ought not to be an organized whole; that free groups and individuals should be allowed within its ranks without any obligation to submit to the decisions of its organs; that every intellectual who sympathized with the Party, as well as "every striker" and "every participant in a demonstration," should be allowed to declare himself a Party member; that the demand for obedience to all the decisions of the Party was "formal and bureaucratic"; that the demand that the minority must submit to the majority meant the "mechanical suppression" of the will of Party members; that the demand that all Party members—both leaders and rank-and-filers— should equally observe Party discipline meant establishing "serfdom" within the Party; that what "we" needed in the Party was not centralism but anarchist "autonomism" which would permit individuals and Party organizations not to obey the decisions of the Party.

This was unbridled propaganda of organizational license, which would undermine the Party principle and Party discipline; it was glorification of the individualism of the intelligentsia, and a justification of the anarchist contempt of discipline.

The Mensheviks were obviously trying to drag the Party back from the Second Congress to the old organizational disunity, to the old parochial outlook of the circles and the old amateurish methods.

A vigorous rebuff had to be given the Mensheviks.

This rebuff was administered by Lenin in his celebrated book, *One Step Forward, Two Steps Back*, published in May 1904.

The following are the main organizational principles which Lenin expounded in his book, and which afterwards came to form the organizational foundations of the Bolshevik Party.

1) The Marxist Party is a part, a detachment, of the working class. But the working class has many detachments, and hence not every detachment of the working class can be called a party of the working class. The Party differs from other detachments of the working class primarily by the fact that it is not an ordinary detachment, but the *vanguard* detachment, a *class-conscious* detachment, a *Marxist* detachment of the working class, armed with a knowledge of the life of society, of the laws of its development and of the laws of the class struggle, and for this reason able to lead the working class and to direct its struggle. The Party must therefore not be confused with the working class, as the part must not be confused with the whole. One cannot demand that every striker be allowed to call himself a member of the Party, for whoever confuses Party and class lowers the level of consciousness of the Party to that of "every striker," destroys the Party as the class-conscious vanguard of the working class. It is not the task of the Party to *lower* its level to that of "every striker," but to *elevate* the masses of the workers, to *elevate* "every striker" to the level of the Party.

"We are the party of a class," Lenin wrote, "and therefore *almost the entire class* (and in times of war, in the period of civil war, the entire class) should act under the leadership of our Party, should adhere to our Party as closely as possible. But it would be Manilovism (smug complacency) and '*khvostism*' (following in the tail) to think that at any time under capitalism the entire class, or almost the entire class, would be able to rise to the level of consciousness and activity of its vanguard, of its Social-Democratic Party. No sensible Social-Democrat has ever yet doubted that under capitalism even the trade union organizations (which are more primitive and more comprehensible to the undeveloped strata) are unable to embrace the entire, or almost the entire working class. To forget the distinction between the vanguard and the whole of the masses which gravitate towards it, to forget the constant duty of the vanguard to *raise* ever wider strata to this most advanced level, means merely to deceive oneself, to shut one's eyes to the immensity of our tasks, and to narrow down these tasks." (Lenin, *Collected Works*, Russ. ed., Vol. VI, pp. 205-06.)

2) The Party is not only the vanguard, the class-conscious detachment of the working class, but also an *organized* detachment of the working class, with its own discipline, which is binding on its members. Hence Party members must necessarily be members of some organization of the Party. If the Party were not an *organized* detachment of the class, not a *system of organization*, but a mere agglomeration of persons who declare themselves to be Party members but do not belong to any Party organization and therefore are *not organized*, hence not obliged to obey Party decisions, the Party would never have a united will, it could never achieve the united action of its members, and, consequently, it would be unable to direct the struggle of the working class. The Party can lead the practical struggle of the working class and direct it towards one aim only if all its members are *organized* in one common detachment, welded together by unity of will, unity of action and unity of discipline.

The objection raised by the Mensheviks that in that case many intellectuals—for example, professors, university and high school students, etc.—would remain outside the ranks of the Party, since they would not want to join any of the organizations of the Party, either because they shrink from Party discipline, or, as Plekhanov said at the Second Congress, because they consider it "beneath their dignity to join some local organization"—this Menshevik objection recoiled on the heads of the Mensheviks themselves; for the Party does not need members who shrink from Party discipline and fear to join the Party organization. Workers did not fear discipline and organization, and they willingly join the organization if they have made up their minds to be Party members. It is the individualistic intellectuals who fear discipline and organization, and they would indeed remain outside the ranks of the Party. But that was all to the good, for the Party would be spared that influx of unstable elements, which had become particularly marked at that time, when the bourgeois-democratic revolution was on the upgrade.

"When I say," Lenin wrote, "that the Party should be a *sum* (and not a mere arithmetical sum, but a complex) of *organizations*

. . . I thereby express clearly and precisely my wish, my demand, that the Party, as the vanguard of the class, should be as *organized* as possible, that the Party should admit to its ranks only such elements *as lend themselves to at least a minimum of organization.* . . ." (*Ibid.*, p. 203.)

And further:

"Martov's formulation *ostensibly* defends the interests of the broad strata of the proletariat, but *in fact,* it serves the interests of the *bourgeois intellectuals,* who fight shy of proletarian discipline and organization.   No one will undertake to deny that it is *precisely its individualism* and incapacity for discipline and organization that in general distinguish *the intelligentsia as a separate stratum* of modern capitalist society." (*Ibid.*, p. 212.)

And again:

"The proletariat is not afraid of organization and discipline. . . . The proletariat will do nothing to have the worthy professors and high school students, who do not want to join an organization, recognized as Party members merely because they work under the control of an organization. . . . It is not the proletariat, but *certain intellectuals* in our Party who lack *self-training* in the spirit of organization and discipline." (*Ibid.*, p. 307.)

3) The Party is not merely an organized detachment, but *"the highest of all forms of organization"* of the working class, and it is its mission to *guide* all the other organizations of the working class.   As the highest form of organization, consisting of the finest members of the class, armed with an advanced theory, with knowledge of the laws of the class struggle and with the experience of the revolutionary movement, the Party has every opportunity of guiding—and is obliged to guide—all the other organizations of the working class.   The attempt of the Mensheviks to belittle and depreciate the leading role of the Party tends to weaken all the other organizations of the proletariat which are guided by the Party, and, consequently, to weaken and disarm the proletariat, for "in its struggle for power the proletariat has no other weapon but organization." (Lenin, *Selected Works*, Vol. II, p. 466.)

4) The Party is an *embodiment of the connection* of the vanguard of the working class with the *working class millions*.   However fine a vanguard the Party may be, and however well it may be organized, it cannot exist and develop without connections with the non-Party masses, and without multiplying and strengthening these connections.   A party

which shuts itself up in its own shell, isolates itself from the masses, and loses, or even relaxes, its connections with its class is bound to lose the confidence and support of the masses, and, consequently, is surely bound to perish. In order to live to the full and to develop, the Party must multiply its connections with the masses and win the confidence of the millions of its class.

"In order to be a Social-Democratic *party*," Lenin said, "we must win the *support* precisely of the *class*." (Lenin, *Collected Works*, Russ. ed., Vol. VI, p. 208.)

5) In order to function properly and to guide the masses systematically, the Party must be organized on the principle of *centralism*, having one set of rules and uniform Party discipline, one leading organ— the Party Congress, and in the intervals between congresses—the Central Committee of the Party; the minority must submit to the majority, the various organizations must submit to the centre, and lower organizations to higher organizations. Failing these conditions, the party of the working class cannot be a real party and cannot carry out its tasks in guiding the class.

Of course, as under the tsarist autocracy the Party existed illegally, the Party organizations could not in those days be built up on the principle of election from below, and as a consequence, the Party had to be strictly conspiratorial. But Lenin considered that this *temporary* feature in the life of our Party would at once lapse with the elimination of tsardom, when the Party would become open and legal, and the Party organizations would be built up on the principles of democratic elections, of *democratic centralism*.

"*Formerly*," Lenin wrote, "our Party was not a formally organized whole, but only the sum of separate groups, and, therefore, no other relations except those of ideological influence were possible between these groups. *Now* we have become an organized Party, and this implies the establishment of authority, the transformation of the power of ideas into the power of authority, the subordination of lower Party bodies to higher Party bodies." (*Ibid.*, p. 291.)

Accusing the Mensheviks of organizational nihilism and of aristocratic anarchism which would not submit to the authority of the Party and its discipline, Lenin wrote:

"This aristocratic anarchism is particularly characteristic of the Russian nihilist. He thinks of the Party organization as a monstrous 'factory'; he regards the subordination of the part to the whole and of the minority to the majority as 'serfdom' . . . division of labour under the direction of a centre evokes from him a tragi-comical out-cry against people being transformed into 'wheels and cogs' (to turn editors into contributors being considered a particularly atrocious species of such transformation); mention of the organizational rules of the Party calls forth a contemptuous grimace and the disdainful remark (intended for the 'formalists') that one could very well dispense with rules altogether." (Lenin, *Selected Works*, Vol. II, pp. 442-43.)

6) In its practical work, if it wants to preserve the *unity* of its ranks, the Party must impose a *common* proletarian discipline, *equally* binding on all Party members, both leaders and rank-and-file. Therefore there should be no division within the Party into the "chosen few," on whom discipline is not binding, and the "many," on whom discipline is binding. If this condition is not observed, the integrity of the Party and the unity of its ranks cannot be maintained.

"The complete absence of *sensible* arguments on the part of Mar-tov and Co. against the editorial board appointed by the congress," Lenin wrote, "is best of all shown by their own catchword: 'We are not serfs!' . . . The mentality of the bourgeois intellectual, who regards himself as one of the 'chosen few' standing above mass organization and mass discipline, is expressed here with remarkable clarity. . . . It seems to the individualism of the intelligentsia . . . that *all* proletarian organization and discipline is *serfdom*." (Lenin, *Collected Works*, Russ. ed., Vol. VI, p. 282.)

And further:

"As we proceed with the building of a *real* party, the class-conscious worker must learn to distinguish the mentality of the soldier of the proletarian army from the mentality of the bourgeois intellectual who makes a display of anarchist phraseology, he must learn to *demand* that the duties of a Party member be fulfilled not only by the rank-and-filers, but by the 'people at the top' as well." (Lenin, *Selected Works*, Vol. II, pp. 445-46.)

Summing up his analysis of the differences, and defining the position of the Mensheviks as "opportunism in matters of organization," Lenin considered that one of the gravest sins of Menshevism lay in its under-estimation of the importance of party *organization* as a weapon of the proletariat in the struggle for its emancipation. The Mensheviks held that the party *organization* of the proletariat was of no great importance for the victory of the revolution. Contrary to the Mensheviks, Lenin held that the *ideological* unity of the proletariat alone was *not enough* for victory; if victory was to be won, ideological unity would have to be *"consolidated"* by the "material unity of *organization"* of the proletariat. Only on this condition, Lenin considered, could the proletariat become an invincible force.

"In its struggle for power," Lenin wrote, "the proletariat has no other weapon but organization. Disunited by the rule of anarchic competition in the bourgeois world, ground down by forced labour for capital, constantly thrust back to the 'lower depths' of utter destitution, savagery and degeneration, the proletariat can become, and inevitably will become, an invincible force only when its ideological unification by the principles of Marxism is consolidated by the material unity of an organization which will weld millions of toilers into an army of the working class. Neither the decrepit rule of Russian tsardom, nor the senile rule of international capital will be able to withstand this army." (*Ibid.*, p. 466.)

With these prophetic words Lenin concludes his book.

Such were the fundamental organizational principles set forth by Lenin in his famous book, *One Step Forward, Two Steps Back.*

The importance of this book lies primarily in the fact that it successfully upheld the Party principle against the circle principle, and the Party against the disorganizers; that it smashed the opportunism of the Mensheviks on questions of organization, and laid the organizational foundations of the Bolshevik Party.

But this does not exhaust its significance. Its historic significance lies in the fact that in it Lenin, for the first time in the history of Marxism, elaborated the *doctrine of the Party* as the leading *organization* of the proletariat, as the principal *weapon* of the proletariat, without which the struggle for the dictatorship of the proletariat cannot be won.

The circulation of Lenin's book, *One Step Forward, Two Steps Back,* among the Party workers led the majority of the local organizations to rally to the side of Lenin.

But the more closely the organizations rallied around the Bolsheviks, the more malicious became the behaviour of the Menshevik leaders.

In the summer of 1904, thanks to Plekhanov's assistance and the treachery of Krassin and Noskov, two demoralized Bolsheviks, the Mensheviks captured the majority on the Central Committee. It was obvious that the Mensheviks were working for a split. The loss of *Iskra* and of the Central Committee put the Bolsheviks in a difficult position. It became necessary for them to organize their own Bolshevik newspaper.

It became necessary to make arrangements for a new Party congress, the Third Congress, so as to set up a new Central Committee and to settle accounts with the Mensheviks.

And this is what the Bolsheviks, headed by Lenin, set to work to do.

The Bolsheviks started a campaign for the summoning of the Third Party Congress. In August 1904, under Lenin's guidance, a conference of twenty-two Bolsheviks was held in Switzerland. The conference adopted an appeal addressed "To the Party." This appeal served the Bolsheviks as a program in their struggle for the summoning of the Third Congress.

At three regional conferences of Bolshevik Committees (Southern, Caucasian and Northern), a Bureau of Committees of the Majority was elected, which undertook the practical preparations for the Third Party Congress.

On January 4, 1905, the first issue of the Bolshevik newspaper *Vperyod* (*Forward*) appeared.

Thus two separate groups arose within the Party, the Bolsheviks and the Mensheviks, each with its own central body and its own press.

BRIEF SUMMARY

In the period 1901-04, with the growth of the revolutionary working-class movement, the Marxist Social-Democratic organizations in Russia grew and gained strength. In the stubborn struggle over principles, waged against the "Economists," the revolutionary line of Lenin's *Iskra* gained the victory, and the ideological confusion and "amateurish methods of work" were overcome.

Iskra linked up the scattered Social-Democratic circles and groups and prepared the way for the convocation of the Second Party Congress. At the Second Congress, held in 1903, the Russian Social-Democratic Labour Party was formed, a Party Program and Rules were adopted, and the central leading organs of the Party were set up.

In the struggle waged at the Second Congress for the complete victory of the *Iskra* trend in the R.S.D.L.P. there emerged two groups —the Bolshevik group and the Menshevik group.

The chief differences between the Bolsheviks and the Mensheviks after the Second Congress centred round questions of organization.

The Mensheviks drew closer to the "Economists" and took their place within the Party. For the time being the opportunism of the Mensheviks revealed itself in questions of organization. The Mensheviks were opposed to a militant revolutionary party of the type advocated by Lenin. They wanted a loose, unorganized, *khvostist* party. They worked to split the ranks of the Party. With Plekhanov's help, they seized *Iskra* and the Central Committee, and used these central organs for their own purposes—to split the Party.

Seeing that the Mensheviks were threatening a split, the Bolsheviks adopted measures to curb the splitters; they mustered the local organizations to back the convocation of a Third Congress, and they started their own newspaper, *Vperyod*.

Thus, on the eve of the first Russian revolution, when the Russo-Japanese war had already begun, the Bolsheviks and the Mensheviks acted as two separate political groups.

CHAPTER THREE

THE MENSHEVIKS AND THE BOLSHEVIKS IN THE PERIOD OF THE RUSSO-JAPANESE WAR AND THE FIRST RUSSIAN REVOLUTION

(1904-1907)

1. RUSSO-JAPANESE WAR. FURTHER RISE OF THE REVOLUTIONARY MOVEMENT IN RUSSIA. STRIKES IN ST. PETERSBURG. WORKERS' DEMONSTRATION BEFORE THE WINTER PALACE ON JANUARY 9, 1905. DEMONSTRATION FIRED UPON. OUTBREAK OF THE REVOLUTION

At the end of the nineteenth century the imperialist states began an intense struggle for mastery of the Pacific and for the partition of China. Tsarist Russia, too, took part in this struggle. In 1900, tsarist troops together with Japanese, German, British and French troops suppressed with unparalleled cruelty an uprising of the Chinese people directed against the foreign imperialists. Even before this the tsarist government had compelled China to surrender to Russia the Liaotung Peninsula with the fortress of Port Arthur. Russia secured the right to build railways on Chinese territory. A railway was built in Northern Manchuria—the Chinese-Eastern Railway—and Russian troops were stationed there to protect it. Northern Manchuria fell under the military occupation of tsarist Russia. Tsardom was advancing towards Korea. The Russian bourgeoisie was making plans for founding a "Yellow Russia" in Manchuria.

Its annexations in the Far East brought tsardom into conflict with another marauder, Japan, which had rapidly become an imperialist country and was also bent on annexing territories on the Asiatic continent, in the first place at the expense of China. Like tsarist Russia, Japan was striving to lay her hands on Korea and Manchuria. Already at that time Japan dreamed of seizing Sakhalin and the Russian Far East. Great Britain, who feared the growing strength of tsarist Russia in the Far East, secretly sided with Japan. War between Russia and Japan was brewing. The tsarist government was pushed to this war by the big bourgeoisie, which was seeking new markets, and by the more reactionary sections of the landlord class.

Without waiting for the tsarist government to declare war, Japan started hostilities herself. She had a good espionage service in Russia and anticipated that her foe would be unprepared for the struggle. In January 1904, without declaring war, Japan suddenly attacked the Russian fortress of Port Arthur and inflicted heavy losses on the Russian fleet lying in the harbour.

That is how the Russo-Japanese War began.

The tsarist government reckoned that the war would help to strengthen its political position and to check the revolution. But it miscalculated. The tsarist regime was shaken more than ever by the war.

Poorly armed and trained, and commanded by incompetent and corrupt generals, the Russian army suffered defeat after defeat.

Capitalists, government officials and generals grew rich on the war. Peculation was rampant. The troops were poorly supplied. When the army was short of ammunition, it would receive, as if in derision, carloads of icons. The soldiers said bitterly: "The Japanese are giving it to us with shells; we're to give it to them with icons." Special trains, instead of being used to evacuate the wounded, were loaded with property looted by the tsarist generals.

The Japanese besieged and subsequently captured Port Arthur. After inflicting a number of defeats on the tsarist army, they finally routed it near Mukden. In this battle the tsarist army of 300,000 men lost about 120,000 men, killed, wounded or taken prisoner. This was followed by the utter defeat and destruction in the Straits of Tsushima of the tsarist fleet dispatched from the Baltic to relieve Port Arthur. The defeat at Tsushima was disastrous: of the twenty warships dispatched by the tsar, thirteen were sunk or destroyed and four captured. Tsarist Russia had definitely lost the war.

The tsarist government was compelled to conclude an ignominious peace with Japan. Japan seized Korea and deprived Russia of Port Arthur and of half the Island of Sakhalin.

The people had not wanted the war and realized how harmful it would be for the country. They paid heavily for the backwardness of tsarist Russia.

The Bolsheviks and the Mensheviks adopted different attitudes towards the war.

The Mensheviks, including Trotsky, were sinking to a position of defending the "fatherland" of the tsar, the landlords and the capitalists.

The Bolsheviks, headed by Lenin, on the other hand, held that the defeat of the tsarist government in this predatory war would be useful, as it would weaken tsardom and strengthen the revolution.

The defeats of the tsarist armies opened the eyes of the masses to the rottenness of tsardom. Their hatred for the tsarist regime grew daily more intense. The fall of Port Arthur meant the beginning of the fall of the autocracy, Lenin wrote.

The tsar wanted to use the war to stifle the revolution. He achieved the very opposite. The Russo-Japanese War hastened the outbreak of the revolution.

In tsarist Russia the capitalist yoke was aggravated by the yoke of tsardom. The workers not only suffered from capitalist exploitation, from inhuman toil, but, in common with the whole people, suffered from a lack of all rights. The politically advanced workers therefore strove to lead the revolutionary movement of all the democratic elements in town and country against tsardom. The peasants were in dire need owing to lack of land and the numerous survivals of serfdom, and lived in a state of bondage to the landlords and kulaks. The nations inhabiting tsarist Russia groaned beneath a double yoke—that of their own land-lords and capitalists and that of the Russian landlords and capitalists. The economic crisis of 1900-03 had aggravated the hardships of the toiling masses; the war intensified them still further. The war defeats added fuel to the hatred of the masses for tsardom. The patience of the people was coming to an end.

As we see, there were grounds enough and to spare for revolution.

In December 1904 a huge and well-organized strike of workers took place in Baku, led by the Baku Committee of the Bolsheviks. The strike ended in a victory for the workers and a collective agreement was concluded between the oilfield workers and owners, the first of its kind in the history of the working-class movement in Russia.

The Baku strike marked the beginning of a revolutionary rise in Transcaucasia and in various parts of Russia.

"The Baku strike was the signal for the glorious actions in January and February all over Russia." (*Stalin.*)

This strike was like a clap of thunder heralding a great revolutionary storm.

The revolutionary storm broke with the events of January 9 (22, New Style), 1905, in St. Petersburg.

On January 3, 1905, a strike began at the biggest of the St. Peters-burg plants, the Putilov (now the Kirov) Works. The strike was caused by the dismissal of four workers. It grew rapidly and was joined by other St. Petersburg mills and factories. The strike became general. The movement grew formidable. The tsarist government decided to crush it while it was still in its earliest phase.

In 1904, prior to the Putilov strike, the police had used the services of an agent-provocateur, a priest by the name of Gapon, to form an organization of the workers known as the Assembly of Russian Factory Workers. This organization had its branches in all the districts of St. Petersburg. When the strike broke out the priest Gapon at the meetings of his society put forward a treacherous plan: all the workers were to gather on January 9 and, carrying church banners and portraits of the tsar, to march in peaceful procession to the Winter Palace and present a petition to the tsar stating their needs. The tsar would appear before the people, listen to them and satisfy their demands. Gapon undertook to assist the tsarist *Okhrana* by providing a pretext for firing on the workers and drowning the working-class movement in blood. But this police plot recoiled on the head of the tsarist government.

The petition was discussed at workers' meetings where amendments were made. Bolsheviks spoke at these meetings without openly announcing themselves as such. Under their influence, the petition was supplemented by demands for freedom of the press, freedom of speech, freedom of association for the workers, the convocation of a Constituent Assembly for the purpose of changing the political system of Russia, equality of all before the law, separation of church from the state, termination of the war, an 8-hour working day, and the handing over of the land to the peasants.

At these meetings the Bolsheviks explained to the workers that liberty could not be obtained by petitions to the tsar, but would have to be won by force of arms. The Bolsheviks warned the workers that they would be fired upon. But they were unable to prevent the procession to the Winter Palace. A large part of the workers still believed that the tsar would help them. The movement had taken a strong hold on the masses.

The petition of the St. Petersburg workers stated:

"We, the workingmen of St. Petersburg, our wives, our children and our helpless old parents, have come to Thee, our Sovereign, to seek truth and protection. We are poverty-stricken, we are oppressed, we are burdened with unendurable toil; we suffer humiliation and are not treated like human beings. ... We have suffered in patience, but we are being driven deeper and deeper into the slough of poverty, lack of rights and ignorance; we are being strangled by despotism and tyranny.... Our patience is exhausted. The dreaded moment has arrived when we would rather die than bear these intolerable sufferings any longer...."

Early in the morning of January 9, 1905, the workers marched to the Winter Palace where the tsar was then residing. They came with their whole families—wives, children and old folk—carrying portraits of the tsar and church banners. They chanted hymns as they marched. They were unarmed. Over 140,000 persons gathered in the streets.

They met with a hostile reception from Nicholas II. He gave orders to fire upon the unarmed workers. That day over a thousand workers were killed and more than two thousand wounded by the tsar's troops. The streets of St. Petersburg ran with workers' blood.

The Bolsheviks had marched with the workers. Many of them were killed or arrested. There, in the streets running with workers' blood, the Bolsheviks explained to the workers who it was that bore the guilt for this heinous crime and how he was to be fought.

January 9 came to be known as "Bloody Sunday." On that day the workers received a bloody lesson. It was their faith in the tsar that was riddled by bullets on that day. They came to realize that they could win their rights only by struggle. That evening barricades were already being erected in the working-class districts. The workers said: "The tsar gave it to us; we'll now give it to him!"

The fearful news of the tsar's bloody crime spread far and wide. The whole working class, the whole country was stirred by indignation and abhorrence. There was not a town where the workers did not strike in protest against the tsar's villainous act and did not put forward political demands. The workers now emerged into the streets with the slogan, "Down with autocracy!" In January the number of strikers reached the immense figure of 440,000. More workers came out on strike in one month than during the whole preceding decade. The working-class movement rose to an unprecedented height.

Revolution in Russia had begun.

2. WORKERS' POLITICAL STRIKES AND DEMONSTRATIONS. GROWTH OF THE REVOLUTIONARY MOVEMENT AMONG THE PEASANTS. REVOLT ON THE BATTLESHIP "POTEMKIN"

After January 9 the revolutionary struggle of the workers grew more acute and assumed a political character. The workers began to pass from economic strikes and sympathy strikes to political strikes, to demonstrations, and in places to armed resistance to the tsarist troops. Particularly stubborn and well organized were the strikes in the big cities such as St. Petersburg, Moscow, Warsaw, Riga and Baku, where large numbers of workers were concentrated. The metal workers marched in the front ranks of the fighting proletariat. By their strikes, the vanguard of the workers stirred up the less class-conscious sections and roused the whole working class to the struggle. The influence of the Social-Democrats grew rapidly.

The May Day demonstrations in a number of towns were marked by clashes with police and troops. In Warsaw, the demonstration was fired upon and several hundred persons were killed or wounded. At the call of the Polish Social-Democrats the workers replied to the shooting in Warsaw by a general protest strike. Strikes and demonstrations did not cease throughout the month of May. In that month over 200,000 workers went on strike throughout Russia. General strikes broke out in Baku, Lodz and Ivanovo-Voznesensk. More and more frequently the strikers and demonstrators clashed with the tsarist troops. Such clashes took place in a number of cities—Odessa, Warsaw, Riga, Lodz and others.

Particularly acute was the struggle in Lodz, a large Polish industrial centre. The workers erected scores of barricades in the streets of Lodz and for three days (June 22-24, 1905) battled in the streets against the tsarist troops. Here armed action merged with a general strike. Lenin regarded these battles as the first armed action of the workers in Russia.

The outstanding strike that summer was that of the workers of Ivanovo-Voznesensk. It lasted for about two and a half months, from the end of May to the beginning of August 1905. About 70,000 workers, among them many women, took part in the strike. It was led by the Bolshevik Northern Committee. Thousands of workers gathered almost daily outside the city on the banks of the River Talka. At these meetings they discussed their needs. The workers' meetings were addressed by Bolsheviks. In order to crush the strike, the tsarist authorities ordered the troops to disperse the workers and to fire upon them. Several scores of workers were killed and several hundred wounded. A state of emergency was proclaimed in the city. But the workers remained firm and would not return to work. They and their families starved, but would not surrender. It was only extreme exhaustion that in the end compelled them to return to work. The strike steeled the workers. It was an example of the courage, staunchness, endurance and solidarity of the working class. It was a real political education for the workers of Ivanovo-Voznesensk.

During the strike the workers of Ivanovo-Voznesensk set up a Council of Representatives, which was actually one of the first Soviets of Workers' Deputies in Russia.

The workers' political strikes stirred up the whole country.

Following the town, the countryside began to rise. In the spring, peasant unrest broke out. The peasants marched in great crowds against the landlords, raided their estates, sugar refineries and distilleries, and set fire to their palaces and manors. In a number of places the peasants seized the land, resorted to wholesale cutting down of forests, and demanded that the landed estates be turned over to the people. They seized the landlords' stores of grain and other products and divided them among the starving. The landlords fled in panic to the towns. The tsarist government dispatched soldiers and Cossacks to crush the peasants' revolts. The troops fired on the peasants, arrested the "ringleaders" and flogged and tortured them. But the peasants would not cease their struggle.

The peasant movement spread ever wider in the central parts of Russia, the Volga region, and in Transcaucasia, especially in Georgia.

The Social-Democrats penetrated deeper into the countryside. The Central Committee of the Party issued an appeal to the peasants entitled: "To You, Peasants, We Address Our Word!" The Social-Democratic committees in the Tver, Saratov, Poltava, Chernigov, Ekaterinoslav, Tiflis and many other provinces issued appeals to the peasants. In the villages, the Social-Democrats would arrange meetings, organize circles among the peasants, and set up peasant committees. In the summer of 1905 strikes of agricultural labourers, organized by Social-Democrats, occurred in many places.

But this was only the beginning of the peasant struggle. The peasant movement affected only 85 uyezds (districts), or roughly one-seventh of the total number of uyezds in the European part of tsarist Russia.

The movement of the workers and peasants and the series of reverses suffered by the Russian troops in the Russo-Japanese War had its influence on the armed forces. This bulwark of tsardom began to totter.

In June 1905 a revolt broke out on the *Potemkin*, a battleship of the Black Sea Fleet. The battleship was at that time stationed near Odessa, where a general strike of the workers was in progress. The insurgent sailors wreaked vengeance on their more detested officers and brought the vessel to Odessa. The battleship *Potemkin* had gone over to the side of the revolution.

Lenin attributed immense importance to this revolt. He considered it necessary for the Bolsheviks to assume the leadership of this movement and to link it up with the movement of the workers, peasants and the local garrisons.

The tsar dispatched several warships against the *Potemkin*, but the sailors of these vessels refused to fire on their insurgent comrades. For several days the red ensign of revolution waved from the mast of the battleship *Potemkin*. But at that time, in 1905, the Bolshevik Party was not the only party leading the movement, as was the case later, in 1917. There were quite a number of Mensheviks, Socialist-Revolutionaries and Anarchists on board the *Potemkin*. Consequently, although individual Social-Democrats took part in the revolt, it lacked proper and sufficiently experienced leadership. At decisive moments part of the sailors wavered. The other vessels of the Black Sea Fleet did not join the revolt of the *Potemkin*. Having run short of coal and provisions, the revolutionary battleship was compelled to make for the Rumanian shore and there surrender to the authorities.

The revolt of the sailors on the battleship *Potemkin* ended in defeat. The sailors who subsequently fell into the hands of the tsarist government were committed for trial. Some were executed and others condemned to exile and penal servitude. But the revolt in itself was an event of the utmost importance. The *Potemkin* revolt was the first instance of mass revolutionary action in the army and navy, the first occasion on which a large unit of the armed forces of the tsar sided with the revolution. This revolt made the idea of the army and navy joining forces with the working class, the people, more comprehensible to and nearer to the heart of the workers and peasants, and especially of the soldiers and sailors themselves.

The workers' recourse to mass political strikes and demonstrations, the growth of the peasant movement, the armed clashes between the people and the police and troops, and, finally, the revolt in the Black Sea Fleet, all went to show that conditions were ripening for an armed uprising of the people. This stirred the liberal bourgeoisie into action. Fearing the revolution, and at the same time frightening the tsar with the spectre of revolution, it sought to come to terms with the tsar against the revolution; it demanded slight reforms "for the people" so as to "pacify" the people, to split the forces of the revolution and thus avert the "horrors of revolution." "Better part with some of our land than part with our heads," said the liberal landlords. The liberal bourgeoisie was preparing to share power with the tsar. "The proletariat is fighting; the bourgeoisie is stealing towards power," Lenin wrote in those days in reference to the tactics of the working class and the tactics of the liberal bourgeoisie.

The tsarist government continued to suppress the workers and peasants with brutal ferocity. But it could not help seeing that it would never cope with the revolution by repressive measures alone. Therefore, without abandoning measures of repression, it resorted to a policy of manœuvring. On the one hand, with the help of its agents-provocateurs, it incited the peoples of Russia against each other, engineering Jewish pogroms and mutual massacres of Armenians and Tatars. On the other hand, it promised to convene a "representative institution" in the shape of a *Zemsky Sobor* or a State Duma, and instructed the Minister Bulygin to draw up a project for such a Duma, stipulating, however, that it was to have no legislative powers. All these measures were adopted in order to split the forces of revolution and to sever from it the moderate sections of the people.

The Bolsheviks declared a boycott of the Bulygin Duma with the aim of frustrating this travesty of popular representation.

The Mensheviks, on the other hand, decided not to sabotage the Duma and considered it necessary to take part in it.

3. TACTICAL DIFFERENCES BETWEEN BOLSHEVIKS AND MEN-SHEVIKS. THIRD PARTY CONGRESS. LENIN'S "TWO TACTICS OF SOCIAL-DEMOCRACY IN THE DEMOCRATIC REVOLUTION." TACTICAL FOUNDATIONS OF THE MARXIST PARTY

The revolution had set in motion all classes of society. The turn in the political life of the country caused by the revolution dislodged them from their old wonted positions and compelled them to regroup themselves in conformity with the new situation. Each class and each party endeavoured to work out its tactics, its line of conduct, its attitude towards other classes, and its attitude towards the government. Even the tsarist government found itself compelled to devise new and unaccustomed tactics, as instanced by the promise to convene a "representative institution"—the Bulygin Duma.

The Social-Democratic Party, too, had to work out its tactics. This was dictated by the growing tide of the revolution. It was dictated by the practical questions that faced the proletariat and brooked no delay: organization of armed uprising, overthrow of the tsarist government, creation of a provisional revolutionary government, participation of the

Social-Democrats in this government, attitude towards the peasantry and towards the liberal bourgeoisie, etc. The Social-Democrats had to work out for themselves carefully considered and uniform Marxist tactics.

But owing to the opportunism of the Mensheviks and their splitting activities, the Russian Social-Democratic Party was at that time divided into two groups. The split could not yet be considered complete, and *formally* the two groups were not yet two separate parties; but *in reality* they very much resembled two separate parties, each with its own leading centre and its own press.

What helped to widen the split was the fact that to their old differences with the majority of the Party over *organizational* questions the Mensheviks added new differences, differences over *tactical* questions.

The absence of a united party resulted in the absence of uniform party tactics.

A way out of the situation may have been found by immediately summoning another congress, the Third Congress of the Party, establishing common tactics and binding the minority to carry out in good faith the decisions of the congress, the decisions of the majority. This was what the Bolsheviks proposed to the Mensheviks. But the Mensheviks would not hear of summoning the Third Congress. Considering it a crime to leave the Party any longer without tactics endorsed by the Party and binding upon all Party members, the Bolsheviks decided to take the initiative of convening the Third Congress into their own hands.

All the Party organizations, both Bolshevik and Menshevik, were invited to the congress. But the Mensheviks refused to take part in the Third Congress and decided to hold one of their own. As the number of delegates at their congress proved to be small, they called it a conference, but actually it was a congress, a Menshevik party congress, whose decisions were considered binding on all Mensheviks.

The Third Congress of the Russian Social-Democratic Party met in London in April 1905. It was attended by 24 delegates representing 20 Bolshevik Committees. All the large organizations of the Party were represented.

The congress condemned the Mensheviks as "a section that had split away from the Party" and passed on to the business on hand, the working out of the tactics of the Party.

At the same time that this congress was held, the Mensheviks held their conference in Geneva.

"Two congresses—two parties," was the way Lenin summed up the situation.

Both the congress and the conference virtually discussed the same tactical questions, but the decisions they arrived at were diametrically opposite. The two sets of resolutions adopted by the congress and the conference respectively revealed the whole depth of the tactical difference between the Third Party Congress and the Menshevik conference, between the Bolsheviks and the Mensheviks.

Here are the main points of these differences.

Tactical line of the Third Party Congress. The congress held that despite the bourgeois-democratic character of the revolution in progress, despite the fact that it could not at the given moment go beyond the limits of what was possible within the framework of capitalism, it was primarily the proletariat that was interested in its complete victory, for the victory of this revolution would enable the proletariat to organize itself, to grow politically, to acquire experience and competence in political leadership of the toiling masses, and to proceed from the bourgeois revolution to the Socialist revolution.

Tactics of the proletariat designed to achieve the complete victory of the bourgeois-democratic revolution could find support only in the peasantry, for the latter could not settle scores with the landlords and obtain possession of their lands without the complete victory of the revolution. The peasantry was therefore the natural ally of the proletariat.

The liberal bourgeoisie was not interested in the complete victory of this revolution, for it needed the tsarist regime as a whip against the workers and peasants, whom it feared more than anything else, and it would strive to preserve the tsarist regime, only somewhat restricting its powers. The liberal bourgeoisie would therefore attempt to end matters by coming to terms with the tsar on the basis of a constitutional monarchy.

The revolution would win only if headed by the proletariat; if the proletariat, as the leader of the revolution, secured an alliance with the peasantry; if the liberal bourgeoisie were isolated; if the Social-Democratic Party took an active part in the organization of the uprising of the people against tsardom; if, as the result of a successful uprising, a provisional revolutionary government were set up that would be capable of destroying the counter-revolution root and branch and convening a Constituent Assembly representing the whole people; and if the Social-Democratic Party did not refuse, the circumstances being favourable, to take part in the provisional revolutionary government in order to carry the revolution to its conclusion.

Tactical line of the Menshevik conference. Inasmuch as the revolution was a bourgeois revolution, only the liberal bourgeoisie could be its leader. The proletariat should not establish close relations with the peasantry, but with the liberal bourgeoisie. The chief thing was not to frighten off the liberal bourgeoisie by a display of revolutionary spirit and not to give it a pretext to recoil from the revolution, for if it were to recoil from the revolution, the revolution would be weakened.

It was possible that the uprising would prove victorious; but after the triumph of the uprising the Social-Democratic Party should step aside so as not to frighten away the liberal bourgeoisie. It was possible that as a result of the uprising a provisional revolutionary government would be set up; but the Social-Democratic Party should under no circumstances take part in it, because this government would not be Socialist in character, and because—and this was the chief thing—by its participation in this government and by its revolutionary spirit, the Social-Democratic Party might frighten off the liberal bourgeoisie and thus undermine the revolution.

It would be better for the prospects of the revolution if some sort of representative institution were convened, of the nature of a *Zemsky Sobor* or a State Duma, which could be subjected to the pressure of the working class from without so as to transform it into a Constituent Assembly or impel it to convene a Constituent Assembly.

The proletariat had its own specific, purely wage-worker interests, and it should attend to these interests only and not try to become the leader of the bourgeois revolution, which, being a general political revolution, concerned all classes and not the proletariat alone.

Such, in brief, were the two tactics of the two groups of the Russian Social-Democratic Labour Party.

In his historic book, *Two Tactics of Social-Democracy in the Democratic Revolution*, Lenin gave a classical criticism of the tactics of the Mensheviks and a brilliant substantiation of the Bolshevik tactics.

This book appeared in July 1905, that is, two months after the Third Party Congress. One might assume from its title that Lenin dealt in it only with tactical questions relating to the period of the bourgeois-democratic revolution and had only the Russian Mensheviks in mind. But as a matter of fact when he criticized the tactics of the Mensheviks he at the same time exposed the tactics of international opportunism; and when he substantiated the Marxist tactics in the period of the bourgeois revolution and drew the distinction between the bourgeois revolution and the Socialist revolution, he at the same time formulated the fundamental principles of the Marxist tactics in the period of transition from the bourgeois revolution to the Socialist revolution.

The fundamental tactical principles expounded by Lenin in his pamphlet, *Two Tactics of Social-Democracy in the Democratic Revolution*, were as follows:

1) The main tactical principle, one that runs through Lenin's whole book, is that the proletariat can and must be the *leader* of the bourgeois-democratic revolution, the *guiding force* of the bourgeois-democratic revolution in Russia.

Lenin admitted the bourgeois character of this revolution, for, as he said, "it is incapable of *directly* overstepping the bounds of a mere democratic revolution." However, he held that it was not a revolution of the upper strata, but a people's revolution, one that would set in motion the whole people, the whole working class, the whole peasantry. Hence the attempts of the Mensheviks to belittle the significance of the bourgeois revolution for the proletariat, to depreciate the role of the proletariat in it, and to keep the proletariat away from it were in Lenin's opinion a betrayal of the interests of the proletariat.

"Marxism," Lenin said, "teaches the proletarian not to keep aloof from the bourgeois revolution, not to be indifferent to it, not to allow the leadership of the revolution to be assumed by the bourgeoisie, but, on the contrary, to take a most energetic part in it, to fight most resolutely for consistent proletarian democracy, for carrying the revolution to its conclusion." (Lenin, *Selected Works*, Vol. III, p. 77.)

"We must not forget," Lenin says further, "that there is not, nor can there be, at the present time, any other means of bringing Socialism nearer, than complete political liberty, than a democratic republic." (*Ibid.*, p. 122.)

Lenin foresaw two possible outcomes of the revolution:

a) Either it would end in a decisive victory over tsardom, in the overthrow of tsardom and the establishment of a democratic republic;

b) Or, if the forces were inadequate, it might end in a deal between the tsar and the bourgeoisie at the expense of the people, in some sort of curtailed constitution, or, most likely, in some caricature of a constitution.

The proletariat was interested in the better outcome of the two, that is, in a decisive victory over tsardom. But such an outcome was possible only if the proletariat succeeded in becoming the leader and guide of the revolution.

"The outcome of the revolution," Lenin said, "depends on whether the working class will play the part of a subsidiary to the bourgeoisie, a subsidiary that is powerful in the force of its onslaught

against the autocracy but impotent politically, or whether it will play
the part of leader of the people's revolution." (*Ibid.*, p. 41.)

Lenin maintained that the proletariat had every *possibility* of escap-
ing the fate of a subsidiary to the bourgeoisie, and of becoming the leader
of the bourgeois-democratic revolution. This possibility, according to
Lenin, arises from the following.

First, "the proletariat, being, by virtue of its very position, the most
advanced and the only consistently revolutionary class, is for that very
reason called upon to play the leading part in the general democratic
revolutionary movement in Russia." (Lenin, *Collected Works*, Russ.
ed., Vol. VIII, p. 75.)

Secondly, the proletariat has its own political party, which is independent of the bourgeoisie and which enables the proletariat to weld
itself "into a united and independent political force." (*Ibid.*, p. 75.)

Thirdly, the proletariat is more interested than the bourgeoisie in
a decisive victory of the revolution, in view of which "*in a certain sense
the bourgeois revolution is *more advantageous* to the proletariat than to
the bourgeoisie." (*Ibid.*, p. 57.)

"It is to the advantage of the bourgeoisie," Lenin wrote, "to
rely on certain remnants of the past as against the proletariat, for
instance, on the monarchy, the standing army, etc. It is to the
advantage of the bourgeoisie if the bourgeois revolution does not too
resolutely sweep away all the remnants of the past, but leaves some
of them, *i.e.*, if this revolution is not fully consistent, if it is not complete and if it is not determined and relentless.... It is of greater
advantage to the bourgeoisie if the necessary changes in the direction
of bourgeois democracy take place more slowly, more gradually,
more cautiously, less resolutely, by means of reforms and not by
means of revolution ... if these changes develop as little as possible
the independent revolutionary activity, initiative and energy of the
common people, *i.e.*, the peasantry and especially the workers, for
otherwise it will be easier for the workers, as the French say, 'to
hitch the rifle from one shoulder to the other,' *i.e.*, to turn against
the bourgeoisie the guns which the bourgeois revolution will place
in their hands, the liberty which the revolution will bring, the democratic institutions which will spring up on the ground that is cleared
of serfdom. On the other hand, it is more advantageous for the
working class if the necessary changes in the direction of bourgeois
democracy take place by way of revolution and not by way of
reform; for the way of reform is the way of delay, of procrastina-

tion, of the painfully slow decomposition of the putrid parts of the national organism. It is the proletariat and the peasantry that suffer first of all and most of all from their putrefaction. The revolutionary way is the way of quick amputation, which is the least painful to the proletariat, the way of the direct removal of the decomposing parts, the way of fewest concessions to and least consideration for the monarchy and the disgusting, vile, rotten and contaminating institutions which go with it." (Lenin, *Selected Works*, Vol. III, pp. 75-6.)

"That," Lenin continues, "is why the proletariat fights in the front ranks for a republic and contemptuously rejects silly and unworthy advice to take care not to frighten away the bourgeoisie." (*Ibid.*, p. 108.)

In order to convert the *possibility* of the proletarian leadership of the revolution into a *reality*, in order that the proletariat might *actually* become the leader, the guiding force of the bourgeois revolution, at least two conditions were needed, according to Lenin.

First, it was necessary for the proletariat to have an ally who was interested in a decisive victory over tsardom and who might be disposed to accept the leadership of the proletariat. This was dictated by the very idea of leadership, for a leader ceases to be a leader if there is nobody to lead, a guide ceases to be a guide if there is nobody to guide. Lenin considered that the peasantry was such an ally.

Secondly, it was necessary that the class, which was fighting the proletariat for the leadership of the revolution and striving to become its sole leader, should be forced out of the arena of leadership and isolated. This too was dictated by the very idea of leadership, which precluded the possibility of there being two leaders of the revolution. Lenin considered that the liberal bourgeoisie was such a class.

"Only the proletariat can be a consistent fighter for democracy," Lenin said. "It may become a victorious fighter for democracy only if the peasant masses join its revolutionary struggle." (*Ibid.*, p. 86.) And further:

"The peasantry includes a great number of semi-proletarian as well as petty-bourgeois elements. This causes it also to be unstable and compels the proletariat to unite in a strictly class party. But the instability of the peasantry differs radically from the instability of the bourgeoisie, for at the present time the peasantry is interested not so much in the absolute preservation of private property as in the confiscation of the landed estates, one of the principal forms of private property. While this does not cause the peasantry to become Socialist or cease to be petty-bourgeois, the peasantry is capable of becoming a whole-hearted and most radical adherent of the democratic revolution. The peasantry will inevitably become such if only the progress of revolutionary events, which is enlightening it, is not interrupted too soon by the treachery of the bourgeoisie and the defeat of the proletariat. Subject to this condition, the peasantry will inevitably become a bulwark of the revolution and the republic, for only a completely victorious revolution can give the peasantry *everything* in the sphere of agrarian reforms—*everything* that the peasants desire, of which they dream, and of which they truly stand in need." (*Ibid.*, pp. 108-09.)

Analysing the objections of the Mensheviks, who asserted that these Bolshevik tactics "will compel the bourgeois classes to recoil from the cause of the revolution and thus curtail its scope," and characterizing these objections as "tactics of betrayal of the revolution," as "tactics which would convert the proletariat into a wretched appendage of the bourgeois classes," Lenin wrote:

"Those who really understand the role of the peasantry in the victorious Russian revolution would not dream of saying that the sweep of the revolution would be diminished if the bourgeoisie recoiled from it. For, as a matter of fact, the Russian revolution will begin to assume its real sweep, will really assume the widest revolutionary sweep possible in the epoch of bourgeois-democratic revolution, only when the bourgeoisie recoils from it and when the masses of the peasantry come out as active revolutionaries side by side with the proletariat. In order that it may be consistently carried to its conclusion, our democratic revolution must rely on such forces as are capable of paralysing the inevitable inconsistency of the bourgeoisie, *i.e.*, capable precisely of 'causing it to recoil from the revolution.'" (*Ibid.*, p. 110.)

Such is the main tactical principle regarding the proletariat as the leader of the bourgeois revolution, the fundamental tactical principle regarding the hegemony (leading role) of the proletariat in the bourgeois revolution, expounded by Lenin in his book, *Two Tactics of Social-Democracy in the Democratic Revolution.*

This was a new line of the Marxist party on questions of tactics in the bourgeois-democratic revolution, a line fundamentally different from the tactical lines hitherto existing in the arsenal of Marxism. The situation before had been that in the bourgeois revolution—in Western Europe, for instance—it was the bourgeoisie that played the leading part, the proletariat willy-nilly playing the part of its subsidiary, while the peasantry was a reserve of the bourgeoisie. The Marxists considered such a combination more or less inevitable, at the same time stipulating that the proletariat must as far as possible fight for its own immediate class demands and have its own political party. Now, under the new historical conditions, according to Lenin, the situation was changing in such a way that the proletariat was becoming the guiding force of the bourgeois revolution, the bourgeoisie was being edged out of the leadership of the revolution, while the peasantry was becoming a reserve of the proletariat.

The claim that Plekhanov "also stood" for the hegemony of the proletariat is based upon a misunderstanding. Plekhanov flirted with the idea of the hegemony of the proletariat and was not averse to recognizing it in words—that is true. But in reality he was opposed to this idea in its essence. The hegemony of the proletariat implies the leading role of the proletariat in the bourgeois revolution, accompanied by a policy of *alliance* between the proletariat and the peasantry and a policy of *isolation* of the liberal bourgeoisie; whereas Plekhanov, as we know, was *opposed* to the policy of isolating the liberal bourgeoisie, *favoured* a policy of *agreement* with the liberal bourgeoisie, and was *opposed* to a policy of alliance between the proletariat and the peasantry. As a matter of fact, Plekhanov's tactical line was the Menshevik line which rejected the hegemony of the proletariat.

2) Lenin considered that the most effective means of overthrowing tsardom and achieving a democratic republic was a victorious armed uprising of the people. Contrary to the Mensheviks, Lenin held that "the general democratic revolutionary movement *has already brought about the necessity* for an armed uprising," that "the organization of the proletariat for uprising" had already "been placed on the order of the day as one of the essential, principal and *indispensable* tasks of the Party," and that it was necessary "to adopt the *most energetic* measures to arm the proletariat and to ensure the possibility of directly leading the uprising." (Lenin, *Collected Works*, Russ. ed., Vol. VIII, p. 75.)

To guide the masses to an uprising and to turn it into an uprising of the whole people, Lenin deemed it necessary to issue such slogans, such appeals to the masses as would set free their revolutionary initiative, organize them for insurrection and disorganize the machinery of power of tsardom. He considered that these slogans were furnished by the tactical decisions of the Third Party Congress, to the defence of which his book *Two Tactics of Social-Democracy in the Democratic Revolution* was devoted.

The following, he considered, were these slogans:

a) "Mass political strikes, which may be of great importance at the beginning and in the very process of the insurrection" (*ibid.*, p. 75);

b) "Immediate realization, in a revolutionary way, of the 8-hour working day and of the other immediate demands of the working class" (*ibid.*, p. 47);

c) "Immediate organization of revolutionary peasant committees in order to carry out" in a revolutionary way "all the democratic changes," including the confiscation of the landed estates (*ibid.*, p. 88);

d) Arming of the workers.

Here two points are of particular interest:

First, the tactics of realizing *in a revolutionary way* the 8-hour day in the towns, and the democratic changes in the countryside, that is, a way which disregards the authorities, disregards the law, which ignores both the authorities and the law, breaks the existing laws and establishes a new order by unauthorized action, as an accomplished fact. This was a new tactical method, the use of which paralysed the machinery of power of tsardom and set free the activity and creative initiative of the masses. These tactics gave rise to the revolutionary strike committees in the towns and the revolutionary peasant committees in the countryside, the former of which later developed into the Soviets of Workers' Deputies and the latter into the Soviets of Peasants' Deputies.

Secondly, the use of *mass political strikes,* the use of general political strikes, which later, in the course of the revolution, were of prime importance in the revolutionary mobilization of the masses. This was a new and very important weapon in the hands of the proletariat, a weapon hitherto unknown in the practice of the Marxist parties and one that subsequently gained recognition.

Lenin held that following the victorious uprising of the people the tsarist government should be replaced by a provisional revolutionary government. It would be the task of the provisional revolutionary government to consolidate the conquests of the revolution, to crush the resistance of the counter-revolution and to give effect to the minimum program of the Russian Social-Democratic Labour Party. Lenin maintained that unless these tasks were accomplished a decisive victory over tsardom would be impossible. And in order to accomplish these tasks and achieve a decisive victory over tsardom, the provisional revolutionary government would have to be not an ordinary kind of government, but a government of the dictatorship of the victorious classes, of the workers and peasants; it would have to be a revolutionary dictatorship of the proletariat and peasantry. Citing Marx's well-known thesis that "after

a revolution every provisional organization of the state requires a dictatorship, and an energetic dictatorship at that," Lenin came to the conclusion
that if the provisional revolutionary government was to ensure a decisive
victory over tsardom, it could be nothing else but a dictatorship of the
proletariat and peasantry.

"A decisive victory of the revolution over tsardom is *the revolu-
tionary-democratic dictatorship of the proletariat and the peasantry,*"
Lenin said. ". . . And such a victory will be precisely a dictatorship,
i.e., it must inevitably rely on military force, on the arming of the
masses, on an uprising and not on institutions of one kind or another, established in a 'lawful' or 'peaceful' way. It can be only a
dictatorship, for the realization of the changes which are urgently and
absolutely indispensable for the proletariat and the peasantry will
call forth the desperate resistance of the landlords, of the big bourgeoisie, and of tsardom. Without a dictatorship it is impossible to
break down that resistance and to repel the counter-revolutionary
attempts. But of course it will be a democratic, not a Socialist dictatorship. It will not be able (without a series of intermediary stages
of revolutionary development) to affect the foundations of capitalism.
At best it may bring about a radical redistribution of landed property
in favour of the peasantry, establish consistent and full democracy,
including the formation of a republic, eradicate all the oppressive
features of Asiatic bondage, not only in village but also in factory
life, lay the foundation for a thorough improvement in the position
of the workers and for a rise in their standard of living, and—last
but not least—carry the revolutionary conflagration into Europe.
Such a victory will by no means as yet transform our bourgeois
revolution into a Socialist revolution; the democratic revolution
will not directly overstep the bounds of bourgeois social and economic
relationships; nevertheless, the significance of such a victory for the
future development of Russia and of the whole world will be immense. Nothing will raise the revolutionary energy of the world
proletariat so much, nothing will shorten the path leading to its
complete victory to such an extent, as this decisive victory of the
revolution that has now started in Russia." (Lenin, *Selected Works,*
Vol. III, p. 82-3.)

As to the attitude of the Social-Democrats towards the provisional
revolutionary government and as to whether it would be permissible for
them to take part in it, Lenin fully upheld the resolution of the Third
Party Congress on the subject, which reads:

"Subject to the relation of forces, and other factors which cannot be exactly determined beforehand, representatives of our Party may participate in the provisional revolutionary government for the purpose of relentless struggle against all counter-revolutionary attempts and of the defence of the independent interests of the working class; an indispensable condition for such participation is that the Party should exercise strict control over its representatives and that the independence of the Social-Democratic Party, which is striving for a complete Socialist revolution and, consequently, is irreconcilably hostile to all the bourgeois parties, should be strictly maintained; whether the participation of Social-Democrats in the provisional revolutionary government prove possible or not, we must propagate among the broadest masses of the proletariat the necessity for permanent pressure to be brought to bear upon the provisional government by the armed proletariat, led by the Social-Democratic Party, for the purpose of defending, consolidating and extending the gains of the revolution." (*Ibid.*, pp. 46-7.)

As to the Mensheviks' objection that the provisional government would still be a bourgeois government, that the Social-Democrats could not be permitted to take part in such a government unless one wanted to commit the same mistake as the French Socialist Millerand when he joined the French bourgeois government, Lenin parried this objection by pointing out that the Mensheviks were here mixing up two *different* things and were betraying their inability to treat the question as Marxists should. In France it was a question of Socialists taking part in a *reactionary* bourgeois government at a time when *there was no* revolutionary situation in the country, which made it incumbent upon the Socialists not to join such a government; in Russia, on the other hand, it was a question of Socialists taking part in a *revolutionary* bourgeois government fighting for the victory *of the revolution* at a time when the revolution was *in full swing*, a circumstance which would make it *permissible* for, and, under favourable circumstances, *incumbent* upon the Social-Democrats to take part in such a government in order to strike at the counter-revolution not only "from below," from without, but also "from above," from within the government.

3) While advocating the victory of the bourgeois revolution and the achievement of a democratic republic, Lenin had not the least intention of coming to a halt in the democratic stage and confining the scope of the revolutionary movement to the accomplishment of bourgeois-democratic tasks. On the contrary, Lenin maintained that following upon the accomplishment of the democratic tasks, the proletariat and the other

exploited masses would have to begin a struggle, this time for the *Socialist* revolution. Lenin knew this and regarded it as the duty of Social-Democrats to do everything to make the bourgeois-democratic revolution *pass into* the Socialist revolution. Lenin held that the dictatorship of the proletariat and the peasantry was necessary not in order to *end* the revolution at the point of consummation of its victory over tsardom, but in order to *prolong* the state of revolution as much as possible, to destroy the last remnants of counter-revolution, to make the flame of revolution spread to Europe, and, having in the meantime given the proletariat the opportunity of educating itself politically and organizing itself into a great army, to begin the direct transition to the Socialist revolution.

Dealing with the scope of the bourgeois revolution, and with the character the Marxist party should lend it, Lenin wrote:

"The proletariat must carry to completion the democratic revolution, by allying to itself the mass of the peasantry in order to crush by force the resistance of the autocracy and to paralyse the instability of the bourgeoisie. The proletariat must accomplish the Socialist revolution by allying to itself the mass of the semi-proletarian elements of the population in order to crush by force the resistance of the bourgeoisie and to paralyse the instability of the peasantry and the petty bourgeoisie. Such are the tasks of the proletariat, which the new *Iskra*-ists (that is, Mensheviks—*Ed.*) *always* present so narrowly in their arguments and resolutions about the scope of the revolution." (*Ibid.*, pp. 110-11.)

And further:

"At the head of the whole of the people, and particularly of the peasantry—for complete freedom, for a consistent democratic revolution, for a republic! At the head of all the toilers and the exploited—for Socialism! Such must in practice be the policy of the revolutionary proletariat, such is the class slogan which must permeate and determine the solution of every tactical problem, of every practical step of the workers' party during the revolution." (*Ibid.*, p. 124.)

In order to leave nothing unclear, two months after the appearance of the *Two Tactics* Lenin wrote an article entitled "Attitude of Social-Democrats to the Peasant Movement," in which he explained:

"From the democratic revolution we shall at once, and just in accordance with the measure of our strength, the strength of the class-conscious and organized proletariat, begin to pass to the Socialist revolution. We stand for uninterrupted revolution. We shall not stop half way." (*Ibid.*, p. 145.)

This was a new line in the question of the relation between the bourgeois revolution and the Socialist revolution, a new theory of a re-grouping of forces around the proletariat, towards the end of the bourgeois revolution, for a direct transition to the Socialist revolution—the theory of the bourgeois-democratic revolution *passing into* the Socialist revolution.

In working out this new line, Lenin based himself, first, on the well-known thesis of uninterrupted revolution advanced by Marx at the end of the forties of the last century in the Address to the Communist League, and, secondly, on the well-known idea of the necessity of combining the peasant revolutionary movement with the proletarian revolution which Marx expressed in a letter to Engels in 1856, saying that: "the whole thing in Germany will depend on the possibility of backing the proletarian revolution by some second edition of the Peasants' War." However, these brilliant ideas of Marx were not developed subsequently in the works of Marx and Engels, while the theoreticians of the Second International did their utmost to bury them and consign them to oblivion. To Lenin fell the task of bringing these forgotten ideas of Marx to light and restoring them to their full rights. But in restoring these Marxian ideas, Lenin did not—and could not—confine himself to merely repeating them, but developed them further and moulded them into a harmonious theory of Socialist revolution by introducing a new factor, an *indispensable* factor of the Socialist revolution, namely, an *alliance* of the proletariat with the semi-proletarian elements of town and country as a *condition* for the victory of the proletarian revolution.

This line confuted the tactical position of the West-European Social-Democratic parties who took it for granted that after the bourgeois revolution the peasant masses, including the poor peasants, would necessarily desert the revolution, as a result of which the bourgeois revolution would be followed by a prolonged *interval*, a long "lull" lasting fifty or a hundred years, if not longer, during which the proletariat would be "peacefully" exploited and the bourgeoisie would "lawfully" enrich itself until the time came round for a new revolution, a Socialist revolution.

This was a new theory which held that the *Socialist* revolution would be accomplished not by the proletariat in isolation as against the *whole* bourgeoisie, but by the proletariat as the leading class which would have as *allies* the semi-proletarian elements of the population, the "toiling and exploited millions."

According to this theory the hegemony of the proletariat in the bourgeois revolution, the proletariat *being in alliance* with the peasantry, would grow into the hegemony of the proletariat in the Socialist revolution, the proletariat now *being in alliance* with the other labouring and exploited masses, while the democratic dictatorship of the proletariat and the peasantry would prepare the ground for the Socialist dictatorship of the proletariat.

It refuted the theory current among the West-European Social-Democrats who denied the revolutionary potentialities of the semi-proletarian masses of town and country and took for granted that "apart from the bourgeoisie and the proletariat we perceive no social forces in our country in which oppositional or revolutionary combinations might find support" (these were Plekhanov's words, typical of the West-European Social-Democrats).

The West-European Social-Democrats held that in the Socialist revolution the proletariat would stand *alone*, against the *whole* bourgeoisie, *without* allies, against *all* the non-proletarian classes and strata. They would not take account of the fact that capital exploits not only the proletarians but also the semi-proletarian millions of town and country, who are crushed by capitalism and who may become allies of the proletariat in the struggle for the emancipation of society from the capitalist yoke. The West-European Social-Democrats therefore held that conditions were not yet ripe for a Socialist revolution in Europe, that the conditions could be considered ripe only when the proletariat became the majority of the nation, the majority of society, as a result of the further economic development of society.

This spurious anti-proletarian standpoint of the West-European Social-Democrats was completely upset by Lenin's theory of the Socialist revolution.

Lenin's theory did not yet contain any direct conclusion regarding the possibility of a victory of Socialism in one country, taken singly. But it did contain all, or nearly all, the fundamental elements necessary for the drawing of such a conclusion sooner or later.

As we know, Lenin arrived at this conclusion ten years later, in 1915.

Such are the fundamental tactical principles expounded by Lenin in his historic book, *Two Tactics of Social-Democracy in the Democratic Revolution*.

The historic significance of this book consists above all in the fact that in it Lenin ideologically shattered the petty-bourgeois tactical line of the Mensheviks, armed the working class of Russia for the further development of the bourgeois-democratic revolution, for a new onslaught on tsardom, and put before the Russian Social-Democrats a clear perspective of the necessity of the bourgeois revolution passing into the Socialist revolution.

But this does not exhaust the significance of Lenin's book. Its invaluable significance consists in that it enriched Marxism with a new theory of revolution and laid the foundation for the revolutionary tactics of the Bolshevik Party with the help of which in 1917 the proletariat of our country achieved the victory over capitalism.

4. FURTHER RISE OF THE REVOLUTION. ALL-RUSSIAN POLITICAL STRIKE OF OCTOBER 1905. RETREAT OF TSARDOM. THE TSAR'S MANIFESTO. RISE OF THE SOVIETS OF WORKERS' DEPUTIES

By the autumn of 1905 the revolutionary movement had swept the whole country and gained tremendous momentum.

On September 19 a printers' strike broke out in Moscow. It spread to St. Petersburg and a number of other cities. In Moscow itself the printers' strike was supported by the workers in other industries and developed into a general political strike.

In the beginning of October a strike started on the Moscow-Kazan Railway. Within two days it was joined by all the railwaymen of the Moscow railway junction and soon all the railways of the country were in the grip of the strike. The postal and telegraph services came to a standstill. In various cities of Russia the workers gathered at huge meetings and decided to down tools. The strike spread to factory after factory, mill after mill, city after city, and region after region. The workers were joined by the minor employees, students and intellectuals —lawyers, engineers and doctors.

The October political strike became an all-Russian strike which embraced nearly the whole country, including the most remote districts, and nearly all the workers, including the most backward strata. About one million industrial workers alone took part in the general political strike, not counting the large number of railwaymen, postal and telegraph employees and others. The whole life of the country came to a standstill. The government was paralysed.

The working class headed the struggle of the masses against the autocracy.

The Bolshevik slogan of a mass political strike had borne fruit.

The October general strike revealed the power and might of the proletarian movement and compelled the mortally frightened tsar to issue his Manifesto of October 17, 1905. This Manifesto promised the people "the unshakable foundations of civil liberty: real inviolability of person, and freedom of conscience, speech, assembly and association." It promised to convene a legislative Duma and to extend the franchise to all classes of the population.

Thus, Bulygin's deliberative Duma was swept away by the tide of revolution. The Bolshevik tactics of boycotting the Bulygin Duma proved to have been right.

Nevertheless, the Manifesto of October 17 was a fraud on the people, a trick of the tsar to gain some sort of respite in which to lull the credulous and to win time to rally his forces and then to strike at the revolution. In words the tsarist government promised liberty, but actually it granted nothing substantial. So far, promises were all that the workers and peasants had received from the government. Instead of the broad political amnesty which was expected, on October 21 amnesty was granted to only a small section of political prisoners. At the same time, with the object of dividing the forces of the people, the government engineered a number of sanguinary Jewish pogroms, in which many thousands of people perished; and in order to crush the revolution it created police-controlled gangster organizations known as the League of the Russian People and the League of Michael the Archangel. These organizations, in which a prominent part was played by reactionary landlords, merchants, priests, and semi-criminal elements of the vagabond type, were christened by the people "Black-Hundreds." The Black-Hundreds, with the support of the police, openly manhandled and murdered politically advanced workers, revolutionary intellectuals and students, burned down meeting places and fired upon assemblies of citizens. These so far were the only results of the tsar's Manifesto.

There was a popular song at the time which ran:
"The tsar caught fright, issued a Manifesto:
Liberty for the dead, for the living—arrest."

The Bolshevists explained to the masses that the Manifesto of October 17 was a trap. They branded the conduct of the government after the promulgation of the Manifesto as provocative. The Bolshevisks called the workers to arms, to prepare for armed uprising.

The workers set about forming fighting squads with greater energy than ever. It became clear to them that the first victory of October 17, wrested by the general political strike, demanded of them further efforts, the continuation of the struggle for the overthrow of tsardom.

Lenin regarded the Manifesto of October 17 as an expression of a certain temporary equilibrium of forces: the proletariat and the peasantry, having wrung the Manifesto from the tsar, *were still not strong enough* to overthrow tsardom, *whereas tsardom was no longer able* to rule by the old methods alone and had been compelled to give a paper *promise* of "civil liberties" and a "legislative" Duma.

In those stormy days of the October political strike, in the fire of the struggle against tsardom, the revolutionary creative initiative of the working-class masses forged a new and powerful weapon—the Soviets of Workers' Deputies.

The Soviets of Workers' Deputies—which were assemblies of delegates from all mills and factories—represented a type of mass political organization of the working class which the world had never seen before. The Soviets that first arose in 1905 were the *prototype* of the Soviet power which the proletariat, led by the Bolshevik Party, set up in 1917. The Soviets were a new revolutionary form of the creative initiative of the people. They were set up exclusively by the revolutionary sections of the population, in defiance of all laws and prescripts of tsardom. They were a manifestation of the independent action of the people who were rising to fight tsardom.

The Bolsheviks regarded the Soviets as the embryo of revolutionary power. They maintained that the strength and significance of the Soviets would depend solely on the strength and success of the uprising.

The Mensheviks regarded the Soviets neither as embryonic organs of revolutionary power nor as organs of uprising. They looked upon the Soviets as organs of local self-government, in the nature of democratized municipal government bodies.

In St. Petersburg, elections to the Soviet of Workers' Deputies took place in all the mills and factories on October 13 (26, New Style) 1905. The first meeting of the Soviet was held that night. Moscow followed St. Petersburg in forming a Soviet of Workers' Deputies.

The St. Petersburg Soviet of Workers' Deputies, being the Soviet of the most important industrial and revolutionary centre of Russia, the capital of the tsarist empire, ought to have played a decisive role in the Revolution of 1905. However, it did not perform its task, owing to its bad, Menshevik leadership. As we know, Lenin had not yet arrived in St. Petersburg; he was still abroad. The Mensheviks took advantage of Lenin's absence to make their way into the St. Petersburg Soviet and to seize hold of its leadership. It was not surprising under such circumstances that the Mensheviks Khrustalev, Trotsky, Parvus and others managed to turn the St. Petersburg Soviet against the policy of an uprising. Instead of bringing the soldiers into close contact with the Soviet and linking them up with the common struggle, they demanded that the soldiers be withdrawn from St. Petersburg. The Soviet, instead of arming the workers and preparing them for an uprising, just marked time and was against preparations for an uprising.

Altogether different was the role played in the revolution by the Moscow Soviet of Workers' Deputies. From the very first the Moscow Soviet pursued a thoroughly revolutionary policy. The leadership of the Moscow Soviet was in the hands of the Bolsheviks. Thanks to them, side by side with the Soviet of Workers' Deputies, there arose in Moscow a Soviet of Soldiers' Deputies. The Moscow Soviet became an organ of armed uprising.

In the period, October to December 1905, Soviets of Workers' Deputies were set up in a number of large towns and in nearly all the working-class centres. Attempts were made to organize Soviets of Soldiers' and Sailors' Deputies and to unite them with the Soviets of Workers' Deputies. In some localities Soviets of Workers' and Peasants' Deputies were formed.

The influence of the Soviets was tremendous. In spite of the fact that they often arose spontaneously, lacked definite structure and were loosely organized, they acted as a governmental power. Without legal authority, they introduced freedom of the press and an 8-hour working day. They called upon the people not to pay taxes to the tsarist government. In some cases they confiscated government funds and used them for the needs of the revolution.

5. DECEMBER ARMED UPRISING. DEFEAT OF THE UPRISING. RETREAT OF THE REVOLUTION. FIRST STATE DUMA. FOURTH (UNITY) PARTY CONGRESS

During October and November 1905 the revolutionary struggle of the masses went on developing with intense vigour. Workers' strikes continued.

The struggle of the peasants against the landlords assumed wide dimensions in the autumn of 1905. The peasant movement embraced over one-third of the uyezds of the country. The provinces of Saratov, Tambov, Chernigov, Tiflis, Kutais and several others were the scenes of veritable peasant revolts. Yet the onslaught of the peasant masses was still inadequate. The peasant movement lacked organization and leadership.

Unrest increased also among the soldiers in a number of cities— Tiflis, Vladivostok, Tashkent, Samarkand, Kursk, Sukhum, Warsaw,

Kiev, and Riga. Revolts broke out in Kronstadt and among the sailors of the Black Sea Fleet in Sevastopol (November 1905). But the revolts were isolated, and the tsarist government was able to suppress them.

Revolts in units of the army and navy were frequently provoked by the brutal conduct of the officers, by bad food ("bean riots"), and similar causes. The bulk of the sailors and soldiers in revolt did not yet clearly realize the necessity for the overthrow of the tsarist government, for the energetic prosecution of the armed struggle. They were still too peaceful and complacent; they frequently made the mistake of releasing officers who had been arrested at the outbreak of the revolt, and would allow themselves to be placated by the promises and coaxing of their superiors.

The revolutionary movement had approached the verge of armed insurrection. The Bolsheviks called upon the masses to rise in arms against the tsar and the landlords, and explained to them that this was inevitable. The Bolsheviks worked indefatigably in preparing for armed uprising. Revolutionary work was carried on among the soldiers and sailors, and military organizations of the Party were set up in the armed forces. Workers' fighting squads were formed in a number of cities, and their members taught the use of arms. The purchase of arms from abroad and the smuggling of them into Russia was organized, prominent members of the Party taking part in arranging for their transportation.

In November 1905 Lenin returned to Russia. He took a direct part in the preparations for armed uprising, while keeping out of the way of the tsar's gendarmes and spies. His articles in the Bolshevik newspaper, *Novaya Zhizn* (*New Life*), served to guide the Party in its day-to-day work.

At this period Comrade Stalin was carrying on tremendous revolutionary work in Transcaucasia. He exposed and lashed the Mensheviks as foes of the revolution and of the armed uprising. He resolutely prepared the workers for the decisive battle against the autocracy. Speaking at a meeting of workers in Tiflis on the day the tsar's Manifesto was announced, Comrade Stalin said:

> "What do we need in order to really win? We need three things: first—arms, second—arms, third—arms and arms again!"

In December 1905 a Bolshevik Conference was held in Tammerfors, Finland. Although the Bolsheviks and Mensheviks formally belonged to one Social-Democratic Party, they actually constituted two different parties, each with its own leading centre. At this conference Lenin and

Stalin met for the first time. Until then they had maintained contact by correspondence and through comrades.

Of the decisions of the Tammerfors Conference, the following two should be noted: one on the restoration of the unity of the Party, which had virtually been split into two parties, and the other on the boycott of the First Duma, known as the Witte Duma.

As by that time the armed uprising had already begun in Moscow, the conference, on Lenin's advice, hastily completed its work and dispersed to enable the delegates to participate personally in the uprising.

But the tsarist government was not dozing either. It too was preparing for a decisive struggle. Having concluded peace with Japan, and thus lessened the difficulties of its position, the tsarist government assumed the offensive against the workers and peasants. It declared martial law in a number of provinces where peasant revolts were rife, issued the brutal commands "take no prisoners" and "spare no bullets," and gave orders for the arrest of .the leaders of the revolutionary movement and the dispersal of the Soviets of Workers' Deputies.

In reply to this, the Moscow Bolsheviks and the Moscow Soviet of Workers' Deputies which they led, and which was connected with the broad masses of the workers, decided to make immediate preparations for armed uprising. On December 5 (18) the Moscow Bolshevik Committee resolved to call upon the Soviet to declare a general political strike with the object of turning it into an uprising in the course of the struggle. This decision was supported at mass meetings of the workers. The Moscow Soviet responded to the will of the working class and unanimously resolved to start a general political strike.

When the Moscow proletariat began the revolt, it had a fighting organization of about one thousand combatants, more than half of whom were Bolsheviks. In addition there were fighting squads in several of the Moscow factories. In all, the insurrectionaries had a force of about two thousand combatants. The workers expected to neutralize the garrison and to win over a part of it to their side.

The political strike started in Moscow on December 7 (20). However, efforts to spread it to the whole country failed; it met with inadequate support in St. Petersburg, and this reduced the chances of success of the uprising from the very outset. The Nikolayevskaya (now the October) Railway remained in the hands of the tsarist government. Traffic on this line was not suspended, which enabled the government to transfer regiments of the Guard from St. Petersburg to Moscow for the suppression of the uprising.

In Moscow itself the garrison vacillated. The workers had begun the uprising partly in expectation of receiving support from the garrison. But the revolutionaries had delayed too long, and the government managed to cope with the unrest in the garrison.

The first barricades appeared in Moscow on December 9 (22). Soon the streets of the city were covered with barricades. The tsarist government brought artillery into action. It concentrated a force many times exceeding the strength of the insurrectionaries. For nine days on end several thousand armed workers waged a heroic fight. It was only by bringing regiments from St. Petersburg, Tver and the Western Territory that the tsarist government was able to crush the uprising. On the very eve of the fighting the leadership of the uprising was partly arrested and partly isolated. The members of the Moscow Bolshevik Committee were arrested. The armed action took the form of disconnected uprisings of separate districts. Deprived of a directing centre, and lacking a common plan of operations for the whole city, the districts mainly confined themselves to defensive action. This was the chief source of weakness of the Moscow uprising and one of the causes of its defeat, as Lenin later pointed out.

The uprising assumed a particularly stubborn and bitter character in the Krasnaya Presnya district of Moscow. This was the main stronghold and centre of the uprising. Here the best of the fighting squads, led by Bolsheviks, were concentrated. But Krasnaya Presnya was suppressed by fire and sword; it was drenched in blood and ablaze with the fires caused by artillery. The Moscow uprising was crushed.

The uprising was not confined to Moscow. Revolutionary uprisings broke out in a number of other cities and districts. There were armed uprisings in Krasnoyarsk, Motovilikha (Perm), Novorossisk, Sormovo, Sevastopol and Kronstadt.

The oppressed nationalities of Russia also rose in armed struggle. Nearly the whole of Georgia was up in arms. A big uprising took place in the Ukraine, in the cities of Gorlovka, Alexandrovsk and Lugansk (now Voroshilovgrad) in the Donetz Basin. A stubborn struggle was waged in Latvia. In Finland the workers formed their Red Guard and rose in revolt.

But all these uprisings, like the uprising in Moscow, were crushed with inhuman ferocity by the autocracy.

The appraisals of the December armed uprising given by the Mensheviks and the Bolsheviks differed.

"They should not have taken to arms," was the rebuke the Menshevik Plekhanov flung at the Party after the uprising. The Mensheviks argued that an uprising was unnecessary and pernicious, that it could be dispensed with in the revolution, that success could be achieved not by armed uprising, but by peaceful methods of struggle.

The Bolsheviks branded this stand as treachery. They maintained that the experience of the Moscow armed uprising had but confirmed that the working class could wage a successful armed struggle. In reply to Plekhanov's rebuke—"they should not have taken to arms"—Lenin said:

> "On the contrary, we should have taken to arms more resolutely, energetically and aggressively; we should have explained to the masses that it was impossible to confine ourselves to a peaceful strike and that a fearless and relentless armed fight was indispensable." (Lenin, *Selected Works*, Vol. III, p. 348.)

The uprising of December 1905 was the climax of the revolution. The tsarist autocracy defeated the uprising. Thereafter the revolution took a turn and began to recede. The tide of revolution gradually subsided.

The tsarist government hastened to take advantage of this defeat to deal the final blow to the revolution. The tsar's hangmen and jailers began their bloody work. Punitive expeditions raged in Poland, Latvia, Esthonia, Transcaucasia and Siberia.

But the revolution was not yet crushed. The workers and revolutionary peasants retreated slowly, putting up a fight. New sections of the workers were drawn into the struggle. Over a million workers took part in strikes in 1906; 740,000 in 1907. The peasant movement embraced about one-half of the uyezds of tsarist Russia in the first half of 1906, and one-fifth in the second half of the year. Unrest continued in the army and navy.

The tsarist government, in combating the revolution, did not confine itself to repressive measures. Having achieved its first successes by repressive measures, it decided to deal a fresh blow at the revolution by convening a new Duma, a "legislative" Duma. It hoped in this way to sever the peasants from the revolution and thus put an end to it. In December 1905 the tsarist government promulgated a law providing for the convocation of a new, a "legislative" Duma as distinct from the old, "deliberative" Bulygin Duma, which had been swept away as the result of the Bolshevik boycott. The tsarist election law was of course anti-democratic. Elections were not universal. Over half the population —for example, women and over two million workers—were deprived of the right of vote altogether. Elections were not equal. The electorate was divided into four curias, as they were called: the agrarian (land-lords), the urban (bourgeoisie), the peasant and the worker curias. Election was not direct, but by several stages. There was actually no secret ballot. The election law ensured the overwhelming preponderance in the Duma of a handful of landlords and capitalists over the millions of workers and peasants.

The tsar intended to make use of the Duma to divert the masses from the revolution. In those days a large proportion of the peasants believed that they could obtain land through the Duma. The Constitutional-Democrats, Mensheviks and Socialist-Revolutionaries deceived workers and peasants by stating that the system the people needed could be obtained without uprising, without revolution. It was to fight this fraud on the people that the Bolsheviks announced and pursued the tactics of boycotting the First State Duma. This was in accordance with the decision passed by the Tammerfors Conference.

In their fight against tsardom, the workers demanded the unity of the forces of the Party, the unification of the party of the proletariat. Armed with the decision of the Tammerfors Conference on unity, the Bolsheviks supported this demand of the workers and proposed to the Mensheviks that a unity congress of the Party be called. Under the pressure of the workers, the Mensheviks had to consent to unification.

Lenin was in favour of unification, but only of such unification as would not cover up the differences that existed over the problems of the revolution. Considerable damage was done to the Party by the conciliators (Bogdanov, Krassin and others), who tried to prove that no serious differences existed between the Bolsheviks and the Mensheviks. Lenin fought the conciliators, insisting that the Bolsheviks should come to the congress with their own platform, so that the workers might clearly see what the position of the Bolsheviks was and on what basis unification was being effected. The Bolsheviks drew up such a platform and submitted it to the Party members for discussion.

The Fourth Congress of the R.S.D.L.P., known as the Unity Congress, met in Stockholm (Sweden) in April 1906. It was attended by 111 delegates with right of vote, representing 57 local organizations of the Party. In addition, there were representatives from the national Social-Democratic parties: 3 from the Bund, 3 from the Polish Social-Democratic Party, and 3 from the Lettish Social-Democratic organization.

Owing to the smash-up of the Bolshevik organizations during and after the December uprising, not all of them were able to send delegates. Moreover, during the "days of liberty" of 1905, the Mensheviks had admitted into their ranks a large number of petty-bourgeois intellectuals who had nothing whatever in common with revolutionary Marxism. It will suffice to say that the Tiflis Mensheviks (and there were very few industrial workers in Tiflis) sent as many delegates to the congress as the largest of the proletarian organizations, the St. Petersburg organization. The result was that at the Stockholm Congress the Mensheviks had a majority, although, it is true, an insignificant one.

This composition of the congress determined the Menshevik character of the decisions on a number of questions.

Only *formal* unity was effected at this congress. In reality, the Bolsheviks and the Mensheviks retained their own views and their own independent organizations.

The chief questions discussed at the Fourth Congress were the agrarian question, the current situation and the class tasks of the proletariat, policy towards the State Duma, and organizational questions.

Although the Mensheviks constituted the majority at this congress they were obliged to agree to Lenin's formulation of the first paragraph of the Party Rules dealing with Party membership, in order not to antagonize the workers.

On the agrarian question, Lenin advocated the *nationalization* of the land. He held that the nationalization of the land would be possible only with the victory of the revolution, after tsardom had been overthrown. Under such circumstances the nationalization of the land would make it easier for the proletariat, in alliance with the poor peasants, to pass to the Socialist revolution. Nationalization of the land meant the confiscation of all the landed estates without compensation and turning them over to the peasantry. The Bolshevik agrarian program called upon the peasants to rise in revolution against the tsar and the landlords.

The Mensheviks took up a different position. They advocated a program of *municipalization*. According to this program, the landed estates were not to be placed at the disposal of the village communities, not even given to the village communities for use, but were to be placed at the disposal of the municipalities (that is, the local organs of self-government, or Zemstvos), and each peasant was to *rent* as much of this land as he could afford.

The Menshevik program of municipalization was one of compromise, and therefore prejudicial to the revolution. It could not mobilize the peasants for a revolutionary struggle and was not designed to achieve the complete abolition of landlord property rights in land. The Menshevik program was designed to stop the revolution halfway. The Mensheviks did not want to rouse the peasants for revolution.

The Menshevik program received the majority of the votes at the congress.

The Mensheviks particularly betrayed their anti-proletarian, opportunist nature during the discussion of the resolution on the current situation and on the State Duma. The Menshevik Martynov frankly spoke in opposition to the hegemony of the proletariat in the revolution. Comrade Stalin, replying to the Mensheviks, put the matter very bluntly:

"Either the hegemony of the proletariat, or the hegemony of the democratic bourgeoisie—that is how the question stands in the Party, that is where we differ."

As to the State Duma, the Mensheviks extolled it in their resolution as the best means of solving the problems of the revolution and of liberating the people from tsardom. The Bolsheviks, on the contrary, regarded the Duma as an impotent appendage of tsardom, as a screen for the evils of tsardom, which the latter would discard as soon as it proved inconvenient.

The Central Committee elected at the Fourth Congress consisted of three Bolsheviks and six Mensheviks. The editorial board of the central press organ was formed entirely of Mensheviks.

It was clear that the internal Party struggle would continue.

After the Fourth Congress the conflict between the Bolsheviks and the Mensheviks broke out with new vigour. In the local organizations, which were formally united, reports on the congress were often made by two speakers: one from the Bolsheviks and another from the Mensheviks. The result of the discussion of the two lines was that in most cases the majority of the members of the organizations sided with the Bolsheviks.

Events proved that the Bolsheviks were right. The Menshevik Central Committee elected at the Fourth Congress increasingly revealed its opportunism and its utter inability to lead the revolutionary struggle of the masses. In the summer and autumn of 1906 the revolutionary struggle of the masses took on new vigour. Sailors' revolts broke out in Kronstadt and Sveaborg; the peasants' struggle against the landlords flared up. Yet the Menshevik Central Committee issued opportunist slogans, which the masses did not follow.

6. DISPERSION OF THE FIRST STATE DUMA. CONVOCATION OF THE
SECOND STATE DUMA. FIFTH PARTY CONGRESS. DISPERSION OF
THE SECOND STATE DUMA. CAUSES OF THE DEFEAT OF THE
FIRST RUSSIAN REVOLUTION

As the First State Duma did not prove docile enough, the tsarist government dispersed it in the summer of 1906. The government resorted to even more drastic repressions against the people, extended the ravaging activities of the punitive expeditions throughout the country, and announced its decision of shortly calling a Second State Duma. The tsarist government was obviously growing more insolent. It no longer feared the revolution, for it saw that the revolution was on the decline.

The Bolsheviks had to decide whether to participate in the Second Duma or to boycott it. By boycott, the Bolsheviks usually meant an active boycott, and not the mere passive abstention from voting in the elections. The Bolsheviks regarded active boycott as a revolutionary means of warning the people against the attempts of the tsar to divert them from the path of revolution to the path of tsarist "constitution," as a means of frustrating these attempts and organizing a new onslaught of the people on tsardom.

The experience of the boycott of the Bulygin Duma had shown that a boycott was "the only correct tactics, as fully proved by events." (Lenin, *Selected Works*, Vol. III, p. 393.) This boycott was successful because it not only warned the people against the danger of the path of tsarist constitutionalism but frustrated the very birth of the Duma. The boycott was successful because it was carried out during the *rising tide* of the revolution and was supported by this tide, and not when the revolution was receding. The summoning of the Duma could be frustrated only during the *high tide* of the revolution.

The boycott of the Witte Duma, *i.e.*, the First Duma, took place after the December uprising had been defeated, when the tsar proved to be the victor, that is, at a time when there was reason to believe that the revolution had begun to recede.

"But," wrote Lenin, "it goes without saying that at that time there were as yet no grounds to regard this victory (of the tsar—*Ed.*) as a decisive victory. The uprising of December 1905 had its sequel in a series of disconnected and partial military uprisings and strikes in the summer of 1906. The call to boycott the Witte Duma was a call to concentrate these uprisings and make them general." (Lenin, *Collected Works*, Russ. ed., Vol. XII, p. 20.)

The boycott of the Witte Duma was unable to frustrate its convocation although it considerably undermined its prestige and weakened the faith of a part of the population in it. The boycott was unable to frustrate the convocation of the Duma because, as subsequently became clear, it took place at a time when the revolution was receding, when it was on the decline. For this reason the boycott of the First Duma in 1906 was unsuccessful. In this connection Lenin wrote in his famous pamphlet, *"Left-Wing" Communism, An Infantile Disorder*:

> "The Bolshevik boycott of 'parliament' in 1905 enriched the revolutionary proletariat with highly valuable political experience and showed that in combining legal with illegal, parliamentary with extra-parliamentary forms of struggle, it is sometimes useful and even essential to reject parliamentary forms.... The boycott of the 'Duma' by the Bolsheviks in 1906 was however a mistake, although a small and easily remediable one.... What applies to individuals applies—with necessary modifications—to politics and parties. Not he is wise who makes no mistakes. There are no such men nor can there be. He is wise who makes not very serious mistakes and who knows how to correct them easily and quickly. (Lenin, *Selected Works*, Vol. X, p. 74.)

As to the Second State Duma, Lenin held that in view of the changed situation and the decline of the revolution, the Bolsheviks "must reconsider the question of boycotting the State Duma." (Lenin, *Selected Works*, Vol. III, p. 392.)

> "History has shown," Lenin wrote, "that when the Duma assembles opportunities arise for carrying on useful agitation both from within the Duma and, in connection with it, outside—that the tactics of joining forces with the revolutionary peasantry against the Constitutional-Democrats can be applied in the Duma." (*Ibid.*, p. 396.)

All this showed that one had to know not only how to advance resolutely, to advance in the front ranks, when the revolution was in the ascendant, but also how to retreat properly, to be the last to retreat, when the revolution was no longer in the ascendant, changing one's tactics as the situation changed; to retreat not in disorder, but in an organized way, calmly and without panic, utilizing every minute opportunity to withdraw the cadres from under enemy fire, to reform one's ranks to muster one's forces and to prepare for a new offensive against the enemy.

The Bolsheviks decided to take part in the elections to the Second Duma.

But the Bolsheviks did not go to the Duma for the purpose of carrying on organic "legislative" work inside it in a bloc with the Constitutional-Democrats, as the Mensheviks did, but for the purpose of utilizing it as a platform in the interests of the revolution.

The Menshevik Central Committee, on the contrary, urged that election agreements be formed with the Constitutional-Democrats, and that support be given to the Constitutional-Democrats in the Duma, for in their eyes the Duma was a legislative body that was capable of bridling the tsarist government.

The majority of the Party organizations expressed themselves against the policy of the Menshevik Central Committee.

The Bolsheviks demanded that a new Party congress be called.

In May 1907 the Fifth Party Congress met in London. At the time of this congress the R.S.D.L.P. (together with the national Social-Democratic organizations) had a membership of nearly 150,000. In all, 336 delegates attended the congress, of whom 105 were Bolsheviks and 97 Mensheviks. The remaining delegates represented the national Social-Democratic organizations—the Polish and Lettish Social-Democrats and the Bund—which had been admitted into the R.S.D.L.P. at the previous congress.

Trotsky tried to knock together a group of his own at the congress, a centrist, that is, semi-Menshevik, group, but could get no following.

As the Bolsheviks had the support of the Poles and the Letts, they had a stable majority at the congress.

One of the main questions at issue at the congress was that of policy towards the bourgeois parties. There had already been a struggle between the Bolsheviks and Mensheviks on this question at the Second Congress. The fifth Congress gave a Bolshevik estimate of all the non-proletarian parties—Black-Hundreds, Octobrists (Union of October Seventeenth), Constitutional-Democrats and Socialist-Revolutionaries—and formulated the Bolshevik tactics to be pursued in regard to these parties.

The congress approved the policy of the Bolsheviks and decided to wage a relentless struggle both against the Black-Hundred parties—the League of the Russian People, the monarchists, the Council of the United Nobility—and against the Octobrists, the Commercial and Industrial Party and the Party of Peaceful Renovation. All these parties were outspokenly counter-revolutionary.

As regards the liberal bourgeoisie, the Constitutional-Democratic Party, the congress recommended a policy of uncompromising exposure; the false and hypocritical "democracy" of the Constitutional-Democratic

Party was to be exposed and the attempts of the liberal bourgeoisie to gain control of the peasant movement combated.

As to the so-called Narodnik or Trudovik parties (the Popular Socialists, the Trudovik Group and the Socialist-Revolutionaries), the congress recommended that their attempts to mask themselves as Socialists be exposed. At the same time the congress considered it permissible now and then to conclude agreements with these parties for a joint and simultaneous attack on tsardom and the Constitutional-Democratic bourgeoisie, inasmuch as these parties were at that time democratic parties and expressed the interests of the petty bourgeoisie of town and country.

Even before this congress, the Mensheviks had proposed that a so-called "labour congress" be convened. The Mensheviks' idea was to call a congress at which Social-Democrats, Socialist-Revolutionaries and Anarchists should all be represented. This "labour" congress was to form something in the nature of a "non-partisan party," or a "broad" petty-bourgeois labour party without a program. Lenin exposed this as a pernicious attempt on the part of the Mensheviks to liquidate the Social-Democratic Labour Party and to dissolve the vanguard of the working class in the petty-bourgeois mass. The congress vigorously condemned the Menshevik call for a "labour congress."

Special attention was devoted at the congress to the subject of the trade unions. The Mensheviks advocated "neutrality" of the trade unions; in other words, they were opposed to the Party playing a leading role in them. The congress rejected the Mensheviks' motion and adopted the resolution submitted by the Bolsheviks. This resolution stated that the Party must gain the ideological and political leadership in the trade unions.

The Fifth Congress was a big victory for the Bolsheviks in the working-class movement. But the Bolsheviks did not allow this to turn their heads; nor did they rest on their laurels. That was not what Lenin taught them. The Bolsheviks knew that more fighting with the Mensheviks was still to come.

In an article entitled "Notes of a Delegate" which appeared in 1907, Comrade Stalin assessed the results of the congress as follows:

> "The actual unification of the advanced workers of all Russia into a single all-Russian party under the banner of *revolutionary* Social-Democracy—that is the significance of the London Congress, that is its general character."

In this article Comrade Stalin cited data showing the *composition* of the congress. They show that the Bolshevik delegates were sent to the congress chiefly by the big industrial centres (St. Petersburg, Moscow, the Urals, Ivanovo-Voznesensk, etc.), whereas the Mensheviks got their mandates from districts where small production prevailed, where artisans, semi-proletarians predominated, as well as from a number of purely rural areas.

"Obviously," says Comrade Stalin, summing up the results of the congress, "the tactics of the Bolsheviks are the tactics of the proletarians in big industry, the tactics of those areas where the class contradictions are especially clear and the class struggle especially acute. Bolshevism is the tactics of the real proletarians. On the other hand, it is no less obvious that the tactics of the Mensheviks are primarily the tactics of the handicraft workers and the peasant semi-proletarians, the tactics of those areas where the class contradictions are not quite clear and the class struggle is masked. Menshevism is the tactics of the semi-bourgeois elements among the proletariat. So say the figures." (*Verbatim Report of the Fifth Congress of the R.S.D.L.P.*, Russ. ed., 1935, pp. xi and xii.)

When the tsar dispersed the First Duma he expected that the Second Duma would be more docile. But the Second Duma, too, belied his expectations. The tsar thereupon decided to disperse it, too, and to convoke a Third Duma on a more restricted franchise, in the hope that this Duma would prove more amenable.

Shortly after the Fifth Congress, the tsarist government effected what is known as the *coup d'état* of June 3. On June 3, 1907, the tsar dispersed the Second State Duma. The sixty-five deputies of the Social-Democratic group in the Duma were arrested and exiled to Siberia. A new election law was promulgated. The rights of the workers and peasants were still further curtailed. The tsarist government continued its offensive.

The tsar's Minister Stolypin intensified the campaign of bloody reprisals against the workers and peasants. Thousands of revolutionary workers and peasants were shot by punitive expeditions, or hanged. In the tsarist dungeons revolutionaries were tortured mentally and physically. Particularly savage was the persecution of the working-class organizations, especially the Bolsheviks. The tsar's sleuths were searching for Lenin, who was living in hiding in Finland. They wanted to wreak their vengeance on the leader of the revolution. In December 1907 Lenin managed at great risk to make his way abroad and again became an exile.

The dark period of the Stolypin reaction set in.

The first Russian revolution thus ended in defeat.

The causes that contributed to this defeat were as follows:

1) In the revolution, there was still no stable alliance of the workers and peasants against tsardom. The peasants rose in struggle against the landlords and were willing to join in an alliance with the workers against them. But they did not yet realize that the landlords could not be overthrown unless the tsar were overthrown, they did not realize that the tsar was acting hand-in-hand with the landlords, and large numbers of the peasants still had faith in the tsar and placed their hopes in the tsarist State Duma. That is why a considerable section of the peasants were disinclined to join in alliance with the workers for the overthrow of tsardom. The peasants had more faith in the compromising Socialist-Revolutionary Party than in the real revolutionaries—the Bolsheviks. As a result, the struggle of the peasants against the landlords was not sufficiently organized. Lenin said:

> "The peasants' actions were too scattered, too unorganized and not sufficiently aggressive, and that was one of the fundamental causes of the defeat of the revolution." (Lenin, *Collected Works*, Russ. ed., Vol. XIX, p. 354.)

2) The disinclination of a large section of the peasants to join the workers for the overthrow of tsardom also influenced the conduct of the army, which largely consisted of peasants' sons clad in soldiers' uniforms. Unrest and revolt broke out in certain units of the tsar's army, but the majority of the soldiers still assisted the tsar in suppressing the strikes and uprisings of the workers.

3) Neither was the action of the workers sufficiently concerted. The advanced sections of the working class started a heroic revolutionary struggle in 1905. The more backward sections—the workers in the less industrialized provinces, those who lived in the villages—came into action more slowly. Their participation in the revolutionary struggle became particularly active in 1906, but by then the vanguard of the working class had already been considerably weakened.

4) The working class was the foremost and principal force of the revolution; but the necessary unity and solidarity in the ranks of the party of the working class were lacking. The R.S.D.L.P.—the party of the working class—was split into two groups: the Bolsheviks and the Mensheviks. The Bolsheviks pursued a consistent revolutionary line and called upon the workers to overthrow tsardom. The Mensheviks, by their compromising tactics, hampered the revolution, confused the minds of large numbers of workers and split the working class. Therefore, the workers did not always act concertedly in the revolution, and the working

class, still lacking unity within its own ranks, could not become the real leader of the revolution.

5) The tsarist autocracy received help in crushing the Revolution of 1905 from the West-European imperialists. The foreign capitalists feared for their investments in Russia and for their huge profits. Moreover, they feared that if the Russian revolution were to succeed the workers of other countries would rise in revolution, too. The West-European imperialists therefore came to the assistance of the hangman-tsar. The French bankers granted a big loan to the tsar for the suppression of the revolution. The German kaiser kept a large army in readiness to intervene in aid of the Russian tsar.

6) The conclusion of peace with Japan in September 1905 was of considerable help to the tsar. Defeat in the war and the menacing growth of the revolution had induced the tsar to hasten the signing of peace. The loss of the war weakened tsardom. The conclusion of peace strengthened the position of the tsar.

BRIEF SUMMARY

The first Russian revolution constituted a whole historical stage in the development of our country. This historical stage consisted of two periods: the first period, when the tide of revolution rose from the general political strike in October to the armed uprising in December and took advantage of the weakness of the tsar, who had suffered defeat on the battlefields of Manchuria, to sweep away the Bulygin Duma and wrest concession after concession from the tsar; and the second period, when tsardom, having recovered after the conclusion of peace with Japan, took advantage of the liberal bourgeoisie's fear of the revolution, took advantage of the vacillation of the peasants, cast them a sop in the form of the Witte Duma, and passed to the offensive against the working class, against the revolution.

In the short period of only three years of revolution (1905-07) the working class and the peasantry received a rich political education, such as they could not have received in thirty years of ordinary peaceful development. A few years of revolution made clear what could not be made clear in the course of decades of peaceful development.

The revolution disclosed that tsardom was the sworn enemy of the people, that tsardom was like the proverbial hunchback whom only the grave could cure.

The revolution showed that the liberal bourgeoisie was seeking an alliance with the tsar, and not with the people, that it was a counter-revolutionary force, an agreement with which would be tantamount to a betrayal of the people.

The revolution showed that only the working class could be the leader of the bourgeois-democratic revolution, that it alone could force aside the liberal Constitutional-Democratic bourgeoisie, destroy its influence over the peasantry, rout the landlords, carry the revolution to its conclusion and clear the way for Socialism.

Lastly, the revolution showed that the labouring peasantry, despite its vacillations, was the only important force capable of forming an alliance with the working class.

Two lines were contending within the R.S.D.L.P. during the revolution, the line of the Bolsheviks and the line of the Mensheviks. The Bolsheviks took as their course the extension of the revolution, the overthrow of tsardom by armed uprising, the hegemony of the working class, the isolation of the Constitutional-Democratic bourgeoisie, an alliance with the peasantry, the formation of a provisional revolutionary government consisting of representatives of the workers and peasants, the victorious completion of the revolution. The Mensheviks, on the contrary, took as their course the liquidation of the revolution. Instead of overthrowing tsardom by uprising, they proposed to reform and "improve" it; instead of the hegemony of the proletariat, they proposed the hegemony of the liberal bourgeoisie; instead of an alliance with the peasantry, they proposed an alliance with the Constitutional-Democratic bourgeoisie; instead of a provisional government, they proposed a State Duma as the centre of the "revolutionary forces" of the country.

Thus the Mensheviks sank into the morass of compromise and became vehicles of the bourgeois influence on the working class, virtual agents of the bourgeoisie within the working class.

The Bolsheviks proved to be the only revolutionary Marxist force in the Party and the country.

It was natural that, in view of such profound differences, the R.S.D.L.P. proved in fact to be split into two parties, the party of the Bolsheviks and the party of the Mensheviks. The Fourth Party Congress changed nothing in the actual state of affairs within the Party. It only preserved and somewhat strengthened *formal* unity in the Party. The Fifth Party Congress took a step towards *actual* unity in the Party, a unity achieved under the banner of Bolshevism.

Reviewing the revolutionary movement, the Fifth Party Congress condemned the line of the Mensheviks as one of compromise, and approved the Bolshevik line as a revolutionary Marxist line. In doing so it once more confirmed what had already been confirmed by the whole course of the first Russian revolution.

The revolution showed that the Bolsheviks knew how to advance when the situation demanded it, that they had learned to advance in the front ranks and to lead the whole people in attack. But the revolution also showed that the Bolsheviks knew how to retreat in an orderly way when the situation took an unfavourable turn, when the revolution was on the decline, and that the Bolsheviks had learned to retreat properly, without panic or commotion, so as to preserve their cadres, rally their forces, and, having reformed their ranks in conformity with the new situation, once again to resume the attack on the enemy.

It is impossible to defeat the enemy without knowing how to attack properly.

It is impossible to avoid utter rout in the event of defeat without knowing how to retreat properly, to retreat without panic and without confusion.

CHAPTER FOUR

THE MENSHEVIKS AND THE BOLSHEVIKS IN THE PERIOD OF THE STOLYPIN REACTION. THE BOLSHEVIKS CONSTITUTE THEMSELVES AN INDEPENDENT MARXIST PARTY

(1908-1912)

1. STOLYPIN REACTION. DISINTEGRATION AMONG THE OPPOSI-
TIONAL INTELLIGENTSIA. DECADENCE. DESERTION OF A SEC-
TION OF THE PARTY INTELLIGENTSIA TO THE ENEMIES OF
MARXISM AND ATTEMPTS TO REVISE THE THEORY OF MARX-
ISM. LENIN'S REBUTTAL OF THE REVISIONISTS IN HIS "MATE-
RIALISM AND EMPIRIO-CRITICISM" AND HIS DEFENCE OF THE
THEORETICAL FOUNDATIONS OF THE MARXIST PARTY

The Second State Duma was dissolved by the tsarist government on
June 3, 1907. This is customarily referred to in history as the *coup
d'état* of June 3. The tsarist government issued a new law on the elections to the Third State Duma, and thus violated its own Manifesto of
October 17, 1905, which stipulated that new laws could be issued only
with the consent of the Duma. The members of the Social-Democratic
group in the Second Duma were committed for trial; the representatives
of the working class were condemned to penal servitude and exile.

The new election law was so drafted as to increase considerably the
number of representatives of the landlords and the commercial and industrial bourgeoisie in the Duma. At the same time the representation
of the peasants and workers, small as it was, was reduced to a fraction
of its former size.

Black-Hundreds and Constitutional-Democrats preponderated in
the Third Duma. Of a total of 442 deputies, 171 were Rights (Black-
Hundreds), 113 were Octobrists or members of kindred groups, 101
were Constitutional-Democrats or members of kindred groups, 13 were
Trudoviki, and 18 were Social-Democrats.

The Rights (so called because they occupied the benches on the
right-hand side of the Duma) represented the worst enemies of the
workers and peasants—the Black-Hundred feudal landlords, who had
subjected the peasants to mass floggings and shootings during the sup-

pression of the peasant movement, and organizers of Jewish pogroms, of the manhandling of demonstrating workers and of the brutal burning of premises where meetings were being held during the revolution.   The Rights stood for the most ruthless suppression of the working people, and for the unlimited power of the tsar; they were opposed to the tsar's Manifesto of October 17, 1905.

The Octobrist Party, or the Union of October Seventeenth, closely adhered to the Rights in the Duma.   The Octobrists represented the interests of big industrial capital, and of the big landlords who ran their estates on capitalist lines (at the beginning of the Revolution of 1905 a large number of the big landlords belonging to the Constitutional-Democratic Party went over to the Octobrists).   The only thing that distinguished the Octobrists from the Rights was their acceptance—only in words at that—of the Manifesto of October 17.   The Octobrists fully supported both the home and foreign policy of the tsarist government.

The Constitutional-Democratic Party had fewer seats in the Third Duma than in the First and Second Dumas.   This was due to the transfer of part of the landlord vote from the Constitutional-Democrats to the Octobrists.

There was a small group of petty-bourgeois democrats, known as Trudoviki, in the Third Duma.   They vacillated between the Constitutional-Democrats and the labour democrats (Bolsheviks).   Lenin pointed out that although the Trudoviki in the Duma were extremely weak, they represented the *masses,* the peasant masses.   The vacillation of the Trudoviki between the Constitutional-Democrats and the labour democrats was an inevitable consequence of the class position of the small owners.   Lenin set before the Bolshevik deputies, the labour democrats, the task of "helping the weak petty-bourgeois democrats, of wresting them from the influence of the liberals, of rallying the democratic camp against the counter-revolutionary Constitutional-Democrats, and not only against the Rights...." (Lenin, *Collected Works,* Russ. ed., Vol. XV, p. 486.)

During the Revolution of 1905, and especially after its defeat, the Constitutional-Democrats increasingly revealed themselves as a counter-revolutionary force.   Discarding their "democratic" mask more and more, they acted like veritable monarchists, defenders of tsardom.   In 1909 a group of prominent Constitutional-Democrat writers published a volume of articles entitled *Vekhi* (*Landmarks*) in which, on behalf of the bourgeoisie, they thanked the tsar for crushing the revolution. Cringing and fawning upon the tsarist government, the government of the knout and the gallows, the Constitutional-Democrats bluntly stated in this book that "we should bless this government, which alone, with its bayonets and jails, protects us (the liberal bourgeoisie) from the ire of the people."

Having dispersed the Second State Duma and disposed of the Social-Democratic group of the Duma, the tsarist government zealously set about destroying the political and economic organizations of the proletariat. Convict prisons, fortresses and places of exile were filled to overflowing with revolutionaries. They were brutally beaten up in the prisons, tormented and tortured. The Black-Hundred terror raged unchecked. The tsar's Minister Stolypin set up gallows all over the country. Several thousand revolutionaries were executed. In those days the gallows was known as the "Stolypin necktie."

In its efforts to crush the revolutionary movement of the workers and peasants the tsarist government could not confine itself to acts of repression, punitive expeditions, shootings, jailings and sentences of penal servitude. It perceived with alarm that the naive faith of the peasants in "the little father, the tsar" was steadily vanishing. It therefore resorted to a broad manœuvre. It conceived the idea of creating a solid support for itself in the countryside, in the large class of rural bourgeoisie —the kulaks.

On November 9, 1906, Stolypin issued a new agrarian law enabling the peasants to leave the communes and to set up separate farms. Stolypin's agrarian law broke down the system of communal land tenure. The peasants were invited to take possession of their allotments as private property and to withdraw from the communes. They could now sell their allotments, which they were not allowed to do before. When a peasant left his commune the latter was obliged to allot land to him in a single tract (*khutor, otrub*).

The rich peasants, the kulaks, now had the opportunity to buy up the land of the poor peasants at low prices. Within a few years after the promulgation of the law, over a million poor peasants had lost their land altogether and had been completely ruined. As the poor peasants lost their land the number of kulak farmholds grew. These were sometimes regular estates employing hired labour—farm hands—on a large scale. The government compelled the peasants to allot the best land of the communes to the kulak farmers.

During the "emancipation" of the peasants the landlords had robbed the peasants of their land; now the kulaks began to rob the communes of their land, securing the best plots and buying up the allotments of poor peasants at low prices.

The tsarist government advanced large loans to the kulaks for the purchase of land and the outfitting of their farms. Stolypin wanted to turn the kulaks into small landlords, into loyal defenders of the tsarist autocracy.

In the nine years 1906-15 alone, over two million households withdrew from the communes.

As a result of the Stolypin policy the condition of the peasants with small land allotments, and of the poor peasants, grew worse than ever. The process of differentiation among the peasantry became more marked. The peasants began to come into collision with the kulak farmers.

At the same time, the peasants began to realize that they would never gain possession of the landed estates as long as the tsarist government and the State Duma of the landlords and Constitutional-Democrats existed.

During the period when kulak farmholds were being formed in large numbers (1907-09), the peasant movement began to decline, but soon after, in 1910, 1911, and later, owing to the clashes between the members of the village communes and the kulak farmers, the peasant movement against the landlords and the kulak farmers grew in intensity.

There were big changes also in industry after the revolution. The concentration of industry in the hands of increasingly powerful capitalist groups proceeded much more rapidly. Even before the Revolution of 1905, the capitalists had begun to form associations with the object of raising prices within the country and of using the super-profits thus obtained for the encouragement of export trade so as to enable them to dump goods abroad at low prices and to capture foreign markets. These capitalist associations (monopolies) were called trusts and syndicates. After the revolution their number became still greater. There was also an increase in the number of big banks, whose role in industry became more important. The flow of foreign capital into Russia increased.

Thus capitalism in Russia was turning into monopoly capitalism, imperialist capitalism, on a growing scale.

After several years of stagnation, industry began to revive: the output of coal, metal, oil, textiles and sugar increased. Grain exports assumed large dimensions.

Although Russia at that time made some industrial progress, she was still backward compared with Western Europe, and still dependent on foreign capitalists. Russia did not produce machinery and machine tools —they were imported from abroad. She had no automobile industry or chemical industry; she did not produce artificial fertilizers. Russia also lagged behind other capitalist countries in the manufacture of armaments.

Pointing to the low level of consumption of metals in Russia as an indication of the country's backwardness, Lenin wrote:

"In the half-century following the emancipation of the peasants the consumption of iron in Russia has increased five-fold; yet Russia remains an incredibly and unprecedentedly backward country, poverty-stricken and semi-barbaric, equipped with modern implements of production to one-fourth the extent of England, one-fifth the extent of Germany, and one-tenth the extent of America." (Lenin, *Collected Works*, Russ. ed., Vol. XVI, p. 543.)

One direct result of Russia's economic and political backwardness was the dependence both of Russian capitalism and of tsardom itself on West-European capitalism.

This found expression in the fact that such highly important branches of industry as coal, oil, electrical equipment, and metallurgy were in the hands of foreign capital, and that tsarist Russia had to import nearly all her machinery and equipment from abroad.

It also found expression in the fettering foreign loans. To pay interest on these loans tsardom squeezed hundreds of millions of rubles out of the people annually.

It moreover found expression in the secret treaties with Russia's "allies," by which the tsarist government undertook in the event of war to send millions of Russian soldiers to support the "allies" on the imperialist fronts and to protect the tremendous profits of the British and French capitalists.

The period of the Stolypin reaction was marked by particularly savage assaults on the working class by the gendarmerie and police, the tsarist agents-provocateurs and Black-Hundred ruffians. But it was not only the underlings of the tsar who harassed and persecuted the workers. No less zealous in this respect were the factory and mill owners, whose offensive against the working class became particularly aggressive in the years of industrial stagnation and increasing unemployment. The factory owners declared mass lockouts and drew up black lists of class-conscious workers who took an active part in strikes. Once a person was blacklisted he could never hope to find employment in any of the plants belonging to the manufacturers' association in that particular branch of industry. Already in 1908 wage rates were cut by 10 to 15 per cent. The working day was everywhere increased to 10 or 12 hours. The system of rapacious fines again flourished.

The defeat of the Revolution of 1905 started a process of disintegration and degeneration in the ranks of the fellow-travelers of the revolution. Degenerate and decadent tendencies grew particularly marked among the intelligentsia. The fellow-travelers who came from the bourgeois camp to join the movement during the upsurge of the revolution deserted the Party in the days of reaction. Some of them joined the camp of the open enemies of the revolution, others entrenched themselves in such legally functioning working-class societies as still survived, and endeavoured to divert the proletariat from the path of revolution and to discredit the revolutionary party of the proletariat. Deserting the revolution the fellow-travelers tried to win the good graces of the reactionaries and to live in peace with tsardom.

The tarist government took advantage of the defeat of the revolution to enlist the more cowardly and self-seeking fellow-travelers of the revolution as agents-provocateurs. These vile Judases were sent by the tsarist *Okhrana* into the working class and Party organizations, where they spied from within and betrayed revolutionaries.

The offensive of the counter-revolution was waged on the ideological front as well. There appeared a whole horde of fashionable writers who "criticized" Marxism, and "demolished" it, mocked and scoffed at the revolution, extolled treachery, and lauded sexual depravity under the guise of the "cult of individuality."

In the realm of philosophy increasing attempts were made to "criticize" and revise Marxism; there also appeared all sorts of religious trends camouflaged by pseudo-scientific theories.

"Criticizing" Marxism became fashionable.

All these gentlemen, despite their multifarious colouring, pursued one common aim: to divert the masses from the revolution.

Decadence and scepticism also affected a section of the Party intelligentsia, those who considered themselves Marxists but had never held firmly to the Marxist position. Among them were writers like Bogdanov, Bazarov, Lunacharsky (who had sided with the Bolsheviks in 1905), Yushkevich and Valentinov (Mensheviks). They launched their "criticism" simultaneously against the philosophical foundations of Marxist theory, *i.e.*, against dialectical materialism, and against the fundamental Marxist principles of historical science, *i.e.*, against historical materialism. This criticism differed from the usual criticism in that it was not conducted openly and squarely, but in a veiled and hypocritical form under the guise of "defending" the fundamental positions of Marxism. These people claimed that in the main they were Marxists, but that they wanted to "improve" Marxism—by ridding it of certain of its fundamental principles. In reality, they were hostile to Marxism, for they tried to undermine its theoretical foundations, although they hypocritically denied their hostility to Marxism and two-facedly continued to style themselves Marx-ists. The danger of this hypocritical criticism lay in the fact that it was calculated to deceive rank-and-file members of the Party and might lead them astray. The more hypocritical grew this criticism, which aimed at undermining the theoretical foundations of Marxism, the more dangerous it was to the Party, for the more it merged with the general campaign of the reactionaries against the Party, against the revolution. Some of the intellectuals who had deserted Marxism went so far as to advocate the founding of a new religion (these were known as "god-seekers" and "god-builders").

It became urgent for the Marxists to give a fitting retort to these renegades from Marxist theory, to tear the mask from their faces and thoroughly expose them, and thus safeguard the theoretical foundations of the Marxist Party.

One might have thought that this task would have been undertaken by Plekhanov and his Menshevik friends who regarded themselves as "eminent Marxist theoreticians." But they preferred to fire off one or two insignificant critical notes of the newspaper type and quit the field.

It was Lenin who accomplished this task in his famous book *Material-ism and Empirio-Criticism*, published in 1909.

"In the course of less than half a year," Lenin wrote, "four books devoted mainly and almost entirely to attacks on dialectical material-ism have made their appearance. These include first and foremost *Studies in* (?—it would have been more proper to say 'against') *the Philosophy of Marxism* (St. Petersburg, 1908), a symposium by Bazarov, Bogdanov, Lunacharsky, Berman, Helfond, Yushkevich and Suvorov; Yushkevich's *Materialism and Critical Realism;* Ber-man's *Dialectics in the Light of the Modern Theory of Knowledge* and Valentinov's *The Philosophic Constructions of Marxism....* All these people, who, despite the sharp divergence of their political views, are united in their hostility toward dialectical materialism, at the same time claim to be Marxists in philosophy! Engels' dialectics is 'mysticism,' says Berman. Engels' views have become 'antiquated,' remarks Bazarov casually, as though it were a self-evident fact. Materialism thus appears to be refuted by our bold warriors, who proudly allude to the 'modern theory of knowledge,' 'recent phi-losophy' (or 'recent positivism'), the 'philosophy of modern natural science,' or even the 'philosophy of natural science of the twentieth century.'" (Lenin, *Selected Works*, Vol. XI, p .89.)

Replying to Lunacharsky, who, in justification of his friends—the revisionists in philosophy—said, "perhaps we have gone astray, but we are seeking," Lenin wrote:

"As for myself, I too am a 'seeker' in philosophy. Namely, the task I have set myself in these comments (*i.e.*, *Materialism and Empirio-Criticism—Ed.*) is to find out what was the stumbling block to these people who under the guise of Marxism are offering something incredibly muddled, confused and reactionary." (*Ibid.*, p. 90.)

But as a matter of fact, Lenin's book went far beyond this modest task. Actually, the book is something more than a criticism of Bogdanov, Yushkevich, Bazarov and Valentinov and their teachers in philosophy, Avenarius and Mach, who endeavoured in their writings to offer a refined and polished idealism as opposed to Marxist materialism; it is at the same time a defence of the theoretical foundations of Marxism—dialectical and historical materialism—and a materialist generalization of everything important and essential acquired by science, and especially the natural sciences, in the course of a whole historical period, the period from Engels' death to the appearance of Lenin's *Materialism and Empirio-Criticism.*

Having effectively criticized in this book the Russian empirio-criticists and their foreign teachers, Lenin comes to the following conclusions regarding philosophical and theoretical revisionism:

1) "An ever subtler falsification of Marxism, an ever subtler presentation of anti-materialist doctrines under the guise of Marxism—this is the characteristic feature of modern revisionism in political economy, in questions of tactics and in philosophy generally." (*Ibid.*, p. 382.)

2) "The whole school of Mach and Avenarius is moving towards idealism." (*Ibid.*, p. 406.)

3) "Our Machians have all got stuck in idealism." (*Ibid.*, p. 396.)

4) "Behind the gnosiological scholasticism of empirio-criticism it is impossible not to see the struggle of parties in philosophy, a struggle which in the last analysis expresses the tendencies and ideology of the antagonistic classes in modern society." (*Ibid.*, p. 407.)

5) "The objective, class role of empirio-criticism reduces itself to nothing but that of servitor of the fideists (the reactionaries who hold faith above science—*Ed.*) in their struggle against materialism in general and historical materialism in particular." (*Ibid.*, p. 407.)

6) "Philosophical idealism is . . . a *road* to clerical obscurantism." (*Ibid.*, p. 84.)

In order to appreciate the tremendous part played by Lenin's book in the history of our Party and to realize what theoretical treasure Lenin safeguarded from the motley crowd of revisionists and renegades of the period of the Stolypin reaction, we must acquaint ourselves, if only briefly, with the fundamentals of dialectical and historical materialism.

This is all the more necessary because dialectical and historical materialism constitute the theoretical basis of Communism, the theoretical foundations of the Marxist party, and it is the duty of every active member of our Party to know these principles and hence to study them.

What, then, is

1) Dialectical materialism?
2) Historical materialism?

2. DIALECTICAL AND HISTORICAL MATERIALISM

Dialectical materialism is the world outlook of the Marxist-Leninist party. It is called dialectical materialism because its approach to the phenomena of nature, its method of studying and apprehending them, is *dialectical*, while its interpretation of the phenomena of nature, its conception of these phenomena, its theory, is *materialistic*.

Historical materialism is the extension of the principles of dialectical materialism to the study of social life, an application of the principles of dialectical materialism to the phenomena of the life of society, to the study of society and its history.

When describing their dialectical method, Marx and Engels usually refer to Hegel as the philosopher who formulated the main features of dialectics. This, however, does not mean that the dialectics of Marx and Engels is identical with the dialectics of Hegel. As a matter of fact, Marx and Engels took from the Hegelian dialectics only its "rational kernel," casting aside its idealistic shell, and developed it further so as to lend it a modern scientific form.

"My dialectic method," says Marx, "is fundamentally not only different from the Hegelian, but is its direct opposite. To Hegel, the process of thinking, which, under the name of 'the Idea,' he even transforms into an independent subject, is the demiurge (creator) of the real world, and the real world is only the external, phenomenal form of 'the Idea.' With me, on the contrary, the ideal is nothing else than the material world reflected by the human mind, and translated into forms of thought." (Karl Marx, *Capital*, Vol, I, p. xxx, International Publishers, 1939.)

When describing their materialism, Marx and Engels usually refer to Feuerbach as the philosopher who restored materialism to its rights. This, however, does not mean that the materialism of Marx and Engels is identical with Feuerbach's materialism. As a matter of fact, Marx and Engels took from Feuerbach's materialism its "inner kernel," developed it into a scientific-philosophical theory of materialism and cast aside its idealistic and religious-ethical encumbrances. We know that Feuerbach, although he was fundamentally a materialist, objected to the name materialism. Engels more than once declared that "in spite of the materialist foundation, Feuerbach remained bound by the traditional idealist fetters," and that "the real idealism of Feuerbach becomes evident as soon as we come to his philosophy of religion and ethics." (Karl Marx, *Selected Works*, Vol. I, pp. 439, 442.)

Dialectics comes from the Greek *dialego*, to discourse, to debate. In ancient times dialectics was the art of arriving at the truth by disclosing the contradictions in the argument of an opponent and overcoming these contradictions. There were philosophers in ancient times who believed that the disclosure of contradictions in thought and the clash of opposite opinions was the best method of arriving at the truth. This dialectical method of thought, later extended to the phenomena of nature, developed into the dialectical method of apprehending nature, which regards the phenomena of nature as being in constant movement and undergoing constant change, and the development of nature as the result of the development of the contradictions in nature, as the result of the interaction of opposed forces in nature.

In its essence, dialectics is the direct opposite of metaphysics.

1) The principal features of the Marxist *dialectical method* are as follows:

a) Contrary to metaphysics, dialectics does not regard nature as an accidental agglomeration of things, of phenomena, unconnected with, isolated from, and independent of, each other, but as a connected and integral whole, in which things, phenomena, are organically connected with, dependent on, and determined by, each other.

The dialectical method therefore holds that no phenomenon in nature can be understood if taken by itself, isolated from surrounding phenomena, inasmuch as any phenomenon in any realm of nature may become meaningless to us if it is not considered in connection with the surrounding conditions, but divorced from them; and that, vice versa, any phenomenon can be understood and explained if considered in its inseparable connection with surrounding phenomena, as one conditioned by surrounding phenomena.

b) Contrary to metaphysics, dialectics holds that nature is not a state of rest and immobility, stagnation and immutability, but a state of continuous movement and change, of continuous renewal and development, where something is always arising and developing, and something always disintegrating and dying away.

The dialectical method therefore requires that phenomena should be considered not only from the standpoint of their interconnection and interdependence, but also from the standpoint of their movement, their change, their development, their coming into being and going out of being.

The dialectical method regards as important primarily not that which at the given moment seems to be durable and yet is already beginning to die away, but that which is arising and developing, even though at the given moment it may appear to be not durable, for the dialectical method considers invincible only that which is arising and developing.

"All nature," says Engels, "from the smallest thing to the biggest, from a grain of sand to the sun, from the protista (the primary living cell—*Ed.*) to man, is in a constant state of coming into being and going out of being, in a constant flux, in a ceaseless state of movement and change." (F. Engels, *Dialectics of Nature.*)

Therefore, dialectics, Engels says, "takes things and their perceptual images essentially in their inter-connection, in their concatenation, in their movement, in their rise and disappearance." (*Ibid.*)

c) Contrary to metaphysics, dialectics does not regard the process of development as a simple process of growth, where quantitative changes do not lead to qualitative changes, but as a development which passes from insignificant and imperceptible quantitative changes to open, fundamental changes, to qualitative changes; a development in which the qualitative changes occur not gradually, but rapidly and abruptly, taking the form of a leap from one state to another; they occur not accidentally but as the natural result of an accumulation of imperceptible and gradual quantitative changes.

The dialectical method therefore holds that the process of development should be understood not as movement in a circle, not as a simple repetition of what has already occurred, but as an onward and upward movement, as a transition from an old qualitative state to a new qualitative state, as a development from the simple to the complex, from the lower to the higher:

"Nature," says Engels, "is the test of dialectics, and it must be said for modern natural science that it has furnished extremely rich and daily increasing materials for this test, and has thus proved that in the last analysis nature's process is dialectical and not metaphysical, that it does not move in an eternally uniform and constantly repeated circle, but passes through a real history. Here prime mention should be made of Darwin, who dealt a severe blow to the metaphysical conception of nature by proving that the organic world of today, plants and animals, and consequently man too, is all a product of a process of development that has been in progress for millions of years." (F. Engels, *Anti-Dühring*.)

Describing dialectical development as a transition from quantitative changes to qualitative changes, Engels says:

"In physics ... every change is a passing of quantity into quality, as a result of quantitative change of some form of movement either inherent in a body or imparted to it. For example, the temperature of water has at first no effect on its liquid state; but as the temperature of liquid water rises or falls, a moment arrives when this state of cohesion changes and the water is converted in one case into steam and in the other into ice. ... A definite minimum current is required to make a platinum wire glow; every metal has its melting temperature; every liquid has a definite freezing point and boiling point at a given pressure, as far as we are able with the means at our disposal to attain the required temperatures; finally, every gas has its critical point at which, by proper pressure and cooling, it can be converted into a liquid state. ... What are known as the constants of physics (the point at which one state passes into another—*Ed.*) are in most cases nothing but designations for the nodal points at which a quantitative (change) increase or decrease of movement causes a qualitative change in the state of the given body, and at which, consequently, quantity is transformed into quality." (*Dialectics of Nature.*)

Passing to chemistry, Engels continues:

"Chemistry may be called the science of the qualitative changes which take place in bodies as the effect of changes of quantitative composition. This was already known to Hegel. ... Take oxygen: if the molecule contains three atoms instead of the customary two, we get ozone, a body definitely distinct in odour and reaction from ordinary oxygen. And what shall we say of the different proportions in which oxygen combines with nitrogen or sulphur, and each of which produces a body qualitatively different from all other bodies!" (*Ibid.*)

Finally, criticizing Dühring, who scolded Hegel for all he was worth, but surreptitiously borrowed from him the well-known thesis that the transition from the insentient world to the sentient world, from the kingdom of inorganic matter to the kingdom of organic life, is a leap to a new state, Engels says:

"This is precisely the Hegelian nodal line of measure relations, in which, at certain definite nodal points, the purely quantitative increase or decrease gives rise to a *qualitative leap*, for example, in the case of water which is heated or cooled, where boiling-point and freezing-point are the nodes at which—under normal pressure—the leap to a new aggregate state takes place, and where consequently quantity is transformed into quality." (F. Engels, *Anti-Dühring*.)

d) Contrary to metaphysics, dialectics holds that internal contradictions are inherent in all things and phenomena of nature, for they all have their negative and positive sides, a past and a future, something dying away and something developing; and that the struggle between these opposites, the struggle between the old and the new, between that which is dying away and that which is being born, between that which is disappearing and that which is developing, constitutes the internal content of the process of development, the internal content of the transformation of quantitative changes into qualitative changes.

The dialectical method therefore holds that the process of development from the lower to the higher takes place not as a harmonious unfolding of phenomena, but as a disclosure of the contradictions inherent in things and phenomena, as a "struggle" of opposite tendencies which operate on the basis of these contradictions.

"In its proper meaning," Lenin says, "dialectics is the study of the contradiction *within the very essence of things*." (Lenin, *Philosophical Notebooks*, Russ. ed., p. 263.)

And further:

"Development is the 'struggle' of opposites." (Lenin, *Selected Works*, Vol. XI, pp. 81-2.)

Such, in brief, are the principal features of the Marxist dialectical method.

It is easy to understand how immensely important is the extension of the principles of the dialectical method to the study of social life and the history of society, and how immensely important is the application of these principles to the history of society and to the practical activities of the party of the proletariat.

If there are no isolated phenomena in the world, if all phenomena are interconnected and interdependent, then it is clear that every social system and every social movement in history must be evaluated not from the standpoint of "eternal justice" or some other preconceived idea, as is not infrequently done by historians, but from the standpoint of the conditions which gave rise to that system or that social movement and with which they are connected.

The slave system would be senseless, stupid and unnatural under modern conditions. But under the conditions of a disintegrating primitive communal system, the slave system is a quite understandable and natural phenomenon, since it represents an advance on the primitive communal system.

The demand for a bourgeois-democratic republic when tsardom and bourgeois society existed, as, let us say, in Russia in 1905, was a quite understandable, proper and revolutionary demand, for at that time a bourgeois republic would have meant a step forward. But now, under the conditions of the U.S.S.R., the demand for a bourgeois-democratic republic would be a meaningless and counter-revolutionary demand, for a bourgeois republic would be a retrograde step compared with the Soviet republic.

Everything depends on the conditions, time and place.

It is clear that without such a *historical* approach to social phenomena, the existence and development of the science of history is impossible, for only such an approach saves the science of history from becoming a jumble of accidents and an agglomeration of most absurd mistakes.

Further, if the world is in a state of constant movement and development, if the dying away of the old and the upgrowth of the new is a law of development, then it is clear that there can be no "immutable" social systems, no "eternal principles" of private property and exploitation, no "eternal ideas" of the subjugation of the peasant to the landlord, of the worker to the capitalist.

Hence the capitalist system can be replaced by the Socialist system, just as at one time the feudal system was replaced by the capitalist system.

Hence we must not base our orientation on the strata of society which are no longer developing, even though they at present constitute the predominant force, but on those strata which are developing and have a future before them, even though they at present do not constitute the predominant force.

In the eighties of the past century, in the period of the struggle between the Marxists and the Narodniks, the proletariat in Russia constituted an insignificant minority of the population, whereas the individual peasants constituted the vast majority of the population. But the proletariat was developing as a class, whereas the peasantry as a class was disintegrating. And just because the proletariat was developing as a class the

Marxists based their orientation on the proletariat. And they were not mistaken, for, as we know, the proletariat subsequently grew from an insignificant force into a first-rate historical and political force.

Hence, in order not to err in policy, one must look forward, not backward.

Further, if the passing of slow quantitative changes into rapid and abrupt qualitative changes is a law of development, then it is clear that revolutions made by oppressed classes are a quite natural and inevitable phenomenon.

Hence the transition from capitalism to Socialism and the liberation of the working class from the yoke of capitalism cannot be effected by slow changes, by reforms, but only by a qualitative change of the capitalist system, by revolution.

Hence, in order not to err in policy, one must be a revolutionary, not a reformist.

Further, if development proceeds by way of the disclosure of internal contradictions, by way of collisions between opposite forces on the basis of these contradictions and so as to overcome these contradictions, then it is clear that the class struggle of the proletariat is a quite natural and inevitable phenomenon.

Hence we must not cover up the contradictions of the capitalist system, but disclose and unravel them; we must not try to check the class struggle but carry it to its conclusion.

Hence, in order not to err in policy, one must pursue an uncompromising proletarian class policy, not a reformist policy of harmony of the interests of the proletariat and the bourgeoisie, not a compromisers' policy of "the growing of capitalism into Socialism."

Such is the Marxist dialectical method when applied to social life, to the history of society.

As to Marxist philosophical materialism, it is fundamentally the direct opposite of philosophical idealism.

2) The principal features of Marxist philosophical *materialism* are as follows:

a) Contrary to idealism, which regards the world as the embodiment of an "absolute idea," a "universal spirit," "consciousness," Marx's philosophical materialism holds that the world is by its very nature *material*, that the multifold phenomena of the world constitute different forms of matter in motion, that interconnection and interdependence of phenomena, as established by the dialectical method, are a law of the development of moving matter, and that the world develops in accordance with the laws of movement of matter and stands in no need of a "universal spirit."

"The materialist world outlook," says Engels, "is simply the conception of nature as it is, without any reservations." (MS of *Ludwig Feuerbach*.)

Speaking of the materialist views of the ancient philosopher Heraclitus, who held that "the world, the all in one, was not created by any god or any man, but was, is and ever will be a living flame, systematically flaring up and systematically dying down," Lenin comments: "A very good exposition of the rudiments of dialectical materialism." (Lenin, *Philosophical Notebooks*, Russ. ed., p. 318.)

b) Contrary to idealism, which asserts that only our mind really exists, and that the material world, being, nature, exists only in our mind, in our sensations, ideas and perceptions, the Marxist materialist philosophy holds that matter, nature, being, is an objective reality existing outside and independent of our mind; that matter is primary, since it is the source of sensations, ideas, mind, and that mind is secondary, derivative, since it is a reflection of matter, a reflection of being; that thought is a product of matter which in its development has reached a high degree of perfection, namely, of the brain, and the brain is the organ of thought; and that therefore one cannot separate thought from matter without committing a grave error. Engels says:

"The question of the relation of thinking to being, the relation of spirit to nature is the paramount question of the whole of philosophy.... The answers which the philosophers gave to this question split them into two great camps. Those who asserted the primacy of spirit to nature ... comprised the camp of *idealism*. The others, who regarded nature as primary, belong to the various schools of *material-ism*." (Karl Marx, *Selected Works*, Vol. I, pp. 430-31.)

And further:

"The material, sensuously perceptible world to which we ourselves belong is the only reality.... Our consciousness and thinking, however supra-sensuous they may seem, are the product of a material, bodily organ, the brain. Matter is not a product of mind, but mind itself is merely the highest product of matter." (*Ibid.*, p. 435.)

Concerning the question of matter and thought, Marx says:

"*It is impossible to separate thought from matter that thinks.* Matter is the subject of all changes." (*Ibid.*, p. 397.)

Describing the Marxist philosophy of materialism, Lenin says:

"Materialism in general recognizes objectively real being (matter) as independent of consciousness, sensation, experience.... Consciousness is only the reflection of being, at best, an approximately true (adequate, ideally exact) reflection of it." (Lenin, *Selected Works*, Vol. XI, p. 378.)

And further:

(a) "Matter is that which, acting upon our sense-organs, produces sensation; matter is the objective reality given to us in sensation. ... Matter, nature, being, the physical—is primary, and spirit, consciousness, sensation, the psychical—is secondary." (*Ibid.*, pp. 208, 209.)

(b) "The world picture is a picture of how matter moves and of how *'matter thinks.'*" (*Ibid.*, p. 403.)

(c) "The brain is the organ of thought." (*Ibid.*, p. 125.)

c) Contrary to idealism, which denies the possibility of knowing the world and its laws, which does not believe in the authenticity of our knowledge, does not recognize objective truth, and holds that the world is full of "things-in-themselves" that can never be known to science, Marxist philosophical materialism holds that the world and its laws are fully knowable, that our knowledge of the laws of nature, tested by experiment and practice, is authentic knowledge having the validity of objective truth, and that there are no things in the world which are unknowable, but only things which are still not known, but which will be disclosed and made known by the efforts of science and practice.

Criticizing the thesis of Kant and other idealists that the world is unknowable and that there are "things-in-themselves" which are unknowable, and defending the well-known materialist thesis that our knowledge is authentic knowledge, Engels writes:

"The most telling refutation of this as of all other philosophical fancies is practice, *viz.*, experiment and industry. If we are able to prove the correctness of our conception of a natural process by making it ourselves, bringing it into being out of its conditions and using it for our own purposes into the bargain, then there is an end of the Kantian 'thing-in-itself.' The chemical substances produced in the bodies of plants and animals remained such 'things-in-themselves' until organic chemistry began to produce them one after another, whereupon the 'thing-in-itself' became a thing for us, as for instance, alizarin, the colouring matter of the madder, which we no longer trouble to grow in the madder roots in the field, but produce much more cheaply and simply from coal tar. For three hundred years the Copernican solar system was a hypothesis, with a hundred, a thousand or ten thousand chances to one in its favour, but still always a hypothesis. But when Leverrier, by means of the data provided by this system, not only deduced the necessity of the existence of an unknown planet, but also calculated the position in the heavens which this planet must necessarily occupy, and when Galle really found this planet, the Copernican system was proved." (Karl Marx, *Selected Works*, Vol. I, pp. 432-33.)

Accusing Bogdanov, Bazarov, Yushkevich and the other followers of Mach of fideism, and defending the well-known materialist thesis that our scientific knowledge of the laws of nature is authentic knowledge, and that the laws of science represent objective truth, Lenin says:

"Contemporary fideism does not at all reject science; all it rejects is the 'exaggerated claims' of science, to wit, its claim to objective truth. If objective truth exists (as the materialists think), if natural science, reflecting the outer world in human 'experience,' is alone capable of giving us objective truth, then all fideism is absolutely refuted." (Lenin, *Selected Works*, Vol. XI, p. 189.)

Such, in brief, are the characteristic features of the Marxist philosophical materialism.

It is easy to understand how immensely important is the extension of the principles of philosophical materialism to the study of social life, of the history of society, and how immensely important is the application of these principles to the history of society and to the practical activities of the party of the proletariat.

If the connection between the phenomena of nature and their interdependence are laws of the development of nature, it follows, too, that the connection and interdependence of the phenomena of social life are laws of the development of society, and not something accidental.

Hence social life, the history of society, ceases to be an agglomeration of "accidents," and becomes the history of the development of society according to regular laws, and the study of the history of society becomes a science.

Hence the practical activity of the party of the proletariat must not be based on the good wishes of "outstanding individuals," not on the dictates of "reason," "universal morals," etc., but on the laws of development of society and on the study of these laws.

Further, if the world is knowable and our knowledge of the laws of development of nature is authentic knowledge, having the validity of objective truth, it follows that social life, the development of society, is also knowable, and that the data of science regarding the laws of development of society are authentic data having the validity of objective truths.

Hence the science of the history of society, despite all the complexity of the phenomena of social life, can become as precise a science as, let us say, biology, and capable of making use of the laws of development of society for practical purposes.

Hence the party of the proletariat should not guide itself in its practical activity by casual motives, but by the laws of development of society, and by practical deductions from these laws.

Hence Socialism is converted from a dream of a better future for humanity into a science.

Hence the bond between science and practical activity, between theory and practice, their unity, should be the guiding star of the party of the proletariat.

Further, if nature, being, the material world, is primary, and mind, thought, is secondary, derivative; if the material world represents objective reality existing independently of the mind of men, while the mind is a reflection of this objective reality, it follows that the material life of society, its being, is also primary, and its spiritual life secondary, derivative, and that the material life of society is an objective reality existing independently of the will of men, while the spiritual life of society is a reflection of this objective reality, a reflection of being.

Hence the source of formation of the spiritual life of society, the origin of social ideas, social theories, political views and political institutions, should not be sought for in the ideas, theories, views and political institutions themselves, but in the conditions of the material life of society, in social being, of which these ideas, theories, views, etc., are the reflection.

Hence, if in different periods of the history of society different social ideas, theories, views and political institutions are to be observed; if under the slave system we encounter certain social ideas, theories, views and political institutions, under feudalism others, and under capitalism others still, this is not to be explained by the "nature," the "properties" of the ideas, theories, views and political institutions themselves but by the different conditions of the material life of society at different periods of social development.

Whatever is the being of a society, whatever are the conditions of material life of a society, such are the ideas, theories, political views and political institutions of that society.

In this connection, Marx says:

"It is not the consciousness of men that determines their being, but, on the contrary, their social being that determines their consciousness." (Karl Marx, *Selected Works*, Vol. I, p. 356.)

Hence, in order not to err in policy, in order not to find itself in the position of idle dreamers, the party of the proletariat must not base its activities on abstract "principles of human reason," but on the concrete conditions of the material life of society, as the determining force of social development; not on the good wishes of "great men," but on the real needs of development of the material life of society.

The fall of the utopians, including the Narodniks, Anarchists and Socialist-Revolutionaries, was due, among other things, to the fact that they did not recognize the primary role which the conditions of the material life of society play in the development of society, and, sinking to idealism, did not base their practical activities on the needs of the development of the material life of society, but, independently of and in spite of these needs, on "ideal plans" and "all-embracing projects" divorced from the real life of society.

The strength and vitality of Marxism-Leninism lie in the fact that it does base its practical activity on the needs of the development of the material life of society and never divorces itself from the real life of society.

It does not follow from Marx's words, however, that social ideas, theories, political views and political institutions are of no significance in the life of society, that they do not reciprocally affect social being, the development of the material conditions of the life of society. We have been speaking so far of the *origin* of social ideas, theories, views and political institutions, of *the way they arise*, of the fact that the spiritual life of society is a reflection of the conditions of its material life. As regards the *significance* of social ideas, theories, views and political institutions, as regards their *role* in history, historical materialism, far from denying them, stresses the role and importance of these factors in the life of society, in its history.

There are different kinds of social ideas and theories. There are old ideas and theories which have outlived their day and which serve the interests of the moribund forces of society. Their significance lies in the fact that they hamper the development, the progress of society. Then there are new and advanced ideas and theories which serve the interests of the advanced forces of society. Their significance lies in the fact that they facilitate the development, the progress of society; and their significance is the greater the more accurately they reflect the needs of development of the material life of society.

New social ideas and theories arise only after the development of the material life of society has set new tasks before society. But once they have arisen they become a most potent force which facilitates the carrying out of the new tasks set by the development of the material life of society, a force which facilitates the progress of society. It is precisely here that the tremendous organizing, mobilizing and transforming value of new ideas, new theories, new political views and new political institutions manifests itself. New social ideas and theories arise precisely because they are necessary to society, because it is *impossible* to carry out the urgent tasks of development of the material life of society without their organizing, mobilizing and transforming action. Arising out of the new tasks set by the development of the material life of society, the new social ideas and theories force their way through, become the possession of the masses, mobilize and organize them against the moribund forces of society, and thus facilitate the overthrow of these forces which hamper the development of the material life of society.

Thus social ideas, theories and political institutions, having arisen on the basis of the urgent tasks of the development of the material life of society, the development of social being, themselves then react upon social being, upon the material life of society, creating the conditions necessary for completely carrying out the urgent tasks of the material life of society, and for rendering its further development possible.

In this connection, Marx says:

> "Theory becomes a material force as soon as it has gripped the masses." (*Zur Kritik der Hegelschen Rechtsphilosophie.*)

Hence, in order to be able to influence the conditions of material life of society and to accelerate their development and their improvement, the party of the proletariat must rely upon such a social theory, such a social idea as correctly reflects the needs of development of the material life of society, and which is therefore capable of setting into motion broad masses of the people and of mobilizing them and organizing them into a great army of the proletarian party, prepared to smash the reactionary forces and to clear the way for the advanced forces of society.

The fall of the "Economists" and Mensheviks was due among other things to the fact that they did not recognize the mobilizing, organizing and transforming role of advanced theory, of advanced ideas and, sinking to vulgar materialism, reduced the role of these factors almost to nothing, thus condemning the Party to passivity and inanition.

The strength and vitality of Marxism-Leninism are derived from the fact that it relies upon an advanced theory which correctly reflects the needs of development of the material life of society, that it elevates theory to a proper level, and that it deems it its duty to utilize every ounce of the mobilizing, organizing and transforming power of this theory.

That is the answer historical materialism gives to the question of the relation between social being and social consciousness, between the conditions of development of material life and the development of the spiritual life of society.

It now remains to elucidate the following question: what, from the viewpoint of historical materialism, is meant by the "conditions of material life of society" which in the final analysis determine the physiognomy of society, its ideas, views, political institutions, etc.?

What, after all, are these "conditions of material life of society," what are their distinguishing features?

There can be no doubt that the concept "conditions of material life of society" includes, first of all, nature which surrounds society, geographical environment, which is one of the indispensable and constant conditions of material life of society and which, of course, influences the development of society. What role does geographical environment play in the development of society? Is geographical environment the chief force determining the physiognomy of society, the character of the social system of men, the transition from one system to another?

Historical materialism answers this question in the negative.

Geographical environment is unquestionably one of the constant and indispensable conditions of development of society and, of course, influences the development of society, accelerates or retards its development. But its influence is not the *determining* influence, inasmuch as the changes and development of society proceed at an incomparably faster rate than the changes and development of geographical environment. In the space of three thousand years three different social systems have been successively superseded in Europe: the primitive communal system, the slave system and the feudal system. In the eastern part of Europe, in the U.S.S.R., even four social systems have been superseded. Yet during this period geographical conditions in Europe have either not changed at all, or have changed so slightly that geography takes no note of them. And that is quite natural. Changes in geographical environment of any importance require millions of years, whereas a few hundred or a couple of thousand years are enough for even very important changes in the system of human society.

It follows from this that geographical environment cannot be the chief cause, the *determining* cause of social development, for that which remains almost unchanged in the course of tens of thousands of years cannot be the chief cause of development of that which undergoes fundamental changes in the course of a few hundred years.

Further, there can be no doubt that the concept "conditions of material life of society" also includes growth of population, density of population of one degree or another, for people are an essential element of the conditions of material life of society, and without a definite minimum number of people there can be no material life of society. Is not growth of population the chief force that determines the character of the social system of man?

Historical materialism answers this question too in the negative.

Of course, growth of population does influence the development of society, does facilitate or retard the development of society, but it cannot be the chief force of development of society, and its influence on the development of society cannot be the *determining* influence because, by itself, growth of population does not furnish the clue to the question why a given social system is replaced precisely by such and such a new system and not by another, why the primitive communal system is succeeded precisely by the slave system, the slave system by the feudal system, and the feudal system by the bourgeois system, and not by some other.

If growth of population were the determining force of social development, then a higher density of population would be bound to give rise to a correspondingly higher type of social system. But we do not find this to be the case. The density of population in China is four times as great as in the U.S.A., yet the U.S.A. stands higher than China in the scale of social development, for in China a semi-feudal system still prevails, whereas the U.S.A. has long ago reached the highest stage of development of capitalism. The density of population in Belgium is nineteen times as great as in the U.S.A., and twenty-six times as great as in the U.S.S.R. Yet the U.S.A. stands higher than Belgium in the scale of social development; and as for the U.S.S.R., Belgium lags a whole historical epoch behind this country, for in Belgium the capitalist system prevails, whereas the U.S.S.R. has already done away with capitalism and has set up a Socialist system.

It follows from this that growth of population is not, and cannot be, the chief force of development of society, the force which *determines* the character of the social system, the physiognomy of society.

What, then, is the chief force in the complex of conditions of material life of society which determines the physiognomy of society, the character of the social system, the development of society from one system to another?

This force, historical materialism holds, is the *method of procuring the means of life* necessary for human existence, the *mode of production of material values*—food, clothing, footwear, houses, fuel, instruments of production, etc.—which are indispensable for the life of development of society.

In order to live, people must have food, clothing, footwear, shelter, fuel, etc.; in order to have these material values, people must produce them; and in order to produce them, people must have the instruments of production with which food, clothing, footwear, shelter, fuel, etc., are produced; they must be able to produce these instruments and to use them.

The *instruments of production* wherewith material values are produced, the *people* who operate the instruments of production and carry on the production of material values thanks to a certain *production experience* and *labour skill*—all these elements jointly constitute the *productive forces* of society.

But the productive forces are only one aspect of production, only one aspect of the mode of production, an aspect that expresses the relation of men to the objects and forces of nature which they make use of for the production of material values. Another aspect of production, another aspect of the mode of production, is the relation of men to each other in the process of production, men's *relations of production*. Men carry on a struggle against nature and utilize nature for the production of material values not in isolation from each other, not as separate individuals, but in common, in groups, in societies. Production, therefore, is at all times and under all conditions *social* production. In the production of material values men enter into mutual relations of one kind or another within production, into relations of production of one kind or another. These may be relations of co-operation and mutual help between people who are free from exploitation; they may be relations of domination and subordination; and, lastly, they may be transitional from one form of relations of production to another. But whatever the character of the relations of production may be, always and in every system, they constitute just as essential an element of production as the productive forces of society.

"In production," Marx says, "men not only act on nature but also on one another. They produce only by co-operating in a certain way and mutually exchanging their activities. In order to produce, they enter into definite connections and relations with one another and only within these social connections and relations does their action on nature, does production, take place." (Karl Marx, *Selected Works*, Vol. I, p. 264.)

Consequently, production, the mode of production, embraces both the productive forces of society and men's relations of production, and is thus the embodiment of their unity in the process of production of material values.

One of the features of production is that it never stays at one point for a long time and is always in a state of change and development, and that, furthermore, changes in the mode of production inevitably call forth changes in the whole social system, social ideas, political views and political institutions—they call forth a reconstruction of the whole social and political order. At different stages of development people make use of different modes of production, or, to put it more crudely, lead different manners of life. In the primitive commune there is one mode of production, under slavery there is another mode of production, under feudalism a third mode of production, and so on. And, correspondingly, men's social system, the spiritual life of men, their views and political institutions also vary.

Whatever is the mode of production of a society, such in the main is the society itself, its ideas and theories, its political views and institutions.

Or, to put it more crudely, whatever is man's manner of life, such is his manner of thought.

This means that the history of development of society is above all the history of the development of production, the history of the modes of production which succeed each other in the course of centuries, the history of the development of productive forces and people's relations of production.

Hence the history of social development is at the same time the history of the producers of material values themselves, the history of the labouring masses who are the chief force in the process of production and who carry on the production of material values necessary for the existence of society.

Hence, if historical science is to be a real science, it can no longer reduce the history of social development to the actions of kings and generals, to the actions of "conquerors" and "subjugators" of states, but must above all devote itself to the history of the producers of material values, the history of the labouring masses, the history of peoples.

Hence the clue to the study of the laws of history of society must not be sought in men's minds, in the views and ideas of society, but in the mode of production practised by society in any given historical period; it must be sought in the economic life of society.

Hence the prime task of historical science is to study and disclose the laws of production, the laws of development of the productive forces and of the relations of production, the laws of economic development of society.

Hence, if the party of the proletariat is to be a real party, it must above all acquire a knowledge of the laws of development of production, of the laws of economic development of society.

Hence, if it is not to err in policy, the party of the proletariat must both in drafting its program and in its practical activities proceed primarily from the laws of development of production, from the laws of economic development of society.

A second feature of production is that its changes and development always begin with changes and development of the productive forces, and, in the first place, with changes and development of the instruments of production. Productive forces are therefore the most mobile and revolutionary element of production. First the productive forces of society change and develop, and then, *depending* on these changes and *in con-*

formity with them, men's relations of production, their economic relations, change. This, however, does not mean that the relations of production do not influence the development of the productive forces and that the latter are not dependent on the former. While their development is dependent on the development of the productive forces, the relations of production in their turn react upon the development of the productive forces, accelerating or retarding it. In this connection it should be noted that the relations of production cannot for too long a time lag behind and be in a state of contradiction to the growth of the productive forces, inasmuch as the productive forces can develop in full measure only when the relations of production correspond to the character, the state of the productive forces and allow full scope for their development. Therefore, however much the relations of production may lag behind the development of the productive forces, they must, sooner or later, come into correspondence with—and actually do come into correspondence with—the level of development of the productive forces, the character of the productive forces. Otherwise we would have a fundamental violation of the unity of the productive forces and the relations of production within the system of production, a disruption of production as a whole, a crisis of production, a destruction of productive forces.

An instance in which the relations of production do not correspond to the character of the productive forces, conflict with them, is the economic crises in capitalist countries, where private capitalist ownership of the means of production is in glaring incongruity with the social character of the process of production, with the character of the productive forces. This results in economic crises, which lead to the destruction of productive forces. Furthermore, this incongruity itself constitutes the economic basis of social revolution, the purpose of which is to destroy the existing relations of production and to create new relations of production corresponding to the character of the productive forces.

In contrast, an instance in which the relations of production completely correspond to the character of the productive forces is the Socialist national economy of the U.S.S.R., where the social ownership of the means of production fully corresponds to the social character of the process of production, and where, because of this, economic crises and the destruction of productive forces are unknown.

Consequently, the productive forces are not only the most mobile and revolutionary element in production, but are also the determining element in the development of production.

Whatever are the productive forces such must be the relations of production.

While the state of the productive forces furnishes an answer to the question—with what instruments of production do men produce the material values they need?—the state of the relations of production furnishes the answer to another question—who owns the *means of production* (the land, forests, waters, mineral resources, raw materials, instruments of production, production premises, means of transportation and communication, etc.), who commands the means of production, whether the whole of society, or individual persons, groups, or classes which utilize them for the exploitation of other persons, groups or classes?

Here is a rough picture of the development of productive forces from ancient times to our day. The transition from crude stone tools to the bow and arrow, and the accompanying transition from the life of hunters to the domestication of animals and primitive pasturage; the transition from stone tools to metal tools (the iron axe, the wooden plough fitted with an iron colter, etc.), with a corresponding transition to tillage and agriculture; a further improvement in metal tools for the working up of materials, the introduction of the blacksmith's bellows, the introduction of pottery, with a corresponding development of handicrafts, the separation of handicrafts from agriculture, the development of an independent handicraft industry and, subsequently, of manufacture; the transition from handicraft tools to machines and the transformation of handicraft and manufacture into machine industry; the transition to the machine system and the rise of modern large-scale machine industry—such is a general and far from complete picture of the development of the productive forces of society in the course of man's history. It will be clear that the development and improvement of the instruments of production were effected by men who were related to production, and not independently of men; and, consequently, the change and development of the instruments of production were accompanied by a change and development of men, as the most important element of the productive forces, by a change and development of their production experience, their labour skill, their ability to handle the instruments of production.

In conformity with the change and development of the productive forces of society in the course of history, men's relations of production, their economic relations also changed and developed.

Five *main* types of relations of production are known to history: primitive communal, slave, feudal, capitalist and Socialist.

The basis of the relations of production under the primitive communal system is that the means of production are socially owned. This in the main corresponds to the character of the productive forces of that period. Stone tools, and, later, the bow and arrow, precluded the possibility of men individually combating the forces of nature and beasts of prey. In order to gather the fruits of the forest, to catch fish, to build some sort of habitation, men were obliged to work in common if they did not want to die of starvation, or fall victim to beasts of prey or to neighbouring societies. Labour in common led to the common ownership of the means of production, as well as of the fruits of production. Here the conception of private ownership of the means of production did not yet exist, except for the personal ownership of certain implements of production which were at the same time means of defence against beasts of prey. Here there was no exploitation, no classes.

The basis of the relations of production under the slave system is that the slave owner owns the means of production; he also owns the worker in production—the slave, whom he can sell, purchase, or kill as though he were an animal. Such relations of production in the main correspond to the state of the productive forces of that period. Instead of stone tools, men now have metal tools at their command; instead of the wretched and primitive husbandry of the hunter, who knew neither pasturage, nor tillage, there now appear pasturage, tillage, handicrafts, and a division of labour between these branches of production. There appears the possibility of the exchange of products between individuals and between societies, of the accumulation of wealth in the hands of a few, the actual accumulation of the means of production in the hands of a minority, and the possibility of subjugation of the majority by a minority and their conversion into slaves. Here we no longer find the common and free labour of all members of society in the production process—here there prevails the forced labour of slaves, who are exploited by the non-labouring slave owners. Here, therefore, there is no common ownership of the means of production or of the fruits of production. It is replaced by private ownership. Here the slave owner appears as the prime and principal property owner in the full sense of the term.

Rich and poor, exploiters and exploited, people with full rights and people with no rights, and a fierce class struggle between them—such is the picture of the slave system.

The basis of the relations of production under the feudal system is that the feudal lord owns the means of production and does not fully own the worker in production—the serf, whom the feudal lord can no longer kill, but whom he can buy and sell. Alongside of feudal ownership there exists individual ownership by the peasant and the handicraftsman of his implements of production and his private enterprise based on his personal labour. Such relations of production in the main correspond to the state of the productive forces of that period. Further improvements in the smelting and working of iron; the spread of the iron plough and the loom; the further development of agriculture, horticulture, viniculture and dairying; the appearance of manufactories alongside of the handicraft workshops—such are the characteristic features of the state of the productive forces.

The new productive forces demand that the labourer shall display some kind of initiative in production and an inclination for work, an interest in work. The feudal lord therefore discards the slave, as a labourer who has no interest in work and is entirely without initiative, and prefers to deal with the serf, who has his own husbandry, implements of production, and a certain interest in work essential for the cultivation of the land and for the payment in kind of a part of his harvest to the feudal lord.

Here private ownership is further developed. Exploitation is nearly as severe as it was under slavery—it is only slightly mitigated. A class struggle between exploiters and exploited is the principal feature of the feudal system.

The basis of the relations of production under the capitalist system is that the capitalist owns the means of production, but not the workers in production—the wage labourers, whom the capitalist can neither kill nor sell because they are personally free, but who are deprived of means of production and, in order not to die of hunger, are obliged to sell their labour power to the capitalist and to bear the yoke of exploitation. Alongside of capitalist property in the means of production, we find, at first on a wide scale, private property of the peasants and handicraftsmen in the means of production, these peasants and handicraftsmen no longer being serfs, and their private property being based on personal labour. In place of the handicraft workshops and manufactories there appear huge mills and factories equipped with machinery. In place of the manorial estates tilled by the primitive implements of production of the peasant, there now appear large capitalist farms run on scientific lines and supplied with agricultural machinery.

The new productive forces require that the workers in production shall be better educated and more intelligent than the downtrodden and ignorant serfs, that they be able to understand machinery and operate it properly. Therefore, the capitalists prefer to deal with wage workers who are free from the bonds of serfdom and who are educated enough to be able properly to operate machinery.

But having developed productive forces to a tremendous extent, capitalism has become enmeshed in contradictions which it is unable to solve. By producing larger and larger quantities of commodities, and reducing their prices, capitalism intensifies competition, ruins the mass of small and medium private owners, converts them into proletarians and reduces their purchasing power, with the result that it becomes impossible to dispose of the commodities produced. On the other hand, by expanding production and concentrating millions of workers in huge mills and factories, capitalism lends the process of production a social character and thus undermines its own foundation, inasmuch as the social character of the process of production demands the social ownership of the means of production; yet the means of production remain private capitalist property, which is incompatible with the social character of the process of production.

These irreconcilable contradictions between the character of the productive forces and the relations of production make themselves felt in periodical crises of overproduction, when the capitalists, finding no effective demand for their goods owing to the ruin of the mass of the population which they themselves have brought about, are compelled to burn products, destroy manufactured goods, suspend production, and destroy productive forces at a time when millions of people are forced to suffer unemployment and starvation, not because there are not enough goods, but because there is an overproduction of goods.

This means that the capitalist relations of production have ceased to correspond to the state of productive forces of society and have come into irreconcilable contradiction with them.

This means that capitalism is pregnant with revolution, whose mission it is to replace the existing capitalist ownership of the means of production by Socialist ownership.

This means that the main feature of the capitalist system is a most acute class struggle between the exploiters and the exploited.

The basis of the relations of production under the Socialist system, which so far has been established only in the U.S.S.R., is the social ownership of the means of production. Here there are no longer exploiters and exploited. The goods produced are distributed according to labour performed, on the principle: "He who does not work, neither shall he eat." Here the mutual relations of people in the process of production are marked by comradely co-operation and the Socialist mutual assistance of workers who are free from exploitation. Here the relations of production fully correspond to the state of productive forces, for the social character of the process of production is reinforced by the social ownership of the means of production.

For this reason Socialist production in the U.S.S.R. knows no periodical crises of overproduction and their accompanying absurdities.

For this reason, the productive forces here develop at an accelerated pace, for the relations of production that correspond to them offer full scope for such development.

Such is the picture of the development of men's relations of production in the course of human history.

Such is the dependence of the development of the relations of production on the development of the production forces of society, and primarily, on the development of the instruments of production, the dependence by virtue of which the changes and development of the productive forces sooner or later lead to corresponding changes and development of the relations of production.

"The use and fabrication of instruments of labour," * says Marx, "although existing in the germ among certain species of animals, is specifically characteristic of the human labour-process, and Franklin therefore defines man as a tool-making animal. Relics of bygone instruments of labour possess the same importance for the investigation of extinct economic forms of society, as do fossil bones for the determination of extinct species of animals. It is not the articles made, but how they are made, and by what instruments that enables us to distinguish different economic epochs. ... Instruments of labour not only supply a standard of the degree of development to which human labour has attained but they are also indicators of the social conditions under which that labour is carried on." (Karl Marx, *Capital*, Vol. I, p. 159.)

And further:

a) "Social relations are closely bound up with productive forces. In acquiring new productive forces men change their mode of production; and in changing their mode of production, in changing the way of earning their living, they change all their social conditions. The hand-mill gives you society with the feudal lord; the steam-mill, society with the industrial capitalist." (Karl Marx, *The Poverty of Philosophy*, p. 92.)

b) "There is a continual movement of growth in productive forces, of destruction in social relations, of formation in ideas; the only immutable thing is the abstraction of movement." (*Ibid.*, p. 93.)

Speaking of historical materialism as formulated in *The Communist Manifesto*, Engels says:

"Economic production and the structure of society of every historical epoch necessarily arising therefrom constitute the foundation for

* By instruments of labour Marx has in mind primarily instruments of production.—*Ed.*

the political and intellectual history of that epoch; ...consequently ever since the dissolution of the primeval communal ownership of land all history has been a history of class struggles, of struggles between exploited and exploiting, between dominated and dominating classes at various stages of social evolution; ...this struggle, however, has now reached a stage where the exploited and oppressed class (the proletariat) can no longer emancipate itself from the class which exploits and oppresses it (the bourgeoisie), without at the same time forever freeing the whole of society from exploitation, oppression and class struggles." (Preface to the German edition of *The Communist Manifesto*—Karl Marx, *Selected Works*, Vol. I, pp. 192-93.)

A third feature of production is that the rise of new productive forces and of the relations of production corresponding to them does not take place separately from the old system, after the disappearance of the old system, but within the old system; it takes place not as a result of the deliberate and conscious activity of man, but spontaneously, unconsciously, independently of the will of man. It takes place spontaneously and independently of the will of man for two reasons.

First, because men are not free to choose one mode of production or another, because as every new generation enters life it finds productive forces and relations of production already existing as the result of the work of former generations, owing to which it is obliged at first to accept and adapt itself to everything it finds ready made in the sphere of production in order to be able to produce material values.

Secondly, because, when improving one instrument of production or another, one element of the productive forces or another, men do not realize, do not understand or stop to reflect what *social* results these improvements will lead to, but only think of their everyday interests, of lightening their labour and of securing some direct and tangible advantage for themselves.

When, gradually and gropingly, certain members of primitive communal society passed from the use of stone tools to the use of iron tools, they, of course, did not know and did not stop to reflect what *social* results this innovation would lead to; they did not understand or realize that the change to metal tools meant a revolution in production, that it would in the long run lead to the slave system. They simply wanted to lighten their labour and secure an immediate and tangible advantage; their conscious activity was confined within the narrow bounds of this everyday personal interest.

When, in the period of the feudal system, the young bourgeoisie of

Europe began to erect, alongside of the small guild workshops, large manufactories, and thus advanced the productive forces of society, it, of course, did not know and did not stop to reflect what *social* consequences this innovation would lead to; it did not realize or understand that this "small" innovation would lead to a regrouping of social forces which was to end in a revolution both against the power of kings, whose favours it so highly valued, and against the nobility, to whose ranks its foremost representatives not infrequently aspired. It simply wanted to lower the cost of producing goods, to throw large quantities of goods on the markets of Asia and of recently discovered America, and to make bigger profits. Its conscious activity was confined within the narrow bounds of this commonplace practical aim.

When the Russian capitalists, in conjunction with foreign capitalists, energetically implanted modern large-scale machine industry in Russia, while leaving tsardom intact and turning the peasants over to the tender mercies of the landlords, they, of course, did not know and did not stop to reflect what *social* consequences this extensive growth of productive forces would lead to, they did not realize or understand that this big leap in the realm of the productive forces of society would lead to a regrouping of social forces that would enable the proletariat to effect a union with the peasantry and to bring about a victorious Socialist revolution. They simply wanted to expand industrial production to the limit, to gain control of the huge home market, to become monopolists, and to squeeze as much profit as possible out of the national economy. Their conscious activity did not extend beyond their commonplace, strictly practical interests. Accordingly, Marx says:

> "In the social production which men carry on (that is, in the production of the material values necessary to the life of men—*Ed.*) they enter into definite relations that are indispensable and *independ-.ent** of their will; these relations of production correspond to a definite stage of development of their material forces of production." (Karl Marx, *Selected Works*, Vol. I, p. 356.)

This, however, does not mean that changes in the relations of production, and the transition from old relations of production to new relations of production proceed smoothly, without conflicts, without upheavals. On the contrary, such a transition usually takes place by means of the revolutionary overthrow of the old relations of production and the establishment of new relations of production. Up to a certain period the development of the productive forces and the changes in the realm of

* Our italics.—*Ed.*

the relations of production proceed spontaneously, independently of the will of men. But that is so only up to a certain moment, until the new and developing productive forces have reached a proper state of maturity. After the new productive forces have matured, the existing relations of production and their upholders—the ruling classes—become that "insuperable" obstacle which can only be removed by the conscious action of the new classes, by the forcible acts of these classes, by revolution. Here there stands out in bold relief the *tremendous role* of new social ideas, of new political institutions, of a new political power, whose mission it is to abolish by force the old relations of production. Out of the conflict between the new productive forces and the old relations of production, out of the new economic demands of society there arise new social ideas; the new ideas organize and mobilize the masses; the masses become welded into a new political army, create a new revolutionary power, and make use of it to abolish by force the old system of relations of production, and firmly to establish the new system. The spontaneous process of development yields place to the conscious actions of men, peaceful development to violent upheaval, evolution to revolution.

> "The proletariat," says Marx, "during its contest with the bourgeoisie is compelled, by the force of circumstances, to organize itself as a class . . . by means of a revolution, it makes itself the ruling class, and, as such, sweeps away by force the old conditions of production." (*The Communist Manifesto*—Karl Marx, *Selected Works*, Vol. I, p. 228.)

And further:

> a) "The proletariat will use its political supremacy to wrest, by degrees, all capital from the bourgeoisie, to centralize all instruments of production in the hands of the state, *i.e.*, of the proletariat organized as the ruling class; and to increase the total of productive forces as rapidly as possible." (*Ibid.*, p. 227.)

> b) "Force is the midwife of every old society pregnant with a new one." (Karl Marx, *Capital*, Vol. I, p. 776.)

Here is the brilliant formulation of the essence of historical materialism given by Marx in 1859 in his historic Preface to his famous book, *Critique of Political Economy*:

> "In the social production which men carry on they enter into definite relations that are indispensable and independent of their will; these relations of production correspond to a definite stage of development of their material forces of production. The sum total of these relations of production constitutes the economic structure of society—

the real foundation, on which rises a legal and political superstructure and to which correspond definite forms of social consciousness. The mode of production in material life determines the social, political and intellectual life process in general. It is not the consciousness of men that determines their being, but, on the contrary, their social being that determines their consciousness. At a certain stage of their development, the material forces of production in society come in conflict with the existing relations of production, or—what is but a legal expression for the same thing—with the property relations within which they have been at work before. From forms of development of the forces of production these relations turn into their fetters. Then begins an epoch of social revolution. With the change of the economic foundation the entire immense superstructure is more or less rapidly transformed. In considering such transformations a distinction should always be made between the material transformation of the economic conditions of production which can be determined with the precision of natural science, and the legal, political, religious, æsthetic or philosophic—in short, ideological forms in which men become conscious of this conflict and fight it out. Just as our opinion of an individual is not based on what he thinks of himself, so can we not judge of such a period of transformation by its own consciousness; on the contrary, this consciousness must be explained rather from the contradictions of material life, from the existing conflict between the social forces of production and the relations of production. No social order ever disappears before all the productive forces for which there is room in it have been developed; and new higher relations of production never appear before the material conditions of their existence have matured in the womb of the old society itself. Therefore, mankind always sets itself only such tasks as it can solve; since, looking at the matter more closely, we will always find that the task itself arises only when the material conditions necessary for its solution already exists or are at least in the process of formation." (Karl Marx, *Selected Works*, Vol. I, pp. 356-57.)

Such is Marxist materialism as applied to social life, to the history of society.

Such are the principal features of dialectical and historical materialism.

It will be seen from this what a theoretical treasure was safeguarded by Lenin for the Party and protected from the attacks of the revisionists and renegades, and how important was the appearance of Lenin's book, *Materialism and Empirio-Criticism*, for the development of our Party.

3. BOLSHEVIKS AND MENSHEVIKS IN THE PERIOD OF THE
   STOLYPIN REACTION. STRUGGLE OF THE BOLSHEVIKS AGAINST
   THE LIQUIDATORS AND OTZOVISTS

During the years of reaction, the work in the Party organizations
was far more difficult than during the preceding period of development
of the revolution. The Party membership had sharply declined. Many
of the petty-bourgeois fellow-travelers of the Party, especially the intellectuals, deserted its ranks from fear of persecution by the tsarist government.

Lenin pointed out that at such moments revolutionary parties should
perfect their knowledge. During the period of rise of the revolution they
learned how to advance; during the period of reaction they should learn
how to retreat properly, how to go underground, how to preserve and
strengthen the illegal party, how to make use of legal opportunities, of
all legally existing, especially mass, organizations in order to strengthen
their connections with the masses.

The Mensheviks retreated in panic, not believing that a new rise in
the tide of revolution was possible; they disgracefully renounced the
revolutionary demands of the program and the revolutionary slogans of
the Party; they wanted to liquidate, to abolish, the revolutionary illegal
party of the proletariat. For this reason, Mensheviks of this type came
to be known as *Liquidators*.

Unlike the Mensheviks, the Bolsheviks were certain that within the
next few years there would be a rise in the tide of revolution, and held
that it was the duty of the Party to prepare the masses for this new rise.
The fundamental problems of the revolution had not been solved. The
peasants had not obtained the landlords' land, the workers had not obtained the 8-hour day, the tsarist autocracy, so detested by the people,
had not been overthrown, and it had again suppressed the meagre political liberties which the people had wrung from it in 1905. Thus the
causes which had given rise to the Revolution of 1905 still remained in
force. That is why the Bolsheviks were certain that there would be a
new rise of the revolutionary movement, prepared for it and mustered the
forces of the working class.

The Bolsheviks derived their certainty that a new rise in the tide
of the revolution was inevitable also from the fact that the Revolution of
1905 had taught the working class to fight for its rights in mass revolutionary struggle. During the period of reaction, when the capitalists took
the offensive, the workers could not forget these lessons of 1905. Lenin
quoted letters from workers in which they told how factory owners were

again oppressing and humiliating them, and in which they said: *"Wait, another 1905 will come!"*

The fundamental political aim of the Bolsheviks remained what it had been in 1905, namely, to overthrow tsardom, to carry the bourgeois-democratic revolution to its conclusion and to proceed to the Socialist revolution. Never for a moment did the Bolsheviks forget this aim, and they continued to put before the masses the principal revolutionary slogans —a democratic republic, the confiscation of the landed estates, and an 8-hour day.

But the *tactics* of the Party could not remain what they had been during the rising tide of the revolution in 1905. For example, it would have been wrong in the immediate future to call the masses to a general political strike or to an armed uprising, for the revolutionary movement was on the decline, the working class was in a state of extreme fatigue, and the position of the reactionary classes had been strengthened considerably. The Party had to reckon with the new situation. Offensive tactics had to be replaced by defensive tactics, the tactics of mustering forces, the tactics of withdrawing the cadres underground and of carrying on the work of the Party from underground, the tactics of combining illegal work with work in the legal working-class organizations.

And the Bolsheviks proved able to accomplish this.

"We knew how to work during the long years preceding the revolution. Not for nothing do they say that we are as firm as a rock. The Social-Democrats have formed a proletarian party which will not lose heart at the failure of the first armed onslaught, will not lose its head, and will not be carried away by adventures," wrote Lenin. (Lenin, *Collected Works*, Russ. ed., Vol. XII, p. 126.)

The Bolsheviks strove to preserve and strengthen the illegal Party organizations. But at the same time they deemed it essential to utilize every legal opportunity, every legal opening to maintain and preserve connections with the masses and thus strengthen the Party.

"This was a period when our Party turned from the open revolutionary struggle against tsardom to roundabout methods of struggle, to the utilization of each and every legal opportunity—from mutual aid societies to the Duma platform. This was a period of retreat after we had been defeated in the Revolution of 1905. This turn made it incumbent upon us to master new methods of struggle, in order to muster our forces and resume the open revolutionary struggle against tsardom." (J. Stalin, *Verbatim Report of the Fifteenth Party Congress*, Russ. ed., pp. 366-67, 1935.)

The surviving legal organizations served as a sort of screen for the underground organizations of the Party and as a means of maintaining connections with the masses. In order to preserve their connections with the masses, the Bolsheviks made use of the trade unions and other legally existing public organizations, such as sick benefit societies, workers' co-operative societies, clubs, educational societies and People's Houses. The Bolsheviks made use of the platform of the State Duma to expose the policy of the tsarist government, to expose the Constitutional-Democrats, and to win the support of the peasants for the proletariat. The preservation of the illegal Party organization, and the direction of all other forms of political work through this organization, enabled the Party to pursue a correct line and to muster forces in preparation for a new rise in the tide of revolution.

The Bolsheviks carried out their revolutionary line in a fight on *two fronts*, a fight against the two varieties of opportunism within the Party—against the *Liquidators*, who were open adversaries of the Party, and against what were known as the *Otzovists*, who were concealed foes of the Party.

The Bolsheviks, headed by Lenin, waged a relentless struggle against liquidationism from the very inception of this opportunist trend. Lenin pointed out that the Liquidators were agents of the liberal bourgeoisie within the Party.

In December 1908, the Fifth (All-Russian) Conference of the R.S.D.L.P. was held in Paris. On Lenin's motion, this conference condemned liquidationism, that is, the attempts of a certain section of the Party intellectuals (Mensheviks) "to liquidate the existing organization of the R.S.D.L.P. and to replace it at all costs, even at the price of down-right renunciation of the program, tactics and traditions of the Party, by an amorphous association functioning legally." (*C.P.S.U.*[*B.*] *in Resolutions*, Russ. ed., Part I, p. 128.)

The conference called upon all Party organizations to wage a resolute struggle against the attempts of the Liquidators.

But the Mensheviks did not abide by this decision of the conference and increasingly committed themselves to liquidationism, betrayal of the revolution, and collaboration with the Constitutional-Democrats. The Mensheviks were more and more openly renouncing the revolutionary program of the proletarian Party, the demands for a democratic republic, for an 8-hour day and for the confiscation of the landed estates. They wanted, at the price of renouncing the program and tactics of the Party, to obtain the consent of the tsarist government to the existence of an open, legal, supposedly "labour" party. They were prepared to make peace with and to adapt themselves to the Stolypin regime. That is why the Liquidators were also called the "Stolypin Labour Party."

Besides fighting the overt adversaries of the revolution, the Liquidators, who were headed by Dan, Axelrod, and Potressov, and assisted by Martov, Trotsky and other Mensheviks, the Bolsheviks also waged a relentless struggle against the covert Liquidators, the Otzovists, who camouflaged their opportunism by "Left" phraseology. Otzovists was the name given to certain former Bolsheviks who demanded the recall (*otzyv* means recall) of the workers' deputies from the State Duma and the discontinuation of work in legally existing organizations altogether.

In 1908 a number of Bolsheviks demanded the recall of the Social-Democratic deputies from the State Duma. Hence, they were called Otzovists. The Otzovists formed their own group (Bogdanov, Lunacharsky, Alexinsky, Pokrovsky, Bubnov and others) which started a struggle against Lenin and Lenin's line. The Otzovists stubbornly refused to work in the trade unions and other legally existing societies. In doing so they did great injury to the workers' cause. The Otzovists were driving a wedge between the Party and the working class, tending to deprive the Party of its connections with the non-party masses; they wanted to seclude themselves within the underground organization, yet at the same time they placed it in jeopardy by denying it the opportunity of utilizing legal cover. The Otzovists did not understand that in the State Duma, and through the State Duma, the Bolsheviks could influence the peasantry, could expose the policy of the tsarist government and the policy of the Constitutional-Democrats, who were trying to gain the following of the peasantry by fraud. The Otzovists hampered the mustering of forces for a new advance of the revolution. The Otzovists were therefore "Liquidators inside-out": they endeavoured to destroy the possibility of utilizing the legally existing organizations and, in fact, renounced proletarian leadership of the broad non-party masses, renounced revolutionary work.

A conference of the enlarged editorial board of the Bolshevik newspaper *Proletary*, summoned in 1909 to discuss the conduct of the Otzovists, condemned them. The Bolsheviks announced that they had nothing in common with the Otzovists and expelled them from the Bolshevik organization.

Both the Liquidators and the Otzovists were nothing but petty-bourgeois fellow-travelers of the proletariat and its Party. When times were hard for the proletariat the true character of the Liquidators and Otzovists became revealed with particular clarity.

4. STRUGGLE OF THE BOLSHEVIKS AGAINST TROTSKYISM. ANTI-PARTY AUGUST BLOC

At a time when the Bolsheviks were waging a relentless struggle on two fronts—against the Liquidators and against the Otzovists—defending the consistent line of the proletarian party, Trotsky supported the Menshevik Liquidators. It was at this period that Lenin branded him "Judas Trotsky." Trotsky formed a group of writers in Vienna (Austria) and began to publish an allegedly non-factional, but in reality Menshevik newspaper. "Trotsky behaves like a most despicable careerist and factionalist. . . . He pays lip service to the Party, but behaves worse than any other factionalist," wrote Lenin at the time.

Later, in 1912, Trotsky organized the August Bloc, a bloc of all the anti-Bolshevik groups and trends directed against Lenin and the Bolshevik Party. The Liquidators and the Otzovists united in this anti-Bolshevik bloc, thus demonstrating their kinship. Trotsky and the Trotskyites took up a liquidationist stand on all fundamental issues. But Trotsky masked his liquidationism under the guise of Centrism, that is, conciliationism; he claimed that he belonged to neither the Bolsheviks nor the Mensheviks and that he was trying to reconcile them. In this connection, Lenin said that Trotsky was more vile and pernicious than the open Liquidators, because he was trying to deceive the workers into believing that he was "above factions," whereas in fact he entirely supported the Menshevik Liquidators. The Trotskyites were the principal group that fostered Centrism.

"Centrism," writes Comrade Stalin, "is a political concept. Its ideology is one of adaptation, of subordination of the interests of the proletariat to the interests of the petty-bourgeoisie *within one common party*. This ideology is alien and abhorrent to Leninism." (Stalin, *Leninism*, Vol. II, "The Industrialization of the Country and the Right Deviation in the C.P.S.U.," p. 97.)

At this period Kamenev, Zinoviev and Rykov were actually covert agents of Trotsky, for they often helped him against Lenin. With the aid of Zinoviev, Kamenev, Rykov and other covert allies of Trotsky, a Plenum of the Central Committee was convened in January 1910 *against Lenin's wishes*. By that time the composition of the Central Committee had changed owing to the arrest of a number of Bolsheviks, and the vacillating elements were able to force through anti-Leninist decisions. Thus, it was decided at this plenum to close down the Bolshevik newspaper *Proletary* and to give financial support to Trotsky's newspaper

Pravda, published in Vienna. Kamenev joined the editorial board of Trotsky's newspaper and together with Zinoviev strove to make it the organ of the Central Committee.

It was only on Lenin's insistence that the January Plenum of the Central Committee adopted a resolution condemning liquidationism and otzovism, but here too Zinoviev and Kamenev insisted on Trotsky's proposal that the Liquidators should not be referred to as such.

It turned out as Lenin had foreseen and forewarned: only the Bolsheviks obeyed the decision of the plenum of the Central Committee and closed down their organ, *Proletary,* whereas the Mensheviks continued to publish their factional liquidationist newspaper *Golos Sotsial-Demokrata* (*Voice of the Social-Democrat*).

Lenin's position was fully supported by Comrade Stalin who published a special article in *Sotsial-Demokrat,* No. 11, in which he condemned the conduct of the accomplices of Trotskyism, and spoke of the necessity of putting an end to the abnormal situation created within the Bolshevik group by the treacherous conduct of Kamenev, Zinoviev and Rykov. The article advanced as immediate tasks what was later carried into effect at the Prague Party Conference, namely, convocation of a general Party conference, publication of a Party newspaper appearing legally, and creation of an illegal practical Party centre in Russia. Comrade Stalin's article was based on decisions of the Baku Committee, which fully supported Lenin.

To counteract Trotsky's anti-Party August Bloc, which consisted exclusively of anti-Party elements, from the Liquidators and Trotskyites to the Otzovists and "god-builders," a Party bloc was formed consisting of people who wanted to preserve and strengthen the illegal proletarian Party. This bloc consisted of the Bolsheviks, headed by Lenin, and a small number of pro-Party Mensheviks, headed by Plekhanov. Plekhanov and his group of pro-Party Mensheviks, while maintaining the Menshevik position on a number of questions, emphatically dissociated themselves from the August Bloc and the Liquidators and sought to reach agreement with the Bolsheviks. Lenin accepted Plekhanov's proposal and consented to a temporary bloc with him against the anti-Party elements on the ground that such a bloc would be advantageous to the Party and fatal to the Liquidators.

Comrade Stalin fully supported this bloc. He was in exile at the time and from there wrote a letter to Lenin, saying:

"In my opinion the line of the bloc (Lenin-Plekhanov) is the only correct one: 1) this line, and it alone, answers to the real interests of the work in Russia, which demands that all Party elements should rally together; 2) this line, and it alone, will expedite the process of emancipation of the legal organizations from the yoke of the Liquidators, by digging a gulf between the Mek * workers and the Liquidators, and dispersing and disposing of the latter." (*Lenin and Stalin,* Russ. ed., Vol. I, pp. 529-30.)

Thanks to a skilful combination of illegal and legal work, the Bolsheviks were able to become a serious force in the legal workers' organizations. This was revealed, incidentally, in the great influence which the Bolsheviks exercised on the workers' groups at four legally held congresses that took place at that period—a congress of people's universities, a women's congress, a congress of factory physicians, and a temperance congress. The speeches of the Bolsheviks at these congresses were of great political value and awakened a response all over the country. For example, at the congress of people's universities, the Bolshevik workers' delegation exposed the policy of tsardom which stifled all cultural activity, and contended that no real cultural progress in the country was conceivable unless tsardom were abolished. The workers' delegation at the congress of factory physicians told of the frightfully unsanitary conditions in which the workers had to live and work, and drew the conclusion that factory hygiene could not be properly ensured until tsardom was overthrown.

The Bolsheviks gradually squeezed the Liquidators out of the various legal organizations that still survived. The peculiar tactics of a united front with the Plekhanov pro-Party group enabled the Bolsheviks to win over a number of Menshevik worker organizations (in the Vyborg district, Ekaterinoslav, etc.).

In this difficult period the Bolsheviks set an example of how legal work should be combined with illegal work.

5. PRAGUE PARTY CONFERENCE, 1912. BOLSHEVIKS CONSTITUTE THEMSELVES AN INDEPENDENT MARXIST PARTY

The fight against the Liquidators and Otzovists, as well as against the Trotskyites, confronted the Bolsheviks with the urgent necessity of uniting all the Bolsheviks and forming them into an independent Bolshevik Party. This was absolutely essential not only in order to put an end to the opportunist trends within the Party which were splitting the work-

* *Mek,* an abbreviation for Menshevik.—*Ed.*

ing class, but also in order to complete the work of mustering the forces of the working class and preparing it for a new upward swing of the revolution.

But before this task could be accomplished the Party had to be rid of opportunists, of Mensheviks.

No Bolshevik now doubted that it was unthinkable for the Bolsheviks to remain in one party with the Mensheviks. The treacherous conduct of the Mensheviks in the period of the Stolypin reaction, their attempts to liquidate the proletarian party and to organize a new, reformist party, made a rupture with them inevitable. By remaining in one party with the Mensheviks, the Bolsheviks in one way or another accepted moral responsibility for the behaviour of the Mensheviks. But for the Bolsheviks to accept moral responsibility for the open treachery of the Mensheviks was unthinkable, unless they themselves wanted to become traitors to the Party and the working class. Unity with the Mensheviks within a single party was thus assuming the character of a betrayal of the working class and its party. Consequently, the actual rupture with the Mensheviks had to be carried to its conclusion: a formal organizational rupture and the expulsion of the Mensheviks from the Party.

Only in this way was it possible to restore the revolutionary party of the proletariat with a single program, single tactics, and a single class organization.

Only in this way was it possible to restore the real (not just formal) unity of the Party, which the Mensheviks had destroyed.

This task was to be performed by the Sixth General Party Conference, for which the Bolsheviks were making preparations.

But this was only one aspect of the matter. A formal rupture with the Mensheviks and the formation by the Bolsheviks of a separate party was, of course, a very important political task. But the Bolsheviks were confronted with another and even more important task. The task of the Bolsheviks was not merely to break with the Mensheviks and formally constitute themselves a separate party, but above all, having broken with the Mensheviks, to create a *new* party, to create a party of a *new type*, different from the usual Social-Democratic parties of the West, one that was free of opportunist elements and capable of leading the proletariat in a struggle for power.

In fighting the Bolsheviks, the Mensheviks of all shades, from Axelrod and Martynov to Martov and Trotsky, invariably used weapons borrowed from the arsenal of the West-European Social-Democrats. They wanted in Russia a party similar, let us say, to the German or French

Social-Democratic Party. They fought the Bolsheviks just because they sensed something new in them, something unusual and different from the Social-Democrats of the West. And what did the Social-Democratic parties of the West represent at that time? A mixture, a hodge-podge of Marxist and opportunist elements, of friends and foes of the revolution, of supporters and opponents of the Party principle, the former gradually becoming ideologically reconciled to the latter, and virtually subordinated to them. Conciliation with the opportunists, with the traitors to the revolution, for the sake of what?—the Bolsheviks asked the West-European Social-Democrats. For the sake of "peace within the Party," for the sake of "unity"—the latter replied. Unity with whom, with the opportunists? Yes, they replied, with the opportunists. It was clear that such parties could not be revolutionary parties.

The Bolsheviks could not help seeing that after Engels' death the West-European Social-Democratic parties had begun to degenerate from parties of social revolution into parties of "social reforms," and that each of these parties, as an organization, had already been converted from a leading force into an appendage of its own parliamentary group.

The Bolsheviks could not help knowing that such a party boded no good to the proletariat, that such a party was not capable of leading the working class to revolution.

The Bolsheviks could not help knowing that the proletariat needed, not such a party, but a different kind of party, a new and genuinely Marxist party, which would be irreconcilable towards the opportunists and revolutionary towards the bourgeoisie, which would be firmly knit and monolithic, which would be a party of social revolution, a party of the dictatorship of the proletariat.

It was this new kind of party that the Bolsheviks wanted. And the Bolsheviks worked to build up such a party. The whole history of the struggle against the "Economists," Mensheviks, Trotskyites, Otzovists and idealists of all shades, down to the empirio-criticists, was a history of the building up of just such a party. The Bolsheviks wanted to create a new party, a *Bolshevist* party, which would serve as a model for all who wanted to have a real revolutionary Marxist party. The Bolsheviks had been working to build up such a party ever since the time of the old *Iskra*. They worked for it stubbornly, persistently, in spite of everything. A fundamental and decisive part was played in this work by the writings of Lenin—*What Is To Be Done?*, *Two Tactics*, etc. Lenin's *What Is To Be Done?* was the *ideological* preparation for such a party. Lenin's *One Step Forward, Two Steps Back* was the *organizational* preparation for such a party. Lenin's *Two Tactics of Social-Democracy in the Dem-*

ocratic Revolution was the *political* preparation for such a party. And, lastly, Lenin's *Materialism and Empirio-Criticism* was the *theoretical* preparation for such a party.

It may be safely said that never in history has any political group been so thoroughly prepared to constitute itself a party as the Bolshevik group was.

The conditions were therefore fully ripe and ready for the Bolsheviks to constitute themselves a party.

It was the task of the Sixth Party Conference to crown the completed work by expelling the Mensheviks and formally constituting the new party, the Bolshevik Party.

The Sixth All-Russian Party Conference was held in Prague in January 1912. Over twenty Party organizations were represented. The conference, therefore, had the significance of a regular Party congress.

In the statement of the conference which announced that the shattered central apparatus of the Party had been restored and a Central Committee set up, it was declared that the period of reaction had been the most difficult the Russian Social-Democratic Party had experienced since it had taken shape as a definite organization. In spite of all persecution, in spite of the severe blows dealt it from without and the treachery and vacillation of the opportunists within, the party of the proletariat had preserved intact its banner and its organization.

"Not only have the banner of the Russian Social-Democratic Party, its program and its revolutionary traditions survived, but so has its organization, which persecution may have undermined and weakened, but could never utterly destroy"—the statement of the conference declared.

The conference recorded the first symptoms of a new rise of the working-class movement in Russia and a revival in Party work.

In its resolution on the reports presented by the local organizations, the conference noted that "energetic work is being conducted everywhere among the Social-Democratic workers with the object of strengthening the local illegal Social-Democratic organizations and groups."

The conference noted that the most important rule of Bolshevik tactics in periods of retreat, namely, to combine illegal work with legal work within the various legally existing workers' societies and unions, was being observed in all the localities.

The Prague Conference elected a Bolshevik Central Committee of the Party, consisting of Lenin, Stalin, Ordjonikidze, Sverdlov, Spandaryan, Goloshchekin and others. Comrades Stalin and Sverdlov were elected to the Central Committee in their absence, as they were in exile at the time.   Among the elected alternate members of the Central Committee was Comrade Kalinin.

For the direction of revolutionary work in Russia a practical centre (the Russian Bureau of the C.C.) was set up with Comrade Stalin at its head and including Comrades Y. Sverdlov, S. Spandaryan, S. Ordjonikidze, M. Kalinin and Goloshchekin.

The Prague Conference reviewed the whole preceding struggle of the Bolsheviks against opportunism and decided to expel the Mensheviks from the Party.

By expelling the Mensheviks from the Party, the Prague Conference formally inaugurated the independent existence of the Bolshevik Party.

Having routed the Mensheviks ideologically and organizationally and expelled them from the Party, the Bolsheviks preserved the old banner of the Party—of the R.S.D.L.P.   That is why the Bolshevik Party continued until 1918 to call itself the Russian Social-Democratic Labour Party, adding the word "Bolsheviks" in brackets.

Writing to Gorky at the beginning of 1912, on the results of the Prague Conference, Lenin said:

> "At last we have succeeded, in spite of the Liquidator scum, in restoring the Party and its Central Committee.   I hope you will rejoice with us over the fact." (Lenin, *Collected Works*, Russ. ed., Vol. XXIX, p. 19.)

Speaking of the significance of the Prague Conference, Comrade Stalin said:

> "This conference was of the utmost importance in the history of our Party, for it drew a boundary line between the Bolsheviks and the Mensheviks and amalgamated the Bolshevik organizations all over the country into a united Bolshevik Party." (*Verbatim Report of the Fifteenth Congress of the C.P.S.U. [B.]*, Russ. ed., pp. 361-362.)

After the expulsion of the Mensheviks and the constitution by the Bolsheviks of an independent party, the Bolshevik Party became firmer and stronger. *The Party strengthens itself by purging its ranks of opportunist elements*—that is one of the maxims of the Bolshevik Party, which is a party of a new type fundamentally different from the Social-Democratic parties of the Second International.   Although the parties of the Second International called themselves Marxist parties, in reality they tolerated foes of Marxism, avowed opportunists, in their ranks and allowed them to corrupt and to ruin the Second International.   The Bol-

sheviks, on the contrary, waged a relentless struggle against the opportunists, purged the proletarian party of the filth of opportunism and
succeeded in creating a party of a new type, a Leninist Party, the Party
which later achieved the dictatorship of the proletariat.

If the opportunists had remained within the ranks of the proletarian
party, the Bolshevik Party could not have come out on the broad high-
way and led the proletariat, it could not have taken power and set up the
dictatorship of the proletariat, it could not have emerged victorious from
the Civil War and built Socialism.

The Prague Conference decided to put forward as the chief immediate political slogans of the Party the demands contained in the minimum
program: a democratic republic, an 8-hour day, and the confiscation of the
landed estates.

It was under these revolutionary slogans that the Bolsheviks conducted their campaign in connection with the elections to the Fourth State
Duma.

It was these slogans that guided the new rise of the revolutionary
movement of the working-class masses in the years 1912-14.

BRIEF SUMMARY

The years 1908-12 were a most difficult period for revolutionary
work. After the defeat of the revolution, when the revolutionary movement was on the decline and the masses were fatigued, the Bolsheviks
changed their tactics and passed from the direct struggle against tsardom
to a roundabout struggle. In the difficult conditions that prevailed during the Stolypin reaction, the Bolsheviks made use of the slightest legal
opportunity to maintain their connections with the masses (from sick
benefit societies and trade unions to the Duma platform). The Bolsheviks indefatigably worked to muster forces for a new rise of the revolutionary movement.

In the difficult conditions brought about by the defeat of the revolution, the disintegration of the oppositional trends, the disappointment with
the revolution, and the increasing endeavours of intellectuals who had
deserted the Party (Bogdanov, Bazarov and others) to revise its theoretical foundations, the Bolsheviks were the only force in the Party
who did not furl the Party banner, who remained faithful to the Party
program, and who beat off the attacks of the "critics" of Marxist theory
(Lenin's *Materialism and Empirio-Criticism*). What helped the leading
core of the Bolsheviks, centred around Lenin, to safeguard the Party

and its revolutionary principles was that this core had been tempered by Marxist-Leninist ideology and had grasped the perspectives of the revolution. "Not for nothing do they say that we are as firm as a rock," Lenin stated in referring to the Bolsheviks.

The Mensheviks at that period were drawing farther and farther away from the revolution. They became Liquidators, demanding the liquidation, abolition, of the illegal revolutionary party of the proletariat; they more and more openly renounced the Party program and the revolutionary aims and slogans of the Party, and endeavoured to organize their own, reformist party, which the workers christened a "Stolypin Labour Party." Trotsky supported the Liquidators, pharisaically using the slogan "unity of the Party" as a screen, but actually meaning unity with the Liquidators.

On the other hand, some of the Bolsheviks, who did not understand the necessity for the adoption of new and roundabout ways of combating tsardom, demanded that legal opportunities should not be utilized and that the workers' deputies in the State Duma be recalled. These Otzovists were driving the Party towards a rupture with the masses and were hampering the mustering of forces for a new rise of the revolution. Using "Left" phraseology as a screen, the Otzovists, like the Liquidators, in essence renounced the revolutionary struggle.

The Liquidators and Otzovists united against Lenin in a common bloc, known as the August Bloc, organized by Trotsky.

In the struggle against the Liquidators and Otzovists, in the struggle against the August Bloc, the Bolsheviks gained the upper hand and succeeded in safeguarding the illegal proletarian party.

The outstanding event of this period was the Prague Conference of the R.S.D.L.P. (January 1912). At this conference the Mensheviks were expelled from the Party, and the formal unity of the Bolsheviks with the Mensheviks within one party was ended forever. From a political group, the Bolsheviks formally constituted themselves an independent party, the Russian Social-Democratic Labour Party (Bolsheviks). The Prague Conference inaugurated a party of a new type, the party of Leninism, the *Bolshevik* Party.

The purge of the ranks of the proletarian party of opportunists, Mensheviks, effected at the Prague Conference, had an important and decisive influence on the subsequent development of the Party and the revolution. If the Bolsheviks had not expelled the betrayers of the workers' cause, the Menshevik compromisers, from the Party, the proletarian party would have been unable in 1917 to rouse the masses for the fight for the dictatorship of the proletariat.

CHAPTER FIVE

THE BOLSHEVIK PARTY DURING THE NEW RISE OF THE WORKING-CLASS MOVEMENT BEFORE THE FIRST IMPERIALIST WAR

(1912-1914)

I. RISE OF THE REVOLUTIONARY MOVEMENT IN THE PERIOD 1912-14

The triumph of the Stolypin reaction was shortlived. A government which would offer the people nothing but the knout and the gallows could not endure. Repressive measures became so habitual that they ceased to inspire fear in the people. The fatigue felt by the workers in the years immediately following the defeat of the revolution began to wear off. The workers resumed the struggle. The Bolsheviks' forecast that a new rise in the tide of revolution was inevitable proved correct. In 1911 the number of strikers already exceeded 100,000, whereas in each of the previous years it had been no more than 50,000 or 60,000. The Prague Party Conference, held in January 1912, could already register the beginnings of a revival of the working-class movement. But the real rise in the revolutionary movement began in April and May 1912, when mass political strikes broke out in connection with the shooting down of workers in the Lena goldfields.

On April 4, 1912, during a strike in the Lena goldfields in Siberia, over 500 workers were killed or wounded upon the orders of a tsarist officer of the gendarmerie. The shooting down of an unarmed body of Lena miners who were peacefully proceeding to negotiate with the management stirred the whole country. This new bloody deed of the tsarist autocracy was committed to break an economic strike of the miners and thus please the masters of the Lena goldfields, the British capitalists. The British capitalists and their Russian partners derived huge profits from the Lena goldfields—over 7,000,000 rubles annually—by most shamelessly exploiting the workers. They paid the workers miserable wages and supplied them with rotten food unfit to eat. Unable to endure the oppression and humiliation any longer, six thousand workers of the Lena goldfields went on strike.

The proletariat of St. Petersburg, Moscow and all other industrial centres and regions replied to the Lena shooting by mass strikes, demonstrations and meetings.

"We were so dazed and shocked that we could not at once find words to express our feelings. Whatever protest we made would be but a pale reflection of the anger that seethed in the hearts of all of us. Nothing can help us, neither tears nor protests, but an organized mass struggle"—the workers of one group of factories declared in their resolution.

The furious indignation of the workers was further aggravated when the tsarist Minister Makarov, who was interpellated by the Social-Democratic group in the State Duma on the subject of the Lena massacre, insolently declared: "So it was, so it will be!" The number of participants in the political protest strikes against the bloody massacre of the Lena workers rose to 300,000.

The Lena events were like a hurricane which rent the atmosphere of "peace" created by the Stolypin regime.

This is what Comrade Stalin wrote in this connection in 1912 in the St. Petersburg Bolshevik newspaper, *Zvezda* (Star):

"The Lena shooting has broken the ice of silence and the river of the people's movement has begun to flow. The ice is broken! ... All that was evil and pernicious in the present regime, all the ills of much-suffering Russia were focussed in the one fact, the Lena events. That is why it was the Lena shooting that served as a signal for the strikes and demonstrations."

The efforts of the Liquidators and Trotskyites to bury the revolution had been in vain. The Lena events showed that the forces of revolution were alive, that a tremendous store of revolutionary energy had accumulated in the working class. The May Day strikes of 1912 involved about 400,000 workers. These strikes bore a marked political character and were held under the Bolshevik revolutionary slogans of a democratic republic, an 8-hour day, and the confiscation of the landed estates. These main slogans were designed to unite not only the broad masses of the workers, but also the peasants and soldiers for a revolutionary onslaught on the autocracy.

"The huge May Day strike of the proletariat of all Russia and the accompanying street demonstrations, revolutionary proclamations, and revolutionary speeches to gatherings of workers have clearly shown that Russia has entered the phase of a rise in the revolution" —wrote Lenin in an article entitled "The Revolutionary Rise." (Lenin, *Collected Works*, Russ. ed., Vol. XV, p. 533.)

Alarmed by the revolutionary spirit of the workers, the Liquidators came out against the strike movement; they called it a "strike fever." The Liquidators and their ally, Trotsky, wanted to substitute for the revolutionary struggle of the proletariat a "petition campaign." They invited the workers to sign a petition, a scrap of paper, requesting the granting of "rights" (abolition of the restrictions on the right of association, the right to strike, etc.), which was then to be sent to the State Duma. The Liquidators managed to collect only 1,300 signatures at a time when hundreds of thousands of workers backed the revolutionary slogans of the Bolsheviks.

The working class followed the path indicated by the Bolsheviks.

The economic situation in the country at that period was as follows:

In 1910 industrial stagnation had already been succeeded by a revival, an extension of production in the main branches of industry. Whereas the output of pig iron had amounted to 186,000,000 poods in 1910, and to 256,000,000 poods in 1912, in 1913 it amounted to 283,000,000 poods. The output of coal rose from 1,522,000,000 poods in 1910 to 2,214,000,000 poods in 1913.

The expansion of capitalist industry was accompanied by a rapid growth of the proletariat. A distinguishing feature of the development of industry was the further concentration of production in large plants. Whereas in 1901 the number of workers engaged in large plants employing 500 workers and over amounted to 46.7 per cent of the total number of workers, the corresponding figure in 1910 was already about 54 per cent, or over half the total number of workers. Such a degree of concentration of industry was unprecedented. Even in a country so industrially developed as the United States only about one-third the total number of workers were employed in large plants at that period.

The growth of the proletariat and its concentration in large enterprises, combined with the existence of such a revolutionary party as the Bolshevik Party, were converting the working class of Russia into the greatest force in the political life of the country. The barbarous methods of exploitation of the workers practised in the factories, combined with the intolerable police regime of the tsarist underlings, lent every big strike a political character. Furthermore, the intertwining of the economic and political struggles imparted exceptional revolutionary force to the mass strikes.

In the van of the revolutionary working-class movement marched the heroic proletariat of St. Petersburg; St. Petersburg was followed by the Baltic Provinces, Moscow and the Moscow Province, the Volga region and the south of Russia. In 1913 the movement spread to the Western

Territory, Poland and the Caucasus. In all, 725,000 workers, according to official figures, and over one million workers according to fuller statistics, took part in strikes in 1912, and 861,000 according to official figures, and 1,272,000 according to fuller statistics, took part in strikes in 1913. In the first half of 1914 the number of strikers already amounted to about one and a half million.

Thus the revolutionary rise of 1912-14, the sweep of the strike movement, created a situation in the country similar to that which had existed at the beginning of the Revolution of 1905.

The revolutionary mass strikes of the proletariat were of moment to the *whole people*. They were directed against the autocracy, and they met with the sympathy of the vast majority of the labouring population. The manufacturers retaliated by locking out the workers. In 1913, in the Moscow Province, the capitalists threw 50,000 textile workers on the streets. In March 1914, 70,000 workers were discharged in St. Petersburg in a single day. The workers of other factories and branches of industry assisted the strikers and their locked-out comrades by mass collections and sometimes by sympathy strikes.

The rising working-class movement and the mass strikes also stirred up the peasants and drew them into the struggle. The peasants again began to rise against the landlords; they destroyed manors and kulak farmholds. In the years 1910-14 there were over 13,000 outbreaks of peasant disaffection.

Revolutionary outbreaks also took place among the armed forces. In 1912 there was an armed revolt of troops in Turkestan. Revolt was brewing in the Baltic Fleet and in Sevastopol.

The revolutionary strike movement and demonstrations, led by the Bolshevik Party, showed that the working class was fighting not for partial demands, not for "reforms," but for the liberation of the people from tsardom. The country was heading for a new revolution.

In the summer of 1912, Lenin removed from Paris to Galicia (formerly Austria) in order to be nearer to Russia. Here he presided over two conferences of members of the Central Committee and leading Party workers, one of which took place in Cracow at the end of 1912, and the other in Poronino, a small town near Cracow, in the autumn of 1913. These conferences adopted decisions on important questions of the working-class movement: the rise in the revolutionary movement, the tasks of the Party in connection with the strikes, the strengthening of the illegal organizations, the Social-Democratic group in the Duma, the Party press, the labour insurance compaign.

2. THE BOLSHEVIK NEWSPAPER "PRAVDA." THE BOLSHEVIK GROUP IN THE FOURTH STATE DUMA

A powerful instrument used by the Bolshevik Party to strengthen its organizations and to spead its influence among the masses was the Bolshevik daily newspaper *Pravda* (*Truth*), published in St. Petersburg. It was founded, according to Lenin's instructions, on the initiative of Stalin, Olminsky and Poletayev. *Pravda* was a mass working-class paper founded simultaneously with the new rise of the revolutionary movement. Its first issue appeared on April 22 (May 5, New Style), 1912. This was a day of real celebration for the workers. In honour of *Pravda's* appearance it was decided henceforward to celebrate May 5 as workers' press day.

Previous to the appearance of *Pravda*, the Bolsheviks already had a weekly newspaper called *Zvezda*, intended for advanced workers. *Zvezda* played an important part at the time of the Lena events. It printed a number of trenchant political articles by Lenin and Stalin which mobilized the working class for the struggle. But in view of the rising revolutionary tide, a weekly newspaper no longer met the requirements of the Bolshevik Party. A daily mass political newspaper designed for the broadest sections of the workers was needed. *Pravda* was such a newspaper.

Pravda played an exceptionally important part at this period. It gained support for Bolshevism among broad masses of the working class. Because of incessant police persecution, fines, and confiscations of issues due to the publication of articles and letters not to the liking of the censor, *Pravda* could exist only with the active support of tens of thousands of advanced workers. *Pravda* was able to pay the huge fines only thanks to large collections made among the workers. Not infrequently, considerable portions of confiscated issues of *Pravda* nevertheless found their way into the hands of readers, because the more active workers would come to the printing shop at night and carry away bundles of the newspaper.

The tsarist government suppressed *Pravda* eight times in the space of two and a half years; but each time, with the support of the workers, it reappeared under a new but similar name, *e.g.*, *Za Pravdu* (*For Truth*), *Put Pravdy* (*Path of Truth*), *Trudovaya Pravda* (*Labour Truth*).

While the average circulation of *Pravda* was 40,000 copies per day, the circulation of *Luch* (*Ray*), the Menshevik daily, did not exceed 15,000 or 16,000.

The workers regarded *Pravda* as their own newspaper; they had great confidence in it and were very responsive to its calls. Every copy was read by scores of readers, passing from hand to hand; it moulded their class-consciousness, educated them, organized them, and summoned them to the struggle.

What did *Pravda* write about?

Every issue contained dozens of letters from workers describing their life, the savage exploitation and the various forms of oppression and humiliation they suffered at the hands of the capitalists, their managers and foremen. These were trenchant and telling indictments of capitalist conditions. *Pravda* often reported cases of suicide of unemployed and starving workers who had lost hope of ever finding jobs again.

Pravda wrote of the needs and demands of the workers of various factories and branches of industry, and told how the workers were fighting for their demands. Almost every issue contained reports of strikes at various factories. In big and protracted strikes, the newspaper helped to organize collections among the workers of other factories and branches of industry for the support of the strikers. Sometimes tens of thousands of rubles were collected for the strike funds, huge sums for those days when the majority of the workers received not more than 70 or 80 kopeks per day. This fostered a spirit of proletarian solidarity among the workers and a consciousness of the unity of interests of all workers.

The workers reacted to every political event, to every victory or defeat, by sending to *Pravda* letters, greetings, protests, etc. In its articles *Pravda* dealt with the tasks of the working-class movement from a consistent Bolshevik standpoint. A legally published newspaper could not call openly for the overthrow of tsardom. It had to resort to hints, which, however, the class-conscious workers understood very well, and which they explained to the masses. When, for example, *Pravda* wrote of the "full and uncurtailed demands of the Year Five," the workers understood that this meant the revolutionary slogans of the Bolsheviks, namely, the overthrow of tsardom, a democratic republic, the confiscation of the landed estates, and an 8-hour day.

Pravda organized the advanced workers on the eve of the elections to the Fourth Duma. It exposed the treacherous position of those who advocated an agreement with the liberal bourgeoisie, the advocates of the "Stolypin Labour Party"—the Mensheviks. *Pravda* called upon the workers to vote for those who advocated the "full and uncurtailed demands of the Year Five," that is, the Bolsheviks. The elections were indirect, held in a series of stages: first, meetings of workers elected delegates; then these delegates chose electors; and it was these electors who participated in the elections of the workers' deputy to the Duma. On the day of the elections of the electors *Pravda* published a list of Bolshevik candidates and recommended the workers to vote for this list. The list could not be published earlier without exposing those on the list to the danger of arrest.

Pravda helped to organize the mass actions of the proletariat. At the time of a big lockout in St. Petersburg in the spring of 1914, when it was inexpedient to declare a mass strike, *Pravda* called upon the workers to resort to other forms of struggle, such as mass meetings in the factories and demonstrations in the streets. This could not be stated openly in the newspaper. But the call was understood by class-conscious workers when they read an article by Lenin bearing the modest title "Forms of the Working-Class Movement" and stating that at the given moment strikes should yield place to a higher form of the working-class movement—which meant a call to organize meetings and demonstrations.

In this way the illegal revolutionary activities of the Bolsheviks were combined with legal forms of agitation and organization of the masses of the workers through *Pravda*.

Pravda not only wrote of the life of the workers, their strikes and demonstrations, but also regularly described the life of the peasants, the famines from which they suffered, their exploitation by the feudal landlords. It described how as a result of the Stolypin "reform" the kulak farmers robbed the peasants of the best parts of their land. *Pravda* drew the attention of the class-conscious workers to the widespread and burning discontent in the countryside. It taught the proletariat that the objectives of the Revolution of 1905 had not been attained, and that a new revolution was impending. It taught that in this second revolution the proletariat must act as the real leader and guide of the people, and that in this revolution it would have so powerful an ally as the revolutionary peasantry.

The Mensheviks worked to get the proletariat to drop the idea of revolution, to stop thinking of the people, of the starvation of the peasants, of the domination of the Black-Hundred feudal landlords, and to fight only for "freedom of association," to present "petitions" to this effect to the tsarist government. The Bolsheviks explained to the workers that this Menshevik gospel of renunciation of revolution, renunciation of an alliance with the peasantry, was being preached in the interests of the bourgeoisie, that the workers would most certainly defeat tsardom if they won over the peasantry as their ally, and that bad shepherds like the Mensheviks should be driven out as enemies of the revolution.

What did *Pravda* write about in its "Peasant Life" section?

Let us take, as an example, several letters relating to the year 1913.

One letter from Samara, headed "An Agrarian Case," reports that of 45 peasants of the village of Novokhasbulat, Bugulma uyezd, accused of interfering with a surveyor who was marking out communal land to be allotted to peasants withdrawing from the commune, the majority were condemned to long terms of imprisonment.

A brief letter from the Pskov Province states that the "peasants of the village of Psitsa (near Zavalye Station) offered armed resistance to the rural police. Several persons were wounded. The clash was due to an agrarian dispute. Rural police have been dispatched to Psitsa, and the vice-governor and the procurator are on their way to the village."

A letter from the Ufa Province reported that peasant's allotments were being sold off in great numbers, and that famine and the law permitting withdrawal from the village communes were causing increasing numbers of peasants to lose their land. Take the hamlet of Borisovka. Here there are 27 peasant households owning 543 dessiatins of arable land between them. During the famine five peasants sold 31 dessiatins outright at prices varying from 25 to 33 rubles per dessiatin, though land is worth three or four times as much. In this village, too, seven peasants have mortgaged between them 177 dessiatins of arable land, receiving 18 to 20 rubles per dessiatin for a term of six years at a rate of 12 per cent per annum. When the poverty of the population and the usurious rate of interest are borne in mind, it may be safely said that half of the 177 dessiatins is bound to pass into the possession of the usurer, for it is not likely that even half the debtors can repay so large a sum in six years.

In an article printed in *Pravda* and entitled "Big Landlord and Small Peasant Land Ownership in Russia," Lenin strikingly demonstrated to the workers and peasants what tremendous landed property was in the hands of the parasite landlords. Thirty thousand big landlords alone owned about 70,000,000 dessiatins of land between them. An equal area fell to the share of 10,000,000 peasant households. On an average, the big landlords owned 2,300 dessiatins each, while peasant households, including the kulaks, owned 7 dessiatins each; moreover, five million households of small peasants, that is, half the peasantry, owned no more than one or two dessiatins each. These figures clearly showed that the root of the poverty of the peasants and the recurrent famines lay in the large landed estates, in the survivals of serfdom, of which the peasants could rid themselves only by a revolution led by the working class.

Through workers connected with the countryside, *Pravda* found its way into the villages and roused the politically advanced peasants to a revolutionary struggle.

At the time *Pravda* was founded the illegal Social-Democratic organizations were entirely under the direction of the Bolsheviks. On the other hand, the legal forms of organization, such as the Duma group, the press, the sick benefit societies, the trade unions, had not yet been fully wrested from the Mensheviks. The Bolsheviks had to wage a determined struggle to drive the Liquidators out of the legally existing organizations of the working class. Thanks to *Pravda*, this fight ended in victory.

Pravda stood in the centre of the struggle for the Party principle, for the building up of a *mass* working-class revolutionary party. *Pravda* rallied the legally existing organizations around the illegal centres of the Bolshevik Party and directed the working-class movement towards one definite aim—preparation for revolution.

Pravda had a vast number of worker correspondents. In one year alone it printed over eleven thousand letters from workers. But it was not only by letters that *Pravda* maintained contact with the working-class masses. Numbers of workers from the factories visited the editorial office every day. In the *Pravda* editorial office was concentrated a large share of the organizational work of the Party. Here meetings were arranged with representatives from Party nuclei; here reports were received of Party work in the mills and factories; and from here were transmitted the instructions of the St. Petersburg Committee and the Central Committee of the Party.

As a result of two and a half years of persistent struggle against the Liquidators for the building up of a mass revolutionary working-class party, by the summer of 1914 the Bolsheviks had succeeded in winning the support of *four-fifths* of the politically active workers of Russia for the Bolshevik Party and for the *Pravda* tactics. This was borne out, for instance, by the fact that out of a total number of 7,000 workers' groups which collected money for the labour press in 1914, 5,600 groups collected for the Bolshevik press, and only 1,400 groups for the Menshevik press. But, on the other hand, the Mensheviks had a large number of "rich friends" among the liberal bourgeoisie and the bourgeois intelligentsia who advanced over half the funds required for the maintenance of the Menshevik newspaper.

The Bolsheviks at that time were called "Pravdists." A whole generation of the revolutionary proletariat was reared by *Pravda*, the generation which subsequently made the October Socialist Revolution. *Pravda* was backed by tens and hundreds of thousands of workers. During the rise of the revolutionary movement (1912-14) the solid foundation was laid of a mass Bolshevik Party, a foundation which no persecution by tsardom could destroy during the imperialist war.

"The *Pravda* of 1912 was the laying of the corner-stone of the victory of Bolshevism in 1917." (*Stalin.*)

Another legally functioning central organ of the Party was the Bolshevik group in the Fourth State Duma.

In 1912 the government decreed elections to the Fourth Duma. Our Party attributed great importance to participation in the elections. The Duma Social-Democratic group and *Pravda* were the chief bases of the revolutionary work of the Bolshevik Party among the masses, functioning legally on a countrywide scale.

The Bolshevik Party acted independently, under its own slogans, in the Duma elections, simultaneously attacking both the government parties and the liberal bourgeoisie (Constitutional-Democrats). The slogans of the Bolsheviks in the election campaign were a democratic republic, an 8-hour day and the confiscation of the landed estates.

The elections to the Fourth Duma were held in the autumn of 1912. At the beginning of October, the government, dissatisfied with the course of the elections in St. Petersburg, tried to encroach on the electoral rights of the workers in a number of the large factories. In reply, the St. Petersburg Committee of our Party, on Comrade Stalin's proposal, called upon the workers of the large factories to declare a one-day strike. Placed in a difficult position, the government was forced to yield, and the workers were able at their meetings to elect whom they wanted. The vast majority of the workers voted for the Mandate (*Nakaz*) to their delegates and the deputy, which had been drawn up by Comrade Stalin. The "Mandate of the Workingmen of St. Petersburg to Their Labour Deputy" called attention to the unaccomplished tasks of 1905.

"We think," the Mandate stated, "that Russia is on the eve of the onset of mass movements, which will perhaps be more profound than in 1905.... As in 1905, in the van of these movements will be the most advanced class in Russian society, the Russian proletariat. Its only ally can be the much-suffering peasantry, which is vitally interested in the emancipation of Russia."

The Mandate declared that the future actions of the people should take the form of a struggle on two fronts—against the tsarist government and against the liberal bourgeoisie, which was seeking to come to terms with tsardom.

Lenin attached great importance to the Mandate, which called the workers to a revolutionary struggle. And in their resolutions the workers responded to this call.

The Bolsheviks scored a victory in the elections, and Comrade Badayev was elected to the Duma by the workers of St. Petersburg.

The workers voted in the elections to the Duma separately from other sections of the population (this was known as the worker curia). Of the nine deputies elected from the worker curia, six were members of the Bolshevik Party: Badayev, Petrovsky, Muranov, Samoilov, Shagov and Malinovsky (the latter subsequently turned out to be an agent-provocateur). The Bolshevik deputies were elected from the big industrial centres, in which not less than four-fifths of the working class were concentrated. On the other hand, several of the elected Liquidators did not get their mandates from the worker curia, that is, were not elected by the workers. The result was that there were seven Liquidators in the Duma as against six Bolsheviks. At first the Bolsheviks and Liquidators formed a joint Social-Democratic group in the Duma. In October 1913, after a stubborn struggle against the Liquidators, who hampered the revolutionary work of the Bolsheviks, the Bolshevik deputies, on the instructions of the Central Commitee of the Party, withdrew from the joint Social-Democratic group and formed an independent Bolshevik group.

The Bolshevik deputies made revolutionary speeches in the Duma in which they exposed the autocratic system and interpellated the government on cases of repression of the workers and on the inhuman exploitation of the workers by the capitalists.

They also spoke in the Duma on the agrarian question, calling upon the peasants to fight the feudal landlords, and exposing the Constitutional-Democratic Party, which was opposed to the confiscation and handing over of the landed estates to the peasants.

The Bolsheviks introduced a bill in the State Duma providing for an 8-hour working day; of course it was not adopted by this Black-Hundred Duma, but it had great agitational value.

The Bolshevik group in the Duma maintained close connections with the Central Committee of the Party and with Lenin, from whom they received instructions. They were directly guided by Comrade Stalin while he was living in St. Petersburg.

The Bolshevik deputies did not confine themselves to work within the Duma, but were very active outside the Duma as well. They visited mills and factories and toured the working-class centres of the country where they made speeches, arranged secret meetings at which they explained the decisions of the Party, and formed new Party organizations. The deputies skilfully combined legal activities with illegal, underground work.

3. VICTORY OF THE BOLSHEVIKS IN THE LEGALLY EXISTING OR-
   GANIZATIONS. CONTINUED RISE OF THE REVOLUTIONARY
   MOVEMENT. EVE OF THE IMPERIALIST WAR

The Bolshevik Party during this period set an example of leadership in all forms and manifestations of the class struggle of the proletariat. It built up illegal organizations. It issued illegal leaflets. It carried on secret revolutionary work among the masses. At the same time it steadily gained the leadership of the various legally existing organizations of the working class. The Party strove to win over the trade unions and gain influence in People's Houses, evening universities, clubs and sick benefit societies. These legally existing organizations had long served as the refuge of the Liquidators. The Bolsheviks started an energetic strug-gle to convert the legally existing societies into strongholds of our Party. By skilfully combining illegal work with legal work, the Bolsheviks won over a majority of the trade union organizations in the two capital cities, St. Petersburg and Moscow. Particularly brilliant was the victory gained in the election of the Executive Committee of the Metal Workers' Union in St. Petersburg in 1913; of the 3,000 metal workers attending the meeting, barely 150 voted for the Liquidators.

The same may be said of so important a legal organization as the Social-Democratic group in the Fourth State Duma. Although the Men-sheviks had seven deputies in the Duma and the Bolsheviks six, the Menshevik deputies, chiefly elected from non-working class districts, rep-resented barely one-fifth of the working class, whereas the Bolshevik deputies, who were elected from the principal industrial centres of the country (St. Petersburg, Moscow, Ivanovo-Voznesensk, Gostroma, Eka-terinoslav and Kharkov), represented over four-fifths of the working class of the country. The workers regarded the six Bolsheviks (Badayev, Petrovsky and the others) and not the seven Mensheviks as their deputies.

The Bolsheviks succeeded in winning over the legally existing organ-izations because, in spite of savage persecution by the tsarist government and vilification by the Liquidators and the Trotskyites, they were able to preserve the illegal Party and maintain firm discipline in their ranks, they staunchly defended the interests of the working class, had close con-nections with the masses, and waged an uncompromising struggle against the enemies of the working-class movement.

Thus the victory of the Bolsheviks and the defeat of the Mensheviks in the legally existing organizations developed all along the line. Both in respect to agitational work from the platform of the Duma and in respect to the labour press and other legally existing organizations, the Mensheviks were forced into the background. The revolutionary movement took strong hold of the working class, which definitely rallied around the Bolsheviks and swept the Mensheviks aside.

To culminate all, the Mensheviks also proved bankrupt as far as the national question was concerned. The revolutionary movement in the border regions of Russia demanded a clear program on the national question. But the Mensheviks had no program, except the "cultural autonomy" of the Bund, which could satisfy nobody. Only the Bolsheviks had a Marxist program on the national question, as set forth in Comrade Stalin's article, "Marxism and the National Question," and in Lenin's articles, "The Right of Nations to Self-Determination" and "Critical Notes on the National Question."

It is not surprising that after the Mensheviks had suffered such defeats, the August Bloc should begin to break up. Composed as it was of heterogeneous elements, it could not withstand the onslaught of the Bolsheviks and began to fall apart. Formed for the purpose of combating Bolshevism, the August Bloc soon went to pieces under the blows of the Bolsheviks. The first to quit the bloc were the *Vperyod*-ites (Bogdanov, Lunacharsky and others); next went the Letts, and the rest followed suit.

Having suffered defeat in their struggle against the Bolsheviks, the Liquidators appealed for help to the Second International. The Second International came to their aid. Under the pretence of acting as a "conciliator" between the Bolsheviks and the Liquidators, and establishing "peace in the Party," the Second International demanded that the Bolsheviks should desist from criticizing the compromising policy of the Liquidators. But the Bolsheviks were irreconcilable: they refused to abide by the decisions of the opportunist Second International and would agree to make no concessions.

The victory of the Bolsheviks in the legally existing organizations was not, and could not have been, accidental. It was not accidental, not only because the Bolsheviks alone had a correct Marxist theory, a clear program, and a revolutionary proletarian party which had been steeled and tempered in battle, but also because the victory of the Bolsheviks reflected the rising tide of revolution.

The revolutionary movement of the workers steadily developed, spreading to town after town and region after region. In the beginning of 1914, the workers' strikes, far from subsiding, acquired a new momentum. They became more and more stubborn and embraced ever larger numbers of workers. On January 9, 250,000 workers were on strike, St. Petersburg accounting for 140,000. On May 1, over half a million workers were on strike, St. Petersburg accounting for more than 250,000. The workers displayed unusual steadfastness in the strikes. A strike at the Obukhov Works in St. Petersburg lasted for over two months, and another at the Lessner Works for about three months. Wholesale poisoning of workers at a number of St. Petersburg factories was the cause of a strike of 115,000 workers which was accompanied by demonstrations. The movement continued to spread. In the first half of 1914 (including the early part of July) a total of 1,425,000 workers took part in strikes.

In May a general strike of oil workers, which broke out in Baku, focussed the attention of the whole proletariat of Russia. The strike was conducted in an organized way. On June 20 a demonstration of 20,000 workers was held in Baku. The police adopted ferocious measures against the Baku workers. A strike broke out in Moscow as a mark of protest and solidarity with the Baku workers and spread to other districts.

On July 3 a meeting was held at the Putilov Works in St. Petersburg in connection with the Baku strike. The police fired on the workers. A wave of indignation swept over the St. Petersburg proletariat. On July 4, at the call of the St. Petersburg Party Committee, 90,000 St. Petersburg workers stopped work in protest; the number rose to 130,000 on July 7, 150,000 on July 8 and 200,000 on July 11.

Unrest spread to all the factories, and meetings and demonstrations were held everywhere. The workers even started to throw up barricades. Barricades were erected also in Baku and Lodz. In a number of places the police fired on the workers. The government adopted "emergency" measures to suppress the movement; the capital was turned into an armed camp; *Pravda* was suppressed.

But at that moment a new factor, one of international import, appeared on the arena. This was the imperialist war, which was to change the whole course of events. It was during the revolutionary developments of July that Poincaré, the French President, arrived in St. Petersburg to discuss with the tsar the war that was about to begin. A few days later Germany declared war on Russia. The tsarist government took advantage of the war to smash the Bolshevik organizations and to crush the working-class movement. The advance of the revolution was interrupted by the World War, in which the tsarist government sought salvation from revolution.

BRIEF SUMMARY

During the period of the new rise of the revolution (1912-14), the Bolshevik Party headed the working-class movement and led it forward to a new revolution under Bolshevik slogans. The Party ably combined illegal work with legal work. Smashing the resistance of the Liquidators and their friends—the Trotskyites and Otzovists—the Party gained the leadership of all forms of the legal movement and turned the legally existing organizations into bases of its revolutionary work.

In the fight against the enemies of the working class and their agents within the working-class movement, the Party consolidated its ranks and extended its connections with the working class. Making wide use of the Duma as a platform for revolutionary agitation, and having founded a splendid mass workers' newspaper, *Pravda*, the Party trained a new generation of revolutionary workers—the Pravdists. During the imperialist war this section of the workers remained faithful to the banner of internationalism and proletarian revolution. It subsequently formed the core of the Bolshevik Party during the revolution of October 1917.

On the eve of the imperialist war the Party led the working class in its revolutionary actions. These were vanguard engagements which were interrupted by the imperialist war only to be resumed three years later to end in the overthrow of tsardom. The Bolshevik Party entered the difficult period of the imperialist war with the banners of proletarian internationalism unfurled.

CHAPTER SIX

THE BOLSHEVIK PARTY IN THE PERIOD OF THE IMPERIALIST WAR. THE SECOND REVOLUTION IN RUSSIA

(1914-MARCH 1917)

1. OUTBREAK AND CAUSES OF THE IMPERIALIST WAR

On July 14 (27, New Style), 1914, the tsarist government proclaimed a general mobilization. On July 19 (August 1, New Style) Germany declared war on Russia.

Russia entered the war.

Long before the actual outbreak of the war the Bolsheviks, headed by Lenin, had foreseen that it was inevitable. At international Socialist congresses Lenin had put forward proposals the purpose of which was to determine a revolutionary line of conduct for the Socialists in the event of war.

Lenin had pointed out that war is an inevitable concomitant of capitalism. Plunder of foreign territory, seizure and spoliation of colonies and the capture of new markets had many times already served as causes of wars of conquest waged by capitalist states. For capitalist countries war is just as natural and legitimate a condition of things as the exploitation of the working class.

Wars became inevitable particularly when, at the end of the nineteenth century and the beginning of the twentieth century, capitalism definitely entered the highest and last stage of its development—imperialism. Under imperialism the powerful capitalist associations (monopolies) and the banks acquired a dominant position in the life of the capitalist states. Finance capital became master in the capitalist states. Finance capital demanded new markets, the seizure of new colonies, new fields for the export of capital, new sources of raw material.

But by the end of the nineteenth century the whole territory of the globe had already been divided up among the capitalist states. Yet in the era of imperialism the development of capitalism proceeds extremely unevenly and by leaps: some countries, which previously held a foremost position, now develop their industry at a relatively slow rate, while others, which were formerly backward, overtake and outstrip them by rapid leaps. The relative economic and military strength of the imperialist states was undergoing a change. There arose a striving for a redivision of the world, and the struggle for this redivision made imperialist war inevitable. The war of 1914 was a war for the redivision of the world and of spheres of influence. All the imperialist states had long been preparing for it. The imperialists of all countries were responsible for the war.

But in particular, preparations for this war were made by Germany and Austria, on the one hand, and by France and Great Britain, as well as by Russia, which was dependent on the latter two, on the other. The Triple Entente, an alliance of Great Britain, France and Russia, was formed in 1907. Germany, Austria-Hungary and Italy formed another imperialist alliance. But on the outbreak of the war of 1914 Italy left this alliance and later joined the Entente. Germany and Austria-Hungary were supported by Bulgaria and Turkey.

Germany prepared for the imperialist war with the design of taking away colonies from Great Britain and France, and the Ukraine, Poland and the Baltic Provinces from Russia. By building the Baghdad railway, Germany created a menace to Britain's domination in the Near East. Great Britain feared the growth of Germany's naval armaments.

Tsarist Russia strove for the partition of Turkey and dreamed of seizing Constantinople and the straits leading from the Black Sea to the Mediterranean (the Dardanelles). The plans of the tsarist government also included the seizure of Galicia, a part of Austria-Hungary.

Great Britain strove by means of war to smash its dangerous competitor—Germany—whose goods before the war were steadily driving British goods out of the world markets. In addition, Great Britain intended to seize Mesopotamia and Palestine from Turkey and to secure a firm foothold in Egypt.

The French capitalists strove to take away from Germany the Saar Basin and Alsace-Lorraine, two rich coal and iron regions, the latter of which Germany had seized from France in the war of 1870-71.

Thus the imperialist war was brought about by profound antagonisms between two groups of capitalist states.

This rapacious war for the redivision of the world affected the interests of all the imperialist countries, with the result that Japan, the United States and a number of other countries were subsequently drawn into it.

The war became a world war.

The bourgeoisie kept the preparations for imperialist war a profound secret from their people. When the war broke out each imperialist government endeavoured to prove that it had not attacked its neighbours, but had been attacked by them. The bourgeoisie deceived the people, concealing the true aims of the war and its imperialist, annexationist character. Each imperialist government declared that it was waging war in defence of its country.

The opportunists of the Second International helped the bourgeoisie to deceive the people. The Social-Democrats of the Second International vilely betrayed the cause of Socialism, the cause of the international solidarity of the proletariat. Far from opposing the war, they assisted the bourgeoisie in inciting the workers and peasants of the belligerent countries against each other on the plea of defending the fatherland.

That Russia entered the imperialist war on the side of the Entente, on the side of France and Great Britain, was not accidental. It should be borne in mind that before 1914 the most important branches of Russian industry were in the hands of foreign capitalists, chiefly those of France, Great Britain and Belgium, that is, the Entente countries. The most important of Russia's metal works were in the hands of French capitalists. In all, about three-quarters (72 per cent) of the metal industry depended on foreign capital. The same was true of the coal industry of the Donetz Basin. Oilfields owned by British and French capital accounted for about half the oil output of the country. A considerable part of the profits of Russian industry flowed into foreign banks, chiefly British and French. All these circumstances, in addition to the thousands of millions borrowed by the tsar from France and Britain in loans, chained tsardom to British and French imperialism and converted Russia into a tributary, a semi-colony of these countries.

The Russian bourgeoisie went to war with the purpose of improving its position: to seize new markets, to make huge profits on war contracts, and at the same time to crush the revolutionary movement by taking advantage of the war situation.

Tsarist Russia was not ready for war. Russian industry lagged far behind that of other capitalist countries. It consisted predominantly of out-of-date mills and factories with worn-out machinery. Owing to the existence of land ownership based on semi-serfdom, and the vast numbers of impoverished and ruined peasants, her agriculture could not provide a solid economic base for a prolonged war.

The chief mainstay of the tsar was the feudal landlords. The Black-Hundred big landlords, in alliance with the big capitalists, domineered the country and the State Duma. They wholly supported the home and foreign policy of the tsarist government. The Russian imperialist bourgeoisie placed its hopes in the tsarist autocracy as a mailed fist that could ensure the seizure of new markets and new territories, on the one hand, and crush the revolutionary movement of the workers and peasants, on the other.

The party of the liberal bourgeoisie—the Constitutional-Democratic Party—made a show of opposition, but supported the foreign policy of the tsarist government unreservedly.

From the very outbreak of the war, the petty-bourgeois parties, the Socialist-Revolutionaries and the Mensheviks, using the flag of Socialism as a screen, helped the bourgeoisie to deceive the people by concealing the imperialist, predatory character of the war. They preached the necessity of defending, of protecting the bourgeois "fatherland" from the "Prussian barbarians"; they supported a policy of "civil peace," and thus helped the government of the Russian tsar to wage war, just as the German Social-Democrats helped the government of the German kaiser to wage war on the "Russian barbarians."

Only the Bolshevik Party remained faithful to the great cause of revolutionary internationalism and firmly adhered to the Marxist position of a resolute struggle against the tsarist autocracy, against the landlords and capitalists, against the imperialist war. From the very outbreak of the war the Bolshevik Party maintained that it had been started, not for the defence of the country, but for the seizure of foreign territory, for the spoliation of foreign nations in the interests of the landlords and capitalists, and that the workers must wage a determined war on this war.

The working class supported the Bolshevik Party.

True, the bourgeois jingoism displayed in the early days of the war by the intelligentsia and the kulak sections of the peasantry also infected a certain section of the workers. But these were chiefly members of the ruffian "League of the Russian People" and some workers who were under the influence of the Socialist-Revolutionaries and Mensheviks. They naturally did not, and could not, reflect the sentiments of the working class. It was these elements who took part in the jingo demonstrations of the bourgeoisie engineered by the tsarist government in the early days of the war.

2. PARTIES OF THE SECOND INTERNATIONAL SIDE WITH THEIR
    IMPERIALIST GOVERNMENTS. DISINTEGRATION OF THE SECOND
    INTERNATIONAL INTO SEPARATE SOCIAL-CHAUVINIST PARTIES

Lenin had time and again warned against the opportunism of the Second International and the wavering attitude of its leaders. He had always insisted that the leaders of the Second International only talked of being opposed to war, and that if war were to break out they would change their attitude, desert to the side of the imperialist bourgeoisie and become supporters of the war. What Lenin had foretold was borne out in the very first days of the war.

In 1910, at the Copenhagen Congress of the Second International, it was decided that Socialists in parliament should vote against war credits. At the time of the Balkan War of 1912, the Basle World Congress of the Second International declared that the workers of all countries considered it a crime to shoot one another for the sake of increasing the profits of the capitalists. That is what they said, that is what they proclaimed in their resolutions.

But when the storm burst, when the imperialist war broke out, and the time had come to put these decisions into effect, the leaders of the Second International proved to be traitors, betrayers of the proletariat and servitors of the bourgeoisie. They became supporters of the war.

On August 4, 1914, the German Social-Democrats in parliament voted for the war credits; they voted to support the imperialist war. So did the overwhelming majority of the Socialists in France, Great Britain, Belgium and other countries.

The Second International ceased to exist. Actually it broke up into separate social-chauvinist parties which warred against each other.

The leaders of the Socialist parties betrayed the proletariat and adopted the position of social-chauvinism and defence of the imperialist bourgeoisie. They helped the imperialist governments to hoodwink the working class and to poison it with the venom of nationalism. Using the defence of the fatherland as a plea, these social-traitors began to incite the German workers against the French workers, and the British and French workers against the German workers. Only an insignificant minority of the Second International kept to the internationalist position and went against the current; true, they did not do so confidently and definitely enough, but go against the current they did.

Only the Bolshevik Party immediately and unhesitatingly raised the banner of determined struggle against the imperialist war. In the theses on the war that Lenin wrote in the autumn of 1914, he pointed out that the fall of the Second International was not accidental. The Second International had been ruined by the opportunists, against whom the foremost representatives of the revolutionary proletariat had long been warning.

The parties of the Second International had already been infected by opportunism before the war. The opportunists had openly preached renunciation of the revolutionary struggle; they had preached the theory of the "peaceful growing of capitalism into Socialism." The Second International did not want to combat opportunism; it wanted to live in peace with opportunism, and allowed it to gain a firm hold. Pursuing a conciliatory policy towards opportunism, the Second International itself became opportunist.

The imperialist bourgeoisie systematically bribed the upper stratum of skilled workers, the so-called labour aristocracy, by means of higher wages and other sops, using for this purpose part of the profits it derived from the colonies, from the exploitation of backward countries. This section of workers had produced quite a number of trade union and co-operative leaders, members of municipal and parliamentary bodies, journalists and functionaries of Social-Democratic organizations. When the war broke out, these people, fearing to lose their positions, became foes of revolution and most zealous defenders of their own bourgeoisies, of their own imperialist governments.

The opportunists became social-chauvinists.

The social-chauvinists, the Russian Mensheviks and Socialist-Revolutionaries among their number, preached *class peace* between the workers and the bourgeoisie at home and war on other nations abroad. They deceived the masses by concealing from them who was really responsible for the war and declaring that the bourgeoisie of their particular country was not to blame. Many social-chauvinists became ministers of the imperialist governments of their countries.

No less dangerous to the cause of the proletariat were the covert social-chauvinists, the so-called Centrists. The Centrists—Kautsky, Trotsky, Martov and others—justified and defended the avowed social-chauvinists, thus joining the social-chauvinists in betraying the proletariat; they masked their treachery by "Leftist" talk about combating the war, talk designed to deceive the working class. As a matter of fact, the Centrists supported the war, for their proposal not to vote against war credits, but merely to abstain when a vote on the credits was being taken, meant supporting the war. Like the social-chauvinists, they demanded the renunciation of the class struggle during the war so as not to hamper their particular imperialist government in waging the war. The Centrist Trotsky opposed Lenin and the Bolshevik Party on all the important questions of the war and Socialism.

From the very outbreak of the war Lenin began to muster forces for the creation of a new International, the Third International. In the manifesto against the war it issued in November 1914, the Central Committee of the Bolshevik Party already called for the formation of the Third International in place of the Second International which had suffered disgraceful bankruptcy.

In February 1915, a conference of Socialists of the Entente countries was held in London. Comrade Litvinov, on Lenin's instructions, spoke at this conference demanding that the Socialists (Vandervelde, Sembat and Guesde) should resign from the bourgeois government of Belgium and France, completely break with the imperialists and refuse to collaborate with them. He demanded that all Socialists should wage a determined struggle against their imperialist governments and condemn the voting of war credits. But no voice in support of Litvinov was raised at this conference.

At the beginning of September 1915 the first conference of internationalists was held in Zimmerwald. Lenin called this conference the "first step" in the development of an international movement against the war. At this conference Lenin formed the Zimmerwald Left group. But within the Zimmerwald Left group only the Bolshevik Party, headed by Lenin, took a correct and thoroughly consistent stand against the war. The Zimmerwald Left group published a magazine in German called the *Vorbote* (*Herald*), to which Lenin contributed articles.

In 1916 the internationalists succeeded in convening a second conference in the Swiss village of Kienthal. It is known as the Second Zimmerwald Conference. By this time groups of internationalists had been formed in nearly every country and the cleavage between the internationalist elements and the social-chauvinists had become more sharply defined. But the most important thing was that by this time the masses themselves had shifted to the Left under the influence of the war and its attendant distress. The manifesto drawn up by the Kienthal Conference was the result of an agreement between various conflicting groups; it was an advance on the Zimmerwald Manifesto.

But like the Zimmerwald Conference, the Kienthal Conference did not accept the basic principles of the Bolshevik policy, namely, the conversion of the imperialist war into a civil war, the defeat of one's own imperialist government in the war, and the formation of the Third International. Nevertheless, the Kienthal Conference helped to crystallize the internationalist elements of whom the Communist Third International was subsequently formed.

Lenin criticized the mistakes of the inconsistent internationalists among the Left Social-Democrats, such as Rosa Luxemburg and Karl Liebknecht, but at the same time he helped them to take the correct position.

3. THEORY AND TACTICS OF THE BOLSHEVIK PARTY ON THE QUESTION OF WAR, PEACE AND REVOLUTION

The Bolsheviks were not mere pacifists who sighed for peace and confined themselves to the propaganda of peace, as the majority of the Left Social-Democrats did. The Bolsheviks advocated an active revolutionary struggle for peace, to the point of overthrowing the rule of the bellicose imperialist bourgeoisie. The Bolsheviks linked up the cause of peace with the cause of the victory of the proletarian revolution, holding that the surest way of ending the war and securing a just peace, a peace without annexations and indemnities, was to overthrow the rule of the imperialist bourgeoisie.

In opposition to the Menshevik and Socialist-Revolutionary renunciation of revolution and their treacherous slogan of preserving "civil peace" in time of war, the Bolsheviks advanced the slogan of *"converting the imperialist war into a civil war."* This slogan meant that the labouring people, including the armed workers and peasants clad in soldiers' uniform, were to turn their weapons against their own bourgeoisie and overthrow its rule if they wanted to put an end to the war and achieve a just peace.

In opposition to the Menshevik and Socialist-Revolutionary policy of defending the bourgeois fatherland, the Bolsheviks advanced the policy of *"the defeat of one's own government in the imperialist war."* This meant voting against war credits, forming illegal revolutionary organizations in the armed forces, supporting fraternization among the soldiers at the front, organizing revolutionary actions of the workers and peasants against the war, and turning these actions into an uprising against one's own imperialist government.

The Bolsheviks maintained that the lesser evil for the people would be the military defeat of the tsarist government in the imperialist war, for this would facilitate the victory of the people over tsardom and the success of the struggle of the working class for emancipation from capitalist slavery and imperialist wars. Lenin held that the policy of working for the defeat of one's own imperialist government must be pursued not only by the Russian revolutionaries, but by the revolutionary parties of the working class in *all* the belligerent countries.

It was not to *every kind* of war that the Bolsheviks were opposed. They were only opposed to wars of conquest, imperialist wars. The Bolsheviks held that there are two kinds of war:

a) *Just* wars, wars that are not wars of conquest but wars of liberation, waged to defend the people from foreign attack and from attempts to enslave them, or to liberate the people from capitalist slavery, or, lastly, to liberate colonies and dependent countries from the yoke of imperialism; and

b) *Unjust* wars, wars of conquest, waged to conquer and enslave foreign countries and foreign nations.

Wars of the first kind the Bolsheviks supported. As to wars of the second kind, the Bolsheviks maintained that a resolute struggle must be waged against them to the point of revolution and the overthrow of one's own imperialist government.

Of great importance to the working class of the world was Lenin's theoretical work during the war. In the spring of 1916 Lenin wrote a book entitled *Imperialism, the Highest Stage of Capitalism*. In this book he showed that imperialism is the highest stage of capitalism, a stage at which it has already become transformed from "progressive" capitalism to parasitic capitalism, decaying capitalism, and that imperialism is moribund capitalism. This, of course, did not mean that capitalism would die away of itself, without a revolution of the proletariat, that it would just rot on the stalk. Lenin always taught that without a revolution of the working class capitalism cannot be overthrown. Therefore, while defining imperialism as moribund capitalism, Lenin at the same time showed that "imperialism is the eve of the social revolution of the proletariat."

Lenin showed that in the era of imperialism the capitalist yoke becomes more and more oppressive, that under imperialism the revolt of the proletariat against the foundations of capitalism grows, and that the elements of a revolutionary outbreak accumulate in capitalist countries.

Lenin showed that in the era of imperialism the revolutionary crisis in the colonial and dependent countries becomes more acute, that the elements of revolt against imperialism, the elements of a war of liberation from imperialism accumulate.

Lenin showed that under imperialism the unevenness of development and the contradictions of capitalism have grown particularly acute, that the struggle for markets and fields for the export of capital, the struggle for colonies, for sources of raw material, makes periodical imperialist wars for the redivision of the world inevitable.

Lenin showed that it is just this unevenness of development of capitalism that gives rise to imperialist wars, which undermine the strength of imperialism and make it possible to break the front of imperialism at its weakest point.

From all this Lenin drew the conclusion that it was quite possible for the proletariat to break the imperialist front in one place or in several

places, that the victory of Socialism was *possible* first in several countries
or even in one country, taken singly, that the simultaneous victory of
Socialism in all countries was *impossible* owing to the unevenness of development of capitalism, and that Socialism would be victorious first in
one country or in several countries, while the others would remain
bourgeois countries for some time longer.

Here is the formulation of this brilliant deduction as given by Lenin
in two articles written during the imperialist war:

1) "Uneven economic and political development is an absolute
law of capitalism. Hence, the victory of Socialism is possible first in
several or even in one capitalist country, taken singly. The victorious
proletariat of that country, having expropriated the capitalists and
organized its own Socialist production, would stand up *against* the
rest of the world, the capitalist world, attracting to its cause the oppressed classes of other countries...." (From the article, "The
United States of Europe Slogan," written in August, 1915.—Lenin,
Selected Works, Vol. V, p. 141.)

2) "The development of capitalism proceeds extremely unevenly
in the various countries. It cannot be otherwise under the commodity
production system. From this it follows irrefutably that Socialism
cannot achieve victory simultaneously *in all* countries. It will achieve
victory first in one or several countries, while the others will remain
bourgeois or pre-bourgeois for some time. This must not only create
friction, but a direct striving on the part of the bourgeoisie of other
countries to crush the victorious proletariat of the Socialist country.
In such cases a war on our part would be a legitimate and just war.
It would be a war for Socialism, for the liberation of other nations
from the bourgeoisie." (From the article, "War Program of the
Proletarian Revolution," written in the autumn of 1916.—Lenin,
Collected Works, Russ. ed., Vol. XIX, p. 325.)

This was a *new* and complete theory of the Socialist revolution, a
theory affirming the possibility of the victory of Socialism in separate
countries, and indicating the conditions of this victory and its prospects,
a theory whose fundamentals were outlined by Lenin as far back as
1905 in his pamphlet, *Two Tactics of Social-Democracy in the Democratic Revolution.*

This theory fundamentally differed from the view current among the
Marxists in the period of *pre-imperialist* capitalism, when they held that
the victory of Socialism in one separate country was impossible, and that
it would take place simultaneously in all the civilized countries. On the

basis of the facts concerning *imperialist* capitalism set forth in his remarkable book, *Imperialism, the Highest Stage of Capitalism*, Lenin displaced this view as obsolete and set forth a new theory, from which it follows that the simultaneous victory of Socialism in all countries is *impossible*, while the victory of Socialism in one capitalist country, taken singly, is *possible.*

The inestimable importance of Lenin's theory of Socialist revolution lies not only in the fact that it has enriched Marxism with a new theory and has advanced Marxism, but also in the fact that it opens up a revolutionary perspective for the proletarians of separate countries, that it unfetters their initiative in the onslaught on their own, national bourgeoisie, that it teaches them to take advantage of a war situation to organize this onslaught, and that it strengthens their faith in the victory of the proletarian revolution.

Such was the theoretical and tactical stand of the Bolsheviks on the questions of war, peace and revolution.

It was on the basis of this stand that the Bolsheviks carried on their practical work in Russia.

At the beginning of the war, in spite of severe persecution by the police, the Bolshevik members of the Duma—Badayev, Petrovsky, Muranov, Samoilov and Shagov—visited a number of organizations and addressed them on the policy of the Bolsheviks towards the war and revolution. In November 1914 a conference of the Bolshevik group in the State Duma was convened to discuss policy towards the war. On the third day of the conference all present were arrested. The court sentenced the Bolshevik members of the State Duma to forfeiture of civil rights and banishment to Eastern Siberia. The tsarist government charged them with "high treason."

The picture of the activities of the Duma members unfolded in court did credit to our Party. The Bolshevik deputies conducted themselves manfully, transforming the tsarist court into a platform from which they exposed the annexationist policy of tsardom.

Quite different was the conduct of Kamenev, who was also tried in this case. Owing to his cowardice, he abjured the policy of the Bolshevik Party at the first contact with danger. Kamenev declared in court that he did not agree with the Bolsheviks on the question of the war, and to prove this he requested that the Menshevik Jordansky be summoned as witness.

The Bolsheviks worked very effectively against the War Industry Committees set up to serve the needs of war, and against the attempts of the Mensheviks to bring the workers under the influence of the imperialist bourgeoisie. It was of vital interest to the bourgeoisie to make everybody believe that the imperialist war was a people's war. During the war the bourgeoisie managed to attain considerable influence in affairs of state and set up a countrywide organization of its own known as the Unions of Zemstvos and Towns. It was necessary for the bourgeoisie to bring the workers, too, under its leadership and influence. It conceived a way to do this, namely, by forming "Workers' Groups" of the War Industry Committees. The Mensheviks jumped at this idea. It was to the advantage of the bourgeoisie to have on these War Industry Committees representatives of the workers who would urge the working class masses to increase productivity of labour in the factories producing shells, guns, rifles, cartridges and other war material. "Everything for the war, all for the war"—was the slogan of the bourgeoisie. Actually, this slogan meant "get as rich as you can on war contracts and seizures of foreign territory." The Mensheviks took an active part in this pseudo-patriotic scheme of the bourgeoisie. They helped the capitalists by conducting an intense campaign among the workers to get them to take part in the elections of the "Workers' Groups" of the War Industry Committees. The Bolsheviks were against this scheme. They advocated a boycott of the War Industry Committees and were successful in securing this boycott. But some of the workers, headed by a prominent Menshevik, Gvozdev, and an agent-provocateur, Abrosimov, did take part in the activities of the War Industry Committees. When, however, the workers' delegates met, in September 1915, for the final elections of the "Workers' Groups" of the War Industry Committees, it turned out that the majority of the delegates were opposed to participation in them. A majority of the workers' delegates adopted a trenchant resolution opposing participation in the War Industry Committees and declared that the workers had made it their aim to fight for peace and for the overthrow of tsardom.

The Bolsheviks also developed extensive activities in the army and navy. They explained to the soldiers and sailors who was to blame for the unparalleled horrors of the war and the sufferings of the people; they explained that there was only one way out for the people from the imperialist shambles, and that was revolution. The Bolsheviks formed nuclei in the army and navy, at the front and in the rear, and distributed leaflets calling for a fight against the war.

In Kronstadt, the Bolsheviks formed a "Central Collective of the Kronstadt Military Organization" which had close connections with the Petrograd Committee of the Party. A military organization of the Petrograd Party Committee was set up for work among the garrison.

In August 1916, the chief of the Petrograd *Okhrana* reported that "in the Kronstadt Collective, things are very well organized, conspiratorially, and its members are all taciturn and cautious people. This Collective also has representatives on shore."

At the front, the Party agitated for fraternization between the soldiers of the warring armies, emphasizing the fact that the world bourgeoisie was the enemy, and that the war could be ended only by converting the imperialist war into a civil war and turning one's weapons against one's own bourgeoisie and its government. Cases of refusal of army units to take the offensive became more and more frequent. There were already such instances in 1915, and even more in 1916.

Particularly extensive were the activities of the Bolsheviks in the armies on the Northern Front, in the Baltic provinces. At the beginning of 1917 General Ruzsky, Commander of the Army on the Northern Front, informed Headquarters that the Bolsheviks had developed intense revolutionary activities on that front.

The war wrought a profound change in the life of the peoples, in the life of the working class of the world. The fate of states, the fate of nations, the fate of the Socialist movement was at stake. The war was therefore a touchstone, a test for all parties and trends calling themselves Socialist. Would these parties and trends remain true to the cause of Socialism, to the cause of internationalism, or would they choose to betray the working class, to furl their banners and lay them at the feet of their national bourgeoisie?—that is how the question stood at the time.

The war showed that the parties of the Second International had not stood the test, that they had betrayed the working class and had surrendered their banners to the imperialist bourgeoisie of their own countries.

And these parties, which had cultivated opportunism in their midst, and which had been brought up to make concessions to the opportunists, to the nationalists, could not have acted differently.

The war showed that the Bolshevik Party was the only party which had passed the test with flying colours and had remained consistently faithful to the cause of Socialism, the cause of proletarian internationalism.

And that was to be expected: only a party of a new type, only a party fostered in the spirit of uncompromising struggle against opportunism, only a party that was free from opportunism and nationalism, only such a party could stand the great test and remain faithful to the cause of the working class, to the cause of Socialism and internationalism.

And the Bolshevik Party was such a party.

4. DEFEAT OF THE TSARIST ARMY. ECONOMIC DISRUPTION. CRISIS
    OF TSARDOM

The war had already been in progress for three years. Millions of
people had been killed in the war, or had died of wounds or from
epidemics caused by war conditions. The bourgeoisie and landlords were
making fortunes out of the war. But the workers and peasants were
suffering increasing hardship and privation. The war was undermining
the economic life of Russia. Some fourteen million able-bodied men
had been torn from economic pursuits and drafted into the army. Mills
and factories were coming to a standstill. The crop area had diminished
owing to a shortage of labour. The population and the soldiers at the
front went hungry, barefoot and naked. The war was eating up the
resources of the country.

The tsarist army suffered defeat after defeat. The German artillery
deluged the tsarist troops with shells, while the tsarist army lacked guns,
shells and even rifles. Sometimes three soldiers had to share one rifle.
While the war was in progress it was discovered that Sukhomlinov, the
tsar's Minister of War, was a traitor, who was connected with German
spies, and was carrying out the instructions of the German espionage
service to disorganize the supply of munitions and to leave the front
without guns and rifles. Some of the tsarist ministers and generals surreptitiously assisted the success of the German army: together with the
tsarina, who had German ties, they betrayed military secrets to the
Germans. It is not surprising that the tsarist army suffered reverses
and was forced to retreat. By 1916 the Germans had already seized
Poland and part of the Baltic provinces.

All this aroused hatred and anger against the tsarist government
among the workers, peasants, soldiers and intellectuals, fostered and intensified the revolutionary movement of the masses against the war and
against tsardom, both in the rear and at the front, in the central and
in the border regions.

Dissatisfaction also began to spread to the Russian imperialist bourgeoisie. It was incensed by the fact that rascals like Rasputin, who were
obviously working for a separate peace with Germany, lorded it at the
tsar's court. The bourgeoisie grew more and more convinced that the
tsarist government was incapable of waging war successfully. It feared
that the tsar might, in order to save his position, conclude a separate
peace with the Germans. The Russian bourgeoisie therefore decided to
engineer a palace coup with the object of deposing Tsar Nicholas II and
replacing him by his brother, Michael Romanov, who was connected

with the bourgeoisie. In this way it wanted to kill two birds with one stone: first, to get into power itself and ensure the further prosecution of the imperialist war, and, secondly, to prevent by a small palace coup the outbreak of a big popular revolution, the tide of which was swelling.

In this the Russian bourgeoisie had the full support of the British and French governments who saw that the tsar was incapable of carrying on the war. They feared that he might end it by concluding a separate peace with the Germans. If the tsarist government were to sign a separate peace, the British and French governments would lose a war ally which not only diverted enemy forces to its own fronts, but also supplied France with tens of thousands of picked Russian soldiers. The British and French governments therefore supported the attempts of the Russian bourgeoisie to bring about a palace coup.

The tsar was thus isolated.

While defeat followed defeat at the front, economic disruption grew more and more acute. In January and February 1917 the extent and acuteness of the disorganization of the food, raw material and fuel supply reached a climax. The supply of foodstuffs to Petrograd and Moscow had almost ceased. One factory after another closed down and this aggravated unemployment. Particularly intolerable was the condition of the workers. Increasing numbers of the people were arriving at the conviction that the only way out of the intolerable situation was to overthrow the tsarist autocracy.

Tsardom was clearly in the throes of a mortal crisis.

The bourgeoisie thought of solving the crisis by a palace coup.

But the people solved it in their own way.

5. THE FEBRUARY REVOLUTION. FALL OF TSARDOM. FORMATION OF SOVIETS OF WORKERS' AND SOLDIERS' DEPUTIES. FORMATION OF THE PROVISIONAL GOVERNMENT. DUAL POWER

The year 1917 was inaugurated by the strike of January 9. In the course of this strike demonstrations were held in Petrograd, Moscow, Baku and Nizhni-Novgorod. In Moscow about one-third of the workers took part in the strike of January 9. A demonstration of two thousand persons on Tverskoi Boulevard was dispersed by mounted police. A demonstration on the Vyborg Chaussée in Petrograd was joined by soldiers.

"The idea of a general strike," the Petrograd police reported, "is daily gaining new followers and is becoming as popular as it was in 1905."

The Mensheviks and Socialist-Revolutionaries tried to direct this incipient revolutionary movement into the channels the liberal bourgeoisie needed. The Mensheviks proposed that a procession of workers to the State Duma be organized on February 14, the day of its opening. But the working-class masses followed the Bolsheviks, and went, not to the Duma, but to a demonstration.

On February 18, 1917, a strike broke out at the Putilov Works in Petrograd. On February 22 the workers of most of the big factories were on strike. On International Women's Day, February 23 (March 8), at the call of the Petrograd Bolshevik Committee, working women came out in the streets to demonstrate against starvation, war and tsardom. The Petrograd workers supported the demonstration of the working women by a city-wide strike movement. The political strike began to grow into a general political demonstration against the tsarist system.

On February 24 (March 9) the demonstration was resumed with even greater vigour. About 200,000 workers were already on strike.

On February 25 (March 10) the whole of working-class Petrograd had joined the revolutionary movement. The political strikes in the districts merged into a general political strike of the whole city. Demonstrations and clashes with the police took place everywhere. Over the masses of workers floated red banners bearing the slogans: "Down with the tsar!" "Down with the war!" "We want bread!"

On the morning of February 26 (March 11) the political strike and demonstration began to assume the character of an uprising. The workers disarmed police and gendarmes and armed themselves. Nevertheless, the clashes with the police ended with the shooting down of a demonstration on Znamenskaya Square.

General Khabalov, Commander of the Petrograd Military Area, announced that the workers must return to work by February 28 (March 13), otherwise they would be sent to the front. On February 25 (March 10) the tsar gave orders to General Khabalov: "I command you to put a stop to the disorders in the capital not later than tomorrow."

But "to put a stop" to the revolution was no longer possible.

On February 26 (March 11) the 4th Company of the Reserve Battalion of the Pavlovsky Regiment opened fire, not on the workers, however, but on squads of mounted police who were engaged in a skirmish with the workers. A most energetic and persistent drive was made to win over the troops, especially by the working women, who addressed themselves directly to the soldiers, fraternized with them and called upon them to help the people to overthrow the hated tsarist autocracy.

The practical work of the Bolshevik Party at that time was directed by the Bureau of the Central Committee of our Party which had its quarters in Petrograd and was headed by Comrade Molotov. On February 26 (March 11) the Bureau of the Central Committee issued a manifesto calling for the continuation of the armed struggle against tsardom and the formation of a Provisional Revolutionary Government.

On February 27 (March 12) the troops in Petrograd refused to fire on the workers and began to line up with the people in revolt. The number of soldiers who had joined the revolt by the morning of February 27 was still no more than 10,000, but by the evening it already exceeded 60,000.

The workers and soldiers who had risen in revolt began to arrest tsarist ministers and generals and to free revolutionaries from jail. The released political prisoners joined the revolutionary struggle.

In the streets, shots were still being exchanged with police and gendarmes posted with machine guns in the attics of houses. But the troops rapidly went over to the side of the workers, and this decided the fate of the tsarist autocracy.

When the news of the victory of the revolution in Petrograd spread to other towns and to the front, the workers and soldiers everywhere began to depose the tsarist officials.

The February bourgeois-democratic revolution had won.

The revolution was victorious because its vanguard was the working class which headed the movement of millions of peasants clad in soldiers' uniform demanding "peace, bread and liberty." It was the hegemony of the proletariat that determined the success of the revolution.

"The revolution was made by the proletariat. The proletariat displayed heroism; it shed its blood; it swept along with it the broadest masses of the toiling and poor population," wrote Lenin in the early days of the revolution. (Lenin, *Collected Works*, Russ. ed., Vol. XX, pp. 23-4.)

The First Revolution, that of 1905, had prepared the way for the swift success of the Second Revolution, that of 1917.

"Without the tremendous class battles," Lenin wrote, "and the revolutionary energy displayed by the Russian proletariat during the three years, 1905-07, the second revolution could not possibly have been so rapid in the sense that its *initial* stage was completed in a few days." (Lenin, *Selected Works*, Vol. VI, pp. 3-4.)

Soviets arose in the very first days of the revolution. The victorious revolution rested on the support of the Soviets of Workers' and Soldiers' Deputies. The workers and soldiers who rose in revolt created Soviets of Workers' and Soldiers' Deputies. The Revolution of 1905 had shown that the Soviets were organs of armed uprising and at the same time the embryo of a new, revolutionary power. The idea of Soviets lived in the minds of the working-class masses, and they put it into effect as soon as tsardom was overthrown, with this difference, however, that in 1905 it was Soviets only of *Workers'* Deputies that were formed, whereas in February 1917, on the initiative of the Bolsheviks, there arose Soviets of *Workers'* and *Soldiers'* Deputies.

While the Bolsheviks were directly leading the struggle of the masses in the streets, the compromising parties, the Mensheviks and Socialist-Revolutionaries, were seizing the seats in the Soviets, and building up a majority there. This was partly facilitated by the fact that the majority of the leaders of the Bolshevik Party were in prison or exile (Lenin was in exile abroad and Stalin and Sverdlov in banishment in Siberia) while the Mensheviks and Socialist-Revolutionaries were freely promenading the streets of Petrograd. The result was that the Petrograd Soviet and its Executive Committee were headed by representatives of the compromising parties: Mensheviks and Socialist-Revolutionaries. This was also the case in Moscow and a number of other cities. Only in Ivanovo-Voznesensk, Krasnoyarsk and a few other places did the Bolsheviks have a majority in the Soviets from the very outset.

The armed people—the workers and soldiers—sent their representatives to the Soviet as to an organ of power of the people. They thought and believed that the Soviet of Workers' and Soldiers' Deputies would carry out all the demands of the revolutionary people, and that, in the first place, peace would be concluded.

But the unwarranted trustfulness of the workers and soldiers served them in evil stead. The Socialist-Revolutionaries and Mensheviks had not the slightest intention of terminating the war, of securing peace. They planned to take advantage of the revolution to continue the war. As to the revolution and the revolutionary demands of the people, the Socialist-Revolutionaries and the Mensheviks considered that the revolution was already over, and that the task now was to seal it and to pass to a "normal" constitutional existence side by side with the bourgeoisie. The Socialist-Revolutionary and Menshevik leaders of the Petrograd Soviet therefore did their utmost to shelve the question of terminating the war, to shelve the question of peace, and to hand over the power to the bourgeoisie.

On February 27 (March 12), 1917, the liberal members of the Fourth State Duma, as the result of a backstairs agreement with the Socialist-Revolutionary and Menshevik leaders, set up a Provisional

Committee of the State Duma, headed by Rodzyanko, the President of the Duma, a landlord and a monarchist.   And a few days later, the Provisional Committee of the State Duma and the Socialist-Revolutionary and Menshevik leaders of the Executive Committee of the Soviet of Workers' and Soldiers' Deputies, acting secretly from the Bolsheviks, came to an agreement to form a new government of Russia—a bourgeois Provisional Government, headed by Prince Lvov, the man whom, prior to the February Revolution, even Tsar Nicholas II was about to make the Prime Minister of his government.   The Provisional Government included Milyukov, the head of the Constitutional-Democrats, Guchkov, the head of the Octobrists, and other prominent representatives of the capitalist class, and, as the representative of the "democracy," the Socialist-Revolutionary Kerensky.

And so it was that the Socialist-Revolutionary and Menshevik leaders of the Executive Committee of the Soviet surrendered the power to the bourgeoisie.   Yet when the Soviet of Workers' and Soldiers' Deputies learned of this, its majority formally approved of the action of the Socialist-Revolutionary and Menshevik leaders, despite the protest of the Bolsheviks.

Thus a new state power arose in Russia, consisting, as Lenin said, of representatives of the "bourgeoisie and landlords who had become bourgeois."

But alongside of the bourgeois government there existed another power—the Soviet of Workers' and Soldiers' Deputies.   The soldier deputies on the Soviet were mostly peasants who had been mobilized for the war.   The Soviet of Workers' and Soldiers' Deputies was an organ of the alliance of workers and peasants against the tsarist regime, and at the same time it was an organ of their power, an organ of the dictatorship of the working class and the peasantry.

The result was a peculiar interlocking of two powers, of two dictatorships: the dictatorship of the bourgeoisie, represented by the Provisional Government, and the dictatorship of the proletariat and peasantry, represented by the Soviet of Workers' and Soldiers' Deputies.

The result was a *dual power*.

How is it to be explained that the majority in the Soviets at first consisted of Mensheviks and Socialist-Revolutionaries?

How is it to be explained that the victorious workers and peasants *voluntarily* surrendered the power to the representatives of the bourgeoisie?

Lenin explained it by pointing out that millions of people, inexperienced in politics, had awakened and pressed forward to political activity.   These were for the most part small owners, peasants, workers who had recently been peasants, people who stood midway between the bourgeoisie and the proletariat. Russia was at that time the most petty-bourgeois of all the big European countries. And in this country, "a gigantic petty-bourgeois wave has swept over everything and over-whelmed the class-conscious proletariat, not only by force of numbers but also ideologically; that is, it has infected and imbued very wide circles of workers with the petty-bourgeois political outlook." (Lenin, *Selected Works*, Vol. VI, p. 49.)

It was this elemental petty-bourgeois wave that swept the petty-bourgeois Menshevik and Socialist-Revolutionary parties to the fore.

Lenin pointed out that another reason was the change in the composition of the proletariat that had taken place during the war and the inadequate class-consciousness and organization of the proletariat at the beginning of the revolution. During the war big changes had taken place in the proletariat itself. About 40 per cent of the regular workers had been drafted into the army. Many small owners, artisans and shop-keepers, to whom the proletarian psychology was alien, had gone to the factories in order to evade mobilization.

It was these petty-bourgeois sections of the workers that formed the soil which nourished the petty-bourgeois politicians—the Mensheviks and Socialist-Revolutionaries.

That is why large numbers of the people, inexperienced in politics, swept into the elemental petty-bourgeois vortex, and intoxicated with the first successes of the revolution, found themselves in its early months under the sway of the compromising parties and consented to surrender the state power to the bourgeoisie in the naive belief that a bourgeois power would not hinder the Soviets in their work.

The task that confronted the Bolshevik Party was, by patient work of explanation, to open the eyes of the masses to the imperialist character of the Provisional Government, to expose the treachery of the Socialist-Revolutionaries and Mensheviks and to show that peace could not be secured unless the Provisional Government were replaced by a government of Soviets.

And to this work the Bolshevik Party addressed itself with the utmost energy.

It resumed the publication of its legal periodicals. The newspaper *Pravda* appeared in Petrograd five days after the February Revolution, and the *Sotsial-Demokrat* in Moscow a few days later. The Party was assuming leadership of the masses, who were losing their confidence in the liberal bourgeoisie and in the Mensheviks and Socialist-Revolution-aries. It patiently explained to the soldiers and peasants the necessity of acting jointly with the working class. It explained to them that the peasants would secure neither peace nor land unless the revolution were further developed and the bourgeois Provisional Government replaced by a government of Soviets.

BRIEF SUMMARY

The imperialist war arose owing to the uneven development of the capitalist countries, to the upsetting of equilibrium between the principal powers, to the imperialists' need for a redivision of the world by means of war and for the creation of a new equilibrium.

The war would not have been so destructive, and perhaps would not even have assumed such dimensions, if the parties of the Second International had not betrayed the cause of the working class, if they had not violated the anti-war decisions of the congresses of the Second International, if they had dared to act and to rouse the working class against their imperialist governments, against the warmongers.

The Bolshevik Party was the only proletarian party which remained faithful to the cause of Socialism and internationalism and which organized civil war against its own imperialist government. All the other parties of the Second International, being tied to the bourgeoisie through their leaders, found themselves under the sway of imperialism and deserted to the side of the imperialists.

The war, while it was a reflection of the general crisis of capitalism, at the same time aggravated this crisis and weakened world capitalism. The workers of Russia and the Bolshevik Party were the first in the world successfully to take advantage of the weakness of capitalism. They forced a breach in the imperialist front, overthrew the tsar and set up Soviets of Workers' and Soldiers' Deputies.

Intoxicated by the first successes of the revolution, and lulled by the assurances of the Mensheviks and Socialist-Revolutionaries that from now on everything would go well, the bulk of the petty-bourgeoisie, the soldiers, as well as the workers, placed their confidence in the Provisional Government and supported it.

The Bolshevik Party was confronted with the task of explaining to the masses of workers and soldiers, who had been intoxicated by the first successes, that the complete victory of the revolution was still a long way off, that as long as the power was in the hands of the bourgeois Provisional Government, and as long as the Soviets were dominated by the compromisers—the Mensheviks and Socialist-Revolutionaries—the people would secure neither peace, nor land, nor bread, and that in order to achieve complete victory, one more step had to be taken and the power transferred to the Soviets.

CHAPTER SEVEN

THE BOLSHEVIK PARTY IN THE PERIOD OF PREPARATION AND REALIZATION OF THE OCTOBER SOCIALIST REVOLUTION

(APRIL 1917-1918)

1. SITUATION IN THE COUNTRY AFTER THE FEBRUARY REVOLUTION. PARTY EMERGES FROM UNDERGROUND AND PASSES TO OPEN POLITICAL WORK. LENIN ARRIVES IN PETROGRAD. LENIN'S APRIL THESES. PARTY'S POLICY OF TRANSITION TO SOCIALIST REVOLUTION

The course of events and the conduct of the Provisional Government daily furnished new proofs of the correctness of the Bolshevik line. It became increasingly evident that the Provisional Government stood not for the people but against the people, not for peace but for war, and that it was unwilling and unable to give the people peace, land or bread. The explanatory work of the Bolsheviks found a fruitful soil.

While the workers and soldiers were overthrowing the tsarist government and destroying the monarchy root and branch, the Provisional Government definitely wanted to preserve the monarchy. On March 2, 1917, it secretly commissioned Guchkov and Shulgin to go and see the tsar. The bourgeoisie wanted to transfer the power to Nicholas Romanov's brother, Michael. But when, at a meeting of railwaymen, Guchkov ended his speech with the words, "Long live Emperor Michael," the workers demanded that Guchkov be immediately arrested and searched. "Horse-radish is no sweeter than radish," they exclaimed indignantly.

It was clear that the workers would not permit the restoration of the monarchy.

While the workers and peasants who were shedding their blood making the revolution expected that the war would be terminated, while they were fighting for bread and land and demanding vigorous measures to end the economic chaos, the Provisional Government remained deaf to these vital demands of the people. Consisting as it did of prominent representatives of the capitalists and landlords, this government had no intention of satisfying the demand of the peasants that the land be turned over to them. Nor could they provide bread for the working people, because to do so they would have to encroach on the interests of the big grain dealers and to take grain from the landlords and the kulaks by every available means; and this the government did not dare to do, for it was itself tied up with the interests of these classes. Nor could it give the people peace. Bound as it was to the British and French imperialists, the Provisional Government had no intention of terminating the war; on the contrary, it endeavoured to take advantage of the revolution to make Russia's participation in the imperialist war even more active, and to realize its imperialist designs of seizing Constantinople, the Straits and Galicia.

It was clear that the people's confidence in the policy of the Provisional Government must soon come to an end.

It was becoming clear that the dual power which had arisen after the February Revolution could not last long, for the course of events demanded the concentration of power in the hands of one authority: either the Provisional Government or the Soviets.

It was true that the compromising policy of the Mensheviks and the Socialist-Revolutionaries still met with support among the masses. There were quite a number of workers, and an even larger number of soldiers and peasants, who still believed that "the Constituent Assembly will soon come and arrange everything in a peaceful way," and who thought that the war was not waged for purposes of conquest, but from necessity— to defend the state. Lenin called such people honestly-mistaken supporters of the war. These people still considered the Socialist-Revolutionary and Menshevik policy, which was one of promises and coaxing, the correct policy. But it was clear that promises and coaxing could not suffice for long, as the course of events and the conduct of the Provisional Government were daily revealing and proving that the compromising policy of the Socialist-Revolutionaries and the Mensheviks was a policy of procrastination and of hoodwinking the credulous.

The Provisional Government did not always confine itself to a covert struggle against the revolutionary movement of the masses, to backstairs scheming against the revolution. It sometimes attempted to make an open assault on the democratic liberties, to "restore discipline," especially among the soldiers, to "establish order," that is, to direct the revolution into channels that suited the needs of the bourgeoisie. But all its efforts in this direction failed, and the people eagerly exercised their democratic liberties, namely, freedom of speech, press, association, assembly and demonstration. The workers and soldiers endeavoured to make full use of their newly-won democratic rights in order to take an active part in the political life of the country, to get an intelligent understanding of the situation and to decide what was to be done next.

After the February Revolution, the organizations of the Bolshevik Party, which had worked illegally under the extremely difficult conditions of tsardom, emerged from underground and began to develop political and organizational work openly. The membership of the Bolshevik organizations at that time did not exceed 40,000 or 45,000. But these were all staunch revolutionaries, steeled in the struggle. The Party Committees were reorganized on the principle of democratic centralism. All Party bodies, from top to bottom, were made elective.

When the Party began its legal existence, differences within its ranks became apparent. Kamenev and several workers of the Moscow organization, for example, Rykov, Bubnov and Nogin, held a semi-Menshevik position of conditionally supporting the Provisional Government and the policy of the partisans of the war. Stalin, who had just returned from exile, Molotov and others, together with the majority of the Party, upheld a policy of no-confidence in the Provisional Government, opposed the partisans of the war, and called for an active struggle for peace, a struggle against the imperialist war. Some of the Party workers vacillated, which was a manifestation of their political backwardness, a consequence of long years of imprisonment or exile.

The absence of the leader of the Party, Lenin, was felt.

On April 3 (16), 1917, after a long period of exile, Lenin returned to Russia.

Lenin's arrival was of tremendous importance to the Party and the revolution.

While still in Switzerland, Lenin, upon receiving the first news of the revolution, had written his "Letters From Afar" to the Party and to the working class of Russia, in which he said:

"Workers, you have displayed marvels of proletarian heroism, the heroism of the people, in the civil war against tsardom. You must now display marvels of organization, organization of the proletariat and of the whole people, in order to prepare the way for your victory in the second stage of the revolution." (Lenin, *Selected Works*, Vol. VI, p. 11.)

Lenin arrived in Petrograd on the night of April 3. Thousands of workers, soldiers and sailors assembled at the Finland Railway Station and in the station square to welcome him. Their enthusiasm as Lenin alighted from the train was indescribable. They lifted their leader shoulder high and carried him to the main waiting room of the station. There the Mensheviks Chkheidze and Skobelev launched into speeches of "welcome" on behalf of the Petrograd Soviet, in which they "expressed the hope" that they and Lenin would find a "common language." But Lenin did not stop to listen; sweeping past them, he went out to the masses of workers and soldiers. Mounting an armoured car, he delivered his famous speech in which he called upon the masses to fight for the victory of the Socialist revolution. "Long live the Socialist revolution!" were the words with which Lenin concluded this first speech after long years of exile.

Back in Russia, Lenin flung himself vigorously into revolutionary work. On the morrow of his arrival he delivered a report on the subject of the war and the revolution at a meeting of Bolsheviks, and then repeated the theses of this report at a meeting attended by Mensheviks as well as Bolsheviks.

These were Lenin's famous April Theses, which provided the Party and the proletariat with a clear revolutionary line for the transition from the bourgeois to the Socialist revolution.

Lenin's theses were of immense significance to the revolution and to the subsequent work of the Party. The revolution was a momentous turn in the life of the country. In the new conditions of the struggle that followed the overthrow of tsardom, the Party needed a new orientation to advance boldly and confidently along the new road. Lenin's theses gave the Party this orientation.

Lenin's April Theses laid down for the Party a brilliant plan of struggle for the transition from the bourgeois-democratic to the Socialist revolution, from the first stage of the revolution to the second stage—the stage of the Socialist revolution. The whole history of the Party had prepared it for this great task. As far back as 1905, Lenin had said in his pamphlet, *Two Tactics of Social-Democracy in the Democratic Revolution*, that after the overthrow of tsardom the proletariat would proceed to bring about the Socialist revolution. The new thing in the theses was that they gave a concrete, theoretically grounded plan for the initial stage of the transition to the Socialist revolution.

The transitional steps in the economic field were: nationalization of all the land and confiscation of the landed estates, amalgamation of all the banks into one national bank to be under the control of the Soviet of Workers' Deputies, and establishment of control over the social production and distribution of products.

In the political field, Lenin proposed the transition from a parliamentary republic to a republic of Soviets. This was an important step forward in the theory and practice of Marxism. Hitherto, Marxist theoreticians had regarded the parliamentary republic as the best political form of transition to Socialism. Now Lenin proposed to replace the parliamentary republic by a Soviet republic as the most suitable form of political organization of society in the period of transition from capitalism to Socialism.

> "The specific feature of the present situation in Russia," the theses stated, "is that it represents a *transition* from the first stage of the revolution—which, owing to the insufficient class-consciousness and organization of the proletariat, placed the power in the hands of the bourgeoisie—*to the second* stage, which must place the power in the hands of the proletariat and the poorest strata of the peasantry." (*Ibid.*, p. 22.)

> "Not a parliamentary republic—to return to a parliamentary republic from the Soviets of Workers' Deputies would be a retrograde step—but a republic of Soviets of Workers', Agricultural Labourers' and Peasants' Deputies throughout the country, from top to bottom." (*Ibid.*, p. 23.)

Under the new government, the Provisional Government, the war continued to be a predatory imperialist war, Lenin said. It was the task of the Party to explain this to the masses and to show them that unless the bourgeoisie were overthrown, it would be impossible to end the war by a truly democratic peace and not a rapacious peace.

As regards the Provisional Government, the slogan Lenin put forward was: "No support for the Provisional Government!"

Lenin further pointed out in the theses that our Party was still in the minority in the Soviets, that the Soviets were dominated by a bloc of Mensheviks and Socialist-Revolutionaries, which was an instrument of bourgeois influence on the proletariat. Hence, the Party's task consisted in the following:

> "It must be explained to the masses that the Soviets of Workers' Deputies are the *only possible* form of revolutionary government, and that therefore our task is, as long as *this* government yields to the influence of the bourgeoisie, to present a patient, systematic, and persistent *explanation* of the errors of their tactics, an explanation especially adapted to the practical needs of the masses. As long as we are in the minority we carry on the work of criticizing and exposing errors and at the same time we preach the necessity of transferring the entire power of state to the Soviets of Workers' Deputies. . . ." (*Ibid.*, p. 23.)

This meant that Lenin was not calling for a revolt against the Provisional Government, which at that moment enjoyed the confidence of the Soviets, that he was not demanding its overthrow, but that he wanted, by means of explanatory and recruiting work, to win a majority in the Soviets, to change the policy of the Soviets, and through the Soviets to alter the composition and policy of the government.

This was a line envisaging a peaceful development of the revolution.

Lenin further demanded that the "soiled shirt" be discarded, that is, that the Party no longer call itself a Social-Democratic Party. The parties of the Second International and the Russian Mensheviks called themselves Social-Democrats. This name had been tarnished and disgraced by the opportunists, the betrayers of Socialism. Lenin proposed that the Party of the Bolsheviks should be called the *Communist Party*, which was the name given by Marx and Engels to their party. This name was scientifically correct, for it was the ultimate aim of the Bolshevik Party to achieve Communism. Mankind can pass directly from capitalism only to Socialism, that is, to the common ownership of the means of production and the distribution of products according to the work performed by each. Lenin said that our Party looked farther ahead. Socialism was inevitably bound to pass gradually into Communism, on the banner of which is inscribed the maxim: "From each according to his abilities, to each according to his needs."

Lastly, Lenin in his theses demanded the creation of a new International, the Third, Communist International, which would be free of opportunism and social-chauvinism.

Lenin's theses called forth a frenzied outcry from the bourgeoisie, the Mensheviks and the Socialist-Revolutionaries.

The Mensheviks issued a proclamation to the workers which began with the warning: "the revolution is in danger." The danger, in the opinion of the Mensheviks, lay in the fact that the Bolsheviks had advanced the demand for the transfer of power to the Soviets of Workers' and Soldiers' Deputies.

Plekhanov in his newspaper, *Yedinstvo (Unity)*, wrote an article in which he termed Lenin's speech a *"raving speech."* He quoted the words of the Menshevik Chkheidze, who said: "Lenin alone will remain outside the revolution, and we shall go our own way."

On April 14 a Petrograd City Conference of Bolsheviks was held. The conference approved Lenin's theses and made them the basis of its work.

Within a short while the local organizations of the Party had also approved Lenin's theses.

The whole Party, with the exception of a few individuals of the type of Kamenev, Rykov and Pyatakov, received Lenin's theses with profound satisfaction.

2. BEGINNING OF THE CRISIS OF THE PROVISIONAL GOVERNMENT. APRIL CONFERENCE OF THE BOLSHEVIK PARTY

While the Bolsheviks were preparing for the further development of the revolution, the Provisional Government continued to work against the people. On April 18, Milyukov, Minister of Foreign Affairs in the Provisional Government, informed the Allies that "the whole people desire to continue the World War until a decisive victory is achieved and that the Provisional Government intends fully to observe the obligations undertaken towards our allies."

Thus the Provisional Government pledged its loyalty to the tsarist treaties and promised to go on shedding as much of the people's blood as the imperialists might require for a "victorious finish."

On April 19 this statement ("Milyukov's note") became known to the workers and soldiers. On April 20 the Central Committee of the Bolshevik Party called upon the masses to protest against the imperialist policy of the Provisional Government. On April 20-21 (May 3-4), 1917, not less than 100,000 workers and soldiers, stirred to indignation by "Milyukov's note," took part in a demonstration. Their banners bore the demands: "Publish the secret treaties!" "Down with the war!" "All power to the Soviets!" The workers and soldiers marched from the outskirts of the city to the centre, where the Provisional Government was sitting. On the Nevsky Prospect and other places clashes with groups of bourgeois took place.

The more outspoken counter-revolutionaries, like General Kornilov, demanded that fire be opened on the demonstrators, and even gave orders to that effect. But the troops refused to carry out the orders.

During the demonstration, a small group of members of the Petrograd Party Committee (Bagdatyev and others) issued a slogan demanding the immediate overthrow of the Provisional Government. The Central Committee of the Bolshevik Party sharply condemned the conduct of these "Left" adventurers, considering this slogan untimely and incorrect, a slogan that hampered the Party in its efforts to win over a majority in the Soviets and ran counter to the Party line of a peaceful development of the revolution.

The events of April 20-21 signified the beginning of the crisis of the Provisional Government.

This was the first serious rift in the compromising policy of the Mensheviks and Socialist-Revolutionaries.

On May 2, 1917, under the pressure of the masses, Milyukov and Guchkov were dropped from the Provisional Government.

The first *coalition* Provisional Government was formed. It included, in addition to representatives of the bourgeoisie, Mensheviks (Skobelev and Tsereteli) and Socialist-Revolutionaries (Chernov, Kerensky and others).

Thus the Mensheviks, who in 1905 had declared it impermissible for representatives of the Social-Democratic Party to take part in a *revolutionary* Provisional Government, now found it permissible for their representatives to take part in a *counter-revolutionary* Provisional Government.

The Mensheviks and Socialist-Revolutionaries had thus deserted to the camp of the counter-revolutionary bourgeoisie.

On April 24, 1917, the Seventh (April) Conference of the Bolshevik Party assembled. For the first time in the existence of the Party a Bolshevik Conference met openly. In the history of the Party this conference holds a place of importance equal to that of a Party Congress.

The All-Russian April Conference showed that the Party was growing by leaps and bounds. The conference was attended by 133 delegates with vote and by 18 with voice but no vote. They represented 80,000 organized members of the Party.

The conference discussed and laid down the Party line on all basic questions of the war and revolution: the current situation, the war, the Provisional Government, the Soviets, the agrarian question, the national question, etc.

In his report, Lenin elaborated the principles he had already set forth in the April Theses. The task of the Party was to effect the transition from the first stage of the revolution, "which placed the power in the hands of the bourgeoisie ... *to the second* stage, which must place the power in the hands of the proletariat and the poorest strata of the peasantry" (*Lenin*). The course the Party should take was to prepare for the Socialist revolution. The immediate task of the Party was set forth by Lenin in the slogan: "All power to the Soviets!"

The slogan, "All power to the Soviets!" meant that it was necessary to put an end to the dual power, that is, the division of power between the Provisional Government and the Soviets, to transfer the *whole* power to the Soviets, and to drive the representatives of the landlords and capitalists out of the organs of government.

The conference resolved that one of the most important tasks of the Party was untiringly to explain to the masses the truth that "the Provisional Government is by its nature an organ of the rule of the landlords and the bourgeoisie," as well as to show how fatal was the compromising policy of the Socialist-Revolutionaries and Mensheviks who were deceiving the people with false promises and subjecting them to the blows of the imperialist war and counter-revolution.

Kamenev and Rykov opposed Lenin at the Conference. Echoing the Mensheviks, they asserted that Russia was not ripe for a Socialist revolution, and that only a bourgeois republic was possible in Russia. They recommended the Party and the working class to confine themselves to "controlling" the Provisional Government. In reality, they, like the Mensheviks, stood for the preservation of capitalism and of the power of the bourgeoisie.

Zinoviev, too, opposed Lenin at the conference; it was on the question whether the Bolshevik Party should remain within the Zimmerwald alliance, or break with it and form a new International. As the years of war had shown, while this alliance carried on propaganda for peace, it did not actually break with the bourgeois partisans of the war. Lenin therefore insisted on immediate withdrawal from this alliance and on the formation of a new, Communist International. Zinoviev proposed that the Party should remain within the Zimmerwald alliance. Lenin vigorously condemned Zinoviev's proposal and called his tactics "archopportunist and pernicious."

The April Conference also discussed the agrarian and national questions.

In connection with Lenin's report on the agrarian question, the conference adopted a resolution calling for the confiscation of the landed estates, which were to be placed at the disposal of the peasant committees, and for the nationalization of all the land. The Bolsheviks called upon the peasants to fight for the land, showing them that the Bolshevik Party was the only revolutionary party, the only party that was really helping the peasants to overthrow the landlords.

Of great importance was Comrade Stalin's report on the national question. Even before the revolution, on the eve of the imperialist war, Lenin and Stalin had elaborated the fundamental principles of the policy of the Bolshevik Party on the national question. Lenin and Stalin declared that the proletarian party must support the national liberation movement of the oppressed peoples against imperialism. Consequently, the Bolshevik Party advocated the right of nations to self-determination even to the point of secession and formation of independent states. This was the view defended by Comrade Stalin, in his report delivered at the conference on behalf of the Central Committee.

Lenin and Stalin were opposed by Pyatakov, who, together with Bukharin, had already during the war taken up a national-chauvinist stand on the national question. Pyatakov and Bukharin were opposed to the right of nations to self-determination.

The resolute and consistent position of the Party on the national question, its struggle for the complete equality of nations and for the abolition of all forms of national oppression and national inequality, secured for the Party the sympathy and support of the oppressed nationalities.

The text of the resolution on the national question adopted by the April Conference is as follows:

"The policy of national oppression, inherited from the autocracy and monarchy, is supported by the landlords, capitalists and petty bourgeoisie in order to protect their class privileges and to cause disunity among the workers of the various nationalities. Modern imperialism, which increases the striving to subjugate weak nations, is a new factor intensifying national oppression.

"To the extent that the elimination of national oppression is achievable at all in capitalist society, it is possible only under a consistently democratic republican system and state administration that guarantee complete equality for all nations and languages.

"The right of all the nations forming part of Russia freely to secede and form independent states must be recognized. To deny them this right, or to fail to take measures guaranteeing its practical realization, is equivalent to supporting a policy of seizure and annexation. It is only the recognition by the proletariat of the right of nations to secede that can ensure complete solidarity among the workers of the various nations and help to bring the nations closer together on truly democratic lines. . . .

"The right of nations freely to secede must not be confused with the expediency of secession of a given nation at a given moment. The party of the proletariat must decide the latter question quite independently in each particular case from the standpoint of the interests of the social development as a whole and of the interests of the class struggle of the proletariat for Socialism.

"The Party demands broad regional autonomy, the abolition of supervision from above, the abolition of a compulsory state language, and the determination of the boundaries of the self-governing and autonomous regions by the local population itself in accordance with the economic and social conditions, the national composition of the population, and so forth.

"The party of the proletariat resolutely rejects what is known as 'national cultural autonomy,' under which education, etc., is removed from the competence of the state and placed within the competence of some kind of national Diets. National cultural autonomy artificially divides the workers living in one locality, and even working in the same industrial enterprise, according to their various 'national cultures'; in other words it strengthens the ties between the workers and the bourgeois culture of individual nations, whereas the aim of the Social-Democrats is to develop the international culture of the world proletariat.

"The Party demands that a fundamental law shall be embodied in the constitution annulling all privileges enjoyed by any nation whatever and all infringements of the rights of national minorities.

"The interests of the working class demand that the workers of all the nationalities of Russia should have common proletarian organizations: political, trade union, educational institutions of the co-operatives and so forth. Only such common organizations of the workers of the various nationalities will make it possible for the proletariat to wage a successful struggle against international capital and bourgeois nationalism." (Lenin and Stalin, *The Russian Revolution*, pp. 52-3.)

Thus the April Conference exposed the opportunist, anti-Leninist stand of Kamenev, Zinoviev, Pyatakov, Bukharin, Rykov and their small following.

The conference unanimously supported Lenin by taking up a precise stand on all important questions and adopting a course leading to the victory of the Socialist revolution.

3. SUCCESSES OF THE BOLSHEVIK PARTY IN THE CAPITAL. ABORTIVE OFFENSIVE OF THE ARMIES OF THE PROVISIONAL GOVERNMENT. SUPPRESSION OF THE JULY DEMONSTRATION OF WORKERS AND SOLDIERS

On the basis of the decisions of the April Conference, the Party developed extensive activities in order to win over the masses, and to train and organize them for battle. The Party line in that period was, by patiently explaining the Bolshevik policy and exposing the compromising policy of the Mensheviks and Socialist-Revolutionaries, to isolate these parties from the masses and to win a majority in the Soviets.

In addition to the work in the Soviets, the Bolsheviks carried on extensive activities in the trade unions and in the factory committees.

Particularly extensive was the work of the Bolsheviks in the army. Military organizations began to arise everywhere. The Bolsheviks worked indefatigably at the front and in the rear to organize the soldiers and sailors. A particularly important part in making the soldiers active revolutionaries was played at the front by the Bolshevik newspaper, *Okopnaya Pravda* (*Trench Truth*).

Thanks to Bolshevik propaganda and agitation, already in the early months of the revolution the workers in many cities held new elections to the Soviets, especially to the district Soviets, drove out the Mensheviks and Socialist-Revolutionaries and elected followers of the Bolshevik Party in their stead.

The work of the Bolsheviks yielded splendid results, especially in Petrograd.

A Petrograd Conference of Factory Committees was held from May 30 to June 3, 1917. At this conference three-quarters of the delegates already supported the Bolsheviks. Almost the entire Petrograd proletariat supported the Bolshevik slogan—"All power to the Soviets!"

On June 3 (16), 1917, the First All-Russian Congress of Soviets met. The Bolsheviks were still in the minority in the Soviets; they had a little over 100 delegates at this congress, compared with 700 or 800 Mensheviks, Socialist-Revolutionaries and others.

At the First Congress of Soviets, the Bolsheviks insistently stressed the fatal consequences of compromise with the bourgeoisie and exposed the imperialist character of the war. Lenin made a speech at the congress in which he showed the correctness of the Bolshevik line and declared that only a government of Soviets could give bread to the working people, land to the peasants, secure peace and lead the country out of chaos.

A mass campaign was being conducted at that time in the working-class districts of Petrograd for the organization of a demonstration and for the presentation of demands to the Congress of Soviets. In its anxiety to prevent the workers from demonstrating without its authorization, and in the hope of utilizing the revolutionary sentiments of the masses for its own ends, the Executive Committee of the Petrograd Soviet decided to call a demonstration for June 18 (July 1). The Mensheviks and Socialist-Revolutionaries expected that it would take place under anti-Bolshevik slogans. The Bolshevik Party began energetic preparations for this demonstration. Comrade Stalin wrote in *Pravda* that ". . . it is our task to make sure that the demonstration in Petrograd on June 18 takes place under our revolutionary slogans."

The demonstration of June 18, 1917, was held at the graves of the martyrs of the revolution. It proved to be a veritable review of the forces of the Bolshevik Party. It revealed the growing revolutionary spirit of the masses and their growing confidence in the Bolshevik Party. The slogans displayed by the Mensheviks and Socialist-Revolutionaries calling for confidence in the Provisional Government and urging the continuation of the war were lost in a sea of Bolshevik slogans. Four hundred thousand demonstrators carried banners bearing the slogans: "Down with the war!" "Down with the ten capitalist Ministers!" "All power to the Soviets!"

It was a complete fiasco for the Mensheviks and Socialist-Revolutionaries, a fiasco for the Provisional Government in the capital of the country.

Nevertheless, the Provisional Government received the support of the First Congress of the Soviets and decided to continue the imperialist policy. On that very day, June 18, the Provisional Government, in obedience to the wishes of the British and French imperialists, drove the soldiers at the front to take the offensive. The bourgeoisie regarded this as the only means of putting an end to the revolution. In the event of the success of the offensive, the bourgeoisie hoped to take the whole power into its own hands, to push the Soviets out of the arena, and to crush the Bolsheviks. Again, in the event of its failure, the entire blame could be thrown upon the Bolsheviks by accusing them of disintegrating the army.

There could be no doubt that the offensive would fail. And fail it did. The soldiers were worn out, they did not understand the purpose of the offensive, they had no confidence in their officers who were alien to them, there was a shortage of artillery and shells. All this made the failure of the offensive a foregone conclusion.

The news of the offensive at the front, and then of its collapse, roused the capital. The indignation of the workers and soldiers knew no bounds. It became apparent that when the Provisional Government proclaimed a policy of peace it was hoodwinking the people, and that it wanted to continue the imperialist war. It became apparent that the All-Russian Central Executive Committee of the Soviets and the Petrograd Soviet were unwilling or unable to check the criminal deeds of the Provisional Government and themselves trailed in its wake.

The revolutionary indignation of the Petrograd workers and soldiers boiled over. On July 3 (16) spontaneous demonstrations started in the Vyborg District of Petrograd. They continued all day. The separate demonstrations grew into a huge general armed demonstration demanding the transfer of power to the Soviets. The Bolshevik Party was opposed to armed action at that time, for it considered that the revolutionary crisis had not yet matured, that the army and the provinces were not yet prepared to support an uprising in the capital, and that an isolated and premature rising might only make it easier for the counter-revolutionaries to crush the vanguard of the revolution. But when it became obviously impossible to keep the masses from demonstrating, the Party resolved to participate in the demonstration in order to lend it a peaceful and organized character. This the Bolshevik Party succeeded in doing. Hundreds of thousands of men and women marched to the headquarters of the Petrograd Soviet and the All-Russian Central Executive Committee of Soviets, where they demanded that the Soviets take the power into their own hands, break with the imperialist bourgeoisie, and pursue an active peace policy.

Notwithstanding the pacific character of the demonstration, reactionary units—detachments of officers and cadets—were brought out against it. The streets of Petrograd ran with the blood of workers and soldiers. The most ignorant and counter-revolutionary units of the army were summoned from the front to suppress the workers.

After suppressing the demonstration of workers and soldiers, the Mensheviks and Socialist-Revolutionaries, in alliance with the bourgeoisie and Whiteguard generals, fell upon the Bolshevik Party. The *Pravda* premises were wrecked. *Pravda, Soldatskaya Pravda* (*Soldiers' Truth*) and a number of other Bolshevik newspapers were suppressed. A worker named Voinov was killed by cadets in the street merely for selling *Listok Pravdy* (*Pravda Bulletin*). Disarming of the Red Guards began. Revolutionary units of the Petrograd garrison were withdrawn from the capital and dispatched to the trenches. Arrests were carried out in the rear and at the front. On July 7 a warrant was issued for Lenin's arrest. A number of prominent members of the Bolshevik Party were arrested. The Trud printing plant, where the Bolshevik publications were printed, was wrecked. The Procurator of the Petrograd Court of Sessions announced that Lenin and a number of other Bolsheviks were being charged with "high treason" and the organization of an armed uprising. The charge against Lenin was fabricated at the headquarters of General Denikin, and was based on the testimony of spies and agents-provocateurs.

Thus the coalition Provisional Government—which included such leading representatives of the Mensheviks and Socialist-Revolutionaries as Tsereteli, Skobelev, Kerensky and Chernov—sank to the depths of downright imperialism and counter-revolution. Instead of a policy of peace, it had adopted the policy of continuing war. Instead of protecting the democratic rights of the people, it had adopted the policy of nullifying these rights and suppressing the workers and soldiers by force of arms.

What Guchkov and Milyukov, the representatives of the bourgeoisie, had hesitated to do, was done by the "socialists" Kerensky and Tsereteli, Chernov and Skobelev.

The dual power had come to an end.

It ended in favour of the bourgeoisie, for the whole power had passed into the hands of the Provisional Government, while the Soviets, with their Socialist-Revolutionary and Menshevik leaders, had become an appendage of the Provisional Government.

The peaceful period of the revolution had ended, for now the bayonet had been placed on the agenda.

In view of the changed situation, the Bolshevik Party decided to change its tactics. It went underground, arranged for a safe hiding place for its leader, Lenin, and began to prepare for an uprising with the object of overthrowing the power of the bourgeoisie by force of arms and setting up the power of the Soviets.

4. THE BOLSHEVIK PARTY ADOPTS THE COURSE OF PREPARING FOR ARMED UPRISING. SIXTH PARTY CONGRESS

The Sixth Congress of the Bolshevik Party met in Petrograd in the midst of a frenzied campaign of Bolshevik-baiting in the bourgeois and petty-bourgeois press. It assembled ten years after the Fifth (London) Congress and five years after the Prague Conference of the Bolsheviks. The congress, which was held secretly, sat from July 26 to August 3, 1917. All that appeared in the press was an announcement of its convocation, the place of meeting was not divulged. The first sittings were held in the Vyborg District, the later ones in a school near the Narva Gate, where a House of Culture now stands. The bourgeois press demanded the arrest of the delegates. Detectives frantically scoured the city trying to discover the meeting place of the congress, but in vain.

And so, five months after the overthrow of tsardom, the Bolsheviks were compelled to meet in secret, while Lenin, the leader of the proletarian party, was forced to go into hiding and took refuge in a shanty near Razliv Station.

He was being hunted high and low by the sleuths of the Provisional Government and was therefore unable to attend the congress; but he

guided its labours from his place of concealment through his close col-
leagues and disciples in Petrograd: Stalin, Sverdlov, Molotov, Ordjonikidze.

The congress was attended by 157 delegates with vote and 128 with
voice but no vote. At that time the Party had a membership of about
240,000. On July 3, *i.e.*, before the workers' demonstration was broken
up, when the Bolsheviks were still functioning legally, the Party had 41
publications, of which 29 were in Russian and 12 in other languages.

The persecution to which the Bolsheviks and the working class were
subjected during the July days, far from diminishing the influence of
our Party, only enhanced it. The delegates from the provinces cited
numerous facts to show that the workers and soldiers had begun to desert
the Mensheviks and Socialist-Revolutionaries en masse, contemptuously
styling them "social-jailers."   Workers and soldiers belonging to the
Menshevik and Socialist-Revolutionary parties were tearing up their
membership cards in anger and disgust and applying for admission to
the Bolshevik Party.

The chief items discussed at the congress were the political report
of the Central Committee and the political situation.   Comrade Stalin
made the reports on both these questions.   He showed with the utmost
clarity how the revolution was growing and developing despite all the
efforts of the bourgeoisie to suppress it. He pointed out that the revolution had placed on the order of the day the task of establishing workers'
control over the production and distribution of products, of turning
over the land to the peasants, and of transferring the power from the
bourgeoisie to the working class and poor peasantry.   He said that the
revolution was assuming the character of a Socialist revolution.

The political situation in the country had changed radically after the
July days. The dual power had come to an end. The Soviets, led by
Socialist-Revolutionaries and Mensheviks, had refused to take over full
power and had therefore lost all power.   The power was now concentrated in the hands of the bourgeois Provisional Government, and the
latter was continuing to disarm the revolution, to smash its organizations
and to destroy the Bolshevik Party. All possibility of a peaceful development of the revolution had vanished. Only one thing remained, Comrade
Stalin said, namely, to take power by force, by overthrowing the Provisional Government.   And only the proletariat, in alliance with the poor
peasants, could take power by force.

The Soviets, still controlled by the Mensheviks and Socialist-Revolutionaries, had landed in the camp of the bourgeoisie, and under existing
conditions could be expected to act only as subsidiaries of the Provisional

Government. Now, after the July days, Comrade Stalin said, the slogan "All power to the Soviets!" had to be withdrawn. However, the temporary withdrawal of this slogan did not in any way imply a renunciation of the struggle for the power of the Soviets. It was not the Soviets in general, as organs of revolutionary struggle, that were in question, but only the existing Soviets, the Soviets controlled by the Mensheviks and Socialist-Revolutionaries.

"The peaceful period of the revolution has ended," said Comrade Stalin, "a non-peaceful period has begun, a period of clashes and explosions." (Lenin and Stalin, *Russian Revolution*, pp. 139-140.)

The Party was headed for armed uprising.

There were some at the congress who, reflecting the bourgeois influence, opposed the adoption of the course of Socialist revolution.

The Trotskyite Preobrazhensky proposed that the resolution on the conquest of power should state that the country could be directed towards Socialism only in the event of a proletarian revolution in the West.

This Trotskyite motion was opposed by Comrade Stalin. He said:

"The possibility is not excluded that Russia will be the country that will lay the road to Socialism.... We must discard the antiquated idea that only Europe can show us the way. There is dogmatic Marxism and creative Marxism. I stand by the latter." (p. 146.)

Bukharin, who held a Trotskyite position, asserted that the peasants supported the war, that they were in a bloc with the bourgeoisie and would not follow the working class.

Retorting to Bukharin, Comrade Stalin showed that there were different kinds of peasants: there were the rich peasants who supported the imperialist bourgeoisie, and there were the poor peasants who sought an alliance with the working class and would support it in a struggle for the victory of the revolution.

The congress rejected Preobrazhensky's and Bukharin's amendments and approved the resolution submitted by Comrade Stalin.

The congress discussed the economic platform of the Bolsheviks and approved it. Its main points were the confiscation of the landed estates and the nationalization of all the land, the nationalization of the banks, the nationalization of large-scale industry, and workers' control over production and distribution.

The congress stressed the importance of the fight for workers' control over production, which was later to play a significant part during the nationalization of the large industrial enterprises.

In all its decisions, the Sixth Congress particularly stressed Lenin's principle of an alliance between the proletariat and the poor peasantry as a condition for the victory of the Socialist revolution.

The congress condemned the Menshevik theory that the trade unions should be neutral. It pointed out that the momentous tasks confronting the working class of Russia could be accomplished only if the trade unions remained militant class organizations recognizing the political leadership of the Bolshevik Party.

The congress adopted a resolution on the Youth Leagues, which at that time frequently sprang up spontaneously. As a result of the Party's subsequent efforts it succeeded in definitely securing the adherence of these young organizations which became a reserve of the Party.

The congress discussed whether Lenin should appear for trial. Kamenev, Rykov, Trotsky and others had held even before the congress that Lenin ought to appear before the counter-revolutionary court. Comrade Stalin was vigorously opposed to Lenin's appearing for trial. This was also the stand of the Sixth Congress, for it considered that it would be a lynching, not a trial. The congress had no doubt that the bourgeoisie wanted only one thing—the physical destruction of Lenin as the most dangerous enemy of the bourgeoisie. The congress protested against the police persecution of the leaders of the revolutionary proletariat by the bourgeoisie, and sent a message of greeting to Lenin.

The Sixth Congress adopted new Party Rules. These rules provided that all Party organizations shall be built on the principle of *democratic centralism*.

This meant:

1) That all directing bodies of the Party, from top to bottom, shall be elected;

2) That Party bodies shall give periodical accounts of their activities to their respective Party organizations;

3) That there shall be strict Party discipline and the subordination of the minority to the majority;

4) That all decisions of higher bodies shall be absolutely binding on lower bodies and on all Party members.

The Party Rules provided that admission of new members to the Party shall be through local Party organizations on the recommendation of two Party members and on the sanction of a general membership meeting of the local organization.

The Sixth Congress admitted the *Mezhrayontsi* and their leader, Trotsky, into the Party. They were a small group that had existed in Petrograd since 1913 and consisted of Trotskyite-Mensheviks and a number of former Bolsheviks who had split away from the Party. During the war, the *Mezhrayontsi* were a Centrist organization. They fought the Bolsheviks, but in many respects disagreed with the Mensheviks, thus occupying an intermediate, centrist, vacillating position. During the Sixth Party Congress the *Mezhrayontsi* declared that they were in agreement with the Bolsheviks on all points and requested admission to the Party. The request was granted by the congress in the expectation that they would in time become real Bolsheviks. Some of the *Mezhrayontsi*, Volodarsky and Uritsky, for example, actually did become Bolsheviks. As to Trotsky and some of his close friends, they, as it later became apparent, had joined not to work in the interests of the Party, but to disrupt and destroy it from within.

The decisions of the Sixth Congress were all intended to prepare the proletariat and the poorest peasantry for an armed uprising. The Sixth Congress headed the Party for armed uprising, for the Socialist revolution.

The congress issued a Party manifesto calling upon the workers, soldiers and peasants to muster their forces for decisive battles with the bourgeoisie. It ended with the words:

> "Prepare, then, for new battles, comrades-in-arms! Staunchly, manfully and calmly, without yielding to provocation, muster your forces and form your fighting columns! Rally under the banner of the Party, proletarians and soldiers! Rally under our banner, downtrodden of the villages!"

5. GENERAL KORNILOV'S PLOT AGAINST THE REVOLUTION. SUPPRESSION OF THE PLOT. PETROGRAD AND MOSCOW SOVIETS GO OVER TO THE BOLSHEVIKS

Having seized all power, the bourgeoisie began preparations to destroy the now weakened Soviets and to set up an open counter-revolutionary dictatorship. The millionaire Ryabushinsky insolently declared that the way out of the situation was "for the gaunt hand of famine, of destitution of the people, to seize the false friends of the people—the democratic Soviets and Committees—by the throat." At the front, courts-martial wreaked savage vengeance on the soldiers, and meted out death sentences wholesale. On August 3, 1917, General Kornilov, the Commander-in-Chief, demanded the introduction of the death penalty behind the lines as well.

On August 12, a Council of State, convened by the Provisional

Government to mobilize the forces of the bourgeoisie and the landlords, opened in the Grand Theatre in Moscow. The Council was attended chiefly by representatives of the landlords, the bourgeoisie, the generals, the officers and Cossacks. The Soviets were represented by Mensheviks and Socialist-Revolutionaries.

In protest against the convocation of the Council of State, the Bolsheviks on the day of its opening called a general strike in Moscow in which the majority of the workers took part. Simultaneously, strikes took place in a number of other cities.

The Socialist-Revolutionary Kerensky threatened in a fit of boasting at the Council to suppress "by iron and blood" every attempt at a revolutionary movement, including unauthorized attempts of the peasants to seize the lands of the landlords.

The counter-revolutionary General Kornilov bluntly demanded that "the Committees and Soviets be abolished."

Bankers, merchants and manufacturers flocked to Kornilov at General Headquarters, promising him money and support.

Representatives of the "Allies," Britain and France, also came to General Kornilov, demanding that action against the revolution be not delayed.

General Kornilov's plot against the revolution was coming to a head.

Kornilov made his preparations openly. In order to distract attention, the conspirators started a rumour that the Bolsheviks were preparing an uprising in Petrograd to take place on August 27—the end of the first six months of the revolution. The Provisional Government, headed by Kerensky, furiously attacked the Bolsheviks, and intensified the terror against the proletarian party. At the same time, General Kornilov massed troops in order to move them against Petrograd, abolish the Soviets and set up a military dictatorship.

Kornilov had come to a preliminary agreement with Kerensky regarding his counter-revolutionary action. But no sooner had Kornilov's action begun than Kerensky made an abrupt right-about-face and dissociated himself from his ally. Kerensky feared that the masses who would rise against the Kornilovites and crush them would at the same time sweep away Kerensky's bourgeois government as well, unless it at once dissociated itself from the Kornilov affair.

On August 25 Kornilov moved the Third Mounted Corps under the command of General Krymov against Petrograd, declaring that he intended to "save the fatherland." In face of the Kornilov revolt, the Central Committee of the Bolshevik Party called upon the workers and soldiers to put up active armed resistance to the counter-revolution. The workers hurriedly began to arm and prepared to resist. The Red Guard detachments grew enormously during these days. The trade unions mobilized their members. The revolutionary military units in Petrograd were also held in readiness for battle. Trenches were dug around Petrograd, barbed wire entanglements erected, and the railway tracks leading to the city were torn up. Several thousand armed sailors arrived from Kronstadt to defend the city. Delegates were sent to the "Savage Division" which was advancing on Petrograd; when these delegates explained the purpose of Kornilov's action to the Caucasian mountaineers of whom the "Savage Division" was made up, they refused to advance. Agitators were also dispatched to other Kornilov units. Wherever there was danger, Revolutionary Committees and headquarters were set up to fight Kornilov.

In those days the mortally terrified Socialist-Revolutionary and Menshevik leaders, Kerensky among them, turned for protection to the Bolsheviks, for they were convinced that the Bolsheviks were the only effective force in the capital that was capable of routing Kornilov.

But while mobilizing the masses to crush the Kornilov revolt, the Bolsheviks did not discontinue their struggle against the Kerensky government. They exposed the government of Kerensky, the Mensheviks and the Socialist-Revolutionaries, to the masses, pointing out that their whole policy was in effect assisting Kornilov's counter-revolutionary plot.

The result of these measures was that the Kornilov revolt was crushed. General Krymov committed suicide. Kornilov and his fellow-conspirators, Denikin and Lukomsky, were arrested. (Very soon, however, Kerensky had them released.)

The rout of the Kornilov revolt revealed in a flash the relative strength of the revolution and the counter-revolution. It showed that the whole counter-revolutionary camp was doomed, from the generals and the Constitutional-Democratic Party to the Mensheviks and Socialist-Revolutionaries who had become entangled in the meshes of the bourgeoisie. It became obvious that the influence of the Mensheviks and Socialist-Revolutionaries among the masses had been completely undermined by the policy of prolonging the unbearable strain of the war, and by the economic chaos caused by the protracted war.

The defeat of the Kornilov revolt further showed that the Bolshevik Party had grown to be the decisive force of the revolution and was capable of foiling any attempt at counter-revolution. Our Party was not yet the ruling party, but during the Kornilov days it acted as the real ruling power, for its instructions were unhesitatingly carried out by the workers and soldiers.

Lastly, the rout of the Kornilov revolt showed that the seemingly dead Soviets actually possessed tremendous latent power of revolutionary resistance. There could be no doubt that it was the Soviets and their Revolutionary Committees that barred the way of the Kornilov troops and broke their strength.

The struggle against Kornilov put new vitality into the languishing Soviets of Workers' and Soldiers' Deputies. It freed them from the sway of the policy of compromise. It led them into the open road of revolutionary struggle, and turned them towards the Bolshevik Party.

The influence of the Bolsheviks in the Soviets grew stronger than ever.

Their influence spread rapidly in the rural districts as well.

The Kornilov revolt made it clear to the broad masses of the peasantry that if the landlords and generals succeeded in smashing the Bolsheviks and the Soviets, they would next attack the peasantry. The mass of the poor peasants therefore began to rally closer to the Bolsheviks. As to the middle peasants, whose vacillations had retarded the development of the revolution in the period from April to August 1917, after the rout of Kornilov they definitely began to swing towards the Bolshevik Party, joining forces with the poor peasants. The broad masses of the peasantry were coming to realize that only the Bolshevik Party could deliver them from the war, and that only this Party was capable of crushing the landlords and was prepared to turn over the land to the peasants. The months of September and October 1917 witnessed a tremendous increase in the number of seizures of landed estates by the peasants. Unauthorized ploughing of the fields of landlords became widespread. The peasants had taken the road of revolution and neither coaxing nor punitive expeditions could any longer halt them.

The tide of revolution was rising.

There ensued a period of revival of the Soviets, of a change in their composition, their *bolshevization*. Factories, mills and military units held new elections and sent to the Soviets representatives of the Bolshevik Party in place of Mensheviks and Socialist-Revolutionaries. On August 31, the day following the victory over Kornilov, the Petrograd Soviet endorsed the Bolshevik policy. The old Menshevik and Socialist-Revolutionary Presidium of the Petrograd Soviet, headed by Chkheidze, resigned, thus clearing the way for the Bolsheviks. On September 5, the Moscow Soviet of Workers' Deputies went over to the Bolsheviks. The Socialist-Revolutionary and Menshevik Presidium of the Moscow Soviet also resigned and left the way clear for the Bolsheviks.

This meant that the chief conditions for a successful uprising were now ripe.

The slogan "All power to the Soviets!" was again on the order of the day.

But it was no longer the old slogan, the slogan of transferring the power to Menshevik and Socialist-Revolutionary Soviets. This time it was a slogan calling for an uprising of the Soviets against the Provisional Government, the object being to transfer the whole power in the country to the Soviets now led by the Bolsheviks.

Disintegration set in among the compromising parties.

Under the pressure of the revolutionary peasants, a Left wing formed within the Socialist-Revolutionary Party, known as the "Left" Socialist-Revolutionaries, who expressed their disapproval of the policy of compromise with the bourgeoisie.

Among the Mensheviks, too, their appeared a group of "Lefts," the so-called "Internationalists," who gravitated towards the Bolsheviks.

As to the Anarchists, a group whose influence was insignificant to start with, they now definitely disintegrated into minute groups, some of which merged with criminal elements, thieves and provocateurs, the dregs of society; others became expropriators "by conviction," robbing the peasants and small townfolk, and appropriating the premises and funds of workers' clubs; while others still openly went over to the camp of the counter-revolutionaries, and devoted themselves to feathering their own nests as menials of the bourgeoisie. They were all opposed to authority of any kind, particularly and especially to the revolutionary authority of the workers and peasants, for they knew that a revolutionary government would not allow them to rob the people and steal public property.

After the rout of Kornilov, the Mensheviks and Socialist-Revolutionaries made one more attempt to stem the rising tide of revolution. With this purpose in view, on September 12, 1917, they convened an All-Russian Democratic Conference, consisting of representatives of the Socialist parties, the compromising Soviets, trade unions, Zemstvos, commercial and industrial circles and military units. The conference set up a Provisional Council of the Republic, known as the Pre-parliament. The compromisers hoped with the help of the Pre-parliament to halt the revolution and to divert the country from the path of a Soviet revolution to the path of bourgeois constitutional development, the path of bourgeois parliamentarism. But this was a hopeless attempt on the part of political bankrupts to turn back the wheel of revolution. It was bound to end in a fiasco, and end in a fiasco it did. The workers jeered at the parliamentary efforts of the compromisers and called the *Predparlament* (Pre-parliament) a *"predbannik"* ("pre-bath-house").

The Central Committee of the Bolshevik Party decided to boycott the Pre-parliament. True, the Bolshevik group in the Pre-parliament, consisting of people like Kamenev and Teodorovich, were loath to leave it, but the Central Committee of the Party compelled them to do so.

Kamenev and Zinoviev stubbornly insisted on participation in the Pre-parliament, striving thereby to divert the Party from its preparations for the uprising. Comrade Stalin, speaking at a meeting of the Bolshevik group of the All-Russian Democratic Conference, vigorously opposed participation in the Pre-parliament. He called the Pre-parliament a "Kornilov abortion."

Lenin and Stalin considered that it would be a grave mistake to participate in the Pre-parliament even for a short time, for it might encourage in the masses the false hope that the Pre-parliament could really do something for the working people.

At the same time, the Bolsheviks made intensive preparations for the convocation of the Second Congress of Soviets, in which they expected to have a majority. Under the pressure of the Bolshevik Soviets, and notwithstanding the subterfuges of the Mensheviks and Socialist-Revolutionaries on the All-Russian Central Executive Committee, the Second All-Russian Congress of Soviets was called for the second half of October 1917.

6. OCTOBER UPRISING IN PETROGRAD AND ARREST OF THE PRO-
VISIONAL GOVERNMENT. SECOND CONGRESS OF SOVIETS AND
FORMATION OF THE SOVIET GOVERNMENT. DECREES OF THE
SECOND CONGRESS OF SOVIETS ON PEACE AND LAND. VICTORY
OF THE SOCIALIST REVOLUTION. REASONS FOR THE VICTORY
OF THE SOCIALIST REVOLUTION

The Bolsheviks began intensive preparations for the uprising. Lenin declared that, having secured a majority in the Soviets of Workers' and Soldiers' Deputies in both the capitals—Moscow and Petrograd—the Bolsheviks could and should take the state power into their own hands. Reviewing the path that had been traversed, Lenin stressed the fact that "the majority of the people are *for* us." In his articles and letters to the Central Committee and the Bolshevik organizations, Lenin outlined a detailed plan for the uprising showing how the army units, the navy and the Red Guards should be used, what key positions in Petrograd should be seized in order to ensure the success of the uprising, and so forth.

On October 7, Lenin secretly arrived in Petrograd from Finland. On October 10, 1917, the historic meeting of the Central Committee of the Party took place at which it was decided to launch the armed uprising within the next few days. The historic resolution of the Central Committee of the Party, drawn up by Lenin, stated:

> "The Central Committee recognizes that the international position of the Russian revolution (the revolt in the German navy which is an extreme manifestation of the growth throughout Europe of the world Socialist revolution; the threat of conclusion of peace by the imperialists with the object of strangling the revolution in Russia) as well as its military position (the indubitable decision of the Russian bourgeoisie and Kerensky and Co. to surrender Petrograd to the Germans), and the fact that the proletarian party has gained a majority in the Soviets—all this, taken in conjunction with the peasant revolt and the swing of popular confidence towards our Party (the elections in Moscow), and, finally, the obvious preparations being made for a second Kornilov affair (the withdrawal of troops from Petrograd, the dispatch of Cossacks to Petrograd, the surrounding of Minsk by Cossacks, etc.)—all this places the armed uprising on the order of the day.
>
> "Considering therefore that an armed uprising is inevitable, and that the time for it is fully ripe, the Central Committee instructs all Party organizations to be guided accordingly, and to discuss and decide all practical questions (the Congress of Soviets of the Northern Region, the withdrawal of troops from Petrograd, the action of our people in Moscow and Minsk, etc.) from this point of view."
> (Lenin, *Selected Works*, Vol. VI, p. 303.)

Two members of the Central Committee, Kamenev and Zinoviev, spoke and voted against this historic decision. Like the Mensheviks, they dreamed of a bourgeois parliamentary republic, and slandered the working class by asserting that it was not strong enough to carry out a Socialist revolution, that it was not mature enough to take power.

Although at this meeting Trotsky did not vote against the resolution directly, he moved an amendment which would have reduced the chances of the uprising to nought and rendered it abortive. He proposed that the uprising should not be started before the Second Congress of Soviets met, a proposal which meant delaying the uprising, divulging its date, and forewarning the Provisional Government.

The Central Committee of the Bolshevik Party sent its represent-
atives to the Donetz Basin, the Urals, Helsingfors, Kronstadt, the South-
Western Front and other places to organize the uprising. Comrades
Voroshilov, Molotov, Dzerzhinsky, Ordjonikidze, Kirov, Kaganovich,
Kuibyshev, Frunze, Yaroslavsky and others were specially assigned by
the Party to direct the uprising in the provinces. Comrade Zhdanov
carried on the work among the armed forces in Shadrinsk, in the Urals.
Comrade Yezhov made preparations for an uprising of the soldiers on the
Western Front, in Byelorussia. The representatives of the Central Committee acquainted the leading members of the Bolshevik organizations
in the provinces with the plan of the uprising and mobilized them in
readiness to support the uprising in Petrograd.

On the instructions of the Central Committee of the Party, a *Revolutionary Military Committee* of the Petrograd Soviet was set up.
This body became the legally functioning headquarters of the uprising.

Meanwhile the counter-revolutionaries, too, were hastily mustering
their forces. The officers of the army formed a counter-revolutionary
organization known as the Officers' League. Everywhere the counter-
revolutionaries set up headquarters for the formation of shock-battalions.
By the end of October the counter-revolutionaries had 43 shock battalions at their command. Special battalions of Cavaliers of the Cross
of St. George were formed.

Kerensky's government considered the question of transferring the
seat of government from Petrograd to Moscow. This made it clear that
it was preparing to surrender Petrograd to the Germans in order to fore-
stall the uprising in the city. The protest of the Petrograd workers and
soldiers compelled the Provisional Government to remain in Petrograd.

On October 16 an enlarged meeting of the Central Committee of
the Party was held. This meeting elected a *Party Centre*, headed by
Comrade Stalin, to direct the uprising. This Party Centre was the
leading core of the Revolutionary Military Committee of the Petrograd
Soviet and had practical direction of the whole uprising.

At the meeting of the Central Committee the capitulators Zinoviev
and Kamenev again opposed the uprising. Meeting with a rebuff, they
came out openly in the press against the uprising, against the Party. On
October 18 the Menshevik newspaper, *Novaya Zhizn*, printed a statement by Kamenev and Zinoviev declaring that the Bolsheviks were
making preparations for an uprising, and that they (Kamenev and
Zinoviev) considered it an adventurous gamble. Kamenev and Zinoviev
thus disclosed to the enemy the decision of the Central Committee regarding the uprising, they revealed that an uprising had been planned

to take place within a few days. This was treachery. Lenin wrote in this connection: "Kamenev and Zinoviev have *betrayed* the decision of the Central Committee of their Party on the armed uprising to Rod-zyanko and Kerensky." Lenin put before the Central Committee the question of Zinoviev's and Kamenev's expulsion from the Party.

Forewarned by the traitors, the enemies of the revolution at once began to take measures to prevent the uprising and to destroy the direct-ing staff of the revolution—the Bolshevik Party. The Provisional Gov-ernment called a secret meeting which decided upon measures for com-bating the Bolsheviks. On October 19 the Provisional Government hastily summoned troops from the front to Petrograd. The streets were heavily patrolled. The counter-revolutionaries succeeded in massing especially large forces in Moscow. The Provisional Government drew up a plan: on the eve of the Second Congress of Soviets, the Smolny—the headquarters of the Bolshevik Central Committee—was to be at-tacked and occupied and the Bolshevik directing centre destroyed. For this purpose the government summoned to Petrograd troops in whose loyalty it believed.

But the days and even the hours of the Provisional Government were already numbered. Nothing could now halt the victorious march of the Socialist revolution.

On October 21 the Bolsheviks sent commissars of the Revolutionary Military Committee to all revolutionary army units. Throughout the remaining days before the uprising energetic preparations for ac-tion were made in the army units and in the mills and factories. Precise instructions were also issued to the warships *Aurora* and *Zarya Svobody*.

At a meeting of the Petrograd Soviet, Trotsky in a fit of boasting blabbed to the enemy the date on which the Bolsheviks had planned to begin the armed uprising. In order not to allow Kerensky's government to frustrate the uprising, the Central Committee of the Party decided to start and carry it through before the appointed time, and set its date for the day before the opening of the Second Congress of Soviets.

Kerensky began his attack on the early morning of October 24 (November 6) by ordering the suppression of the central organ of the Bolshevik Party, *Rabochy Put* (*Workers' Path*), and the dispatch of armoured cars to its editorial premises and to the printing plant of the Bolsheviks. By 10 a.m., however, on the instructions of Comrade Stalin, Red Guards and revolutionary soldiers pressed back the armoured cars and placed a reinforced guard over the printing plant and the *Rabochy Put* editorial offices. Towards 11 a.m. *Rabochy Put* came out with a call for the *overthrow* of the Provisional Government.   Simultaneously, on the instructions of the Party Centre of the uprising, detachments of revolutionary soldiers and Red Guards were rushed to the Smolny.

The uprising had begun.

On the night of October 24 Lenin arrived at the Smolny and assumed personal direction of the uprising.   All that night revolutionary units of the army and detachments of the Red Guard kept arriving at the Smolny.   The Bolsheviks directed them to the centre of the capital, to surround the Winter Palace, where the Provisional Government had entrenched itself.

On October 25 (November 7), Red Guards and revolutionary troops occupied the railway stations, post office, telegraph office, the Ministries and the State Bank.

The Pre-parliament was dissolved.

The Smolny, the headquarters of the Petrograd Soviet and of the Bolshevik Central Committee, became the headquarters of the revolution, from which all fighting orders emanated.

The Petrograd workers in those days showed what a splendid schooling they had received under the guidance of the Bolshevik Party.   The revolutionary units of the army, prepared for the uprising by the work of the Bolsheviks, carried out fighting orders with precision and fought side by side with the Red Guard.   The navy did not lag behind the army.   Kronstadt was a stronghold of the Bolshevik Party, and had long since refused to recognize the authority of the Provisional Government.   The cruiser *Aurora* trained its guns on the Winter Palace, and on October 25 their thunder ushered in a new era, the era of the Great Socialist Revolution.

On October 25 (November 7) the Bolsheviks issued a manifesto "To the Citizens of Russia" announcing that the bourgeois Provisional Government had been deposed and that state power had passed into the hands of the Soviets.

The Provisional Government had taken refuge in the Winter Palace under the protection of cadets and shock battalions.   On the night of October 25 the revolutionary workers, soldiers and sailors took the Winter Palace by storm and arrested the Provisional Government.

The armed uprising in Petrograd had won.

The Second All-Russian Congress of Soviets opened in the Smolny at 10:45 p.m. on October 25 (November 7), 1917, when the uprising in Petrograd was already in the full flush of victory and the power in the capital had actually passed into the hands of the Petrograd Soviet.

The Bolsheviks secured an overwhelming majority at the congress.

The Mensheviks, Bundists and Right Socialist-Revolutionaries, seeing that their day was done, left the congress, announcing that they refused to take any part in its labours. In a statement which was read at the Congress of Soviets they referred to the October Revolution as a "military plot." The congress condemned the Mensheviks and Socialist-Revolutionaries and, far from regretting their departure, welcomed it, for, it declared, thanks to the withdrawal of the traitors the congress had become a real revolutionary congress of workers' and soldiers' deputies.

The congress proclaimed that all power had passed to the Soviets:

> "Backed by the will of the vast majority of the workers, soldiers and peasants, backed by the victorious uprising of the workers and the garrison which had taken place in Petrograd, the Congress takes the power into its own hands"—the proclamation of the Second Congress of Soviets read.

On the night of October 26 (November 8), 1917, the Second Congress of Soviets adopted the *Decree on Peace*. The congress called upon the belligerent countries to conclude an immediate armistice for a period of not less than three months to permit negotiations for peace. While addressing itself to the governments and peoples of all the belligerent countries, the congress at the same time appealed to "the class-conscious workers of the three most advanced nations of mankind and the largest states participating in the present war, namely, Great Britain, France and Germany." It called upon these workers to help "to bring to a successful conclusion the cause of peace, and at the same time the cause of the emancipation of the toiling and exploited masses of the population from all forms of slavery and all forms of exploitation."

That same night the Second Congress of Soviets adopted the *Decree on Land*, which proclaimed that "landlord ownership of land is abolished forthwith without compensation." The basis adopted for this agrarian law was a Mandate (*Nakaz*) of the peasantry, compiled from 242 mandates of peasants of various localities. In accordance with this Mandate private ownership of land was to be abolished forever and replaced by public, or state ownership of the land. The lands of the landlords, of the tsar's family and of the monasteries were to be turned over to all the toilers for their free use.

By this decree the peasantry received from the October Socialist Revolution over 150,000,000 dessiatins (over 400,000,000 acres) of land that had formerly belonged to the landlords, the bourgeoisie, the tsar's family, the monasteries and the churches.

Moreover, the peasants were released from paying rent to the landlords, which had amounted to about 500,000,000 gold rubles annually.

All mineral resources (oil, coal, ores, etc.), forests and waters became the property of the people.

Lastly, the Second All-Russian Congress of Soviets formed the first Soviet Government—the Council of People's Commissars—which consisted entirely of Bolsheviks. Lenin was elected Chairman of the first Council of People's Commissars.

This ended the labours of the historic Second Congress of Soviets.

The congress delegates dispersed to spread the news of the victory of the Soviets in Petrograd and to ensure the extension of the power of the Soviets to the whole country.

Not everywhere did power pass to the Soviets at once. While in Petrograd the Soviet Government was already in existence, in Moscow fierce and stubborn fighting continued in the streets several days longer. In order to prevent the power from passing into the hands of the Moscow Soviet, the counter-revolutionary Menshevik and Socialist-Revolutionary parties, together with Whiteguards and cadets, started an armed fight against the workers and soldiers. It took several days to rout the rebels and to establish the power of the Soviets in Moscow.

In Petrograd itself, and in several of its districts, counter-revolutionary attempts to overthrow the Soviet power were made in the very first days of the victory of the revolution. On November 10, 1917, Kerensky, who during the uprising had fled from Petrograd to the Northern Front, mustered several Cossack units and dispatched them against Petrograd under the command of General Krasnov. On November 11, 1917, a counter-revolutionary organization calling itself the "Committee for the Salvation of the Fatherland and the Revolution," headed by Socialist-Revolutionaries, raised a mutiny of cadets in Petrograd. But the mutiny was suppressed by sailors and Red Guards without much difficulty by the evening of the same day, and on November 13 General Krasnov was routed near the Pulkovo Hills. Lenin personally directed the suppression of the anti-Soviet mutiny, just as he had personally directed the October uprising. His inflexible firmness and calm confidence of victory inspired and welded the masses. The enemy was smashed. Krasnov was taken prisoner and pledged his "word of honour" to terminate the struggle against the Soviet power. And on his "word of honour" he was released. But, as it later transpired, the general violated his word of honour. As to Kerensky, disguised as a woman, he managed to "disappear in an unknown direction."

In Moghilev, at the General Headquarters of the Army, General Dukhonin, the Commander-in-Chief, also attempted a mutiny. When the Soviet Government instructed him to start immediate negotiations for an armistice with the German Command, he refused to obey. Thereupon Dukhonin was dismissed by order of the Soviet Government. The counter-revolutionary General Headquarters was broken up and Dukhonin himself was killed by the soldiers, who had risen against him.

Certain notorious opportunists within the Party—Kamenev, Zinoviev, Rykov, Shlyapnikov and others—also made a sally against the Soviet power. They demanded the formation of an "all-Socialist government" to include Mensheviks and Socialist-Revolutionaries, who had just been overthrown by the October Revolution. On November 15, 1917, the Central Committee of the Bolshevik Party adopted a resolution rejecting agreement with these counter-revolutionary parties, and proclaiming Kamenev and Zinoviev strikebreakers of the revolution. On November 17, Kamenev, Zinoviev, Rykov and Milyutin, disagreeing with the policy of the Party, announced their resignation from the Central Committee. That same day, November 17, Nogin, in his own name and in the names of Rykov, V. Milyutin, Teodorovich, A. Shlyapnikov, D. Ryazanov, Yurenev and Larin, members of the Council of People's Commissars, announced their disagreement with the policy of the Central Committee of the Party and their resignation from the Council of People's Commissars. The desertion of this handful of cowards caused jubilation among the enemies of the October Revolution. The bourgeoisie and its henchmen proclaimed with malicious glee the collapse of Bolshevism and presaged the early end of the Bolshevik Party. But not for a moment was the Party shaken by this handful of deserters. The Central Committee of the Party contemptuously branded them as deserters from the revolution and accomplices of the bourgeoisie, and proceeded with its work.

As to the "Left" Socialist-Revolutionaries, they, desirous of retaining their influence over the peasant masses, who definitely sympathized with the Bolsheviks, decided not to quarrel with the latter and for the time being to maintain a united front with them. The Congress of Peasant Soviets which took place in November 1917 recognized all the gains of the October Socialist Revolution and endorsed the decrees of the Soviet Government. An agreement was concluded with the "Left" Socialist-Revolutionaries and several of their number were given posts on the Council of People's Commissars (Kolegayev, Spiridonova, Proshyan and Steinberg). However, this agreement lasted only until the signing of the Peace of Brest-Litovsk and the formation of the Committees of the Poor Peasants, when a deep cleavage took place among the peasantry and when the "Left" Socialist-Revolutionaries, coming more and more to reflect the interests of the kulaks, started a revolt against the Bolsheviks and were routed by the Soviet Government.

In the interval from October 1917 to February 1918 the Soviet revolution spread throughout the vast territory of the country at such a rapid rate that Lenin referred to it as a "triumphal march" of Soviet power.

The Great October Socialist Revolution had won.

There were several reasons for this comparatively easy victory of the Socialist revolution in Russia. The following chief reasons should be noted:

1) The October Revolution was confronted by an enemy so comparatively weak, so badly organized and so politically inexperienced as the Russian bourgeoisie. Economically still weak, and completely dependent on government contracts, the Russian bourgeoisie lacked sufficient political self-reliance and initiative to find a way out of the situation. It had neither the experience of the French bourgeoisie, for example, in political combination and political chicanery on a broad scale nor the schooling of the British bourgeoisie in broadly conceived crafty compromise. It had but recently sought to reach an understanding with the tsar; yet now that the tsar had been overthrown by the February Revolution, and the bourgeoisie itself had come to power, it was unable to think of anything better than to continue the policy of the detested tsar in all its essentials. Like the tsar, it stood for "war to a victorious finish," although the war was beyond the country's strength and had reduced the people and the army to a state of utter exhaustion. Like the tsar, it stood for the preservation in the main of big landed property, although the peasantry was perishing from lack of land and the weight of the landlord's yoke. As to its labour policy the Russian bourgeoisie outstripped even the tsar in its hatred of the working class, for it not only strove to preserve and strengthen the yoke of the factory owners, but to render it intolerable by wholesale lockouts.

It is not surprising that the people saw no essential difference between the policy of the tsar and the policy of the bourgeoisie, and that they transferred their hatred of the tsar to the Provisional Government of the bourgeoisie.

As long as the compromising Socialist-Revolutionary and Menshevik parties possessed a certain amount of influence among the people, the bourgeoisie could use them as a screen and preserve its power. But after the Mensheviks and Socialist-Revolutionaries had exposed themselves as agents of the imperialist bourgeoisie, thus forfeiting their influence among the people, the bourgeoisie and its Provisional Government were left without a support.

2) The October Revolution was headed by so revolutionary a class

as the working class of Russia, a class which had been steeled in battle, which had in a short space passed through two revolutions, and which by the eve of the third revolution had won recognition as the leader of the people in the struggle for peace, land, liberty and Socialism. If the revolution had not had a leader like the working class of Russia, a leader that had earned the confidence of the people, there would have been no alliance between the workers and peasants, and without such an alliance the victory of the October Revolution would have been impossible.

3) The working class of Russia had so effective an ally in the revolution as the poor peasantry, which comprised the overwhelming majority of the peasant population. The experience of eight months of revolution —which may unhesitatingly be compared to the experience of several decades of "normal" development—had not been in vain as far as the mass of the labouring peasants were concerned. During this period they had had the opportunity to test all the parties of Russia in practice and convince themselves that neither the Constitutional-Democrats, nor the Socialist-Revolutionaries and Mensheviks would seriously quarrel with the landlords or sacrifice themselves for the interests of the peasants; that there was only one party in Russia—the Bolshevik Party—which was in no way connected with the landlords and which was prepared to crush them in order to satisfy the needs of the peasants. This served as a solid basis for the alliance of the proletariat and the poor peasantry. The existence of this alliance between the working class and the poor peasantry determined the conduct of the middle peasants, who had long been vacillating and only on the eve of the October uprising wholeheartedly swung over towards the revolution and joined forces with the poor peasants.

It goes without saying that without this alliance the October Revolution could not have been victorious.

4) The working class was headed by a party so tried and tested in political battles as the Bolshevik Party. Only a party like the Bolshevik Party, courageous enough to lead the people in decisive attack, and cautious enough to keep clear of all the submerged rocks in its path to the goal—only such a party could so skilfully merge into one common revolutionary torrent such diverse revolutionary movements as the general democratic movement for peace, the peasant democratic movement for the seizure of the landed estates, the movement of the oppressed nationalities for national liberation and national equality, and the Socialist movement of the proletariat for the overthrow of the bourgeoisie and the establishment of the dictatorship of the proletariat.

Undoubtedly, the merging of these diverse revolutionary streams into one common powerful revolutionary torrent decided the fate of capitalism in Russia.

5) The October Revolution began at a time when the imperialist war was still at its height, when the principal bourgeois states were split into two hostile camps, and when, absorbed in mutual war and undermining each other's strength, they were unable to intervene effectively in "Russian affairs" and actively to oppose the October Revolution.

This undoubtedly did much to facilitate the victory of the October Socialist Revolution.

7. STRUGGLE OF THE BOLSHEVIK PARTY TO CONSOLIDATE THE SOVIET POWER. PEACE OF BREST-LITOVSK. SEVENTH PARTY CONGRESS

In order to consolidate the Soviet power, the old, bourgeois state machine had to be shattered and destroyed and a new, Soviet state machine set up in its place. Further, it was necessary to destroy the survivals of the division of society into estates and the regime of national oppression, to abolish the privileges of the church, to suppress the counter-revolutionary press and counter-revolutionary organizations of all kinds, legal and illegal, and to dissolve the bourgeois Constitutent Assembly. Following on the nationalization of the land, all large-scale industry had also to be nationalized. And, lastly, the state of war had to be ended, for the war was hampering the consolidation of the Soviet power more than anything else.

All these measures were carried out in the course of a few months, from the end of 1917 to the middle of 1918.

The sabotage of the officials of the old Ministries, engineered by the Socialist-Revolutionaries and Mensheviks, was smashed and overcome. The Ministries were abolished and replaced by Soviet administrative machinery and appropriate People's Commissariats. The Supreme Council of National Economy was set up to administer the industry of the country. The All-Russian Extraordinary Commission (Vecheka) was created to combat counter-revolution and sabotage, and F. Dzerzhinsky was placed at its head. The formation of a Red Army and Navy was decreed. The Constituent Assembly, the elections to which had largely been held prior to the October Revolution, and which refused to recognize the decrees of the Second Congress of Soviets on peace, land and the transfer of power to the Soviets, was dissolved.

In order to put an end to the survivals of feudalism, the estates system, and inequality in all spheres of social life, decrees were issued abolishing the estates, removing restrictions based on nationality or religion, separating the church from the state and the schools from the church, establishing equality for women and the equality of all the nationalities of Russia.

A special edict of the Soviet Government known as "The Declaration of Rights of the Peoples of Russia" laid down as a law the right of the peoples of Russia to unhampered development and complete equality.

In order to undermine the economic power of the bourgeoisie and to create a new, Soviet national economy, and, in the first place, to create a new, Soviet industry, the banks, railways, foreign trade, the mercantile fleet and all large enterprises in all branches of industry— coal, metal, oil, chemicals, machine-building, textiles, sugar, etc.—were nationalized.

To render our country financially independent of the foreign capitalists and free from exploitation by them, the foreign loans contracted by the Russian tsar and the Provisional Government were annulled. The people of our country refused to pay debts which had been incurred for the continuation of the war of conquest and which had placed our country in bondage to foreign capital.

These and similar measures undermined the very root of the power of the bourgeoisie, the landlords, the reactionary officials and the counter-revolutionary parties, and considerably strengthened the position of the Soviet Government within the country.

But the position of the Soviet Government could not be deemed fully secure as long as Russia was in a state of war with Germany and Austria. In order finally to consolidate the Soviet power, the war had to be ended. The Party therefore launched the fight for peace from the moment of the victory of the October Revolution.

The Soviet Government called upon "all the belligerent peoples and their governments to start immediate negotiations for a just, democratic peace." But the "allies"—Great Britain and France—refused to accept the proposal of the Soviet Government. In view of this refusal, the Soviet Government, in compliance with the will of the Soviets, decided to start negotiations with Germany and Austria.

The negotiations began on December 3 in Brest-Litovsk. On December 5 an armistice was signed.

The negotiations took place at a time when the country was in a state of economic disruption, when war-weariness was universal, when our troops were abandoning the trenches and the front was collapsing. It became clear in the course of the negotiations that the German imperialists were out to seize huge portions of the territory of the former tsarist empire, and to turn Poland, the Ukraine and the Baltic countries into dependencies of Germany.

To continue the war under such conditions would have meant staking the very existence of the new-born Soviet Republic. The working class and the peasantry were confronted with the necessity of accepting onerous terms of peace, of retreating before the most dangerous marauder of the time—German imperialism—in order to secure a respite in which to strengthen the Soviet power and to create a new army, the Red Army, which would be able to defend the country from enemy attack.

All the counter-revolutionaries, from the Mensheviks and Socialist-Revolutionaries to the most arrant Whiteguards, conducted a frenzied campaign against the conclusion of peace. Their policy was clear: they wanted to wreck the peace negotiations, provoke a German offensive and thus imperil the still weak Soviet power and endanger the gains of the workers and peasants.

Their allies in this sinister scheme were Trotsky and his accomplice Bukharin, the latter, together with Radek and Pyatakov, heading a group which was hostile to the Party but camouflaged itself under the name of "Left Communists." Trotsky and the group of "Left Communists" began a fierce struggle within the Party against Lenin, demanding the continuation of the war. These people were clearly playing into the hands of the German imperialists and the counter-revolutionaries within the country, for they were working to expose the young Soviet Republic, which had not yet any army, to the blows of German imperialism.

This was really a policy of provocateurs, skilfully masked by Left phraseology.

On February 10, 1918, the peace negotiations in Brest-Litovsk were broken off. Although Lenin and Stalin, in the name of the Central Committee of the Party, had insisted that peace be signed, Trotsky, who was chairman of the Soviet delegation at Brest-Litovsk, treacherously violated the direct instructions of the Bolshevik Party. He announced that the Soviet Republic refused to conclude peace on the terms proposed by Germany. At the same time he informed the Germans that the Soviet Republic would not fight and would continue to demobilize the army.

This was monstrous. The German imperialists could have desired nothing more from this traitor to the interests of the Soviet country.

The German government broke the armistice and assumed the offensive. The remnants of our old army crumbled and scattered before the onslaught of the German troops. The Germans advanced swiftly, seizing enormous territory and threatening Petrograd. German imperialism invaded the Soviet land with the object of overthrowing the Soviet power and converting our country into its colony. The ruins of the old tsarist army could not withstand the armed hosts of German imperialism, and steadily retreated under their blows.

But the armed intervention of the German imperialists was the signal for a mighty revolutionary upsurge in the country. The Party and the Soviet Government issued the call—"The Socialist fatherland is in danger!" And in response the working class energetically began to form regiments of the Red Army. The young detachments of the new army—the army of the revolutionary people—heroically resisted the German marauders who were armed to the teeth. At Narva and Pskov the German invaders met with a resolute repulse. Their advance on Petrograd was checked. February 23—the day the forces of German imperialism were repulsed—is regarded as the birthday of the Red Army.

On February 18, 1918, the Central Committee of the Party had approved Lenin's proposal to send a telegram to the German government offering to conclude an immediate peace. But in order to secure more advantageous terms, the Germans continued to advance, and only on February 22 did the German government express its willingness to sign peace. The terms were now far more onerous than those originally proposed.

Lenin, Stalin and Sverdlov had to wage a stubborn fight on the Central Committee against Trotsky, Bukharin and the other Trotsky-ites before they secured a decision in favour of the conclusion of peace. Bukharin and Trotsky, Lenin declared, "actually *helped* the German imperialists and *hindered* the growth and development of the revolution in Germany." (Lenin, *Collected Works*, Russ. ed., Vol. XXII, p. 307.)

On February 23, the Central Committee decided to accept the terms of the German Command and to sign the peace treaty. The treachery of Trotsky and Bukharin cost the Soviet Republic dearly. Latvia, Esthonia, not to mention Poland, passed into German hands; the Ukraine was severed from the Soviet Republic and converted into a vassal of the German state. The Soviet Republic undertook to pay an indemnity to the Germans.

Meanwhile, the "Left Communists" continued their struggle against Lenin, sinking deeper and deeper into the slough of treachery.

The Moscow Regional Bureau of the Party, of which the "Left Communists" (Bukharin, Ossinsky, Yakovleva, Stukov and Mantsev) had temporarily seized control, passed a resolution of no-confidence in the Central Committee, a resolution designed to split the Party. The Bureau declared that it considered "a split in the Party in the very near future scarcely avoidable." The "Left Communists" even went so far in their resolution as to adopt an anti-Soviet stand. "In the interests of the international revolution," they declared, "we consider it expedient to consent to the possible loss of the Soviet power, which has now become purely formal."

Lenin branded this decision as "strange and monstrous."

At that time the real cause of this anti-Party behaviour of Trotsky and the "Left Communists" was not yet clear to the Party. But the recent trial of the Anti-Soviet "Bloc of Rights and Trotskyites" (beginning of 1938) has now revealed that Bukharin and the group of "Left Communists" headed by him, together with Trotsky and the "Left" Socialist-Revolutionaries, were at that time secretly conspiring against the Soviet Government. Now it is known that Bukharin, Trotsky and their fellow-conspirators had determined to wreck the Peace of Brest-Litovsk, arrest V. I. Lenin, J. V. Stalin and Y. M. Sverdlov, assassinate them, and form a new government consisting of Bukharinites, Trotskyites and "Left" Socialist-Revolutionaries.

While hatching this clandestine counter-revolutionary plot, the group of "Left Communists," with the support of Trotsky, openly attacked the Bolshevik Party, trying to split it and to disintegrate its ranks. But at this grave juncture the Party rallied around Lenin, Stalin and Sverdlov and supported the Central Committee on the question of peace as on all other questions.

The "Left Communist" group was isolated and defeated.

In order that the Party might pronounce its final decision on the question of peace the Seventh Party Congress was summoned.

The congress opened on March 6, 1918. This was the first congress held after our Party had taken power. It was attended by 46 delegates with vote and 58 delegates with voice but no vote, representing 145,000 Party members. Actually, the membership of the Party at that time was not less than 270,000. The discrepancy was due to the fact that, owing to the urgency with which the congress met, a large number of the organizations were unable to send delegates in time; and the organizations in the territories then occupied by the Germans were unable to send delegates at all.

Reporting at this congress on the Brest-Litovsk Peace, Lenin said that "... the severe crisis which our Party is now experiencing, owing to the formation of a Left opposition within it, is one of the gravest crises the Russian revolution has experienced." (Lenin, *Selected Works*, Vol. VII, pp. 293-94.)

The resolution submitted by Lenin on the subject of the Brest-Litovsk Peace was adopted by 30 votes against 12, with 4 abstentions.

On the day following the adoption of this resolution, Lenin wrote an article entitled "A Distressful Peace," in which he said:

> "Intolerably severe are the terms of peace. Nevertheless, history will claim its own. . . . Let us set to work to organize, organize and organize. Despite all trials, the future is ours." (Lenin, *Collected Works*, Russ. ed., Vol. XXII, p. 288.)

In its resolution, the congress declared that further military attacks by imperialist states on the Soviet Republic were inevitable, and that therefore the congress considered it the fundamental task of the Party to adopt the most energetic and resolute measures to strengthen the self-discipline and discipline of the workers and peasants, to prepare the masses for self-sacrificing defence of the Socialist country, to organize the Red Army, and to introduce universal military training.

Endorsing Lenin's policy with regard to the Peace of Brest-Litovsk, the congress condemned the position of Trotsky and Bukharin and stigmatized the attempt of the defeated "Left Communists" to continue their splitting activities at the congress itself.

The Peace of Brest-Litovsk gave the Party a respite in which to consolidate the Soviet power and to organize the economic life of the country.

The peace made it possible to take advantage of the conflicts within the imperialist camp (the war of Austria and Germany with the Entente, which was still in progress) to disintegrate the forces of the enemy, to organize a Soviet economic system and to create a Red Army.

The peace made it possible for the proletariat to retain the support of the peasantry and to accumulate strength for the defeat of the Whiteguard generals in the Civil War.

In the period of the October Revolution Lenin taught the Bolshevik Party how to advance fearlessly and resolutely when conditions favoured an advance. In the period of the Brest-Litovsk Peace Lenin taught the Party how to retreat in good order when the forces of the enemy are obviously superior to our own, in order to prepare with the utmost energy for a new offensive.

History has fully proved the correctness of Lenin's line.

It was decided at the Seventh Congress to change the name of the Party and to alter the Party Program. The name of the Party was changed to the Russian Communist Party (Bolsheviks)—R.C.P.(B.). Lenin proposed to call our Party a Communist Party because this name precisely corresponded to the aim of the Party, namely, the achievement of Communism.

A special commission, which included Lenin and Stalin, was elected to draw up a new Party program, Lenin's draft program having been accepted as a basis.

Thus the Seventh Congress accomplished a task of profound historical importance: it defeated the enemy hidden within the Party's ranks— the "Left Communists" and Trotskyites; it succeeded in withdrawing the country from the imperialist war; it secured peace and a respite; it enabled the Party to gain time for the organization of the Red Army; and it set the Party the task of introducing Socialist order in the national economy.

8. LENIN'S PLAN FOR THE INITIAL STEPS IN SOCIALIST CONSTRUCTION. COMMITTEES OF THE POOR PEASANTS AND THE CURBING OF THE KULAKS. REVOLT OF THE "LEFT" SOCIALIST-REVOLUTIONARIES AND ITS SUPPRESSION. FIFTH CONGRESS OF SOVIETS AND ADOPTION OF THE CONSTITUTION OF THE R.S.F.S.R.

Having concluded peace and thus gained a respite, the Soviet Government set about the work of Socialist construction. Lenin called the period from November 1917 to February 1918 the stage of "the Red Guard attack on capital." During the first half of 1918 the Soviet Government succeeded in breaking the economic might of the bourgeoisie, in concentrating in its own hands the key positions of the national economy (mills, factories, banks, railways, foreign trade, mercantile fleet, etc.), smashing the bourgeois machinery of state power, and victoriously crushing the first attempts of the counter-revolution to overthrow the Soviet power.

But this was by no means enough. If there was to be progress, the destruction of the old order had to be followed by the building of a new. Accordingly, in the spring of 1918, a transition was begun "from the expropriation of the expropriators" to a new stage of Socialist construction—the organizational consolidation of the victories gained, the building of the Soviet national economy. Lenin held that the utmost advantage should be taken of the respite in order to begin to lay the foundation of the Socialist economic system. The Bolsheviks had to learn to organize and manage production in a new way. The Bolshevik Party had convinced Russia, Lenin wrote; the Bolshevik Party had wrested Russia for the people from the hands of the rich, and now the Bolsheviks must learn to govern Russia.

Lenin held that the chief task at the given stage was to keep account of everything the country produced and to exercise control over the distribution of all products. Petty-bourgeois elements predominated in the economic system of the country. The millions of small owners in town and country were a breeding ground for capitalism. These small owners recognized neither labour discipline nor civil discipline; they would not submit to a system of state accounting and control. What was particularly dangerous at this difficult juncture was the petty-bourgeois welter of speculation and profiteering, the attempts of the small owners and traders to profit by the people's want.

The Party started a vigorous war on slovenliness in work, on the absence of labour discipline in industry. The masses were slow in acquiring new habits of labour. The struggle for labour discipline consequently became the major task of the period.

Lenin pointed to the necessity of developing Socialist emulation in industry; of introducing the piece rate system; of combating wage equalization; of resorting—in addition to methods of education and persuasion—to methods of compulsion with regard to those who wanted to grab as much as possible from the state, with regard to idlers and profiteers. He maintained that the new discipline—the discipline of labour, the discipline of comradely relations, Soviet discipline—was something that would be evolved by the labouring millions in the course of their daily, practical work, and that "this task will take up a whole historical epoch." (Lenin, *Selected Works*, Vol. VII, p. 393.)

All these problems of Socialist construction, of the new, Socialist relations of production, were dealt with by Lenin in his celebrated work, *The Immediate Tasks of the Soviet Government.*

The "Left Communists," acting in conjunction with the Socialist-Revolutionaries and Mensheviks, fought Lenin over these questions too. Bukharin, Ossinsky and others were opposed to the introduction of discipline, one-man management in the enterprises, the employment of bourgeois experts in industry, and the introduction of efficient business methods. They slandered Lenin by claiming that this policy would mean a return to bourgeois conditions. At the same time, the "Left Communists" preached the Trotskyite view that Socialist construction and the victory of socialism in Russia were impossible.

The "Left" phraseology of the "Left Communists" served to camouflage their defence of the kulaks, idlers and profiteers who were opposed to discipline and hostile to the state regulation of economic life, to accounting and control.

Having settled on the principles of organization of the new, Soviet industry, the Party proceeded to tackle the problems of the countryside, which at this period was in the throes of a struggle between the poor peasants and the kulaks. The kulaks were gaining strength and seizing the lands confiscated from the landlords. The poor peasants needed assistance. The kulaks fought the proletarian government and refused to sell grain to it at fixed prices. They wanted to starve the Soviet state into renouncing Socialist measures. The Party set the task of smashing the counter-revolutionary kulaks. Detachments of industrial workers were sent into the countryside with the object of organizing the poor peasants and ensuring the success of the struggle against the kulaks, who were holding back their grain surpluses.

"Comrades, workers, remember that the revolution is in a critical situation," Lenin wrote. "Remember that *you alone* can save the revolution, nobody else. What we need is tens of thousands of picked, politically advanced workers, loyal to the cause of Socialism, incapable of succumbing to bribery and the temptations of pilfering, and capable of creating an iron force against the kulaks, profiteers, marauders, bribers and disorganizers." (Lenin, *Collected Works*, Russ. ed., Vol XXIII, p. 25.)

"The struggle for bread is a struggle for Socialism," Lenin said. And it was under this slogan that the sending of workers' detachments to the rural districts was organized. A number of decrees were issued establishing a food dictatorship and conferring emergency powers on the organs of the People's Commissariat of Food for the purchase of grain at fixed prices.

A decree was issued on June 11, 1918, providing for the creation of *Committees of the Poor Peasants*. These committees played an important part in the struggle against the kulaks, in the redistribution of the confiscated land and the distribution of agricultural implements, in the collection of food surpluses from the kulaks, and in the supply of food-stuffs to the working-class centres and the Red Army. Fifty million hectares of kulak land passed into the hands of the poor and middle peasants. A large portion of the kulaks' means of production was confiscated and turned over to the poor peasants.

The formation of the Committees of the Poor Peasants was a further stage in the development of the Socialist revolution in the countryside. The committees were strongholds of the dictatorship of the proletariat in the villages. It was largely through them that enlistment for the Red Army was carried out among the peasants.

The proletarian campaign in the rural districts and the organization of the Committees of the Poor Peasants consolidated the Soviet power in the countryside and were of tremendous political importance in winning over the middle peasants to the side of the Soviet Government.

At the end of 1918, when their task had been completed, the Committees of the Poor Peasants were merged with the rural Soviets and their existence was thus terminated.

At the Fifth Congress of Soviets which opened on July 4, 1918, the "Left" Socialist-Revolutionaries launched a fierce attack on Lenin in defence of the kulaks. They demanded the discontinuation of the fight against the kulaks and of the dispatch of workers' food detachments into the countryside. When the "Left" Socialist-Revolutionaries saw that the majority of the congress was firmly opposed to their policy, they started a revolt in Moscow and seized Tryokhsvyatitelsky Alley, from which they began to shell the Kremlin. This foolhardy outbreak was put down by the Bolsheviks within a few hours. Attempts at revolt were made by "Left" Socialist-Revolutionaries in other parts of the country, but everywhere these outbreaks were speedily suppressed.

As the trial of the Anti-Soviet "Block of Rights and Trotskyites" has now established, the revolt of the "Left" Socialist-Revolutionaries was started with the knowledge and consent of Bukharin and Trotsky and was part of a general counter-revolutionary conspiracy of the Bukharinites, Trotskyites and "Left" Socialist-Revolutionaries against the Soviet power.

At this juncture, too, a "Left" Socialist-Revolutionary by name of Blumkin, afterwards an agent of Trotsky, made his way into the German Embassy and assassinated Mirbach, the German Ambassador in Moscow, with the object of provoking a war with Germany. But the Soviet Government managed to avert war and to frustrate the provocateur designs of the counter-revolutionaries.

The Fifth Congress of Soviets adopted the First Soviet Constitution —the Constitution of the Russian Soviet Federative Socialist Republic.

BRIEF SUMMARY

During the eight months, February to October 1917, the Bolshevik Party accomplished the very difficult task of winning over the majority of the working class and the majority in the Soviets, and enlisting the support of millions of peasants for the Socialist revolution. It wrested these masses from the influence of the petty-bourgeois parties (Socialist-Revolutionaries, Mensheviks and Anarchists), by exposing the policy of these parties step by step and showing that it ran counter to the interests of the working people. The Bolshevik Party carried on extensive political work at the front and in the rear, preparing the masses for the October Socialist Revolution.

The events of decisive importance in the history of the Party at this period were Lenin's arrival from exile abroad, his April Theses, the April Party Conference and the Sixth Party Congress. The Party decisions were a source of strength to the working class and inspired it with confidence in victory; in them the workers found solutions to the important problems of the revolution. The April Conference directed the efforts of the Party to the struggle for the transition from the bourgeois-democratic revolution to the Socialist revolution. The Sixth Congress headed the Party for an armed uprising against the bourgeoisie and its Provisional Government.

The compromising Socialist-Revolutionary and Menshevik parties, the Anarchists, and the other non-Communist parties completed the cycle of their development: they all became bourgeois parties even before the October Revolution and fought for the preservation and integrity of the capitalist system. The Bolshevik Party was the only party which led the struggle of the masses for the overthrow of the bourgeoisie and the establishment of the power of the Soviets.

At the same time, the Bolsheviks defeated the attempts of the capitulators within the Party—Zinoviev, Kamenev, Rykov, Bukharin, Trotsky and Pyatakov—to deflect the Party from the path of Socialist revolution.

Headed by the Bolshevik Party, the working class, in alliance with the poor peasants, and with the support of the soldiers and sailors, overthrew the power of the bourgeoisie, established the power of the Soviets, set up a new type of state—a Socialist Soviet state—abolished the landlords' ownership of land, turned over the land to the peasants for their use, nationalized all the land in the country, expropriated the capitalists, achieved the withdrawal of Russia from the war and obtained peace, that is, obtained a much-needed respite, and thus created the conditions for the development of Socialist construction.

The October Socialist Revolution smashed capitalism, deprived the bourgeoisie of the means of production and converted the mills, factories, land, railways and banks into the property of the whole people, into public property.

It established the dictatorship of the proletariat and turned over the government of the vast country to the working class, thus making it the ruling class.

The October Socialist Revolution thereby ushered in a new era in the history of mankind—the era of proletarian revolutions.

CHAPTER EIGHT

THE BOLSHEVIK PARTY IN THE PERIOD OF FOREIGN MILITARY INTERVENTION AND CIVIL WAR

(1918-1920)

I. BEGINNING OF FOREIGN MILITARY INTERVENTION. FIRST PERIOD OF THE CIVIL WAR

The conclusion of the Peace of Brest-Litovsk and the consolidation of the Soviet power, as a result of a series of revolutionary economic measures adopted by it, at a time when the war in the West was still in full swing, created profound alarm among the Western imperialists, especially those of the Entente countries.

The Entente imperialists feared that the conclusion of peace between Germany and Russia might improve Germany's position in the war and correspondingly worsen the position of their own armies. They feared, moreover, that peace between Russia and Germany might stimulate the craving for peace in all countries and on all fronts, and thus interfere with the prosecution of the war and damage the cause of the imperialists. Lastly, they feared that the existence of a Soviet government on the territory of a vast country, and the success it had achieved at home after the overthrow of the power of the bourgeoisie, might serve as an infectious example for the workers and soldiers of the West. Profoundly discontented with the protracted war, the workers and soldiers might follow in the footsteps of the Russians and turn their bayonets against their masters and oppressors. Consequently, the Entente governments decided to intervene in Russia by armed force with the object of overthrowing the Soviet Government and establishing a bourgeois government, which would restore the bourgeois system in the country, annul the peace treaty with the Germans and re-establish the military front against Germany and Austria.

The Entente imperialists launched upon this sinister enterprise all the more readily because they were convinced that the Soviet Government was unstable; they had no doubt that with some effort on the part of its enemies its early fall would be inevitable.

The achievements of the Soviet Government and its consolidation created even greater alarm among the deposed classes—the landlords

and capitalists; in the ranks of the vanquished parties—the Constitutional-Democrats, Mensheviks, Socialist-Revolutionaries, Anarchists and
the bourgeois nationalists of all hues; and among the Whiteguard generals, Cossack officers, etc.

From the very first days of the victorious October Revolution, all
these hostile elements began to shout from the housetops that there was
no ground in Russia for a Soviet power, that it was doomed, that it was
bound to fall within a week or two, or a month, or two or three months
at most.   But as the Soviet Government, despite the imprecations of its
enemies, continued to exist and gain strength, its foes within Russia
were forced to admit that it was much stronger than they had imagined,
and that its overthrow would require great efforts and a fierce struggle
on the part of all the forces of counter-revolution.   They therefore decided to embark upon counter-revolutionary insurrectionary activities on
a broad scale: to mobilize the forces of counter-revolution, to assemble
military cadres and to organize revolts, especially in the Cossack and
kulak districts.

Thus, already in the first half of 1918, two definite forces took
shape that were prepared to embark upon the overthrow of the Soviet
power, namely, the foreign imperialists of the Entente and the counter-
revolutionaries at home.

Neither of these forces possessed all the requisites needed to undertake
the overthrow of the Soviet Government singly.   The counter-revolutionaries in Russia had certain military cadres and man-power, drawn
principally from the upper classes of the Cossacks and from the kulaks,
enough to start a rebellion against the Soviet Government.   But they
possessed neither money nor arms.   The foreign imperialists, on the other
hand, had the money and the arms, but could not "release" a sufficient
number of troops for purposes of intervention; they could not do so, not
only because these troops were required for the war with Germany and
Austria, but because they might not prove altogether reliable in a war
against the Soviet power.

The conditions of the struggle against the Soviet power dictated a
union of the two anti-Soviet forces, foreign and domestic.   And this
union was effected in the first half of 1918.

This was how the foreign military intervention against the Soviet
power supported by counter-revolutionary revolts of its foes at home
originated.

This was the end of the respite in Russia and the beginning of the
Civil War, which was a war of the workers and peasants of the nations
of Russia against the foreign and domestic enemies of the Soviet power.

The imperialists of Great Britain, France, Japan and America started their military intervention without any declaration of war, although the intervention was a war, a war against Russia, and the worst kind of war at that. These "civilized" marauders secretly and stealthily made their way to Russian shores and landed their troops on Russia's territory.

The British and French landed troops in the north, occupied Archangel and Murmansk, supported a local Whiteguard revolt, overthrew the Soviets and set up a White "Government of North Russia."

The Japanese landed troops in Vladivostok, seized the Maritime Province, dispersed the Soviets and supported the Whiteguard rebels, who subsequently restored the bourgeois system.

In the North Caucasus, Generals Kornilov, Alexeyev and Denikin, with the support of the British and French, formed a Whiteguard "Volunteer Army," raised a revolt of the upper classes of the Cossacks and started hostilities against the Soviets.

On the Don, Generals Krasnov and Mamontov, with the secret support of the German imperialists (the Germans hesitated to support them openly owing to the peace treaty between Germany and Russia), raised a revolt of Don Cossacks, occupied the Don region and started hostilities against the Soviets.

In the Middle Volga region and in Siberia, the British and French instigated a revolt of the Czechoslovak Corps. This corps, which consisted of prisoners of war, had received permission from the Soviet Government to return home through Siberia and the Far East. But on the way it was used by the Socialist-Revolutionaries and by the British and French for a revolt against the Soviet Government. The revolt of the corps served as a signal for a revolt of the kulaks in the Volga region and in Siberia, and of the workers of the Votkinsk and Izhevsk Works, who were under the influence of the Socialist-Revolutionaries. A Whiteguard-Socialist-Revolutionary government was set up in the Volga region, in Samara, and a Whiteguard government of Siberia, in Omsk.

Germany took no part in the intervention of this British-French-Japanese-American bloc; nor could she do so, since she was at war with this bloc if for no other reason. But in spite of this, and notwithstanding the existence of a peace treaty between Russia and Germany, no Bolshevik doubted that Kaiser Wilhelm's government was just as rabid an enemy of Soviet Russia as the British-French-Japanese-American invaders. And, indeed, the German imperialists did their utmost to isolate, weaken and destroy Soviet Russia. They snatched from it the Ukraine—true, it was in accordance with a "treaty" with the

Whiteguard Ukrainian Rada (Council)—brought in their troops at the request of the Rada and began mercilessly to rob and oppress the Ukrainian people, forbidding them to maintain any connections whatever with Soviet Russia. They severed Transcaucasia from Soviet Russia, sent German and Turkish troops there at the request of the Georgian and Azerbaidjan nationalists and began to play the masters in Tiflis and in Baku. They supplied, not openly, it is true, abundant arms and provisions to General Krasnov, who had raised a revolt against the Soviet Government on the Don.

Soviet Russia was thus cut off from her principal sources of food, raw material and fuel.

Conditions were hard in Soviet Russia at that period. There was a shortage of bread and meat. The workers were starving. In Moscow and Petrograd a bread ration of one-eighth of a pound was issued to them every other day, and there were times when no bread was issued at all. The factories were at a standstill, or almost at a standstill, owing to a lack of raw materials and fuel. But the working class did not lose heart. Nor did the Bolshevik Party. The desperate struggle waged to overcome the incredible difficulties of that period showed how inexhaustible is the energy latent in the working class and how immense the prestige of the Bolshevik Party.

The Party proclaimed the country an armed camp and placed its economic, cultural and political life on a war footing. The Soviet Government announced that "the Socialist fatherland is in danger," and called upon the people to rise in its defence. Lenin issued the slogan, "All for the front!"—and hundreds of thousands of workers and peasants volunteered for service in the Red Army and left for the front. About half the membership of the Party and of the Young Communist League went to the front. The Party roused the people for a *war for the fatherland*, a war against the foreign invaders and against the revolts of the exploiting classes whom the revolution had overthrown. The Council of Workers' and Peasants' Defence, organized by Lenin, directed the work of supplying the front with reinforcements, food, clothing and arms. The substitution of compulsory military service for the volunteer system brought hundreds of thousands of new recruits into the Red Army and very shortly raised its strength to over a million men.

Although the country was in a difficult position, and the young Red Army was not yet consolidated, the measures of defence adopted soon yielded their first fruits. General Krasnov was forced back from Tsaritsyn, whose capture he had regarded as certain, and driven beyond the River Don. General Denikin's operations were localized within a small area in the North Caucasus, while General Kornilov was killed in action against the Red Army. The Czechoslovaks and the White-guard-Socialist-Revolutionary bands were ousted from Kazan, Simbirsk and Samara and driven to the Urals. A revolt in Yaroslavl headed by the Whiteguard Savinkov and organized by Lockhart, chief of the British Mission in Moscow, was suppressed, and Lockhart himself arrested. The Socialist-Revolutionaries, who had assassinated Comrades Uritsky and Volodarsky and had made a villainous attempt on the life of Lenin, were subjected to a Red terror in retaliation for their White terror against the Bolsheviks, and were completely routed in every important city in Central Russia.

The young Red Army matured and hardened in battle.

The work of the Communist Commissars was of decisive importance in the consolidation and political education of the Red Army and in raising its discipline and fighting efficiency.

But the Bolshevik Party knew that these were only the first, not the decisive successes of the Red Army. It was aware that new and far more serious battles were still to come, and that the country could recover the lost food, raw material and fuel regions only by a prolonged and stubborn struggle with the enemy. The Bolsheviks therefore undertook intense preparations for a protracted war and decided to place the whole country at the service of the front. The Soviet Government introduced *War Communism*. It took under its control the middle-sized and small industries, in addition to large-scale industry, so as to accumulate goods for the supply of the army and the agricultural population. It introduced a state monopoly of the grain trade, prohibited private trading in grain and established the surplus-appropriation system, under which all surplus produce in the hands of the peasants was to be registered and acquired by the state at fixed prices, so as to accumulate stores of grain for the provisioning of the army and the workers. Lastly, it introduced universal labour service for all classes. By making physical labour compulsory for the bourgeoisie and thus releasing workers for other duties of greater importance to the front, the Party was giving practical effect to the principle: "He who does not work, neither shall he eat."

All these measures, which were necessitated by the exceptionally difficult conditions of national defence, and bore a temporary character, were in their entirety known as War Communism.

The country prepared itself for a long and exacting civil war, for a war against the foreign and internal enemies of the Soviet power. By the end of 1918 it had to increase the strength of the army threefold, and to accumulate supplies for this army.

Lenin said at that time:

"We had decided to have an army of one million men by the spring; now we need an army of three million. We can get it. And we will get it."

2. DEFEAT OF GERMANY IN THE WAR. REVOLUTION IN GER-
MANY. FOUNDING OF THE THIRD INTERNATIONAL. EIGHTH
PARTY CONGRESS

While the Soviet country was preparing for new battles against the forces of foreign intervention, in the West decisive events were taking place in the belligerent countries, both on the war fronts and in their interior. Germany and Austria were suffocating in the grip of war and a food crisis. Whereas Great Britain, France and the United States were continually drawing upon new resources, Germany and Austria were consuming their last meagre stocks. The situation was such that Germany and Austria, having reached the stage of extreme exhaustion, were on the brink of defeat.

At the same time, the peoples of Germany and Austria were seething with indignation against the disastrous and interminable war, and against their imperialist governments who had reduced them to a state of exhaustion and starvation. The revolutionary influence of the October Revolution also had a tremendous effect, as did the fraternization of the Soviet soldiers with the Austrian and German soldiers at the front even before the Peace of Brest-Litovsk, the actual termination of the war with Soviet Russia and the conclusion of peace with her. The people of Russia had brought about the end of the detested war by overthrowing their imperialist government, and this could not but serve as an object lesson to the Austrian and German workers. And the German soldiers who had been stationed on the Eastern front and who after the Peace of Brest-Litovsk were transferred to the Western front could not but undermine the morale of the German army on that front by their accounts of the fraternization with the Soviet soldiers and of the way the Soviet soldiers had got rid of the war. The disintegration of the Austrian army from the same causes had begun even earlier.

All this served to accentuate the craving for peace among the German soldiers; they lost their former fighting efficiency and began to retreat in face of the onslaught of the Entente armies. In November 1918 a revolution broke out in Germany, and Wilhelm and his government were overthrown.

Germany was obliged to acknowledge defeat and to sue for peace.

Thus at one stroke Germany was reduced from a first-rate power to a second-rate power.

As far as the position of the Soviet Government was concerned, this circumstance had certain disadvantages, inasmuch as it made the Entente countries, which had started armed intervention against the Soviet power, the dominant force in Europe and Asia, and enabled them to intervene more actively in the Soviet country and to blockade her, to draw the noose more tightly around the Soviet power. And this was what actually happened, as we shall see later. On the other hand, it had its advantages, which outweighed the disadvantages and fundamentally improved the position of Soviet Russia. In the first place, the Soviet Government was now able to annul the predatory Peace of Brest-Litovsk, to stop paying the indemnities, and to start an open struggle, military and political, for the liberation of Esthonia, Latvia, Byelorussia, Lithuania, the Ukraine and Transcaucasia from the yoke of German imperialism. Secondly, and chiefly, the existence in the centre of Europe, in Germany, of a republican regime and of Soviets of Workers' and Soldiers' Deputies was bound to revolutionize, and actually did revolutionize, the countries of Europe, and this could not but strengthen the position of the Soviet power in Russia. True, the revolution in Germany was not a Socialist but a bourgeois revolution, and the Soviets were an obedient tool of the bourgeois parliament, for they were dominated by the Social-Democrats, who were compromisers of the type of the Russian Mensheviks. This in fact explains the weakness of the German revolution. How weak it really was is shown, for example, by the fact that it allowed the German Whiteguards to assassinate such prominent revolutionaries as Rosa Luxemburg and Karl Liebknecht with impunity. Nevertheless, it was a revolution: Wilhelm had been overthrown, and the workers had cast off their chains; and this in itself was bound to unloose the revolution in the West, was bound to call forth a rise in the revolution in the European countries.

The tide of revolution in Europe began to mount. A revolutionary movement started in Austria, and a Soviet Republic arose in Hungary. With the rising tide of the revolution Communist parties came to the surface.

A real basis now existed for a union of the Communist parties, for the formation of the Third, Communist International.

In March 1919, on the initiative of the Bolsheviks, headed by Lenin, the First Congress of the Communist Parties of various countries, held in Moscow, founded the Communist International. Although many of the delegates were prevented by the blockade and imperialist persecution from arriving in Moscow, the most important countries of Europe and America were represented at this First Congress. The work of the congress was guided by Lenin.

Lenin reported on the subject of bourgeois democracy and the dictatorship of the proletariat. He brought out the importance of the Soviet system, showing that it meant genuine democracy for the working people. The congress adopted a manifesto to the proletariat of all countries, calling upon them to wage a determined struggle for the dictatorship of the proletariat and for the triumph of Soviets all over the world.

The congress set up an Executive Committee of the Third, Communist International (E.C.C.I.).

Thus was founded an international revolutionary proletarian organization of a new type—the Communist International—the Marxist-Leninist International.

The Eighth Congress of our Party met in March 1919. It assembled in the midst of a conflict of contradictory factors—on the one hand, the reactionary bloc of the Entente countries against the Soviet Government had grown stronger, and, on the other, the rising tide of revolution in Europe, especially in the defeated countries, had considerably improved the position of the Soviet country.

The congress was attended by 301 delegates with vote, representing 313,766 members of the Party, and 102 delegates with voice but no vote.

In his inaugural speech, Lenin paid homage to the memory of Y. M. Sverdlov, one of the finest organizing talents in the Bolshevik Party, who had died on the eve of the congress.

The congress adopted a new Party Program. This program gives a description of capitalism and of its highest phase—imperialism. It compares two systems of state—the bourgeois-democratic system and the Soviet system. It details the specific tasks of the Party in the struggle for Socialism: completion of the expropriation of the bourgeoisie; administration of the economic life of the country in accordance with a single Socialist plan; participation of the trade unions in the organization of the national economy; Socialist labour discipline; utilization of bourgeois experts in the economic field under the control of Soviet bodies; gradual and systematic enlistment of the middle peasantry in the work of Socialist construction.

The congress adopted Lenin's proposal to include in the program, in addition to a definition of imperialism as the highest stage of capitalism, the description of industrial capitalism and simple commodity production contained in the old program adopted at the Second Party Congress. Lenin considered it essential that the program should take account of the complexity of our economic system and note the existence of diverse economic formations in the country, including small commodity production, as represented by the middle peasants. Therefore, during the debate on the program, Lenin vigorously condemned the anti-Bolshevik views of Bukharin, who proposed that the clauses dealing with capitalism, small commodity production, the economy of the middle peasant, be left out of the program. Bukharin's views represented a Menshevik-Trotskyite denial of the role played by the middle peasant in the development of the Soviet state. Furthermore, Bukharin glossed over the fact that the small commodity production of the peasants bred and nourished kulak elements.

Lenin further refuted the anti-Bolshevik views of Bukharin and Pyatakov on the national question. They spoke against the inclusion in the program of a clause on the right of nations to self-determination; they were against the equality of nations, claiming that it was a slogan that would hinder the victory of the proletarian revolution and the union of the proletarians of different nationalities. Lenin overthrew these utterly pernicious, imperialist, chauvinist views of Bukharin and Pyatakov.

An important place in the deliberations of the Eighth Congress was devoted to policy towards the middle peasants. The Decree on the Land had resulted in a steady growth in the number of middle peasants, who now comprised the majority of the peasant population. The attitude and conduct of the middle peasantry, which vacillated between the bourgeoisie and the proletariat, was of momentous importance for the fate of the Civil War and Socialist construction. The outcome of the Civil War largely depended on which way the middle peasant would swing, which class would win his allegiance—the proletariat or the bourgeoisie. The Czechoslovaks, the Whiteguards, the kulaks, the Socialist-Revolutionaries and the Mensheviks were able to overthrow the Soviet power in the Volga region in the summer of 1918 because they were supported by a large section of the middle peasantry. The same was true during the revolts raised by the kulaks in Central Russia. But in the autumn of 1918 the mass of the middle peasants began to swing over to the Soviet power. The peasants saw that victories of the Whites were followed by the restoration of the power of the landlords, the seizure of peasants' land, and the robbery, flogging and torture of peasants. The activities of the Committees of the Poor Peasants, which crushed the kulaks, also contributed to the change in the attitude of the peasantry. Accordingly, in November 1918, Lenin issued the slogan:

"Learn to come to an agreement with the middle peasant, while
not for a moment renouncing the struggle against the kulak and at
the same time firmly relying solely on the poor peasant." (Lenin,
Selected Works, Vol. VIII, p. 150.)

Of course, the middle peasants did not cease to vacillate entirely,
but they drew closer to the Soviet Government and began to support it
more solidly. This to a large extent was facilitated by the policy towards
the middle peasants laid down by the Eighth Party Congress.

The Eighth Congress marked a turning point in the policy of the
Party towards the middle peasants. Lenin's report and the decisions of
the congress laid down a new line of the Party on this question. The
congress demanded that the Party organizations and all Communists
should draw a strict distinction and division between the middle peasant
and the kulak, and should strive to win the former over to the side of the
working class by paying close attention to his needs. The backwardness
of the middle peasants had to be overcome by persuasion and not by
compulsion and coercion. The congress therefore gave instructions that
no compulsion be used in the carrying out of Socialist measures in the
countryside (formation of communes and agricultural artels). In all
cases affecting the vital interests of the middle peasant, a practical agreement should be reached with him and concessions made with regard to
the *methods* of realizing Socialist changes. The congress laid down the
policy of a *stable alliance* with the middle peasant, the *leading role* in this
alliance to be maintained by the proletariat.

The new policy towards the middle peasant proclaimed by Lenin at
the Eighth Congress required that the proletariat should rely on the poor
peasant, maintain a stable alliance with the middle peasant and fight the
kulak. The policy of the Party before the Eighth Congress was in general one of *neutralizing* the middle peasant. This meant that the Party
strove to prevent the middle peasant from siding with the kulak and with
the bourgeoisie in general. But now this was not enough. The Eighth
Congress passed from a policy of neutralization of the middle peasant
to a policy of *stable alliance* with him for the purpose of the struggle
against the Whiteguards and foreign intervention and for the successful
building of Socialism.

The policy adopted by the congress towards the middle peasants,
who formed the bulk of the peasantry, played a decisive part in ensuring
success in the Civil War against foreign intervention and its Whiteguard
henchmen. In the autumn of 1919, when the peasants had to choose
between the Soviet power and Denikin, they supported the Soviets, and
the proletarian dictatorship was able to vanquish its most dangerous enemy.

The problems connected with the building up of the Red Army held a special place in the deliberations of the congress, where the so-called "Military Opposition" appeared in the field. This "Military Opposition" comprised quite a number of former members of the now shattered group of "Left Communists"; but it also included some Party workers who had never participated in any opposition, but were dissatisfied with the way Trotsky was conducting the affairs of the army. The majority of the delegates from the army were distinctly hostile to Trotsky; they resented his veneration for the military experts of the old tsarist army, some of whom were betraying us outright in the Civil War, and his arrogant and hostile attitude towards the old Bolshevik cadres in the army. Instances of Trotsky's "practices" were cited at the congress. For example, he had attempted to shoot a number of prominent army Communists serving at the front, just because they had incurred his displeasure. This was directly playing into the hands of the enemy. It was only the intervention of the Central Committee and the protests of military men that saved the lives of these comrades.

But while fighting Trotsky's distortions of the military policy of the Party, the "Military Opposition" held incorrect views on a number of points concerning the building up of the army. Lenin and Stalin vigorously came out against the "Military Opposition," because the latter defended the survivals of the guerrilla spirit and resisted the creation of a regular Red Army, the utilization of the military experts of the old army and the establishment of that iron discipline without which no army can be a real army. Comrade Stalin rebutted the "Military Opposition" and demanded the creation of a regular army inspired with the spirit of strictest discipline.

He said:

> "Either we create a real worker and peasant—primarily a peasant—army, strictly disciplined army, and defend the Republic, or we perish."

While rejecting a number of proposals made by the "Military Opposition," the congress dealt a blow at Trotsky by demanding an improvement in the work of the central military institutions and the enhancement of the role of the Communists in the army.

A Military Commission was set up at the congress; thanks to its efforts the decision on the military question was adopted by the congress unanimously.

The effect of this decision was to strengthen the Red Army and to bring it still closer to the Party.

The congress further discussed Party and Soviet affairs and the guiding role of the Party in the Soviets. During the debate on the latter question the congress repudiated the view of the opportunist Sapronov-Ossinsky group which held that the Party should not guide the work of the Soviets.

Lastly, in view of the huge influx of new members into the Party, the congress outlined measures to improve the social composition of the Party and decided to conduct a re-registration of its members.

This initiated the first purge of the Party ranks.

3. EXTENSION OF INTERVENTION. BLOCKADE OF THE SOVIET COUNTRY. KOLCHAK'S CAMPAIGN AND DEFEAT. DENIKIN'S CAMPAIGN AND DEFEAT. A THREE-MONTHS' RESPITE. NINTH PARTY CONGRESS

Having vanquished Germany and Austria, the Entente states decided to hurl large military forces against the Soviet country. After Germany's defeat and the evacuation of her troops from the Ukraine and Trans-caucasia, her place was taken by the British and French, who dispatched their fleets to the Black Sea and landed troops in Odessa and in Trans-caucasia. Such was the brutality of the Entente forces of intervention that they did not hesitate to shoot whole batches of workers and peasants in the occupied regions. Their outrages reached such lengths in the end that after the occupation of Turkestan they carried off to the Trans-caspian region twenty-six leading Baku Bolsheviks—including Comrades Shaumyan, Fioletov, Djaparidze, Malygin, Azizbekov, Korganov—and with the aid of the Socialist-Revolutionaries, had them brutally shot.

The interventionists soon proclaimed a *blockade* of Russia. All sea routes and other lines of communication with the external world were cut.

The Soviet country was surrounded on nearly every side.

The Entente countries placed their chief hopes in Admiral Kolchak, their puppet in Omsk, Siberia. He was proclaimed "supreme ruler of Russia" and all the counter-revolutionary forces in the country placed themselves under his command.

The Eastern Front thus became the main front.

Kolchak assembled a huge army and in the spring of 1919 almost reached the Volga. The finest Bolshevik forces were hurled against him; Young Communist Leaguers and workers were mobilized. In April 1919, Kolchak's army met with severe defeat at the hands of the Red Army and very soon began to retreat along the whole front.

At the height of the advance of the Red Army on the Eastern Front, Trotsky put forward a suspicious plan: he proposed that the advance should be halted before it reached the Urals, the pursuit of Kolchak's army discontinued, and troops transferred from the Eastern Front to the Southern Front. The Central Committee of the Party fully realized that the Urals and Siberia could not be left in Kolchak's hands, for there, with the aid of the Japanese and British, he might recuperate and retrieve his former position. It therefore rejected this plan and gave instructions to proceed with the advance. Trotsky disagreed with these instructions and tendered his resignation, which the Central Committee declined, at the same time ordering him to refrain at once from all participation in the direction of the operations on the Eastern Front. The Red Army pursued its offensive against Kolchak with greater vigour than ever; it inflicted a number of new defeats on him and freed of the Whites the Urals and Siberia, where the Red Army was supported by a powerful partisan movement in the Whites' rear.

In the summer of 1919, the imperialists assigned to General Yudenich, who headed the counter-revolutionaries in the north-west (in the Baltic countries, in the vicinity of Petrograd), the task of diverting the attention of the Red Army from the Eastern Front by an attack on Petrograd. Influenced by the counter-revolutionary agitation of former officers, the garrisons of two forts in the vicinity of Petrograd mutinied against the Soviet Government. At the same time a counter-revolutionary plot was discovered at the Front Headquarters. The enemy threatened Petrograd. But thanks to the measures taken by the Soviet Government with the support of the workers and sailors, the mutinous forts were cleared of Whites, and Yudenich's troops were defeated and driven back into Esthonia.

The defeat of Yudenich near Petrograd made it easier to cope with Kolchak, and by the end of 1919 his army was completely routed. Kolchak himself was taken prisoner and shot by sentence of the Revolutionary Committee in Irkutsk.

That was the end of Kolchak.

The Siberians had a popular song about Kolchak at that time:

> "Uniform British,
> Epaulettes from France,
> Japanese tobacco,
> Kolchak leads the dance.
> Uniform in tatters,
> Epaulettes all gone,
> So is the tobacco,
> Kolchak's day is done."

Since Kolchak had not justified their hopes, the interventionists altered their plan of attack on the Soviet Republic. The troops landed in Odessa had to be withdrawn, for contact with the army of the Soviet Republic had infected them with the revolutionary spirit and they were beginning to rebel against their imperialist masters. For example, there was the revolt of French sailors in Odessa led by André Marty. Accordingly, now that Kolchak had been defeated, the Entente centred its attention on General Denikin, Kornilov's confederate and the organizer of the "Volunteer Army." Denikin at that time was operating against the Soviet Government in the south, in the Kuban region. The Entente supplied his army with large quantities of ammunition and equipment and sent it north against the Soviet Government.

The Southern Front now became the chief front.

Denikin began his main campaign against the Soviet Government in the summer of 1919. Trotsky had disrupted the Southern Front, and our troops suffered defeat after defeat. By the middle of October the Whites had seized the whole of the Ukraine, had captured Orel and were nearing Tula, which supplied our army with cartridges, rifles and machine-guns. The Whites were approaching Moscow. The situation of the Soviet Republic became grave in the extreme. The Party sounded the alarm and called upon the people to resist. Lenin issued the slogan, "All for the fight against Denikin!" Inspired by the Bolsheviks, the workers and peasants mustered all their forces to smash the enemy.

The Central Committee sent Comrades Stalin, Voroshilov, Ordjoni-kidze and Budyonny to the Southern Front to prepare the rout of Denikin. Trotsky was removed from the direction of the operations of the Red Army in the south. Before Comrade Stalin's arrival, the Command of the Southern Front, in conjunction with Trotsky, had drawn up a plan to strike the main blow at Denikin from Tsaritsyn in the direction of Novorossisk, through the Don Steppe, where there were no roads and where the Red Army would have to pass through regions inhabited by Cossacks, who were at that time largely under the influence of the Whiteguards. Comrade Stalin severely criticized this plan and submitted to the Central Committee his own plan for the defeat of Denikin. According to this plan the main blow was to be delivered by way of Kharkov-Donetz Basin-Rostov. This plan would ensure the rapid advance of our troops against Denikin, for they would be moving through working class and peasant regions where they would have the open sympathy of the population. Furthermore, the dense network of railway lines in this region would ensure our armies the regular supply of all they required.

Lastly, this plan would make it possible to release the Donetz Coal Basin and thus supply our country with fuel.

The Central Committee of the Party accepted Comrade Stalin's plan. In the second half of October 1919, after fierce resistance, Denikin was defeated by the Red Army in the decisive battles of Orel and Voronezh. He began a rapid retreat, and, pursued by our forces, fled to the south. At the beginning of 1920 the whole of the Ukraine and the North Caucasus had been cleared of Whites.

During the decisive battles on the Southern Front, the imperialists again hurled Yudenich's corps against Petrograd in order to divert our forces from the south and thus improve the position of Denikin's army. The Whites approached the very gates of Petrograd. The heroic proletariat of the premier city of the revolution rose in a solid wall for its defence. The Communists, as always, were in the vanguard. After fierce fighting, the Whites were defeated and again flung beyond our borders back into Esthonia.

And that was the end of Denikin.

The defeat of Kolchak and Denikin was followed by a brief respite.

When the imperialists saw that the Whiteguard armies had been smashed, that intervention had failed, and that the Soviet Government was consolidating its position all over the country, while in Western Europe the indignation of the workers against military intervention in the Soviet Republic was rising, they began to change their attitude towards the Soviet state. In January 1920, Great Britain, France, and Italy decided to call off the blockade of Soviet Russia.

This was an important breach in the wall of intervention.

It did not, of course, mean that the Soviet country was done with intervention and the Civil War. There was still the danger of attack by imperialist Poland. The forces of intervention had not yet been finally driven out of the Far East, Transcaucasia and the Crimea. But Soviet Russia had secured a temporary breathing space and was able to divert more forces to economic development. The Party could now devote its attention to economic problems.

During the Civil War many skilled workers had left industry owing to the closing down of mills and factories. The Party now took measures to return them to industry to work at their trades. The railways were in a grave condition and several thousand Communists were assigned to the work of restoring them, for unless this was done the restoration of the major branches of industry could not be seriously undertaken. The organization of the food supply was extended and improved. The drafting of a plan for the electrification of Russia was begun. Nearly five million Red Army men were under arms and could not be demobilized owing to the danger of war. A part of the Red Army was therefore converted into *labour armies* and used in the economic field. The Council of Workers' and Peasants' Defence was transformed into the *Council of Labour and Defence,* and a *State Planning Commission* (Gosplan) set up to assist it.

Such was the situation when the Ninth Party Congress opened.

The congress met at the end of March 1920. It was attended by 554 delegates with vote, representing 611,978 Party members, and 162 delegates with voice but no vote.

The congress defined the immediate tasks of the country in the sphere of transportation and industry. It particularly stressed the necessity of the trade unions taking part in the building up of the economic life.

Special attention was devoted by the congress to a single economic plan for the restoration, in the first place, of the railways, the fuel industry and the iron and steel industry. The major item in this plan was a project for the electrification of the country, which Lenin advanced as "a great program for the next ten or twenty years." This formed the basis of the famous plan of the State Commission for the Electrification of Russia (GOELRO), the provisions of which have today been far exceeded.

The congress rejected the views of an anti-Party group which called itself "The Group of Democratic-Centralism" and was opposed to one-man management and the undivided responsibility of industrial directors. It advocated unrestricted "group management" under which nobody would be personally responsible for the administration of industry. The chief figures in this anti-Party group were Sapronov, Ossinsky and V. Smirnov. They were supported at the congress by Rykov and Tomsky.

4. POLISH GENTRY ATTACK SOVIET RUSSIA. GENERAL WRANGEL'S CAMPAIGN. FAILURE OF THE POLISH PLAN. ROUT OF WRANGEL. END OF THE INTERVENTION.

Notwithstanding the defeat of Kolchak and Denikin, notwithstanding the fact that the Soviet Republic was steadily regaining its territory by clearing the Whites and the forces of intervention out of the Northern Territory, Turkestan, Siberia, the Don region, the Ukraine, etc., notwithstanding the fact that the Entente states were obliged to call off the blockade of Russia, they still refused to reconcile themselves to the idea that the Soviet power had proved impregnable and had come out victorious. They therefore resolved to make one more attempt at intervention in Soviet Russia. This time they decided to utilize both Pilsudski, a bourgeois counter-revolutionary nationalist, the virtual head of the Polish state, and General Wrangel, who had rallied the remnants of Denikin's army in the Crimea and from there was threatening the Donetz Basin and the Ukraine.

The Polish gentry and Wrangel, as Lenin put it, were the two hands with which international imperialism attempted to strangle Soviet Russia.

The plan of the Poles was to seize the Soviet Ukraine west of the Dnieper, to occupy Soviet Byelorussia, to restore the power of the Polish magnates in these regions, to extend the frontiers of the Polish state so that they stretched "from sea to sea," from Danzig to Odessa, and, in return for his aid, to help Wrangel smash the Red Army and restore the power of the landlords and capitalists in Soviet Russia.

This plan was approved by the Entente states.

The Soviet Government made vain attempts to enter into negotiations with Poland with the object of preserving peace and averting war. Pilsudski refused to discuss peace. He wanted war. He calculated that the Red Army, fatigued by its battles with Kolchak and Denikin, would not be able to withstand the attack of the Polish forces.

The short breathing space had come to an end.

In April 1920 the Poles invaded the Soviet Ukraine and seized Kiev. At the same time, Wrangel took the offensive and threatened the Donetz Basin.

In reply, the Red Army started a counter-offensive against the Poles along the whole front. Kiev was recaptured and the Polish warlords driven out of the Ukraine and Byelorussia. The impetuous advance of the Red troops on the Southern Front brought them to the very gates of Lvov in Galicia, while the troops on the Western Front were nearing Warsaw. The Polish armies were on the verge of utter defeat.

But success was frustrated by the suspicious actions of Trotsky and his followers at the General Headquarters of the Red Army. Through the fault of Trotsky and Tukhachevsky, the advance of the Red troops on the Western Front, towards Warsaw, proceeded in an absolutely unorganized manner: the troops were allowed no opportunity to consolidate the positions that they won, the advance detachments were led too far ahead, while reserves and ammunition were left too far in the rear. As a result, the advance detachments were left without ammunition and reserves and the front was stretched out endlessly. This made it easy to force a breach in the front. The result was that when a small force of Poles broke through our Western Front at one point, our troops, left without ammunition, were obliged to retreat. As regards the troops on the Southern Front, who had reached the gates of Lvov and were pressing the Poles hard, they were forbidden by Trotsky, that ill-famed "chairman of the Revolutionary Military Council," to capture Lvov. He ordered the transfer of the Mounted Army, the main force on the Southern Front, far to the north-east. This was done on the pretext of helping the Western Front, although it was not difficult to see that the best, and in fact only possible, way of helping the Western Front was to capture Lvov. But the withdrawal of the Mounted Army from the Southern Front, its departure from Lvov, virtually meant the retreat of our forces on the Southern Front as well. This wrecker's order issued by Trotsky thus forced upon our troops on the Southern Front an incomprehensible and absolutely unjustified retreat—to the joy of the Polish gentry.

This was giving direct assistance, indeed—not to our Western Front, however, but to the Polish gentry and the Entente.

Within a few days the advance of the Poles was checked and our troops began preparations for a new counter-offensive. But, unable to continue the war, and alarmed by the prospect of a Red counter-offensive, Poland was obliged to renounce her claims to the Ukrainian territory west of the Dnieper and to Byelorussia and preferred to conclude peace. On October 20, 1920, the Peace of Riga was signed. In accordance with this treaty Poland retained Galicia and part of Byelorussia.

Having concluded peace with Poland, the Soviet Republic decided to put an end to Wrangel. The British and French had supplied him with guns, rifles, armoured cars, tanks, aeroplanes and ammunition of the latest type. He had Whiteguard shock regiments, mainly consisting of officers. But Wrangel failed to rally any considerable number of peasants and Cossacks in support of the troops he had landed in the Kuban and the Don regions. Nevertheless, he advanced to the very gates of the Donetz Basin, creating a menace to our coal region. The position of the Soviet Government at that time was further complicated by the fact that the Red Army was suffering greatly from fatigue. The troops were obliged to advance under extremely difficult conditions: while conducting an offensive against Wrangel, they had at the same time to smash Makhno's anarchist bands who were assisting Wrangel. But although Wrangel had the superiority in technical equipment, although the Red Army had no tanks, it drove Wrangel into the Crimean Peninsula and there bottled him up. In November 1920 the Red forces captured the fortified position of Perekop, swept into the Crimea, smashed Wrangel's forces and cleared the Peninsula of the Whiteguards and the forces of intervention. The Crimea became Soviet territory.

The failure of Poland's imperialist plans and the defeat of Wrangel ended the period of intervention.

At the end of 1920 there began the liberation of Transcaucasia: Azerbaidjan was freed from the yoke of the bourgeois nationalist Mussavatists, Georgia from the Menshevik nationalists, and Armenia from the Dashnaks. The Soviet power triumphed in Azerbaidjan, Armenia and Georgia.

This did not yet mean the end of all intervention. That of the Japanese in the Far East lasted until 1922. Moreover, new attempts at intervention were made (Ataman Semyonov and Baron Ungern in the East, the Finnish Whites in Karelia in 1921). But the principal enemies of the Soviet country, the principal forces of intervention, were shattered by the end of 1920.

The war of the foreign interventionists and the Russian Whiteguards against the Soviets ended in a victory for the Soviets.

The Soviet Republic preserved its independence and freedom.

This was the end of foreign military intervention and Civil War.

This was a historic victory for the Soviet power.

5. HOW AND WHY THE SOVIET REPUBLIC DEFEATED THE COM-
   BINED FORCES OF BRITISH-FRENCH-JAPANESE-POLISH INTER-
   VENTION AND OF THE BOURGEOIS-LANDLORD-WHITEGUARD
   COUNTER-REVOLUTION IN RUSSIA

If we study the leading European and American newspapers and periodicals of the period of intervention, we shall easily find that there was not a single prominent writer, military or civilian, not a single military expert who believed that the Soviet Government could win. On the contrary, all prominent writers, military experts and historians of revolution of all countries and nations, all the so-called savants, were unanimous in declaring that the days of the Soviets were numbered, that their defeat was inevitable.

They based their certainty of the victory of the forces of intervention on the fact that whereas Soviet Russia had no organized army and had to create its Red Army under fire, so to speak, the interventionists and Whiteguards did have an army more or less ready to hand.

Further, they based their certainty on the fact that the Red Army had no experienced military men, the majority of them having gone over to the counter-revolution, whereas the interventionists and Whiteguards did have such men.

Furthermore, they based their certainty on the fact that, owing to the backwardness of Russia's war industry, the Red Army was suffering from a shortage of arms and ammunition; that what it did have was of poor quality, while it could not obtain supplies from abroad because Russia was hermetically sealed on all sides by the blockade. The army of the interventionists and Whiteguards, on the other hand, was abundantly supplied, and would continue to be supplied, with first-class arms, ammunition and equipment.

Lastly, they based their certainty on the fact that the army of the interventionists and Whiteguards occupied the richest food-producing regions of Russia, whereas the Red Army had no such regions and was suffering from a shortage of provisions.

And it was a fact that the Red Army did suffer from all these handicaps and deficiencies.

In this respect—but only in this respect—the gentlemen of the intervention were absolutely right.

How then is it to be explained that the Red Army, although suffering from such grave shortcomings, was able to defeat the army of the interventionists and Whiteguards which did not suffer from such shortcomings?

1. The Red Army was victorious because the Soviet Government's policy for which the Red Army was fighting was a right policy, one that corresponded to the interests of the people, and because the people understood and realized that it was the right policy, their own policy, and supported it unreservedly.

The Bolsheviks knew that an army that fights for a wrong policy, for a policy that is not supported by the people, cannot win. The army of the interventionists and Whiteguards was such an army. It had everything: experienced commanders and first-class arms, ammunition, equipment and provisions. It lacked only one thing—the support and sympathy of the peoples of Russia; for the peoples of Russia could not and would not support the policy of the interventionists and Whiteguard "rulers" because it was a policy hostile to the people. And so the interventionist and Whiteguard army was defeated.

2. The Red Army was victorious because it was absolutely loyal and faithful to its people, for which reason the people loved and supported it and looked upon it as their own army. The Red Army is the offspring of the people, and if it is faithful to its people, as a true son is to his

mother, it will have the support of the people and is bound to win. An army, however, that goes against its people must suffer defeat.

3. The Red Army was victorious because the Soviet Government was able to muster the whole rear, the whole country, to serve the needs of the front. An army without a strong rear to support the front in every way is doomed to defeat. The Bolsheviks knew this and that is why they converted the country into an armed camp to supply the front with arms, ammunition, equipment, food and reinforcements.

4. The Red Army was victorious because: a) the Red Army men understood the aims and purposes of the war and recognized their justice; b) the recognition of the justice of the aims and purposes of the war strengthened their discipline and fighting efficiency; and c) as a result, the Red Army throughout displayed unparalleled self-sacrifice and unexampled mass heroism in battle against the enemy.

5. The Red Army was victorious because its leading core, both at the front and in the rear, was the Bolshevik Party, united in its solidarity and discipline, strong in its revolutionary spirit and readiness for any sacrifice in the common cause, and unsurpassed in its ability to organize millions and to lead them properly in complex situations.

"It is only because of the Party's vigilance and its strict discipline," said Lenin, "because the authority of the Party united all government departments and institutions, because the slogans issued by the Central Committee were followed by tens, hundreds, thousands and finally millions of people as one man, because incredible sacrifices were made, that the miracle took place and we were able to win, in spite of repeated campaigns of the imperialists of the Entente and of the whole world." (Lenin, *Collected Works*, Russ. ed., Vol. XXV, p. 96.)

6. The Red Army was victorious because: a) it was able to produce from its own ranks military commanders of a new type, men like Frunze, Voroshilov, Budyonny, and others; b) in its ranks fought such talented heroes who came from the people as Kotovsky, Chapayev, Lazo, Shchors, Parkhomenko, and many others; c) the political education of the Red Army was in the hands of men like Lenin, Stalin, Molotov, Kalinin, Sverdlov, Kaganovich, Ordjonikidze, Kirov, Kuibyshev, Mikoyan, Zhdanov, Andreyev, Petrovsky, Yaroslavsky, Yezhov, Dzerzhinsky, Shchadenko, Mekhlis, Khrushchev, Shvernik, Shkiryatov, and others; d) the Red Army possessed such outstanding organizers and agitators as the military commissars, who by their work cemented the ranks of the Red Army men, fostered in them the spirit of discipline and military daring,

and energetically—swiftly and relentlessly—cut short the treacherous activities of certain of the commanders, while on the other hand, they boldly and resolutely supported the prestige and renown of commanders, Party and non-Party, who had proved their loyalty to the Soviet power and who were capable of leading the Red Army units with a firm hand.

"Without the military commissars we would not have had a Red Army," Lenin said.

7. The Red Army was victorious because in the rear of the White armies, in the rear of Kolchak, Denikin, Krasnov and Wrangel, there secretly operated splendid Bolsheviks, Party and non-Party, who raised the workers and peasants in revolt against the invaders, against the Whiteguards, undermined the rear of the foes of the Soviet Government, and thereby facilitated the advance of the Red Army. Everybody knows that the partisans of the Ukraine, Siberia, the Far East, the Urals, Byelorussia and the Volga region, by undermining the rear of the Whiteguards and the invaders, rendered invaluable service to the Red Army.

8. The Red Army was victorious because the Soviet Republic was not alone in its struggle against Whiteguard counter-revolution and foreign intervention, because the struggle of the Soviet Government and its successes enlisted the sympathy and support of the proletarians of the whole world. While the imperialists were trying to stifle the Soviet Republic by intervention and blockade, the workers of the imperialist countries sided with the Soviets and helped them. Their struggle against the capitalists of the countries hostile to the Soviet Republic helped in the end to force the imperialists to call off the intervention. The workers of Great Britain, France and the other intervening powers called strikes, refused to load munitions consigned to the invaders and the Whiteguard generals, and set up Councils of Action whose work was guided by the slogan—"Hands off Russia!"

"The international bourgeoisie has only to raise its hand against us to have it seized by its own workers," Lenin said. (*Ibid.,* p. 405.)

BRIEF SUMMARY

Vanquished by the October Revolution, the landlords and capitalists, in conjunction with the Whiteguard generals, conspired with the governments of the Entente countries against the interests of their own country for a joint armed attack on the Soviet land and for the overthrow of the Soviet Government. This formed the basis of the military intervention of the Entente and of the Whiteguard revolts in the border regions of Russia, as a result of which Russia was cut off from her sources of food and raw material.

The military defeat of Germany and the termination of the war between the two imperialist coalitions in Europe served to strengthen the Entente and to intensify the intervention, and created new difficulties for Soviet Russia.

On the other hand, the revolution in Germany and the incipient revolutionary movement in the European countries created favourable international conditions for the Soviet power and relieved the position of the Soviet Republic.

The Bolshevik Party roused the workers and peasants for a war *for the fatherland,* a war against the foreign invaders and the bourgeois and landlord Whiteguards. The Soviet Republic and its Red Army defeated one after another the puppets of the Entente—Kolchak, Yudenich, Denikin, Krasnov and Wrangel, drove out of the Ukraine and Byelorussia another puppet of the Entente, Pilsudski, and thus beat off the forces of foreign intervention and drove them out of the Soviet country.

Thus the first armed attack of international capital on the land of Socialism ended in a complete fiasco.

In the period of intervention, the parties which had been smashed by the revolution, the Socialist-Revolutionaries, Mensheviks, Anarchists and nationalists, supported the Whiteguard generals and the invaders, hatched counter-revolutionary plots against the Soviet Republic and resorted to terrorism against Soviet leaders. These parties, which had enjoyed a certain amount of influence among the working class before the October Revolution, completely exposed themselves before the masses as counter-revolutionary parties during the Civil War.

The period of Civil War and intervention witnessed the political collapse of these parties and the final triumph of the Communist Party in Soviet Russia.

CHAPTER NINE

THE BOLSHEVIK PARTY IN THE PERIOD OF TRANSITION TO THE PEACEFUL WORK OF ECONOMIC RESTORATION

(1921-1925)

1. SOVIET REPUBLIC AFTER THE DEFEAT OF THE INTERVENTION AND END OF THE CIVIL WAR. DIFFICULTIES OF THE RESTORATION PERIOD

Having ended the war, the Soviet Republic turned to the work of peaceful economic development. The wounds of war had to be healed. The shattered economic life of the country had to be rebuilt, its industry, railways and agriculture restored.

But the work of peaceful development had to be undertaken in extremely difficult circumstances. The victory in the Civil War had not been an easy one. The country had been reduced to a state of ruin by four years of imperialist war and three years of war against the intervention.

The gross output of agriculture in 1920 was only about *one-half* of the pre-war output—that of the poverty-stricken Russian countryside of tsarist days. To make matters worse, in 1920 there was a harvest failure in many of the provinces. Agriculture was in sore straits.

Even worse was the plight of industry, which was in a state of complete dislocation. The output of large-scale industry in 1920 was a little over *one-seventh* of pre-war. Most of the mills and factories were at a standstill; mines and collieries were wrecked and flooded. Gravest of all was the condition of the iron and steel industry. The total output of pig-iron in 1921 was only 116,300 tons, or about 3 per cent of the pre-war output. There was a shortage of fuel. Transport was disrupted. Stocks of metal and textiles in the country were nearly exhausted. There was an acute shortage of such prime necessities as bread, fats, meat, footwear, clothing, matches, salt, kerosene, and soap.

While the war was on, people put up with the shortage and scarcity, and were sometimes even oblivious to it. But now that the war was over, they suddenly felt that this shortage and scarcity were intolerable and began to demand that they be immediately remedied.

Discontent appeared among the peasants. The fire of the Civil War had welded and steeled a military and political alliance of the working class and the peasantry. This alliance rested on a definite basis: the peasants received from the Soviet Government land and protection against the landlords and kulaks; the workers received from the peasantry foodstuffs under the surplus-appropriation system.

Now this basis was no longer adequate.

The Soviet state had been compelled to appropriate all surplus produce from the peasants for the needs of national defence. Victory in the Civil War would have been impossible without the surplus-appropriation system, without the policy of War Communism. This policy was necessitated by the war and intervention. As long as the war was on, the peasantry had acquiesced in the surplus-appropriation system and had paid no heed to the shortage of commodities; but when the war ended and there was no longer any danger of the landlords returning, the peasants began to express dissatisfaction with having to surrender all their surpluses, with the surplus-appropriation system, and to demand a sufficient supply of commodities.

As Lenin pointed out, the whole system of War Communism had come into collision with the interests of the peasantry.

The spirit of discontent affected the working class as well. The proletariat had borne the brunt of the Civil War, had heroically and self-sacrificingly fought the Whiteguard and foreign hordes, and the ravages of economic disruption and famine. The best, the most class-conscious, self-sacrificing and disciplined workers were inspired by Socialist enthusiasm. But the utter economic disruption had its influence on the working class, too. The few factories and plants still in operation were working spasmodically. The workers were reduced to doing odd jobs for a living, making cigarette lighters and engaging in petty bartering for food in the villages ("bag-trading"). The class basis of the dictatorship of the proletariat was being weakened; the workers were scattering, decamping for the villages, ceasing to be workers and becoming declassed. Some of the workers were beginning to show signs of discontent owing to hunger and weariness.

The Party was confronted with the necessity of working out a new line of policy on all questions affecting the economic life of the country, a line that would meet the new situation.

And the Party proceeded to work out such a line of policy on questions of economic development.

But the class enemy was not dozing. He tried to exploit the distressing economic situation and the discontent of the peasants for his own purposes. Kulak revolts, engineered by Whiteguards and Socialist-Revolutionaries, broke out in Siberia, the Ukraine and the Tambov province (Antonov's rebellion). All kinds of counter-revolutionary elements—Mensheviks, Socialist-Revolutionaries, Anarchists, Whiteguards, bourgeois nationalists—became active again. The enemy adopted new tactics of struggle against the Soviet power. He began to borrow a Soviet garb, and his slogan was no longer the old bankrupt "Down with the Soviets!" but a new slogan: "For the Soviets, but without Communists!"

A glaring instance of the new tactics of the class enemy was the counter-revolutionary mutiny in Kronstadt. It began in March 1921, a week before the Tenth Party Congress. Whiteguards, in complicity with Socialist-Revolutionaries, Mensheviks and representatives of foreign states, assumed the lead of the mutiny. The mutineers at first used a "Soviet" signboard to camouflage their purpose of restoring the power and property of the capitalists and landlords. They raised the cry: "Soviets without Communists!" The counter-revolutionaries tried to exploit the discontent of the petty bourgeois masses in order to overthrow the power of the Soviets under a pseudo-Soviet slogan.

Two circumstances facilitated the outbreak of the Kronstadt mutiny: the deterioration in the composition of the ships' crews, and the weakness of the Bolshevik organization in Kronstadt. Nearly all the old sailors who had taken part in the October Revolution were at the front, heroically fighting in the ranks of the Red Army. The naval replenishments consisted of new men, who had not been schooled in the revolution. These were a perfectly raw peasant mass who gave expression to the peasantry's discontent with the surplus-appropriation system. As for the Bolshevik organization in Kronstadt, it had been greatly weakened by a series of mobilizations for the front. This enabled the Socialist-Revolutionaries, Mensheviks and Whiteguards to worm their way into Kronstadt and to seize control of it.

The mutineers gained possession of a first-class fortress, the fleet, and a vast quantity of arms and ammunition. The international counter-revolutionaries were triumphant. But their jubilation was premature. The mutiny was quickly put down by Soviet troops. Against the Kronstadt mutineers the Party sent its finest sons—delegates to the Tenth Congress, headed by Comrade Voroshilov. The Red Army men advanced on Kronstadt across a thin sheet of ice; it broke in places and many were drowned. The almost impregnable forts of Kronstadt had to be taken by storm; but loyalty to the revolution, bravery and readiness to die for the Soviets won the day. The fortress of Kronstadt fell before the onslaught of the Red troops. The Kronstadt mutiny was suppressed.

2. PARTY DISCUSSION ON THE TRADE UNIONS. TENTH PARTY CONGRESS. DEFEAT OF THE OPPOSITION. ADOPTION OF THE NEW ECONOMIC POLICY (NEP)

The Central Committee of the Party, its Leninist majority, saw clearly that now that the war was over and the country had turned to peaceful economic development, there was no longer any reason for maintaining the rigid regime of War Communism—the product of war and blockade.

The Central Committee realized that the need for the surplus-appropriation system had passed, that it was time to supersede it by a tax in kind so as to enable the peasants to use the greater part of their surpluses at their own discretion. The Central Committee realized that this measure would make it possible to revive agriculture, to extend the cultivation of grain and industrial crops required for the development of industry, to revive the circulation of commodities, to improve supplies to the towns, and to create a new foundation, an economic foundation for the alliance of workers and peasants.

The Central Committee realized also that the prime task was to revive industry, but considered that this could not be done without enlisting the support of the working class and its trade unions; it considered that the workers could be enlisted in this work by showing them that the economic disruption was just as dangerous an enemy of the people as the intervention and the blockade had been, and that the Party and the trade unions could certainly succeed in this work if they exercised their influence on the working class not by military commands, as had been the case at the front, where commands were really essential, but by methods of persuasion, by convincing it.

But not all members of the Party were of the same mind as the Central Committee. The small opposition groups—the Trotskyites, "Workers' Opposition," "Left Communists," "Democratic-Centralists," etc.—wavered and vacillated in face of the difficulties attending the transition to peaceful economic construction. There were in the Party quite a number of ex-members of the Menshevik, Socialist-Revolutionary, Bund and Borotbist parties, and all kinds of semi-nationalists from the border regions of Russia. Most of them allied themselves with one opposition group or another. These people were not real Marxists, they were ignorant of the laws of economic development, and had not had a Leninist-Party schooling, and they only helped to aggravate the confusion and vacillations of the opposition groups. Some of them thought that it would be wrong to relax the rigid regime of War Communism, that, on the contrary, "the screws must be tightened." Others thought that the Party and the state should stand aside from the economic restoration, and that it should be left entirely in the hands of the trade unions.

It was clear that with such confusion reigning among certain groups in the Party, lovers of controversy, opposition "leaders" of one kind or another were bound to try to force a discussion upon the Party.

And that is just what happened.

The discussion started over the role of the trade unions, although the trade unions were not the chief problem of Party policy at the time.

It was Trotsky who started the discussion and the fight against Lenin, against the Leninist majority of the Central Committee. With the intention of aggravating the situation, he came out at a meeting of Communist delegates to the Fifth All-Russian Trade Union Conference, held at the beginning of November 1920, with the dubious slogans of "tightening the screws" and "shaking up the trade unions." Trotsky demanded that the trade unions be immediately "governmentalized." He was against the use of persuasion in relations with the working class, and was in favour of introducing military methods in the trade unions. Trotsky was against any extension of democracy in the trade unions, against the principle of electing trade union bodies.

Instead of methods of persuasion, without which the activities of working-class organizations are inconceivable, the Trotskyites proposed methods of sheer compulsion, of dictation. Applying this policy wherever they happened to occupy leading positions in the trade unions, the Trotskyites caused conflicts, disunity and demoralization in the unions. By their policy the Trotskyites were setting the mass of the non-Party workers against the Party, were splitting the working class.

As a matter of fact, the discussion on the trade unions was of much broader import than the trade union question. As was stated later in the resolution of the Plenum of the Central Committee of the Russian Communist Party (Bolsheviks) adopted on January 17, 1925, the actual point at issue was "the policy to be adopted towards the peasantry, who were rising against War Communism, the policy to be adopted towards the mass of the non-Party workers, and, in general, what was to be the approach of the Party to the masses in the period when the Civil War was coming to an end." (*Resolutions of the C.P.S.U.*[*B.*] Russ ed., Part I, p. 651.)

Trotsky's lead was followed by other anti-Party groups: the "Workers' Opposition" (Shlyapnikov, Medvedyev, Kollontai and others), the

"Democratic-Centralists" (Sapronov, Drobnis, Boguslavsky, Ossinsky, V. Smirnov and others), the "Left Communists" (Bukharin, Preobra-zhensky).

The "Workers' Opposition" put forward a slogan demanding that the administration of the entire national economy be entrusted to an "All-Russian Producers' Congress." They wanted to reduce the role of the Party to nought, and denied the importance of the dictatorship of the proletariat to economic development. The "Workers' Opposition" contended that the interests of the trade unions were opposed to those of the Soviet state and the Communist Party. They held that the trade unions, and not the Party, were the highest form of working-class or-ganization. The "Workers' Opposition" was essentially an anarcho-syndicalist anti-Party group.

The "Democratic-Centralists" (Decists) demanded complete free-dom for factions and groupings. Like the Trotskyites, the "Democratic-Centralists" tried to undermine the leadership of the Party in the Soviets and in the trade unions. Lenin spoke of the "Democratic-Centralists" as a faction of "champion shouters," and of their platform as a Socialist-Revolutionary-Menshevik platform.

Trotsky was assisted in his fight against Lenin and the Party by Bukharin. With Preobrazhensky, Serebryakov and Sokolnikov, Bukharin formed a "buffer" group. This group defended and shielded the Trot-skyites, the most vicious of all factionalists. Lenin said that Bukharin's behaviour was the "acme of ideological depravity." Very soon, the Buk-harinites openly joined forces with the Trotskyites against Lenin.

Lenin and the Leninists concentrated their fire on the Trotskyites as the backbone of the anti-Party groupings. They condemned the Trot-skyites for ignoring the difference between trade unions and military bodies and warned them that military methods could not be applied to the trade unions. Lenin and the Leninists drew up a platform of their own, entirely contrary in spirit to the platforms of the opposition groups. In this platform, the trade unions were defined as a school of adminis-tration, a school of management, a school of Communism. The trade unions should base all their activities on methods of persuasion. Only then would the trade unions rouse the workers as a whole to combat the economic disruption and be able to enlist them in the work of Socialist construction.

In this fight against the opposition groupings, the Party organiza-tions rallied around Lenin. The struggle took an especially acute form in Moscow. Here the opposition concentrated its main forces, with the object of capturing the Party organization of the capital. But these

factionalist intrigues were frustrated by the spirited resistance of the
Moscow Bolsheviks. An acute struggle broke out in the Ukrainian Party
organizations as well. Led by Comrade Molotov, then the secretary of
the Central Committee of the Communist Party of the Ukraine, the
Ukrainian Bolsheviks routed the Trotskyites and Shlyapnikovites. The
Communist Party of the Ukraine remained a loyal support of Lenin's
Party. In Baku, the routing of the opposition was led by Comrade
Ordjonikidze. In Central Asia, the fight against the anti-Party group-
ings were headed by Comrade L. Kaganovich.

All the important local organizations of the Party endorsed Lenin's
platform.

On March 8, 1921, the Tenth Party Congress opened. The congress was attended by 694 delegates with vote, representing 732,521
Party members, and 296 delegates with voice but no vote.

The congress summed up the discussion on the trade unions and
endorsed Lenin's platform by an overwhelming majority.

In opening the congress, Lenin said that the discussion had been an
inexcusable luxury. He declared that the enemies had speculated on the
inner Party strife and on a split in the ranks of the Communist Party.

Realizing how extremely dangerous the existence of factional groups
was to the Bolshevik Party and the dictatorship of the proletariat, the
Tenth Congress paid special attention to *Party unity*. The report on
this question was made by Lenin. The congress passed condemnation
on all the opposition groups and declared that they were "in fact helping
the class enemies of the proletarian revolution."

The congress ordered the immediate dissolution of all factional
groups and instructed all Party organizations to keep a strict watch to
prevent any outbreaks of factionalism, non-observance of the congress
decision to be followed by unconditional and immediate expulsion from
the Party. The congress authorized the Central Committee, in the event
of members of that body violating discipline, or reviving or tolerating
factionalism, to apply to them all Party penalties, including expulsion
from the Central Committee and from the Party.

These decisions were embodied in a special resolution on "Party
Unity," moved by Lenin and adopted by the congress.

In this resolution, the congress reminded all Party members that
unity and solidarity of the ranks of the Party, unanimity of will of the
vanguard of the proletariat were particularly essential at that juncture,
when a number of circumstances had, during the time of the Tenth
Congress, increased the vacillation among the petty-bourgeois population
of the country.

"Notwithstanding this," read the resolution, "even before the general Party discussion on the trade unions, certain signs of factionalism had been apparent in the Party, *viz.*, the formation of groups with separate platforms, striving to a certain degree to segregate and create their own group discipline. All class-conscious workers must clearly realize the perniciousness and impermissibility of factionalism of any kind, for in practice factionalism inevitably results in weakening team work. At the same time it inevitably leads to intensified and repeated attempts by the enemies of the Party, who have fastened themselves onto it because it is the governing party, to widen the cleavage (in the Party) and to use it for counter-revolutionary purposes."

Further, in the same resolution, the congress said:

"The way the enemies of the proletariat take advantage of every deviation from the thoroughly consistent Communist line was most strikingly shown in the case of the Kronstadt mutiny, when the bourgeois counter-revolutionaries and Whiteguards in all countries of the world immediately expressed their readiness to accept even the slogans of the Soviet system, if only they might thereby secure the overthrow of the dictatorship of the proletariat in Russia, and when the Socialist-Revolutionaries and the bourgeois counter-revolutionaries in general resorted in Kronstadt to slogans calling for an insurrection against the Soviet Government of Russia ostensibly in the interest of Soviet power. These facts fully prove that the Whiteguards strive, and are able to disguise themselves as Communists, and even as people "more Left" than the Communists, solely for the purpose of weakening and overthrowing the bulwark of the proletarian revolution in Russia. Menshevik leaflets distributed in Petrograd on the eve of the Kronstadt mutiny likewise show how the Mensheviks took advantage of the disagreements in the R.C.P. actually in order to egg on and support the Kronstadt mutineers, the Socialist-Revolutionaries and Whiteguards, while claiming to be opponents of mutiny and supporters of the Soviet power, only with supposedly slight modifications."

The resolution declared that in its propaganda the Party must explain in detail the harm and danger of factionalism to Party unity and to the unity of purpose of the vanguard of the proletariat, which is a fundamental condition for the success of the dictatorship of the proletariat.

On the other hand, the congress resolution stated, the Party must explain in its propaganda the *peculiarity* of the latest tactical methods employed by the enemies of the Soviet power.

> "These enemies," read the resolution, "having realized the hopelessness of counter-revolution under an openly Whiteguard flag, are now doing their utmost to utilize the disagreements within the R.C.P. and to further the counter-revolution in one way or another by transferring the power to the political groupings which outwardly are closest to the recognition of the Soviet power." (*Resolutions of the C.P.S.U.[B.]*, Russ. ed., Part I, pp. 373-74.)

The resolution further stated that in its propaganda the Party "must also teach the lessons of preceding revolutions in which the counter-revolutionaries usually supported the petty-bourgeois groupings which stood closest to the extreme revolutionary Party, in order to undermine and overthrow the revolutionary dictatorship, and thus pave the way for the subsequent complete victory of the counter-revolution, of the capitalists and landlords."

Closely allied to the resolution on "Party Unity" was the resolution on "The Syndicalist and Anarchist Deviation in our Party," also moved by Lenin and adopted by the congress. In this resolution the Tenth Congress passed condemnation on the so-called "Workers' Opposition." The congress declared that the propaganda of the ideas of the anarchosyndicalist deviation was incompatible with membership in the Communist Party, and called upon the Party vigorously to combat this deviation.

The Tenth Congress passed the highly important decision to replace the surplus-appropriation system by a tax in kind, to adopt the *New Economic Policy* (NEP).

This turn from War Communism to NEP is a striking instance of the wisdom and farsightedness of Lenin's policy.

The resolution of the congress dealt with the substitution of a tax in kind for the surplus-appropriation system. The tax in kind was to be lighter than the assessments under the surplus-appropriation system. The total amount of the tax was to be announced each year before the spring sowing. The dates of delivery under the tax were to be strictly specified. All produce over and above the amount of the tax was to be entirely at the disposal of the peasant, who would be at liberty to sell these surpluses at will. In his speech, Lenin said that freedom of trade would at first lead to a certain revival of capitalism in the country. It would be necessary to permit private trade and to allow private manufacturers to open small businesses. But no fears need be entertained on this score. Lenin considered that a certain freedom of trade would give the peasant an economic incentive, induce him to produce more and would lead to a rapid improvement of agriculture; that, on this basis, the state-owned industries would be restored and private capital displaced; that strength and resources having been accumulated, a powerful industry could be created as the economic foundation of Socialism, and that then a determined offensive could be undertaken to destroy the remnants of capitalism in the country.

War Communism had been an attempt to take the fortress of the capitalist elements in town and countryside by assault, by a frontal attack. In this offensive the Party had gone too far ahead, and ran the risk of being cut off from its base. Now Lenin proposed to retire a little, to retreat for a while nearer to the base, to change from an assault of the fortress to the slower method of siege, so as to gather strength and resume the offensive.

The Trotskyites and other oppositionists held that NEP was *nothing but* a retreat. This interpretation suited their purpose, for their line was to restore capitalism. This was a most harmful, anti-Leninist interpretation of NEP. The fact is that only a year after NEP was introduced Lenin declared at the Eleventh Party Congress that *the retreat had come to an end,* and he put forward the slogan: *"Prepare for an offensive on private capital."* (Lenin, *Collected Works,* Russ. ed., Vol. XXVII (p. 213.)

The oppositionists, poor Marxists and crass ignoramuses in questions of Bolshevik policy as they were, understood neither the meaning of NEP nor the character of the retreat undertaken at the beginning of NEP. We have dealt with the meaning of NEP above. As for the character of the retreat, there are retreats and retreats. There are times when a party or an army has to retreat because it has suffered defeat. In such cases, the army or party retreats to preserve itself and its ranks for new battles. It was no such retreat that Lenin proposed when NEP was introduced, because, far from having suffered defeat or discomfiture, the Party had itself defeated the interventionists and Whiteguards in the Civil War. But there are other times, when in its advance a victorious party or army runs too far ahead, without providing itself with an adequate base in the rear. This creates a serious danger. So as not to lose connection with its base, an experienced party or army generally finds it necessary in such cases to fall back a little, to draw closer to and establish better contact with its base, in order to provide itself with all it needs, and then resume the offensive more confidently and with guarantee of success. It was this kind of temporary retreat that Lenin effected by the New Economic Policy. Reporting to the Fourth Congress of the Communist International on the reasons that prompted the introduction of NEP, Lenin plainly said, "in our economic offensive we ran too far ahead, we did not provide ourselves with an adequate base," and so it was necessary to make a temporary retreat to a secure rear.

The misfortune of the opposition was that, in their ignorance, they did not understand, and never understood to the end of their days, this feature of the retreat under NEP.

The decision of the Tenth Congress on the New Economic Policy ensured a durable economic alliance of the working class and the peasantry for the building of Socialism.

This prime object was served by yet another decision of the congress —the decision on the national question. The report on the national question was made by Comrade Stalin. He said that we had abolished national oppression, but that this was not enough. The task was to do away with the evil heritage of the past—the economic, political and cultural backwardness of the formerly oppressed peoples. They had to be helped to catch up with Central Russia.

Comrade Stalin further referred to two anti-Party deviations on the national question: dominant-nation (Great-Russian) chauvinism and local nationalism. The congress condemned both deviations as harmful and dangerous to Communism and proletarian internationalism. At the same time, it directed its main blow at the bigger danger, dominant-nation chauvinism, *i.e.*, the survivals and hangovers of the attitude towards the nationalities such as the Great-Russian chauvinists had displayed towards the non-Russian peoples under tsardom.

3. FIRST RESULTS OF NEP. ELEVENTH PARTY CONGRESS. FORMATION OF THE UNION OF SOVIET SOCIALIST REPUBLICS. LENIN'S ILLNESS. LENIN'S CO-OPERATIVE PLAN. TWELFTH PARTY CONGRESS

The New Economic Policy was resisted by the unstable elements in the Party. The resistance came from two quarters. First there were the "Left" shouters, political freaks like Lominadze, Shatskin and others, who argued that NEP meant a renunciation of the gains of the October Revolution, a return to capitalism, the downfall of the Soviet power. Because of their political illiteracy and ignorance of the laws of economic development, these people did not understand the policy of the Party, fell into a panic, and sowed dejection and discouragement. Then there were the downright capitulators, like Trotsky, Radek, Zinoviev, Sokolnikov, Kamenev, Shlyapnikov, Bukharin, Rykov and others, who did not believe that the Socialist development of our country was possible, bowed before the "omnipotence" of capitalism and, in their endeavour to strengthen the position of capitalism in the Soviet country, demanded far-reaching concessions to private capital, both home and foreign, and the surrender of a number of key positions of the Soviet power in the economic field to private capitalists, the latter to act either as concessionaries or as partners of the state in mixed joint stock companies.

Both groups were alien to Marxism and Leninism.

Both were exposed and isolated by the Party, which passed severe stricture on the alarmists and the capitulators.

This resistance to the Party policy was one more reminder that the Party needed to be purged of unstable elements. Accordingly, the Central Committee in 1921 organized a Party purge, which helped to considerably strengthen the Party. The purging was done at open meetings, in the presence and with the participation of non-Party people. Lenin advised that the Party be thoroughly cleansed "of rascals, bureaucrats, dishonest or wavering Communists, and of Mensheviks who have repainted their 'façade' but who have remained Mensheviks at heart." (Lenin, *Collected Works*, Russ. ed., Vol. XXVII, p. 13.)

Altogether, nearly 170,000 persons, or about 25 per cent of the total membership, were expelled from the Party as a result of the purge.

The purge greatly strengthened the Party, improved its social composition, increased the confidence of the masses in it, and heightened its prestige. The Party became more closely welded and better disciplined.

The correctness of the New Economic Policy was proved in its very first year. Its adoption served greatly to strengthen the alliance of workers and peasants on a new basis. The dictatorship of the proletariat gained in might and strength. Kulak banditry was almost completely liquidated. The middle peasants, now that the surplus-appropriation system had been abolished, helped the Soviet Government to fight the kulak bands. The Soviet Government retained all the key positions in the economic field: large-scale industry, the means of transport, the banks, the land, and home and foreign trade. The Party achieved a definite turn for the better on the economic front. Agriculture soon began to forge ahead. Industry and the railways could record their first successes. An economic revival began, still very slow but sure. The workers and the peasants felt and perceived that the Party was on the right track.

In March 1922, the Party held its Eleventh Congress. It was attended by 522 voting delegates, representing 532,000 Party members, which was less than at the previous congress. There were 165 delegates with voice but no vote. The reduction in the membership was due to the Party purge which had already begun.

At this congress the Party reviewed the results of the first year of the New Economic Policy. These results entitled Lenin to declare at the congress:

"For a year we have been retreating. In the name of the Party we must now call a halt. The purpose pursued by the retreat has been achieved. This period is drawing, or has drawn, to a close. Now our purpose is different—to regroup our forces." (*Ibid.*, p. 238.)

Lenin said that NEP meant a life and death struggle between capitalism and Socialism. "Who will win?"—that was the question. In order that we might win, the bond between the working class and the peasantry, between Socialist industry and peasant agriculture, had to be made secure by developing the exchange of goods between town and country to the utmost. For this purpose the art of management and of efficient trading would have to be learned.

At that period, trade was the main link in the chain of problems that confronted the Party. Unless this problem were solved it would be impossible to develop the exchange of goods between town and country, to strengthen the economic alliance between the workers and peasants, impossible to advance agriculture, or to extricate industry from its state of disruption.

Soviet trade at that time was still very undeveloped. The machinery of trade was highly inadequate. Communists had not yet learned the art of trade; they had not studied the enemy, the Nepman, or learned how to combat him. The private traders, or Nepmen, had taken advantage of the undeveloped state of Soviet trade to capture the trade in textiles and other goods in general demand. The organization of state and co-operative trade became a matter of utmost importance.

After the Eleventh Congress, work in the economic sphere was resumed with redoubled vigour. The effects of the recent harvest failure were successfully remedied. Peasant farming showed rapid recovery. The railways began to work better. Increasing numbers of factories and plants resumed operation.

In October 1922, the Soviet Republic celebrated a great victory: Vladivostok, the last piece of Soviet territory to remain in the hands of the invaders, was wrested by the Red Army and the Far Eastern partisan from the hands of the Japanese.

The whole territory of the Soviet republic having been cleared of interventionists, and the needs of Socialist construction and national defence demanding a further consolidation of the union of the Soviet peoples, the necessity now arose of welding the Soviet republics closer together in a single federal state. All the forces of the people had to be combined for the work of building Socialism. The country had to be made impregnable. Conditions had to be created for the all-round development of every nationality in our country. This required that all the Soviet nations should be brought into still closer union.

In December 1922 the First All-Union Congress of Soviets was held, at which, on the proposal of Lenin and Stalin, a voluntary state union of the Soviet nations was formed—the Union of Soviet Socialist Republics (U.S.S.R.). Originally, the U.S.S.R. comprised the Russian Soviet Federative Socialist Republic (R.S.F.S.R.), the Trancaucasian Soviet Federative Socialist Republic (T.S.F.S.R.), the Ukrainian Soviet Socialist Republic (Ukr. S.S.R.) and the Byelorussian Soviet Socialist Republic (B.S.S.R.). Somewhat later, three independent Union Soviet Republics—the Uzbek, Turkmen and Tadjik—were formed in Central Asia. All these republics have now united in a single union of Soviet states—the U.S.S.R.—on a voluntary and equal basis, each of them being reserved the right of freely seceding from the Soviet Union.

The formation of the Union of Soviet Socialist Republics meant the consolidation of the Soviet power and a great victory for the Leninist-Stalinist policy of the Bolshevik Party on the national question.

In November 1922, Lenin made a speech at a plenary meeting of the Moscow Soviet in which he reviewed the five years of Soviet rule and expressed the firm conviction that "NEP Russia will become Socialist Russia." This was his last speech to the country. That same autumn a great misfortune overtook the Party: Lenin fell seriously ill. His illness was a deep and personal affliction to the whole Party and to all the working people. All lived in trepidation for the life of their beloved Lenin. But even in illness Lenin did not discontinue his work. When already a very sick man, he wrote a number of highly important articles. In these last writings he reviewed the work already performed and outlined a plan for the building of Socialism in our country by enlisting the peasantry in the cause of Socialist construction. This contained his co-operative plan for securing the participation of the peasantry in the work of building Socialism.

Lenin regarded co-operative societies in general, and agricultural co-operative societies in particular, as a means of transition—a means within the reach and understanding of the peasant millions—from small, individual farming to large-scale producing associations, or collective farms. Lenin pointed out that the line to be followed in the development of agriculture in our country was to draw the peasants into the work of building Socialism through the co-operative societies, gradually to introduce the collective principle in agriculture, first in the selling, and then in the growing of farm produce. With the dictatorship of the proletariat and the alliance of the working class and the peasantry, with the leadership of the peasantry by the proletariat made secure, and with the existence of a Socialist industry, Lenin said, a properly organized producing co-operative system embracing millions of peasants was the means whereby a complete Socialist society could be built in our country.

In April 1923, the Party held its Twelfth Congress. Since the seizure of power by the Bolsheviks this was the first congress at which Lenin was unable to be present. The congress was attended by 408 voting delegates, representing 386,000 Party members. This was less than was represented at the previous congress, the reduction being due to the fact that in the interval the Party purge had continued and had resulted in the expulsion of a considerable percentage of the Party membership. There were 417 delegates with voice but no vote.

The Twelfth Party Congress embodied in its decisions the recommendations made by Lenin in his recent articles and letters.

The congress sharply rebuked those who took NEP to mean a retreat from the Socialist position, a surrender to capitalism, and who advocated a return to capitalist bondage. Proposals of this kind were made at the congress by Radek and Krassin, followers of Trotsky. They proposed that we should throw ourselves on the tender mercies of foreign capitalists, surrender to them, in the form of concessions, branches of industry that were of vital necessity to the Soviet state. They proposed that we pay the tsarist government's debts annulled by the October Revolution. The Party stigmatized these capitulatory proposals as treachery. It did not reject the policy of granting concessions, but favoured it only in such industries and in such dimensions as would be of advantage to the Soviet state.

Bukharin and Sokolnikov had even prior to the congress proposed the abolition of the state monopoly of foreign trade. The proposal was also based on the conception that NEP was a surrender to capitalism. Lenin had branded Bukharin as a champion of the profiteers, Nepmen and kulaks. The Twelfth Congress firmly repelled the attempts to undermine the monopoly of foreign trade.

The congress also repelled Trotsky's attempt to foist upon the Party a policy towards the peasantry that would have been fatal, and stated that the predominance of small peasant farming in the country was a fact not to be forgotten. It emphatically declared that the development of industry, including heavy industry, must not run counter to the interests of the peasant masses, but must be based on a close bond with the peasants, in the interests of the whole working population. These decisions were an answer to Trotsky, who had proposed that we should build up our industry by exploiting the peasants, and who in fact did not accept the policy of an alliance of the proletariat with the peasantry.

At the same time, Trotsky had proposed that big plants like the Putilov, Bryansk and others, which were of importance to the country's defence, should be closed down allegedly on the grounds that they were unprofitable. The congress indignantly rejected Trotsky's proposals.

On Lenin's proposal, sent to the congress in written form, the Twelfth Congress united the Central Control Commission of the Party and the Workers' and Peasants' Inspection into one body. To this united body were entrusted the important duties of safeguarding the unity of our Party, strengthening Party and civil discipline, and improving the Soviet state apparatus in every way.

An important item on the agenda of the congress was the national question, the report on which was made by Comrade Stalin. Comrade Stalin stressed the international significance of our policy on the national question. To the oppressed peoples in the East and West, the Soviet Union was a model of the solution of the national question and the abolition of national oppression. He pointed out that energetic measures were needed to put an end to economic and cultural inequality among the peoples of the Soviet Union. He called upon the Party to put up a determined fight against deviations in the national question—Great-Russian chauvinism and local bourgeois nationalism.

The nationalist deviators and their dominant-nation policy towards the national minorities were exposed at the congress. At that time the Georgian nationalist deviators, Mdivani and others, were opposing the Party. They had been against the formation of the Trancaucasian Federation and were against the promotion of friendship between the peoples of Transcaucasia. The deviators were behaving like outright dominant-nation chauvinists towards the other nationalities of Georgia. They were expelling non-Georgians from Tiflis wholesale, especially Armenians; they had passed a law under which Georgian women who married non-Georgians lost their Georgian citizenship. The Georgian nationalist deviators were supported by Trotsky, Radek, Bukharin, Skrypnik and Rakovsky.

Shortly after the congress, a special conference of Party workers from the national republics was called to discuss the national question. Here were exposed a group of Tatar bourgeois nationalists—Sultan-Galiev and others—and a group of Uzbek nationalist deviators—Faizulla Khodjayev and others.

The Twelfth Party Congress reviewed the results of the New Economic Policy for the past two years. They were very heartening results and inspired confidence in ultimate victory.

"Our Party has remained solid and united; it has stood the test of a momentous turn, and is marching on with flying colours," Comrade Stalin declared at the congress.

4. STRUGGLE AGAINST THE DIFFICULTIES OF ECONOMIC RESTORATION. TROTSKYITES TAKE ADVANTAGE OF LENIN'S ILLNESS TO INCREASE THEIR ACTIVITY. NEW PARTY DISCUSSION. DEFEAT OF THE TROTSKYITES. DEATH OF LENIN. THE LENIN ENROLMENT. THIRTEENTH PARTY CONGRESS

The struggle to restore the national economy yielded substantial results in its very first year. By 1924 progress was to be observed in all fields. The crop area had increased considerably since 1921, and peasant farming was steadily improving. Socialist industry was growing and expanding. The working class had greatly increased in numbers. Wages had risen. Life had become easier and better for the workers and peasants as compared with 1920 and 1921.

But the effects of the economic disruption still made themselves felt. Industry was still below the pre-war level, and its development was still far behind the country's demand. At the end of 1923 there were about a million unemployed; the national economy was progressing too slowly to absorb unemployment. The development of trade was being hindered by the excessive prices of manufactured goods, prices which the Nepmen, and the Nepman elements in our trading organizations, were imposing on the country. Owing to this, the Soviet ruble began to fluctuate violently and to fall in value. These factors impeded the improvement of the condition of the workers and peasants.

In the autumn of 1923, the economic difficulties were somewhat

aggravated owing to violations of the Soviet price policy by our industrial
and commercial organizations.   There was a yawning gap between the
prices of manufactures and the prices of farm produce.   Grain prices
were low, while prices of manufacturers were inordinately high. Industry
was burdened with excessive overhead costs which increased the price
of goods.   The money which the peasants received for their grain rapidly
depreciated.   To make matters worse, the Trotskyite Pyatakov, who
was at that time on the Supreme Council of National Economy, gave
managers and directors criminal instructions to grind all the profit
they could out of the sale of manufactured goods and to force up prices
to the maximum, ostensibly for the purpose of developing industry.   As
a matter of fact, this Nepman policy could only narrow the base of
industry and undermine it.   It became unprofitable for the peasantry to
purchase manufactured goods, and they stopped buying them.   The
result was a sales crisis, from which industry suffered.   Difficulties arose
in the payment of wages.   This provoked discontent among the workers.
At some factories the more backward workers stopped work.

The Central Committee of the Party adopted measures to remove
these difficulties and anomalies.   Steps were taken to overcome the sales
crisis.   Prices of consumers' goods were reduced.   It was decided to reform the currency and to adopt a firm and stable currency unit, the cher-
vonetz.   The normal payment of wages was resumed.   Measures were
outlined for the development of trade through state and co-operative
channels and for the elimination of private traders and profiteers.

What was now required was that everybody should join in the common effort, roll up his sleeves, and set to work with gusto.   That is the
way all who were loyal to the Party thought and acted.   But not so the
Trotskyites.   They took advantage of the absence of Lenin, who was
incapacitated by grave illness, to launch a new attack on the Party and
its leadership.   They decided that this was a favourable moment to smash
the Party and overthrow its leadership.   They used everything they could
as a weapon against the Party: the defeat of the revolution in Germany
and Bulgaria in the autumn of 1923, the economic difficulties at home,
and Lenin's illness.   It was at this moment of difficulty for the Soviet
state, when the Party's leader was stricken by sickness, that Trotsky
started his attack on the Bolshevik Party.   He mustered all the anti-
Leninist elements in the Party and concocted an opposition platform
against the Party, its leadership, and its policy.   This platform was called
the Declaration of the Forty-Six Oppositionists.   All the opposition groupings—the Trotskyites, Democratic-Centralists, and the remnants of the
"Left Communist" and "Workers' Opposition" groups—united to fight

the Leninist Party. In their declaration, they prophesied a grave economic crisis and the fall of the Soviet power, and demanded freedom of factions and groups as the only way out of the situation.

This was a fight for the restoration of factionalism which the Tenth Party Congress, on Lenin's proposal, had prohibited.

The Trotskyites did not make a single definite proposal for the improvement of agriculture or industry, for the improvement of the circulation of commodities, or for the betterment of the condition of the working people. This did not even interest them. The only thing that interested them was to take advantage of Lenin's absence in order to restore factions within the Party, to undermine its foundations and its Central Committee.

The platform of the forty-six was followed up by the publication of a letter by Trotsky in which he vilified the Party cadres and levelled new slanderous accusations against the Party. In this letter Trotsky harped on the old Menshevik themes which the Party had heard from him many times before.

First of all the Trotskyites attacked the Party apparatus. They knew that without a strong apparatus the Party could not live and function. The opposition tried to undermine and destroy the Party apparatus, to set the Party members against it, and the young members against the old stalwarts of the Party. In this letter Trotsky played up to the students, the young Party members who were not acquainted with the history of the Party's fight against Trotskyism. To win the support of the students, Trotsky flatteringly referred to them as the "Party's surest barometer," at the same time declaring that the Leninist old guard had degenerated. Alluding to the degeneration of the leaders of the Second International, he made the foul insinuation that the old Bolshevik guard was going the same way. By this outcry about the degeneration of the Party, Trotsky tried to hide his own degeneration and his anti-Party scheming.

The Trotskyites circulated both oppositionist documents, *viz.*, the platform of the forty-six and Trotsky's letter, in the districts and among the Party nuclei and put them up for discussion by the Party membership.

They challenged the Party to a discussion.

Thus the Trotskyites forced a general discussion on the Party, just as they did at the time of the controversy over the trade union question before the Tenth Party Congress.

Although the Party was occupied with the far more important problems of the country's economic life, it accepted the challenge and opened the discussion.

The whole Party was involved in the discussion. The fight took a most bitter form. It was fiercest of all in Moscow, for the Trotskyites endeavoured above all to capture the Party organization in the capital. But the discussion was of no help to the Trotskyites. It only disgraced them. They were completely routed both in Moscow and all other parts of the Soviet Union. Only a small number of nuclei in universities and offices voted for the Trotskyites.

In January 1924 the Party held its Thirteenth Conference. The conference heard a report by Comrade Stalin, summing up the results of the discussion. The conference condemned the Trotskyite opposition, declaring that it was a *petty-bourgeois deviation* from Marxism. The decisions of the conference were subsequently endorsed by the Thirteenth Party Congress and the Fifth Congress of the Communist International. The international Communist proletariat supported the Bolshevik Party in its fight against Trotskyism.

But the Trotskyites did not cease their subversive work. In the autumn of 1924, Trotsky published an article entitled, "The Lessons of October" in which he attempted to substitute Trotskyism for Leninism. It was a sheer slander on our Party and its leader, Lenin. This defamatory broadsheet was seized upon by all enemies of Communism and of the Soviet Government. The Party was outraged by this unscrupulous distortion of the heroic history of Bolshevism. Comrade Stalin denounced Trotsky's attempt to substitute Trotskyism for Leninism. He declared that "it is the duty of the Party to bury Trotskyism as an ideological trend."

An effective contribution to the ideological defeat of Trotskyism and to the defense of Leninism was Comrade Stalin's theoretical work, *Foundations of Leninism*, published in 1924. This book is a masterly exposition and a weighty theoretical substantiation of Leninism. It was, and is today, a trenchant weapon of Marxist-Leninist theory in the hands of Bolsheviks all over the world.

In the battles against Trotskyism, Comrade Stalin rallied the Party around its Central Committee and mobilized it to carry on the fight for the victory of Socialism in our country. Comrade Stalin proved that Trotskyism had to be ideologically demolished if the further victorious advance to Socialism was to be ensured.

Reviewing this period of the fight against Trotskyism, Comrade Stalin said:

> "Unless Trotskyism is defeated, it will be impossible to achieve victory under the conditions of NEP, it will be impossible to convert present-day Russia into a Socialist Russia."

But the successes attending the Party's Leninist policy were clouded by a most grievous calamity which now befell the Party and the working class.   On January 21, 1924, Lenin, our leader and teacher, the creator of the Bolshevik Party, passed away in the village of Gorki, near Moscow. Lenin's death was received by the working class of the whole world as a most cruel loss.   On the day of Lenin's funeral the international proletariat proclaimed a five-minute stoppage of work.   Railways, mills and factories came to a standstill.   As Lenin was borne to the grave, the working people of the whole world paid homage to him in overwhelming sorrow, as to a father and teacher, their best friend and defender.

The loss of Lenin caused the working class of the Soviet Union to rally even more solidly around the Leninist Party.   In those days of mourning every class-conscious worker defined his attitude to the Communist Party, the executor of Lenin's behest.   The Central Committee of the Party received thousands upon thousands of applications from workers for admission to the Party.   The Central Committee responded to this movement and proclaimed a mass admission of politically advanced workers into the Party ranks.   Tens of thousands of workers flocked into the Party; they were people prepared to give their lives for the cause of the Party, the cause of Lenin.   In a brief space of time over two hundred and forty thousand workers joined the ranks of the Bolshevik Party.   They were the foremost section of the working class, the most class-conscious and revolutionary, the most intrepid and disciplined.   This was the *Lenin Enrolment*.

The reaction to Lenin's death demonstrated how close are our Party's ties with the masses, and how high a place the Leninist Party holds in the hearts of the workers.

In the days of mourning for Lenin, at the Second Congress of Soviets of the U.S.S.R., Comrade Stalin made a solemn vow in the name of the Party.   He said:

"We Communists are people of a special mould.   We are made of a special stuff.   We are those who form the army of the great proletarian strategist, the army of Comrade Lenin.   There is nothing higher than the honour of belonging to this army.   There is nothing higher than the title of member of the Party whose founder and leader is Comrade Lenin. . . .

"Departing from us, Comrade Lenin adjured us to hold high and guard the purity of the great title of member of the Party.   We vow to you, Comrade Lenin, that we will fulfil your behest with honour! . . .

"Departing from us, Comrade Lenin adjured us to guard the unity of our Party as the apple of our eye. We vow to you, Comrade Lenin, that this behest, too, we will fulfil with honour! ...

"Departing from us, Comrade Lenin adjured us to guard and strengthen the dictatorship of the proletariat. We vow to you, Comrade Lenin, that we will spare no effort to fulfil this behest, too, with honour! ...

"Departing from us, Comrade Lenin adjured us to strengthen with all our might the alliance of the workers and the peasants. We vow to you, Comrade Lenin, that this behest, too, we will fulfil with honour! ...

"Comrade Lenin untiringly urged upon us the necessity of maintaining the voluntary union of the nations of our country, the necessity for fraternal co-operation between them within the framework of the Union of Republics. Departing from us, Comrade Lenin adjured us to consolidate and extend the Union of Republics. We vow to you, Comrade Lenin, that this behest, too, we will fulfil with honour! ...

"More than once did Lenin point out to us that the strengthening of the Red Army and the improvement of its condition is one of the most important tasks of our Party.... Let us vow then, comrades, that we will spare no effort to strengthen our Red Army and our Red Navy....

"Departing from us, Comrade Lenin adjured us to remain faithful to the principles of the Communist International. We vow to you, Comrade Lenin, that we will not spare our lives to strengthen and extend the union of the toilers of the whole world—the Communist International!" (Joseph Stalin, *The Lenin Heritage.*)

This was the vow made by the Bolshevik Party to its leader, Lenin, whose memory will live throughout the ages.

In May 1924 the Party held its Thirteenth Congress. It was attended by 748 voting delegates, representing a Party membership of 735,881. This marked increase in membership in comparison with the previous congress was due to the admission of some 250,000 new members under the Lenin Enrolment. There were 416 delegates with voice but no vote.

The congress unanimously condemned the platform of the Trotskyite opposition, defining it as a petty-bourgeois deviation from Marxism, as a revision of Leninism, and endorsed the resolutions of the Thirteenth

Party Conference on "Party Affairs" and "The Results of the Discussion."

With the purpose of strengthening the bond between town and country, the congress gave instructions for a further expansion of industry, primarily of the light industries, while placing particular stress on the necessity for a rapid development of the iron and steel industry.

The congress endorsed the formation of the People's Commissariat of Internal Trade and set the trading bodies the task of gaining control of the market and ousting private capital from the sphere of trade.

The congress gave instructions for the increase of cheap state credit to the peasantry so as to oust the usurer from the countryside.

The congress called for the maximum development of the co-operative movement among the peasantry as the paramount task in the countryside.

Lastly, the congress stressed the profound importance of the Lenin Enrolment and drew the Party's attention to the necessity of devoting greater efforts to educating the young Party members—and above all the recruits of the Lenin Enrolment—in the principles of Leninism.

5. THE SOVIET UNION TOWARDS THE END OF THE RESTORATION PERIOD. THE QUESTION OF SOCIALIST CONSTRUCTION AND THE VICTORY OF SOCIALISM IN OUR COUNTRY. ZINOVIEV-KAMENEV "NEW OPPOSITION." FOURTEENTH PARTY CONGRESS. POLICY OF SOCIALIST INDUSTRIALIZATION OF THE COUNTRY

For over four years the Bolshevik Party and the working class had been working strenuously along the lines of the New Economic Policy. The heroic work of economic restoration was approaching completion. The economic and political might of the Soviet Union was steadily growing.

By this time the international situation had undergone a change. Capitalism had withstood the first revolutionary onslaught of the masses after the imperialist war. The revolutionary movement in Germany, Italy, Bulgaria, Poland and a number of other countries had been crushed. The bourgeoisie had been aided in this by the leaders of the compromising Social-Democratic parties. A temporary ebb in the tide of revolution set in. There began a temporary, partial stabilization of capitalism in Western Europe, a partial consolidation of the position of capitalism. But the stabilization of capitalism did not eliminate the basic contradictions rending capitalist society. On the contrary, the partial stabilization of capitalism aggravated the contradictions between the workers and the capitalists, between imperialism and the colonial nations, between the imperialist groups of the various countries. The stabilization of capitalism was preparing for a new explosion of contradictions, for new crises in the capitalist countries.

Parallel with the stabilization of capitalism, proceeded the stabilization of the Soviet Union. But these two processes of stabilization were fundamentally different in character. Capitalist stabilization presaged a new crisis of capitalism. The stabilization of the Soviet Union meant a further growth of the economic and political might of the Socialist country.

Despite the defeat of the revolution in the West, the position of the Soviet Union in the international arena continued to grow stronger, although, it is true, at a slower rate.

In 1922, the Soviet Union had been invited to an international economic conference in Genoa, Italy. At the Genoa Conference the imperialist governments, emboldened by the defeat of the revolution in the capitalist countries, tried to bring new pressure to bear on the Soviet Republic, this time in diplomatic form. The imperialists presented brazen demands to the Soviet Republic. They demanded that the factories and plants which had been nationalized by the October Revolution be returned to the foreign capitalists; they demanded the payment of the debts of the tsarist government. In return, the imperialist states promised some trifling loans to the Soviet Government.

The Soviet Union rejected these demands.

The Genoa Conference was barren of result.

The threat of a new intervention contained in the ultimatum of Lord Curzon, the British Foreign Secretary, in 1923, also met with the rebuff it deserved.

Having tested the strength of the Soviet Government and convinced themselves of its stability, the capitalist states began one after another to resume diplomatic relations with our country. In 1924 diplomatic relations were restored with Great Britain, France, Japan and Italy.

It was plain that the Soviet Union had been able to win a prolonged breathing space, a period of peace.

The domestic situation had also changed. The self-sacrificing efforts of the workers and peasants, led by the Bolshevik Party, had borne fruit. The rapid development of the national economy was manifest. In the fiscal year 1924-25, agricultural output had already approached the pre-war level, amounting to 87 per cent of the pre-war output. In 1925 the large-scale industries of the U.S.S.R. were already producing about *three-quarters* of the pre-war industrial output. In the fiscal year 1924-25, the Soviet Union was able to invest 385,000,000 rubles in capital construction work. The plan for the electrification of the country was proceeding successfully. Socialism was consolidating its key positions in the national economy. Important successes had been won in the struggle against private capital in industry and trade.

Economic progress was accompanied by a further improvement in the condition of the workers and peasants. The working class was growing rapidly. Wages had risen, and so had productivity of labour. The standard of living of the peasants had greatly improved. In 1924-25, the Workers' and Peasants' Government was able to assign nearly 290,000,000 rubles for the purpose of assisting the small peasants. The improvement in the condition of the workers and peasants led to greater political activity on the part of the masses. The dictatorship of the proletariat was now more firmly established. The prestige and influence of the Bolshevik Party had grown.

The restoration of the national economy was approaching completion. But mere economic restoration, the mere attainment of the pre-war level, was not enough for the Soviet Union, the land of Socialism in construction. The pre-war level was the level of a backward country. The advance had to be continued beyond that point. The prolonged breathing space gained by the Soviet state ensured the possibility of further development.

But this raised the question in all its urgency: what were to be the perspectives, the character of our development, of our construction, what was to be the destiny of Socialism in the Soviet Union? In what direction was economic development in the Soviet Union to be carried on, in the direction of Socialism, or in some other direction? Should we and could we build a Socialist economic system; or were we fated but to manure the soil for another economic system, the capitalist economic system? Was it possible at all to build a Socialist economic system in the U.S.S.R., and, if so, could it be built in spite of the delay of the revolution in the capitalist countries, in spite of the stabilization of capitalism? Was it at all possible to build a Socialist economic system by way of the New Economic Policy, which, while it was strengthening and augmenting the forces of Socialism in the country in every way, nevertheless still promoted a certain growth of capitalism? How was a Socialist economic system to be constructed, from which end should its construction begin?

All these questions confronted the Party towards the end of the restoration period, and no longer as theoretical questions, but as practical questions, as questions of everyday economic policy.

All these questions needed straightforward and plain answers, so that our Party members engaged in the development of industry and agriculture, as well as the people generally, might know in what direction to work, towards Socialism, or towards capitalism.

Unless plain answers were given to these questions, all our practical work of construction would be without perspective, work in the dark, labour in vain.

The Party gave plain and definite answers to all these questions.

Yes, replied the Party, a Socialist economic system could be and should be built in our country, for we had everything needed for the building of a Socialist economic system, for the building of a complete Socialist society. In October 1917 the working class had vanquished capitalism *politically*, by establishing its own political dictatorship. Since then the Soviet Government had been taking every measure to shatter the economic power of capitalism and to create conditions for the building of a Socialist economic system. These measures were: the expropriation of the capitalists and landlords; the conversion of the land, factories, mills, railways and the banks into public property; the adoption of the New Economic Policy; the building up of a state-owned Socialist industry; and the application of Lenin's co-operative plan. Now the main task was to proceed to build a new, Socialist economic system all over the country and thus smash capitalism *economically* as well. All our practical work, all our actions must be made to serve this main purpose. The working class could do it, and would do it. The realization of this colossal task must begin with the industrialization of the country. The Socialist industrialization of the country was the chief link in the chain; with it the construction of a Socialist economic system must begin. Neither the delay of the revolution in the West, nor the partial stabilization of capitalism in the non-Soviet countries could stop our advance— to Socialism. The New Economic Policy could only make this task easier, for it had been introduced by the Party with the specific purpose of facilitating the laying of a Socialist foundation for our economic system.

Such was the Party's answer to the question—was the victory of Socialist construction possible in our country?

But the Party knew that the problem of the victory of Socialism in one country did not end there. The construction of Socialism in the Soviet Union would be a momentous turning point in the history of mankind, a victory for the working class and peasantry of the U.S.S.R., marking a new epoch in the history of the world. Yet this was an internal affair of the U.S.S.R. and was only a part of the problem of the victory of Socialism. The other part of the problem was its international aspect. In substantiating the thesis that Socialism could be victorious in one country, Comrade Stalin had repeatedly pointed out that the question should be viewed from two aspects, the domestic and the international. As for the domestic aspect of the question, *i.e.*, the class relations within the country, the working class and the peasantry of the U.S.S.R. were fully capable of vanquishing their own bourgeoisie *economically* and building a complete Socialist society. But there was also the international aspect of the question, namely, the sphere of foreign relations, the sphere of the relations between the Soviet Union and the capitalist countries, between the Soviet people and the international bourgeoisie, which hated the Soviet system and was seeking the chance to start again armed intervention in the Soviet Union, to make new attempts to restore capitalism in the U.S.S.R. And since the U.S.S.R. was as yet the only Socialist country, all the other countries remaining capitalist, the U.S.S.R. continued to be encircled by a capitalist world, which gave rise to the danger of capitalist intervention. Clearly, there would be a danger of capitalist intervention as long as this capitalist encirclement existed. Could the Soviet people by their own efforts destroy this external danger, the danger of capitalist intervention in the U.S.S.R.? No, they could not. They could not, because in order to destroy the danger of capitalist intervention the capitalist encirclement would have to be destroyed; and the capitalist encirclement could be destroyed only as a result of victorious proletarian revolutions in at least several countries. It followed from this that the victory of Socialism in the U.S.S.R., as expressed in the abolition of the capitalist economic system and the building of a Socialist economic system, could not be considered a *final* victory, inasmuch as the danger of foreign armed intervention and of attempts to restore capitalism had not been eliminated, and inasmuch as the Socialist country had no guarantee against this danger. To destroy the danger of foreign capitalist intervention, the capitalist encirclement would have to be destroyed.

Of course, as long as the Soviet Government pursued a correct policy, the Soviet people and their Red Army would be able to beat off a new foreign capitalist intervention just as they had beaten off the first capitalist intervention of 1918-20. But this would not mean that the danger of new capitalist intervention would be eliminated. The defeat of the first intervention did not destroy the danger of new intervention, inasmuch as the source of the danger of intervention—the capitalist en-circlement—continued to exist. Neither would the danger of intervention be destroyed by the defeat of the new intervention if the capitalist en-circlement continued to exist.

It followed from this that the victory of the proletarian revolution in the capitalist countries was a matter of vital concern to the working people of the U.S.S.R.

Such was the Party's line on the question of the victory of Socialism in our country.

The Central Committee demanded that this line be discussed at the forthcoming Fourteenth Party Conference, and that it be endorsed and accepted as the line of the Party, as a Party law, *binding* upon all Party members.

This line of the Party came as a thunderbolt to the oppositionists, above all, because the Party lent it a specific and practical character, linked it with a practical plan for the Socialist industrialization of the country, and demanded that it be formulated as a Party law, as a resolution of the Fourteenth Party Conference, binding upon all Party members.

The Trotskyites opposed this Party line and set up against it the Menshevik "theory of permanent revolution," which it would be an insult to Marxism to call a Marxist theory, and which denied the possibil-ity of the victory of Socialist construction in the U.S.S.R.

The Bukharinites did not venture to oppose the Party line out-spokenly. But they furtively set up against it their own "theory" of the peaceful growing of the bourgeoisie into Socialism, amplifying it with a "new" slogan—"Get Rich!" According to the Bukharinites, the victory of Socialism meant fostering and encircling the bourgeoisie, not destroying it.

Zinoviev and Kamenev ventured forth with the assertion that the victory of Socialism in the U.S.S.R. was impossible because of the coun-try's technical and economic backwardness, but they soon found it pru-dent to hide under cover.

The Fourteenth Party Conference (April, 1925) condemned all these capitulatory "theories" of the open and covert oppositionists and affirmed the Party line of working for the victory of Socialism in the U.S.S.R., adopting a resolution to this effect.

Driven to the wall, Zinoviev and Kamenev preferred to vote for this resolution. But the Party knew that they had only postponed their struggle and had decided to "give battle to the Party" at the Fourteenth Party Congress. They were mustering a following in Leningrad and forming the so-called "New Opposition."

The Fourteenth Party Congress opened in December 1925.

The situation within the Party was tense and strained. Never in its history had there been a case when the whole delegation from an important Party centre like Leningrad had prepared to come out in opposition to their Central Committee.

The congress was attended by 665 delegates with vote and 641 with voice but no vote, representing 643,000 Party members and 445,000 candidate members, or a little less than at the previous congress. The reduction was due to a partial purge, a purge of the Party organizations in universities and offices to which anti-Party elements had gained entrance.

The political report of the Central Committee was made by Comrade Stalin. He drew a vivid picture of the growth of the political and economic might of the Soviet Union. Thanks to the advantages of the Soviet economic system, both industry and agriculture had been restored in a comparatively short space of time and were approaching the pre-war level. But good as these results were, Comrade Stalin proposed that we should not rest there, for they could not nullify the fact that our country still remained a backward, agrarian country. Two-thirds of the total production of the country was provided by agriculture and only one-third by industry. Comrade Stalin said that the Party was now squarely confronted with the problem of converting our country into an industrial country, economically independent of capitalist countries. This could be done, and must be done. It was now the cardinal task of the Party to fight for the Socialist industrialization of the country, for the victory of Socialism.

"The conversion of our country from an agrarian into an industrial country able to produce the machinery it needs by its own efforts—that is the essence, the basis of our general line," said Comrade Stalin.

The industrialization of the country would ensure its economic independence, strengthen its power of defence and create the conditions for the victory of Socialism in the U.S.S.R.

The Zinovievites opposed the general line of the Party. As against Stalin's plan of Socialist industrialization, the Zinovievite Sokolnikov put forward a bourgeois plan, one that was then in vogue among the imperialist sharks. According to this plan, the U.S.S.R. was to remain an agrarian country, chiefly producing raw materials and foodstuffs, exporting them, and importing machinery, which it did not and should not produce itself. As conditions were in 1925, this was tantamount to a plan for the economic enslavement of the U.S.S.R. by the industrially-developed foreign countries, a plan for the perpetuation of the industrial backwardness of the U.S.S.R. for the benefit of the imperialist sharks of the capitalist countries.

The adoption of this plan would have converted our country into an impotent agrarian, agricultural appendage of the capitalist world; it would have left it weak and defenceless against the surrounding capitalist world, and in the end would have been fatal to the cause of Socialism in the U.S.S.R.

The congress condemned the economic "plan" of the Zinovievites as a plan for the enslavement of the U.S.S.R.

Equally unsuccessful were the other sorties of the "New Opposition" as, for instance, when they asserted (in defiance of Lenin) that our state industries were not Socialist industries, or when they declared (again in defiance of Lenin) that the middle peasant could not be an ally of the working class in the work of Socialist construction.

The congress condemned these sorties of the "New Opposition" as anti-Leninist.

Comrade Stalin laid bare the Trotskyite-Menshevik essence of the "New Opposition." He showed that Zinoviev and Kamenev were only harping on the old tunes of the enemies of the Party with whom Lenin had waged so relentless a struggle.

It was clear that the Zinovievites were nothing but ill-disguised Trotskyites.

Comrade Stalin stressed the point that the main task of our Party was to maintain a firm alliance between the working class and the middle peasant in the work of building Socialism. He pointed to two deviations on the peasant question existing in the Party at that time, both of which constituted a menace to this alliance. The first deviation was the one that underestimated and belittled the kulak danger, the second was the one that stood in panic fear of the kulak and underestimated the role of the middle peasant. To the question, which deviation was worse, Comrade Stalin replied: "One is as bad as the other. And if these deviations are allowed to develop they may disintegrate and destroy the Party. Fortunately there are forces in our Party capable of ridding it of both deviations."

And the Party did indeed rout both deviations, the "Left" and the Right, and rid itself of them.

Summing up the debate on the question of economic development, the Fourteenth Party Congress unanimously rejected the capitulatory plans of the oppositionists and recorded in its now famous resolution:

"In the sphere of economic development, the congress holds that in our land, the land of the dictatorship of the proletariat, there is 'every requisite for the building of a complete Socialist society' (*Lenin*). The congress considers that the main task of our Party is to fight for the victory of Socialist construction in the U.S.S.R."

The Fourteenth Party Congress adopted new Party Rules.

Since the Fourteenth Congress our Party has been called the Communist Party of the Soviet Union (Bolsheviks)—the C.P.S.U. (B.).

Though defeated at the congress, the Zinovievites did not submit to the Party. They started a fight against the decisions of the Fourteenth Congress. Immediately following the congress, Zinoviev called a meeting of the Leningrad Provincial Committee of the Young Communist League, the leading group of which had been reared by Zinoviev, Zalutsky, Bakayev, Yevdokimov, Kuklin, Safarov and other double-dealers in a spirit of hatred of the Leninist Central Committee of the Party. At this meeting, the Leningrad Provincial Committee passed a resolution unparalleled in the history of the Y.C.L.: it refused to abide by the decisions of the Fourteenth Party Congress.

But the Zinovievite leaders of the Leningrad Y.C.L. did not in any way reflect the mind of the mass of Young Communist Leaguers of Leningrad. They were therefore easily defeated, and soon the Leningrad organization recovered the place in the Y.C.L. to which it was entitled.

Towards the close of the Fourteenth Congress a group of congress delegates—Comrades Molotov, Kirov, Voroshilov, Kalinin, Andreyev and others—were sent to Leningrad to explain to the members of the Leningrad Party organization the criminal, anti-Bolshevik nature of the stand taken up at the congress by the Leningrad delegation, who had secured their mandates under false pretences. The meetings at which the reports on the congress were made were marked by stormy scenes. An extraordinary conference of the Leningrad Party organization was called. The overwhelming majority of the Party members of Leningrad (over 97 per cent) fully endorsed the decisions of the Fourteenth Party Congress and condemned the anti-Party Zinovievite "New Opposition." The latter already at that time were generals without an army.

The Leningrad Bolsheviks remained in the front ranks of the Party of Lenin-Stalin.

Summing up the results of the Fourteenth Party Congress, Comrade Stalin wrote:

"The historical significance of the Fourteenth Congress of the C.P.S.U. lies in the fact that it was able to expose the very roots of the mistakes of the New Opposition, that it spurned their scepticism and sniveling, that it clearly and distinctly indicated the path of the further struggle for Socialism, opened before the Party the prospect of victory, and thus armed the proletariat with an invincible faith in the victory of Socialist construction." (Stalin, *Leninism*, Vol. I, p. 319.)

BRIEF SUMMARY

The years of transition to the peaceful work of economic restoration constituted one of the most crucial periods in the history of the Bolshevik Party. In a tense situation, the Party was able to effect the difficult turn from the policy of War Communism to the New Economic Policy. The Party reinforced the alliance of the workers and peasants on a new economic foundation. The Union of Soviet Socialist Republics was formed.

By means of the New Economic Policy, decisive results were obtained in the restoration of the economic life of the country. The Soviet Union emerged from the period of economic restoration with success and entered a new period, the period of industrialization of the country.

The transition from Civil War to peaceful Socialist construction was accompanied by great difficulties, especially in the early stages. The enemies of Bolshevism, the anti-Party elements in the ranks of the C.P.S.U.(B.), waged a desperate struggle against the Leninist Party all through this period. These anti-Party elements were headed by Trotsky. His henchmen in this struggle were Kamenev, Zinoviev and Bukharin. After the death of Lenin, the oppositionists calculated on demoralizing the ranks of the Bolshevik Party, on splitting the Party, and infecting it with disbelief in the possibility of the victory of Socialism in the U.S.S.R. In point of fact, the Trotskyites were trying to form another party in the U.S.S.R., a political organization of the new bourgeoisie, a party of capitalist restoration.

The Party rallied under the banner of Lenin around its Leninist Central Committee, around Comrade Stalin, and inflicted defeat both on the Trotskyites and on their new friends in Leningrad, the Zinoviev-Kamenev New Opposition.

Having accumulated strength and resources, the Bolshevik Party brought the country to a new stage in its history—the stage of Socialist industrialization.

CHAPTER TEN

THE BOLSHEVIK PARTY IN THE STRUGGLE FOR THE SOCIALIST INDUSTRIALIZATION OF THE COUNTRY

(1926-1929)

I. DIFFICULTIES IN THE PERIOD OF SOCIALIST INDUSTRIALIZA-
TION AND THE FIGHT TO OVERCOME THEM. FORMATION OF
THE ANTI-PARTY BLOC OF TROTSKYITES AND ZINOVIEVITES.
ANTI-SOVIET ACTIONS OF THE BLOC. DEFEAT OF THE BLOC

After the Fourteenth Congress, the Party launched a vigorous struggle for the realization of the general line of the Soviet Government—
the *Socialist industrialization* of the country.

In the restoration period the task had been to revive agriculture before all else, so as to obtain raw materials and foodstuffs, to restore and
to set going the industries, the existing mills and factories.

The Soviet Government coped with this task with comparative ease.

But in the restoration period there were three major shortcomings:

First, the mills and factories were old, equipped with worn-out
and antiquated machinery, and might soon go out of commission. The task
now was to re-equip them on up-to-date lines.

Secondly, industry in the restoration period rested on too narrow a
foundation: it lacked machine-building plants absolutely indispensable to
the country. Hundreds of these plants had to be built, for without them
no country can be considered as being really industrialized. The task
now was to build these plants and to equip them on up-to-date lines.

Thirdly, the industries in this period were mostly light industries.
These were developed and put on their feet. But, beyond a certain
point, the further development even of the light industries met an
obstacle in the weakness of heavy industry, not to mention the fact
that the country had other requirements which could be satisfied only
by a well-developed heavy industry. The task now was to tip the scales
in favour of heavy industry.

All these new tasks were to be accomplished by the policy of Socialist
industrialization.

It was necessary to build up a large number of *new* industries, industries which had not existed in tsarist Russia—new machinery, machine-

tool, automobile, chemical, and iron and steel plants—to organize the production of engines and power equipment, and to increase the mining of
ore and coal. This was essential for the victory of Socialism in the U.S.S.R.

It was necessary to create a new munitions industry, to erect new
works for the production of artillery, shells, aircraft, tanks and machine
guns. This was essential for the defence of the U.S.S.R., surrounded
as it was by a capitalist world.

It was necessary to build tractor works and plants for the production
of modern agricultural machinery, and to furnish agriculture with these
machines, so as to enable millions of small individual peasant farms to
pass to large-scale collective farming. This was essential for the victory
of Socialism in the countryside.

All this was to be achieved by the policy of industrialization, for that
is what the Socialist industrialization of the country meant.

Clearly, construction work on so large a scale would necessitate the
investment of thousands of millions of rubles. To count on foreign
loans was out of the question, for the capitalist countries refused to grant
loans. We had to build with our own resources, without foreign assistance. But we were then a poor country.

There lay one of the chief difficulties.

Capitalist countries as a rule built up their heavy industries with
funds obtained from abroad, whether by colonial plunder, or by exacting
indemnities from vanquished nations, or else by foreign loans. The Soviet
Union could not as a matter of principle resort to such infamous means
of obtaining funds as the plunder of colonies or of vanquished nations.
As for foreign loans, that avenue was closed to the U.S.S.R., as the
capitalist countries refused to lend it anything. The funds had to be
found *inside* the country.

And they were found. Financial sources were tapped in the U.S.S.R.
such as could not be tapped in any capitalist country. The Soviet
state had taken over all the mills, factories, and lands which the October
Socialist Revolution had wrested from the capitalists and landlords, all
the means of transportation, the banks, and home and foreign trade.
The profits from the state-owned mills and factories, and from the means
of transportation, trade and the banks now went to further the expansion
of industry, and not into the pockets of a parasitic capitalist class.

The Soviet Government had annulled the tsarist debts, on which the
people had annually paid hundreds of millions of gold rubles in interest
alone. By abolishing the right of the landlords to the land, the Soviet
Government had freed the peasantry from the annual payment of about

500,000,000 gold rubles in rent. Released from this burden, the peasantry was in a position to help the state to build a new and powerful industry. The peasants had a vital interest in obtaining tractors and other agricultural machinery.

All these sources of revenue were in the hands of the Soviet state. They could yield hundreds and thousands of millions of rubles for the creation of a heavy industry. All that was needed was a business-like approach, the strictly economical expenditure of funds, rationalization of industry, reduction of costs of production, elimination of unproductive expenditure, etc.

And this was the course the Soviet Government adopted.

Thanks to a regime of strict economy, the funds available for capital development increased from year to year. This made it possible to start on gigantic construction works like the Dnieper Hydro-Electric Power Station, the Turkestan-Siberian Railway, the Stalingrad Tractor Works, a number of machine-tool works, the AMO (ZIS) Automobile Works and others.

Whereas in 1926-27 about 1,000,000,000 rubles were invested in industry, three years later it was found possible to invest about 5,000,000,000 rubles.

Industrialization was making steady headway.

The capitalist countries looked upon the growing strength of the Socialist economic system in the U.S.S.R. as a threat to the existence of the capitalist system. Accordingly, the imperialist governments did everything they could to bring new pressure to bear on the U.S.S.R., to create a feeling of uncertainty and uneasiness in the country, and to frustrate, or at least to impede, the industrialization of the U.S.S.R.

In May 1927, the British Conservative Die-hards, then in office, organized a provocative raid on Arcos (the Soviet trading body in Great Britain). On May 26, 1927, the British Conservative Government broke off diplomatic and trade relations with the U.S.S.R.

On June 7, 1927, Comrade Voikov, the Soviet Ambassador in Warsaw, was assassinated by a Russian Whiteguard, a naturalized Polish subject.

About this time, too, in the U.S.S.R itself, British spies and diversionists hurled bombs at a meeting in a Party club in Leningrad, wounding about 30 people, some of them severely.

In the summer of 1927, almost simultaneous raids were made on the Soviet Embassies and Trade Representations in Berlin, Peking, Shanghai and Tientsin.

This created additional difficulties for the Soviet Government.

But the U.S.S.R. refused to be intimidated and easily repulsed the provocative attempts of the imperialists and their agents.

No less were the difficulties caused to the Party and the Soviet state by the subversive activities of the Trotskyites and other oppositionists. Comrade Stalin had good reason to say that "something like a united front from Chamberlain to Trotsky is being formed" against the Soviet Government. In spite of the decisions of the Fourteenth Party Congress and the professions of loyalty of the oppositionists, the latter had not laid down their arms. On the contrary, they intensified their efforts to undermine and split the Party.

In the summer of 1926, the Trotskyites and Zinovievites united to form an anti-Party bloc, made it a rallying point for the remnants of all the defeated opposition groups, and laid the foundation of their secret anti-Leninist party, thereby grossly violating the Party Rules and the decisions of Party congresses forbidding the formation of factions. The Central Committee of the Party gave warning that unless this anti-Party bloc—which resembled the notorious Menshevik August Bloc— were dissolved, matters might end badly for its adherents. But the supporters of the bloc would not desist.

That autumn, on the eve of the Fifteenth Party Conference, they made a sortie at Party meetings in the factories of Moscow, Leningrad and other cities, attempting to force a new discussion on the Party. The platform they tried to get the Party members to discuss was a rehash of the usual Trotskyite-Menshevik anti-Leninist platform. The Party members gave the oppositionists a severe rebuff, and in some places simply ejected them from the meetings. The Central Committee again warned the supporters of the bloc, stating that the Party could not tolerate their subversive activities any longer.

The opposition then submitted to the Central Committee a statement signed by Trotsky, Zinoviev, Kamenev and Sokolnikov condemning their own factional work and promising to be loyal in the future. Nevertheless, the bloc continued to exist and its adherents did not stop their underhand work against the Party. They went on banding together their anti-Leninist party, started an illegal printing press, collected membership dues from their supporters and circulated their platform.

In view of the behaviour of the Trotskyites and Zinovievites, the Fifteenth Party Conference (November 1926) and the Enlarged Plenum of the Executive Committee of the Communist International (December 1926) discussed the question of the bloc of Trotskyites and Zinovievites and adopted resolutions stigmatizing the adherents of this bloc as splitters whose platform was downright Menshevism.

But even this failed to bring them to their senses. In 1927, just when the British Conservatives broke off diplomatic and trade relations with the U.S.S.R., the bloc attacked the Party with renewed vigour. It concocted a new anti-Leninist platform, the so-called "Platform of the Eighty-Three" and began to circulate it among Party members, at the same time demanding that the Central Committee open a new general Party discussion.

This was perhaps the most mendacious and pharisaical of all opposition platforms.

In their platform, the Trotskyites and Zinovievites professed that they had no objection to observing Party decisions and that they were all in favour of loyalty, but in reality they grossly violated the Party decisions, and scoffed at the very idea of loyalty to the Party and to its Central Committee.

In their platform, they professed they had no objection to Party unity and were against splits, but in reality they grossly violated Party unity, worked for a split, and already had their own, illegal, anti-Leninist party which had all the makings of an anti-Soviet, counter-revolutionary party.

In their platform, they professed they were all in favour of the policy of industrialization, and even accused the Central Committee of not proceeding with industrialization fast enough, but in reality they did nothing but carp at the Party resolution on the victory of Socialism in the U.S.S.R., scoffed at the policy of Socialist industrialization, demanded the surrender of a number of mills and factories to foreigners in the form of concessions, and pinned their main hopes on foreign capitalist concessions in the U.S.S.R.

In their platform, they professed they were all in favour of the collective-farm movement, and even accused the Central Committee of not proceeding with collectivization fast enough, but in reality they scoffed at the policy of enlisting the peasants in the work of Socialist construction, preached the idea that "unresolvable conflicts" between the working class and the peasantry were inevitable, and pinned their hopes on the "cultured leaseholders" in the countryside, in other words, on the kulaks.

This was the most mendacious of all the platforms of the opposition.

It was meant to deceive the Party.

The Central Committee refused to open a general discussion immediately. It informed the opposition that a general discussion could be opened only in accordance with the Party Rules, namely, two months before a Party congress.

In October 1927, that is, two months before the Fifteenth Congress, the Central Committee of the Party announced a general Party discussion, and the fight began. Its result was truly lamentable for the bloc of Trotskyites and Zinovievites: 724,000 Party members voted for the policy of the Central Committee; 4,000, or less than one per cent, for the bloc of Trotskyites and Zinovievites. The anti-Party bloc was completely routed. The overwhelming majority of the Party members were unanimous in rejecting the platform of the bloc.

Such was the clearly expressed will of the Party, for whose judgment the oppositionists themselves had appealed.

But even this lesson was lost on the supporters of the bloc. Instead of submitting to the will of the Party they decided to frustrate it. Even before the discussion had closed, perceiving that ignominious failure awaited them, they decided to resort to more acute forms of struggle against the Party and the Soviet Government and to stage an open demonstration of protest in Moscow and Leningrad. The day they chose for their demonstration was November 7, the anniversary of the October Revolution, the day on which the working people of the U.S.S.R. annually hold their countrywide revolutionary demonstration. Thus, the Trotskyites and Zinovievites planned to hold a parallel demonstration. As was to be expected, the supporters of the bloc managed to bring out into the streets only a miserable handful of their satellites. These satellites and their patrons were overwhelmed by the general demonstration and swept off the streets.

Now there was no longer any doubt that the Trotskyites and Zinovievites had become definitely anti-Soviet. During the general Party discussion they had appealed to the Party against the Central Committee; now, during their puny demonstration, they had taken the course of appealing to the hostile classes against the Party and the Soviet state. Once they had made it their aim to undermine the Bolshevik Party, they were bound to go to the length of undermining the Soviet state, for in the Soviet Union the Bolshevik Party and the state are inseparable. That being the case, the ringleaders of the bloc of Trotskyites and Zinovievites had outlawed themselves from the Party, for men who had sunk to the depths of anti-Soviet action could no longer be tolerated in the ranks of the Bolshevik Party.

On November 14, 1927, a joint meeting of the Central Committee and the Central Control Commission expelled Trotsky and Zinoviev from the Party.

2. PROGRESS OF SOCIALIST INDUSTRIALIZATION. AGRICULTURE LAGS. FIFTEENTH PARTY CONGRESS. POLICY OF COLLECTIVIZATION IN AGRICULTURE. ROUT OF THE BLOC OF TROTSKYITES AND ZINOVIEVITES. POLITICAL DUPLICITY

By the end of 1927 the decisive success of the policy of Socialist industrialization was unmistakable. Under the New Economic Policy industrialization had made considerable progress in a short space of time. The gross output of industry and agriculture (including the timber industry and fisheries) had reached and even surpassed the pre-war level. Industrial output had risen to 42 per cent of the total output of the country, which was the pre-war ratio.

The Socialist sector of industry was rapidly growing at the expense of the private sector, its output having risen from 81 per cent of the total output in 1924-25 to 86 per cent in 1926-27, the output of the private sector dropping from 19 per cent to 14 per cent in the same period.

This meant that industrialization in the U.S.S.R was of a pronounced Socialist character, that industry was developing towards the victory of the Socialist system of production, and that as far as industry was concerned, the question—"Who will win?"—had already been decided in favour of Socialism.

No less rapid was the displacement of the private dealer in the sphere of trade, his share in the retail market having fallen from 42 per cent in 1924-25 to 32 per cent in 1926-27, not to mention the wholesale market, where the share of the private dealer had fallen from 9 per cent to 5 per cent in the same period.

Even more rapid was the rate of growth of *large-scale* Socialist industry, which in 1927, the first year *after* the restoration period, increased its output over the previous year by 18 per cent. This was a record increase, one beyond the reach of the large-scale industry of even the most advanced capitalist countries.

But in agriculture, especially grain growing, the picture was different. Although agriculture as a whole had passed the pre-war level, the gross yield of its most important branch—grain growing—was only 91 per cent of pre-war, while the marketed share of the harvest, that is, the amount of grain sold for the supply of the towns, scarcely attained 37 per cent of the pre-war figure. Furthermore, all the signs pointed to the danger of a further decline in the amount of marketable grain.

This meant that the process of the splitting up of the large farms that used to produce for the market, into small farms, and of the small farms into dwarf farms, a process which had begun in 1918, was still going on; that these small and dwarf peasant farms were reverting practically to a natural form of economy and were able to supply only a negligible quantity of grain for the market; that while in the 1927 period the grain crop was only slightly below that of the pre-war period, the marketable surplus for the supply of the towns was only a little more than one-third of the pre-war marketable surplus.

There could be no doubt that if such a state of affairs in grain farming were to continue, the army and the urban population would be faced with chronic famine.

This was a crisis in grain farming which was bound to be followed by a crisis in livestock farming.

The only escape from this predicament was a change to large-scale farming which would permit the use of tractors and agricultural machines and secure a several-fold increase of the marketable surplus of grain. The country had the alternative: either to adopt large-scale *capitalist* farming, which would have meant the ruin of the peasant masses, destroyed the alliance between the working class and the peasantry, increased the strength of the kulaks, and led to the downfall of Socialism in the countryside; or to take the course of amalgamating the small peasant holdings into large *Socialist* farms, collective farms, which would be able to use tractors and other modern machines for a rapid advancement of grain farming and a rapid increase in the marketable surplus of gain.

It is clear that the Bolshevik Party and the Soviet state could only take the second course, the collective farm way of developing agriculture.

In this, the Party was guided by the following precepts of Lenin regarding the necessity of passing from small peasant farming to large-scale, co-operative, collective farming:

a) "There is no escape from poverty for the small farm." (Lenin, *Selected Works*, Vol. VIII, p. 195.)

b) "If we continue as of old on our small farms, even as free citizens on free land, we shall still be faced with inevitable ruin." (Lenin, *Selected Works*, Vol. VI, p. 370.)

c) "If peasant farming is to develop further, we must firmly assure also its transition to the next stage, and this next stage must inevitably be one in which the small, isolated peasant farms, the least profitable and most backward, will by a process of gradual amalgamation form large-scale collective farms." (Lenin, *Selected Works*, Vol. IX, p. 151.)

d) "Only if we succeed in proving to the peasants in practice the advantages of common, collective, co-operative, artel cultivation of the soil, only if we succeed in helping the peasant by means of co-operative or artel farming, will the working class, which holds the state power, be really able to convince the peasant of the correctness of its policy and to secure the real and durable following of the millions of peasants." (Lenin, *Selected Works*, Vol. VIII, p. 198.)

Such was the situation prior to the Fifteenth Party Congress.

The Fifteenth Party Congress opened on December 2, 1927. It was attended by 898 delegates with vote and 771 delegates with voice but no vote, representing 887,233 Party members and 348,957 candidate members.

In his report on behalf of the Central Committee, Comrade Stalin referred to the good results of industrialization and the rapid expansion of Socialist industry, and set the Party the following task:

"To extend and consolidate our Socialist key position in all economic branches in town and country and to pursue a course of eliminating the capitalist elements from the national economy."

Comparing agriculture with industry and noting the backwardness of the former, especially of grain growing, owing to the scattered state of agriculture, which precluded the use of modern machinery, Comrade Stalin emphasized that such an unenviable state of agriculture was endangering the entire national economy.

"What is the way out?" Comrade Stalin asked.

"The way out," he said, "is to turn the small and scattered peasant farms into large united farms based on the common cultivation of the soil, to introduce collective cultivation of the soil on the basis of a new and higher technique. The way out is to unite the small and dwarf peasant farms gradually but surely, not by pressure, but by example and persuasion, into large farms based on common, co-operative, collective cultivation of the soil with the use of agricultural machines and tractors and scientific methods of intensive agriculture. There is no other way out."

The Fifteenth Congress passed a resolution calling for the fullest development of *collectivization* in agriculture. The congress adopted a plan for the extension and consolidation of the collective farms and state farms and formulated explicit instructions concerning the methods to be used in the struggle for collectivization in agriculture.

At the same time, the congress gave directions:

"To develop further the offensive against the kulaks and to adopt a number of new measures which would restrict the development of capitalism in the countryside and guide peasant farming towards Socialism." (*Resolutions of the C.P.S.U.* [*B.*], Russ. ed., Part II, p. 260.)

Finally, in view of the fact that economic planning had taken firm root, and with the object of organizing a systematic offensive of Socialism against the capitalist elements along the entire economic front, the congress gave instructions to the proper bodies for the drawing up of the *First Five-Year Plan* for the development of the national economy.

After passing decisions on the problems of Socialist construction, the congress proceeded to discuss the question of liquidating the bloc of Trotsykites and Zinovievites.

The congress recognized that "the opposition has ideologically broken with Leninism, has degenerated into a Menshevik group, has taken the course of capitulation to the forces of the international and home bourgeoisie, and has objectively become a tool of counter-revolution against the regime of the proletarian dictatorship." (*Ibid.*, p. 232.)

The congress found that the differences between the Party and the opposition had developed into differences of program, and that the Trotsky opposition had taken the course of struggle against the Soviet power. The congress therefore declared that adherence to the Trotsky opposition and the propagation of its views were incompatible with membership of the Bolshevik Party.

The congress approved the decision of the joint meeting of the Central Committee and the Central Control Commission to expel Trotsky and Zinoviev from the Party and resolved on the expulsion of all active members of the bloc of Trotskyites and Zinovievites, such as Radek, Preobrazhensky, Rakovsky, Pyatakov, Serebryakov, I. Smirnov, Kamenev, Sarkis, Safarov, Lifshitz, Mdivani, Smilga and the whole "Democratic-Centralism" group (Sapronov, V. Smirnov, Boguslavsky, Drobnis and others).

Defeated ideologically and routed organizationally, the adherents of the bloc of Trotskyites and Zinovievites lost the last vestiges of their influence among the people.

Shortly after the Fifteenth Party Congress, the expelled anti-Leninists began to hand in statements, recanting Trotskyism and asking to be reinstated in the Party. Of course, at that time the Party could not yet know that Trotsky, Rakovsky, Radek, Krestinsky, Sokolnikov and others had long been enemies of the people, spies recruited by foreign espionage services, and that Kamenev, Zinoviev, Pyatakov and others were already forming connections with enemies of the U.S.S.R in capitalist countries for the purpose of "collaboration" with them against the Soviet people. But experience had taught the Party that any knavery might be expected from these individuals, who had often attacked Lenin and the Leninist Party at the most crucial moments. It was therefore sceptical of the statements they had made in their applications for reinstatement. As a preliminary test of their sincerity, it made their reinstatement in the Party dependent on the following conditions:

a) They must publicly denounce Trotskyism as an anti-Bolshevik and anti-Soviet ideology.

b) They must publicly acknowledge the Party policy as the only correct policy.

c) They must unconditionally abide by the decisions of the Party and its bodies.

d) They must undergo a term of probation, during which the Party would test them; on the expiration of this term, the Party would consider the reinstatement of each applicant separately, depending on the results of the test.

The Party considered that in any case the public acceptance of these points by the expelled would be all to the good of the Party, because it would break the unity of the Trotskyite-Zinovievite ranks, undermine their morale, demonstrate once more the right and the might of the Party, and enable the Party, if the applicants were sincere, to reinstate its former workers in its ranks, and if they were not sincere, to unmask them in the public eye, no longer as misguided individuals, but as unprincipled careerists, deceivers of the working class and incorrigible double-dealers.

The majority of the expelled accepted the terms of reinstatement and made public statements in the press to this effect.

Desiring to be clement to them, and loath to deny them an opportunity of once again becoming men of the Party and of the working class, the Party reinstated them in its ranks.

However, time showed that, with few exceptions, the recantations of the "leading lights" of the bloc of Trotskyites and Zinovievites were false and hypocritical from beginning to end.

It turned out that even before they had handed in their applications, these gentry had ceased to represent a political trend ready to defend their views before the people, and had become an unprincipled gang of careerists who were prepared publicly to trample on the last remnants of their own views, publicly to praise the views of the Party, which were alien to them, and—like chameleons—to adopt any colouring, provided they could maintain themselves in the ranks of the Party and the working class and have the opportunity to do harm to the working class and to its Party.

The "leading lights" of the bloc of Trotskyites and Zinovievites proved to be political swindlers, political double-dealers.

Political double-dealers usually begin with deceit and prosecute their nefarious ends by deceiving the people, the working class, and the Party of the working class. But political double-dealers are not to be regarded as mere humbugs. Political double-dealers are an unprincipled gang of political careerists who, having long ago lost the confidence of the people, strive to insinuate themselves once more into their confidence by deception, by chameleon-like changes of colour, by fraud, by any means, only that they might retain the title of political figures. Political double-dealers are an unprincipled gang of political careerists who are ready to seek support anywhere, even among criminal elements, even among the scum of society, even among the mortal enemies of the people, only that they might be able, at a "propitious" moment, again to mount the political stage and to clamber on to the back of the people as their "rulers."

The "leading lights" of the bloc of Trotskyites and Zinovievites were political double-dealers of this very description.

3. OFFENSIVE AGAINST THE KULAKS. THE BUKHARIN-RYKOV ANTI-PARTY GROUP. ADOPTION OF THE FIRST FIVE-YEAR PLAN. SOCIALIST EMULATION. BEGINNING OF THE MASS COLLECTIVE-FARM MOVEMENT

The agitation conducted by the bloc of Trotskyites and Zinovievites against the Party policy, against the building of Socialism, and against collectivization, as well as the agitation conducted by the Bukharinites, who said that nothing would come of the collective farms, that the kulaks should be let alone because they would "grow" into Socialism of themselves, and that the enrichment of the bourgeoisie represented no danger to Socialism—all found an eager response among the capitalist elements in the country, and above all among the kulaks. The kulaks now knew from comments in the press that they were not alone, that they had defenders and intercessors in the persons of Trotsky, Zinoviev, Kamenev, Bukharin, Rykov and others. Naturally, this could not but stiffen the kulaks' spirit of resistance against the policy of the Soviet Government. And, in fact, the resistance of the kulaks became increasingly stubborn. They refused en masse to sell to the Soviet state their grain surpluses, of which they had considerable hoards. They resorted to terrorism against the collective farmers, against Party workers and government officials in the countryside, and burned down collective farms and state granaries.

The Party realized that until the resistance of the kulaks was broken, until they were defeated in open fight in full view of the peasantry, the working class and the Red Army would suffer from a food shortage, and the movement for collectivization among the peasants could not assume a mass character.

In pursuance of the instructions of the Fifteenth Party Congress, the Party launched a determined offensive against the kulaks, putting into effect the slogan: rely firmly on the poor peasantry, strengthen the alliance with the middle peasantry, and wage a resolute struggle against the kulaks. In answer to the kulaks' refusal to sell their grain surpluses to the state at the fixed prices, the Party and the Government adopted a number of emergency measures against the kulaks, applied Article 107 of the Criminal Code empowering the courts to confiscate grain surpluses from kulaks and profiteers in case they refused to sell them to the state at the fixed prices, and granted the poor peasants a number of privileges, under which 25 per cent of the confiscated kulak grain was placed at their disposal.

These emergency measures had their effect: the poor and middle peasants joined in the resolute fight against the kulaks; the kulaks were isolated, and the resistance of the kulaks and the profiteers was broken. By the end of 1928, the Soviet state already had sufficient stocks of grain at its disposal, and the collective-farm movement began to advance with surer strides.

That same year, a large organization of wreckers, consisting of bourgeois experts, was discovered in the Shakhty district of the Donetz Coal Basin. The Shakhty wreckers were closely connected with the former mine owners—Russian and foreign capitalists—and with a foreign military espionage service. Their aim was to disrupt the development of Socialist industry and to facilitate the restoration of capitalism in the U.S.S.R. The wreckers had deliberately mismanaged the mines in order to reduce the output of coal, spoiled machinery and ventilation apparatus, caused roof-falls and explosions, and set fire to pits, plants and power-stations. The wreckers had deliberately obstructed the improvement of the workers' conditions and had infringed the Soviet labour protection laws.

The wreckers were put on trial and met with their deserts.

The Central Committee of the Party directed all Party organizations to draw the necessary conclusions from the Shakhty case. Comrade Stalin declared that Bolshevik business executives must themselves become experts in the technique of production, so as no longer to be the dupes of the wreckers among the old bourgeois experts, and that the training of new technical personnel from the ranks of the working class must be accelerated.

In accordance with a decision of the Central Committee, the training of young experts in the technical colleges was improved. Thousands of Party members, members of the Young Communist League and non-Party people devoted to the cause of the working class were mobilized for study.

Before the Party took the offensive against the kulaks, and while it was engaged in liquidating the bloc of Trotskyites and Zinovievites, the Bukharin-Rykov group had been more or less lying low, holding themselves as a reserve of the anti-Party forces, not venturing to support the Trotskyites openly, and sometimes even acting together with the Party against the Trotskyites. But when the Party assumed the offensive against the kulaks, and adopted emergency measures against them, the Bukharin-Rykov group threw off their mask and began to attack the Party policy openly. The kulak soul of the Bukharin-Rykov group got the better of them, and they began to come out openly in defence of the kulaks. They demanded the repeal of the emergency measures, frightening the simple-minded with the argument that otherwise agriculture would begin to "decay," and even affirming that this process had already begun. Blind to the growth of the collective farms and state farms, those superior forms of agricultural organization, and perceiving the decline of kulak farming, they represented the decay of the latter as the decay of agriculture. In order to provide a theoretical backing for their case, they concocted the absurd "theory of the subsidence of the class-struggle," maintaining, on the strength of this theory, that the class struggle would grow milder with every victory gained by Socialism against the capitalist elements, that the class struggle would soon subside altogether and the class enemy would surrender all his positions without a fight, and that, consequently, there was no need for an offensive against the kulaks. In this way they tried to furbish up their threadbare bourgeois theory that the kulaks would peaceably grow into Socialism, and rode roughshod over the well-known thesis of Leninism that the resistance of the class enemy would assume more acute forms as the progress of Socialism cut the ground from under his feet and that the class struggle could "subside" only after the class enemy was destroyed.

It was easy to see that in the Bukharin-Rykov group the Party was faced with a group of Right opportunists who differed from the bloc of Trotskyites and Zinovievites only in form, only in the fact that the Trotskyite and Zinovievite capitulators had had some opportunity of masking their true nature with Left, revolutionary vociferations about "permanent revolution," whereas the Bukharin-Rykov group, attacking the Party as they did for taking the offensive against the kulaks, could not possibly mask their capitulatory character and had to defend the reactionary forces in our country, the kulaks in particular, openly, without mask or disguise.

The Party understood that sooner or later the Bukharin-Rykov group was bound to join hands with the remnants of the bloc of Trotskyites and Zinovievites for common action against the Party.

Parallel with their political pronouncements, the Bukharin-Rykov group "worked" to muster and organize their following. Through Bukharin, they banded together young bourgeois elements like Slepkov, Maretsky, Eichenwald, Goldenberg; through Tomsky—high bureaucrats in the trade unions (Melnichansky, Dogadov and others); through Rykov—demoralized high Soviet officials (A. Smirnov, Eismont, V. Schmidt, and others). The group readily attracted people who had degenerated politically, and who made no secret of their capitulatory sentiments.

About this time the Bukharin-Rykov group gained the support of high functionaries in the Moscow Party organization (Uglanov, Kotov, Ukhanov, Ryutin, Yagoda, Polonsky, and others). A section of the Rights kept under cover, abstaining from open attacks on the Party line. In the Moscow Party press and at Party meetings, it was advocated that concessions must be made to the kulaks, that heavy taxation of kulaks was inadvisable, that industrialization was burdensome to the people, and that the development of heavy industry was premature. Uglanov opposed the Dnieper hydro-electric scheme and demanded that funds be diverted from heavy industry to the light industries. Uglanov and the other Right capitulators maintained that Moscow was and would remain a gingham city, and that there was no need to build engineering works in Moscow.

The Moscow Party organization unmasked Uglanov and his followers, gave them a final warning and rallied closer than ever around the Central Committee of the Party. At a plenary meeting of the Moscow Committee of the C.P.S.U.(B.), held in 1928, Comrade Stalin said that a fight must be waged on two fronts, with the fire concentrated on the Right deviation. The Rights, Comrade Stalin said, were kulak agents inside the Party.

> "The triumph of the Right deviation in our Party would un-leash the forces of capitalism, undermine the revolutionary position of the proletariat and increase the chances of restoring capitalism in our country," said Comrade Stalin. (Stalin, *Leninism*, Vol. II.)

At the beginning of 1929 it was discovered that Bukharin, authorized by the group of Right capitulators, had formed connections with the Trotskyites, through Kamenev, and was negotiating an agreement with them for a joint struggle against the Party. The Central Committee exposed these criminal activities of the Right capitulators and warned them that this affair might end lamentably for Bukharin, Rykov, Tom-sky and the rest. But the Right capitulators would not heed the warning. At a meeting of the Central Committee they advanced a new anti-Party platform, in the form of a declaration, which the Central Com-mittee condemned. It warned them again, reminding them of what had happened to the bloc of Trotskyites and Zinovievites. In spite of this, the Bukharin-Rykov group persisted in their anti-Party activities. Rykov, Tomsky and Bukharin tendered to the Central Committee their resignations, believing that they would intimidate the Party thereby. The Central Committee passed condemnation on this saboteur policy of resignations. Finally, a plenum of the Central Committee, held in November 1929, declared that the propaganda of the views of the Right opportunists was incompatible with membership of the Party; it resolved that Bukharin, as the instigator and leader of the Right capitulators, be removed from the Political Bureau of the Central Committee, and issued a grave warning to Rykov, Tomsky and other members of the Right opposition.

Perceiving that matters had taken a lamentable turn, the chieftains of the Right capitulators submitted a statement acknowledging their errors and the correctness of the political line of the Party.

The Right capitulators decided to effect a temporary retreat so as to preserve their ranks from debâcle.

This ended the first stage of the Party's fight against the Right capitulators.

The new differences within the Party did not escape the attention of the external enemies of the Soviet Union. Believing that the "new dissensions" in the Party were a sign of its weakness, they made a new attempt to involve the U.S.S.R. in war and to thwart the work of industrialization before it had got properly under way. In the summer of 1929, the imperialists provoked a conflict between China and the Soviet Union, and instigated the seizure of the Chinese Eastern Railway (which belonged to the U.S.S.R.) by the Chinese militarists, and an attack on our Far-Eastern frontier by troops of the Chinese Whites. But this raid of the Chinese militarists was promptly liquidated, the militarists, routed by the Red Army, retreated and the conflict ended in the signing of a peace agreement with the Manchurian authorities.

The peace policy of the U.S.S.R. once more triumphed in the face of all obstacles, notwithstanding the intrigues of external enemies and the "dissensions" within the Party.

Soon after this diplomatic and trade relations between the U.S.S.R. and Great Britain, which had been severed by the British Conservatives, were resumed.

While successfully repulsing the attacks of the external and internal enemies, the Party was busily engaged in developing heavy industry, organizing Socialist emulation, building up state farms and collective farms, and, lastly, preparing the ground for the adoption and execution of the First Five-Year Plan for the development of the national economy.

In April 1929, the Party held its Sixteenth Conference, with the First Five-Year Plan as the main item on the agenda. The conference rejected the "minimal" variant of the Five-Year Plan advocated by the Right capitulators and adopted the "optimal" variant as binding under all circumstances.

Thus, the Party adopted the celebrated First Five-Year Plan for the construction of Socialism.

The Five-Year-Plan fixed the volume of capital investments in the national economy in the period 1928-33 at 64,600,000,000 rubles. Of this sum, 19,500,000,000 rubles were to be invested in industrial and electric-power development, 10,000,000,000 rubles in transport development and 23,200,000,000 rubles in agriculture.

This was a colossal plan for the equipment of industry and agriculture of the U.S.S.R. with modern technique.

"The fundamental task of the Five-Year Plan," said Comrade Stalin, "was to create such an industry in our country as would be able to re-equip and reorganize, not only the whole of industry, but also transport and agriculture—on the basis of Socialism." (Stalin, *Problems of Leninism*, Russ. ed., p. 485.)

For all the immensity of this plan, it did not nonplus or surprise the Bolsheviks. The way for it had been prepared by the whole course of development of industrialization and collectivization and it had been preceded by a wave of labour enthusiasm which caught up the workers and peasants and which found expression in *Socialist emulation.*

The Sixteenth Party Conference adopted an appeal to all working people, calling for the further development of Socialist emulation.

Socialist emulation had produced many an instance of exemplary labour and of a new attitude to labour. In many factories, collective farms and state farms, the workers and collective farmers drew up *counter-plans* for an output exceeding that provided for in the state plans. They displayed heroism in labour. They not only fulfilled, but exceeded the plans of Socialist development laid down by the Party and the Government. The attitude to labour had changed. From the involuntary and penal servitude it had been under capitalism, it was becoming "a matter of honour, a matter of glory, a matter of valour and heroism." (*Stalin.*)

New industrial construction on a gigantic scale was in progress all over the country. The Dnieper hydro-electric scheme was in full swing. Construction work on the Kramatorsk and Gorlovka Iron and Steel Works and the reconstruction of the Lugansk Locomotive Works had begun in the Donetz Basin. New collieries and blast furnaces came into being. The Urals Machine-Building Works and the Bereznik and Solikamsk Chemical Works were under construction in the Urals. Work was begun on the construction of the iron and steel mills of Magnitogorsk. The erection of big automobile plants in Moscow and Gorky was well under way, as was the construction of giant tractor plants, harvester combine plants, and a mammoth agricultural machinery plant in Rostov-on-Don. The Kuznetsk collieries, the Soviet Union's second coal base, were being extended. An immense tractor works sprang up in the steppe near Stalingrad in the space of eleven months. In the erection of the Dnieper Hydro-Electric Station and the Stalingrad Tractor Works, the workers beat world records in productivity of labour.

History had never known industrial construction on such a gigantic scale, such enthusiasm for new development, such labour heroism on the part of the working-class millions.

It was a veritable upsurge of labour enthusiasm, produced and stimulated by Socialist emulation.

This time the peasants did not lag behind the workers. In the countryside, too, this labour enthusiasm began to spread among the peasant masses who were organizing their collective farms. The peasants definitely began to turn to collective farming. In this a great part was played by the state farms and the machine and tractor stations. The

peasants would come in crowds to the state farms and machine and
tractor stations to watch the operation of the tractors and other agricultural machines, admire their performance and there and then resolve:
"Let's join the collective farm." Divided and disunited, each on his
tiny, dwarf individually-run farm, destitute of anything like serviceable
implements or traction, having no way of breaking up large tracts of
virgin soil, without prospect of any improvement on their farms, crushed
by poverty, isolated and left to their own devices, the peasants had at
last found a way out, an avenue to a better life, in the amalgamation
of their small farms into co-operative undertakings, collective farms; in
tractors, which are able to break up any "hard ground," any virgin soil;
in the assistance rendered by the state in the form of machines, money,
men, and counsel; in the opportunity to free themselves from bondage
to the kulaks, who had been quite recently defeated by the Soviet Government and forced to the ground, to the joy of the millions of peasants.

On this basis began the mass collective-farm movement, which later
developed rapidly, especially towards the end of 1929, progressing at
an unprecedented rate, a rate unknown even to our Socialist industry.

In 1928 the total crop area of the collective farms was 1,390,000
hectares, in 1929 it was 4,262,000 hectares, while in 1930 the ploughing plan of the collective farms was already 15,000,000 hectares.

"It must be admitted," said Comrade Stalin in his article,
"A Year of Great Change" (1929), in reference to the collective
farms, "that such an impetuous speed of development is unequalled
even in our socialized large-scale industry, which in general is noted
for its outstanding speed of development."

This was a turning point in the development of the collective-farm
movement.

This was the beginning of a mass collective-farm movement.

"What is the *new* feature of the present collective-farm movement?" asked Comrade Stalin in his article, "A Year of Great
Change." And he answered:

"The new and decisive feature of the present collective-farm
movement is that the peasants are joining the collective farms not
in separate groups, as was formerly the case, but in whole villages,
whole *volosts* (rural districts), whole districts and even whole areas.
And what does that mean? It means that *the middle peasant has
joined the collective-farm movement*. And that is the basis of that
radical change in the development of agriculture which represents
the most important achievement of the Soviet Government. . . ."

This meant that the time was becoming ripe, or had already become ripe, for the elimination of the kulaks as a class, on the basis of solid collectivization.

BRIEF SUMMARY

During the period 1926-29, the Party grappled with and overcame immense difficulties on the home and foreign fronts in the fight for the Socialist industrialization of the country. The efforts of the Party and the working class ended in the victory of the policy of Socialist industrialization.

In the main, one of the most difficult problems of industrialization had been solved, namely, the problem of accumulating funds for the building of a heavy industry. The foundations were laid of a heavy industry capable of re-equipping the entire national economy.

The First Five-Year Plan of Socialist construction was adopted. The building of new factories, state farms and collective farms was developed on a vast scale.

This advance towards Socialism was attended by a sharpening of the class struggle in the country and a sharpening of the struggle within the Party. The chief results of this struggle were that the resistance of the kulaks was crushed, the bloc of Trotskyite and Zinovievite capitulators was exposed as an anti-Soviet bloc, the Right capitulators were exposed as agents of the kulaks, the Trotskyites were expelled from the Party, and the views of the Trotskyites and the Right opportunists were declared incompatible with membership of the C.P.S.U.(B.).

Defeated ideologically by the Bolshevik Party, and having lost all support among the working class, the Trotskyites ceased to be a political trend and became an unprincipled, careerist clique of political swindlers, a gang of political double-dealers.

Having laid the foundations of a heavy industry, the Party mustered the working class and the peasantry for the fulfilment of the First Five-Year Plan for the Socialist reconstruction of the U.S.S.R. Socialist emulation developed all over the country among millions of working people, giving rise to a mighty wave of labour enthusiasm and originating a new labour discipline.

This period ended with a year of great change, signalized by sweeping victories of Socialism in industry, the first important successes in agriculture, the swing of the middle peasant towards the collective farms, and the beginning of a mass collective-farm movement.

CHAPTER ELEVEN

THE BOLSHEVIK PARTY IN THE STRUGGLE FOR THE COLLECTIVIZATION OF AGRICULTURE

(1930-1934)

1. INTERNATIONAL SITUATION IN 1930-34. ECONOMIC CRISIS IN THE CAPITALIST COUNTRIES. JAPANESE ANNEXATION OF MANCHURIA. FASCISTS' ADVENT TO POWER IN GERMANY. TWO SEATS OF WAR

While in the U.S.S.R. important progress had been made in the Socialist industrialization of the country and industry was rapidly developing, in the capitalist countries a devastating world economic crisis of unprecedented dimensions had broken out at the end of 1929 and grew steadily more acute in the three following years. The industrial crisis was interwoven with an agrarian crisis, which made matters still worse for the capitalist countries.

In the three years of economic crisis (1930-33), industrial output in the U.S.A. had sunk to 65 per cent, in Great Britain to 86 per cent, in Germany to 66 per cent and in France to 77 per cent of the 1929 output. Yet in this same period industrial output in the U.S.S.R. more than doubled, amounting in 1933 to 201 per cent of the 1929 output.

This was but an additional proof of the superiority of the Socialist economic system over the capitalist economic system. It showed that the country of Socialism is the only country in the world which is exempt from economic crises.

The world economic crisis condemned 24,000,000 unemployed to starvation, poverty and misery. The agrarian crisis brought suffering to tens of millions of peasants.

The world economic crisis further aggravated the contradictions between the imperialist states, between the victor countries and the vanquished countries, between the imperialist states and the colonial and dependent countries, between the workers and the capitalists, between the peasants and the landlords.

In his report on behalf of the Central Committee to the Sixteenth Party Congress, Comrade Stalin pointed out that the bourgeoisie would seek a way out of the economic crisis, on the one hand, by crushing the working class through the establishment of fascist dictatorship, *i.e.*, the dictatorship of the most reactionary, most chauvinistic, most imperialistic capitalist elements, and, on the other hand, by fomenting war for the re-division of colonies and spheres of influence at the expense of the poorly defended countries.

That is just what happened.

In 1932 the war danger was aggravated by Japan. Perceiving that, owing to the economic crisis, the European powers and the U.S.A. were wholly engrossed in their domestic affairs, the Japanese imperialists decided to seize the opportunity and bring pressure to bear on poorly defended China, in an attempt to subjugate her and to lord it over the country. Unscrupulously exploiting "local incidents" they themselves had provoked, the Japanese imperialists, like robbers, without declaring war on China, marched their troops into Manchuria. The Japanese soldiery seized the whole of Manchuria, thereby preparing a convenient *place d'armes* for the conquest of North China and for an attack on the U.S.S.R. Japan withdrew from the League of Nations in order to leave her hands free, and began to arm at a feverish pace.

This impelled the U.S.A., Britain and France to strengthen their naval armaments in the Far East. It was obvious that Japan was out to subjugate China and to eject the European and American imperialist powers from that country. They replied by increasing their armaments.

But Japan was pursuing another purpose, too, namely, to seize the Soviet Far East. Naturally, the U.S.S.R. could not shut its eyes to this danger, and began intensively to strengthen the defences of its Far Eastern territory.

Thus, in the Far East, thanks to the Japanese fascist imperialists, there arose the first seat of war.

But it was not only in the Far East that the economic crisis aggravated the contradictions of capitalism. It aggravated them in Europe too. The prolonged crisis in industry and agriculture, the huge volume of unemployment, and the growing insecurity of the poorer classes fanned the discontent of the workers and peasants. The discontent of the working class grew into revolutionary disaffection. This was particularly the case in Germany, which was economically exhausted by the war, by the payment of reparations to the Anglo-French victors, and by the economic crisis, and the working class of which languished under a double yoke, that of the home and the foreign, the British and French, bourgeoisie. The extent of this discontent was clearly indicated by the six million votes cast for the German Communist Party at the last Reichstag elections, before the fascists came to power. The German bourgeoisie perceived that the bourgeois-democratic liberties preserved in Germany might play them an evil trick, that the working class might use these liberties to extend the revolutionary movement. They therefore decided that there was only one way of maintaining the power of the bourgeoisie in Germany, and that was to abolish the bourgeois liberties, to reduce the Reichstag to a cipher, and to establish a terrorist bourgeois-nationalist dictatorship, which would be able to suppress the working class and base itself on the petty-bourgeois masses who wanted to revenge Germany's defeat in the war. And so they called to power the fascist party—which in order to hoodwink the people calls itself the National-*Socialist* Party—well knowing that the fascist party, first, represents that section of the imperialist bourgeoisie which is the most reactionary and most hostile to the working class, and, secondly, that it is the most pronounced party of revenge, one capable of beguiling the millions of the nationalistically minded petty bourgeoisie. In this they were assisted by the traitors to the working class, the leaders of the German Social-Democratic Party, who paved the way for fascism by their policy of compromise.

These were the conditions which brought about the accession to power of the German fascists in 1933.

Analysing the events in Germany in his report to the Seventeenth Party Congress, Comrade Stalin said:

> "The victory of fascism in Germany must be regarded not only as a symptom of the weakness of the working class and a result of the betrayals of the working class by the Social-Democratic Party, which paved the way for fascism; it must also be regarded as a symptom of the weakness of the bourgeoisie, of the fact that the bourgeoisie is already unable to rule by the old methods of parliamentarism and bourgeois democracy, and, as a consequence, is compelled in its home policy to resort to terroristic methods of rule...."
> (J. Stalin, *Seventeenth Congress of the. C.P.S.U.*, "Report on the Work of the Central Committee of the C.P.S.U.[B.]," p. 17.)

The German fascists inaugurated their home policy by setting fire to the Reichstag, brutally suppressing the working class, destroying its organizations, and abolishing the bourgeois-democratic liberties. They inaugurated their foreign policy by withdrawing from the League of Nations and openly preparing for a war for the *forcible* revision of the frontiers of the European states to the advantage of Germany.

Thus, in the centre of Europe, thanks to the German fascists, there arose a second seat of war.

Naturally, the U.S.S.R. could not shut its eyes to so serious a fact, and began to keep a sharp watch on the course of events in the West and to strengthen its defences on the Western frontiers.

2. FROM THE POLICY OF RESTRICTING THE KULAK ELEMENTS TO THE POLICY OF ELIMINATING THE KULAKS AS A CLASS. STRUGGLE AGAINST DISTORTIONS OF THE PARTY POLICY IN THE COLLECTIVE-FARM MOVEMENT. OFFENSIVE AGAINST THE CAPITALIST ELEMENTS ALONG THE WHOLE LINE. SIXTEENTH PARTY CONGRESS

The mass influx of the peasants into the collective farms in 1929 and 1930 was a result of the whole preceding work of the Party and the Government. The growth of Socialist industry, which had begun the mass production of tractors and machines for agriculture; the vigorous measures taken against the kulaks during the grain-purchasing campaigns of 1928 and 1929; the spread of agricultural co-operative societies, which gradually accustomed the peasants to collective farming; the good results obtained by the first collective farms and state farms—all this prepared the way for solid collectivization, when the peasants of entire villages, districts and regions joined the collective farms.

Solid collectivization was not just a peaceful process—the overwhelming bulk of the peasantry simply joining the collective farms—but was a struggle of the peasant masses against the kulaks. Solid collectivization meant that all the land in a village area in which a collective farm was formed passed into the hands of the collective farm; but a considerable portion of this land was held by the kulaks, and therefore the peasants would expropriate them, driving them from the land, dispossessing them of their cattle and machinery and demanding their arrest and eviction from the district by the Soviet authorities.

Solid collectivization therefore meant the elimination of the kulaks.

This was a policy of eliminating the kulaks as a class, on the basis of solid collectivization.

By this time, the U.S.S.R. had a strong enough material base to allow it to put an end to the kulaks, break their resistance, eliminate them as a class and replace kulak farming by collective and state farming.

In 1927 the kulaks still produced over 600,000,000 poods of grain, of which about 130,000,000 poods were available for sale. In that year the collective and state farms had only 35,000,000 poods of grain available for sale. In 1929, thanks to the Bolshevik Party's firm policy of developing state farms and collective farms, and likewise to the progress made by Socialist industry in supplying the countryside with tractors and agricultural machinery, the collective farms and state farms had become an important factor. In that year the collective farms and state farms already produced no less than 400,000,000 poods of grain, of which over 130,000,000 poods were marketed. This was more than the kulaks had marketed in 1927. And in 1930 the collective farms and state farms were to produce, and actually did produce, over 400,000,000 poods of grain for the market, which was incomparably more than had been marketed by the kulaks in 1927.

Thus, thanks to the changed alignment of class forces in the economic life of the country, and the existence of the necessary material base for the replacement of the kulak grain output by that of the collective and state farms, the Bolshevik Party was able to proceed from the policy of *restricting* the kulaks to a new policy, the policy of *eliminating them as a class*, on the basis of solid collectivization.

Prior to 1929, the Soviet Government had pursued a policy of restricting the kulaks. It had imposed higher taxes on the kulak, and had required him to sell grain to the state at fixed prices; by the law on the renting of land it had to a certain extent restricted the amount of land he could use; by the law on the employment of hired labour on private farms it had limited the scope of his farm. But it had not yet pursued a policy of eliminating the kulaks, since the laws on the renting of land and the hiring of labour allowed them to carry on, while the prohibition of their expropriation gave them a certain guarantee in this respect. The effect of this policy was to arrest the growth of the kulak class, some sections of which, unable to withstand the pressure of these restrictions, were forced out of business and ruined. But this policy did not destroy the economic foundations of the kulaks as a class, nor did it tend to eliminate them. It was a policy of restricting the kulaks, not of eliminating them. This policy was essential up to a certain time, that is, as long as the collective farms and state farms were still weak and unable to replace the kulaks in the production of grain.

At the end of 1929, with the growth of the collective farms and state farms, the Soviet Government turned sharply from this policy to the policy of eliminating the kulaks, of destroying them as a class. It repealed the laws on the renting of land and the hiring of labour, thus depriving the kulaks both of land and of hired labourers. It lifted the ban on the expropriation of the kulaks. It permitted the peasants to confiscate cattle, machines and other farm property from the kulaks for the benefit of the collective farms. The kulaks were expropriated. They were expropriated just as the capitalists had been expropriated in the sphere of industry in 1918, with this difference, however, that the kulaks' means of production did not pass into the hands of the state, but into the hands of the peasants united in the collective farms.

This was a profound revolution, a leap from an old qualitative state of society to a new qualitative state, equivalent in its consequences to the revolution of October 1917.

The distinguishing feature of this revolution is that it was accomplished *from above*, on the initiative of the state, and directly supported *from below* by the millions of peasants, who were fighting to throw off kulak bondage and to live in freedom in the collective farms.

This revolution, at one blow, solved three fundamental problems of Socialist construction:

a) It eliminated the most numerous class of exploiters in our country, the kulak class, the mainstay of capitalist restoration;

b) It transferred the most numerous labouring class in our country, the peasant class, from the path of individual farming, which breeds capitalism, to the path of co-operative, collective, Socialist farming;

c) It furnished the Soviet regime with a Socialist base in agriculture—the most extensive and vitally necessary, yet least developed, branch of national economy.

This destroyed the last mainsprings of the restoration of capitalism within the country and at the same time created new and decisive conditions for the building up of a Socialist economic system.

Explaining the reasons for the policy of eliminating the kulaks as a class, and summing up the results of the mass movement of the peasants for solid collectivization, Comrade Stalin wrote in 1929:

"The last hope of the capitalists of all countries, who are dreaming of restoring capitalism in the U.S.S.R.—'the sacred principle of private property'—is collapsing and vanishing. The peasants, whom they regarded as material manuring the soil for capitalism, are abandoning en masse the lauded banner of 'private property' and are taking to the path of collectivism, the path of Socialism. The last hope for the restoration of capitalism is crumbling." (Stalin, *Leninism*, Vol. II, "A Year of Great Change.")

The policy of eliminating the kulaks as a class was embodied in the historic resolution on "The Rate of Collectivization and State Measures to Assist the Development of Collective Farms" adopted by the Central Committee of the C.P.S.U.(B.) on January 5, 1930. In this decision, full account was taken of the diversity of conditions in the various districts of the U.S.S.R. and the varying degrees to which the regions were ripe for collectivization.

Different rates of collectivization were established, for which purpose the Central Committee of the C.P.S.U.(B.) divided the regions of the U.S.S.R. into three groups.

The first group included the principal grain-growing areas: *viz.*, the North Caucasus (the Kuban, Don and Terek), the Middle Volga and the Lower Volga, which were ripest for collectivization since they had the most tractors, the most state farms, and the most experience in fighting the kulaks, gained in past grain-purchasing campaigns. The Central Committee proposed that in this group of grain-growing areas collectivization should in the main be completed in the spring of 1931.

The second group of grain-growing areas, the Ukraine, the Central Black-Earth Region, Siberia, the Urals, Kazakhstan and others could complete collectivization in the main in the spring of 1932.

The other regions, territories and republics (Moscow Region, Trans-caucasia, the republics of Central Asia, etc.) could extend the process of collectivization to the end of the Five-Year Plan, that is, to 1933.

In view of the growing speed of collectivization, the Central Committee of the Party considered it necessary to accelerate the construction of plants for the production of tractors, harvester combines, tractor-drawn machinery, etc. Simultaneously, the Central Committee demanded that "the tendency to underestimate the importance of horse traction at the present stage of the collective-farm movement, a tendency which was leading to the reckless disposal and sale of horses, be resolutely checked."

State loans to collective farms for the year 1929-30 were doubled (500,000,000 rubles) as compared with the original plan.

The expense of the surveying and demarcation of the lands of the collective farms was to be borne by the state.

The resolution contained the highly important direction that the *chief form* of the collective-farm movement at the given stage must be the agricultural artel, in which only the *principal* means of production are collectivized.

The Central Committee most seriously warned Party organizations "against any attempts whatsoever to force the collective-farm movement by 'decrees' from above, which might involve the danger of the substitution of mock-collectivization for real Socialist emulation in the organization of collective farms." (*Resolutions of the C.P.S.U.[B.]* Russ. ed., Part II, page 662.)

In this resolution the Central Committee made it clear how the Party's new policy in the countryside should be applied.

The policy of eliminating the kulaks as a class and of solid collectivization stimulated a powerful collective-farm movement. The peasants of whole villages and districts joined the collective farms, sweeping the kulaks from their path and freeing themselves from kulak bondage.

But with all the phenomenal progress of collectivization, certain faults on the part of Party workers, distortions of the Party policy in collective farm development, soon revealed themselves. Although the Central Committee had warned Party workers not to be carried away by the success of collectivization, many of them began to force the pace of collectivization artificially, without regard to the conditions of time and place, and heedless of the degree of readiness of the peasants to join the collective farms.

It was found that the *voluntary* principle of forming collective farms was being violated, and that in a number of districts the peasants were being *forced* into the collective farms under threat of being dispossessed, disfranchised, and so on.

In a number of districts, preparatory work and patient explanation of the underlying principles of the Party's policy with regard to collectivization were being replaced by bureaucratic decreeing from above, by exaggerated, fictitious figures regarding the formation of collective farms, by an artificial inflation of the percentage of collectivization.

Although the Central Committee had specified that the chief form of the collective-farm movement must be the agricultural artel, in which only the *principal* means of production are collectivized, in a number of places pigheaded attempts were made to skip the artel form and pass straight to the commune; dwellings, milch-cows, small livestock, poultry, etc., not exploited for the market, were collectivized.

Carried away by the initial success of collectivization, persons in authority in certain regions violated the Central Committee's explicit instructions regarding the pace and time limits of collectivization. In their zeal for inflated figures, the leadership of the Moscow Region gave the cue to their subordinates to complete collectivization by the spring of 1930, although they had no less than three years (till the end of 1932) for this purpose. Even grosser were the violations in Transcaucasia and Central Asia.

Taking advantage of these distortions of policy for their own provocative ends, the kulaks and their toadies would themselves propose that communes be formed instead of agricultural artels, and that dwellings, small livestock and poultry be collectivized forthwith. Furthermore, the kulaks instigated the peasants to slaughter their animals before entering the collective farms, arguing that "they will be taken away anyhow."

The class enemy calculated that the distortions and mistakes committed by the local organizations in the process of collectivization would incense the peasantry and provoke revolts against the Soviet Government.

As a result of the mistakes of Party organizations and the downright provocateur actions of the class enemy, in the latter half of February 1930, against the general background of the unquestionable success of collectivization, there were dangerous signs of serious discontent among the peasantry in a number of districts. Here and there, the kulaks and their agents even succeeded in inciting the peasants to outright anti-Soviet actions.

Having received a number of alarming signals of distortions of the Party line that might jeopardize collectivization, the Central Committee of the Party immediately proceeded to remedy the situation, to set the Party workers the task of rectifying the mistakes as quickly as possible. On March 2, 1930, by decision of the Central Committee, Comrade Stalin's article, "Dizzy With Success," was published. This article was a warning to all who had been so carried away by the success of collectivization as to commit gross mistakes and depart from the Party line, to all who were trying to coerce the peasants to join the collective farms. The article laid the utmost emphasis on the principle that the formation of collective farms must be voluntary, and on the necessity of making allowances for the diversity of conditions in the various districts of the U.S.S.R. when determining the pace and methods of collectivization. Comrade Stalin reiterated that the chief form of the collective-farm movement was the agricultural artel, in which only the principal means of production, chiefly those used in grain growing, are collectivized, while household land, dwellings, part of the dairy cattle, small livestock, poultry, etc., are not collectivized.

Comrade Stalin's article was of the utmost political moment. It helped the Party organizations to rectify their mistakes and dealt a severe blow to the enemies of the Soviet Government who had been hoping to take advantage of the distortions of policy to set the peasants against the Soviet Government. The broad mass of the peasants now saw that the line of the Bolshevik Party had nothing in common with the pigheaded "Left" distortions of local authorities. The article set the minds of the peasants at rest.

In order to complete the work begun by Comrade Stalin's article in rectifying distortions and mistakes, the Central Committee of the C.P.S.U.(B.) decided to strike another blow at them, and on March 15, 1930, published its resolution on "Measures to Combat the Distortions of the Party Line in the Collective-Farm Movement."

This resolution made a detailed analysis of the mistakes committed, showing that they were the result of a departure from the Leninist-Stalinist line of the Party, the result of a flagrant breach of Party instructions.

The Central Committee pointed out that these "Left" distortions were of direct service to the class enemy.

The Central Committee gave directions that "persons who are unable or unwilling earnestly to combat distortions of the Party line must be *removed* from their posts and *replaced*." (*Resolutions of the C.P.S.U.[B.]*, Part II, p. 663.)

The Central Committee changed the leadership of certain regional and territorial Party organizations (Moscow Region, Transcaucasia) which had committed political mistakes and proved incapable of rectifying them.

On April 3, 1930, Comrade Stalin's "Reply to Collective Farm Comrades" was published, in which he indicated the *root cause* of the mistakes in the peasant question and the major mistakes committed in the collective-farm movement, *viz.*, an incorrect approach to the middle peasant, violation of the Leninist principle that the formation of collective farms must be voluntary, violation of the Leninist principle that allowance must be made for the diversity of conditions in the various districts of the U.S.S.R., and the attempts to skip the artel form and to pass straight to the commune.

The result of all these measures was that the Party secured the correction of the distortions of policy committed by local Party workers in a number of districts.

It required the utmost firmness on the part of the Central Committee and its ability to go *against the current* in order to promptly correct that considerable body of Party workers who, carried away by success, had been rapidly straying from the Party line.

The Party succeeded in correcting the distortions of the Party line in the collective-farm movement.

This made it possible to consolidate the success of the collective-farm movement.

It also made possible a new and powerful advance of the collective-farm movement.

Prior to the Party's adoption of the policy of eliminating the kulaks as a class, an energetic offensive against the capitalist elements with the object of eliminating them had been waged chiefly in the towns, on the industrial front. So far, the countryside, agriculture, had been lagging behind the towns, behind industry. Consequently, the offensive had not borne an all-round, complete and general character. But now that the backwardness of the countryside was becoming a thing of the past, now that the peasants' fight for the elimination of the kulak class had taken clear shape, and the Party had adopted the policy of eliminating the kulak class, the offensive against the capitalist elements assumed a general character, the partial offensive developed into an offensive along the whole front. By the time the Sixteenth Party Congress was convened, the general offensive against the capitalist elements was proceeding all along the line.

The Sixteenth Party Congress met on June 26, 1930. It was attended by 1,268 delegates with vote and 891 delegates with voice but no vote, representing 1,260,874 Party members and 711,609 candidate members.

The Sixteenth Party Congress is known in the annals of the Party as "the congress of the sweeping offensive of Socialism *along the whole front,* of the elimination of the kulaks as a class, and of the realization of solid collectivization." (*Stalin.*)

Presenting the political report of the Central Committee, Comrade Stalin showed what big victories had been won by the Bolshevik Party in developing the Socialist offensive.

Socialist industrialization had progressed so far that the share of industry in the total production of the country now predominated over that of agriculture. In the fiscal year 1929-30, the share of industry already comprised no less than 53 per cent of the total production of the country, while the share of agriculture was about 47 per cent.

In the fiscal year 1926-27, at the time of the Fifteenth Party Congress, the *total* output of industry had been only 102.5 per cent of the pre-war output; in the year 1929-30, at the time of the Sixteenth Congress, it was already about 180 per cent.

Heavy industry—the production of means of production, machine-building—was steadily growing in power.

"...We are on the eve of the transformation of our country from an *agrarian* to an *industrial* country," declared Comrade Stalin at the congress, amidst hearty acclamation.

Still, the high *rate* of industrial development, Comrade Stalin explained, was not to be confused with the *level* of industrial development. Despite the unprecedented rate of development of Socialist industry, we were still *far behind* the advanced capitalist countries as regards the *level* of industrial development. This was so in the case of electric power, in spite of the phenomenal progress of electrification in the U.S.S.R. This was the case with metal. According to the plan, the output of pig-iron in the U.S.S.R. was to be 5,500,000 tons in the year 1929-30, when the output of pig-iron in Germany in 1929 was 13,400,000 tons, and in France 10,450,000 tons. In order to make good our technical and economic backwardness in the minimum of time, our rate of industrial development had to be further accelerated, and a most resolute fight waged against the opportunists who were striving to reduce the rate of development of Socialist industry.

"... People who talk about the necessity of *reducing* the rate of development of our industry are enemies of Socialism, agents of our class enemies," said Comrade Stalin. (Stalin, *Leninism*, Vol. II, "Political Report of the Central Committee to the Sixteenth Congress of the C.P.S.U.")

After the program of the first year of the First Five-Year Plan had been successfully fulfilled and surpassed, a slogan originated among the masses—"*Fulfil the Five-Year Plan in Four Years.*" A number of branches of industry (oil, peat, general machine-building, agricultural machinery, electrical equipment) were carrying out their plans so successfully that their five-year-plans could be fulfilled in two and a half or three years. This proved that the slogan "The Five-Year Plan in Four Years" was quite feasible, and thus exposed the opportunism of the sceptics who doubted it.

The Sixteenth Congress instructed the Central Committee of the Party to "ensure that the *spirited Bolshevik tempo* of Socialist construction be maintained, and that the *Five-Year Plan be actually fulfilled in four years.*"

By the time of the Sixteenth Party Congress, a momentous change had taken place in the development of agriculture in the U.S.S.R. The broad masses of the peasantry had turned towards Socialism. On May 1, 1930, collectivization in the principal grain-growing regions embraced 40-50 per cent of the peasant households (as against 2-3 per cent in the spring of 1928). The crop area of the collective farms reached 36,000,000 hectares.

Thus the increased program (30,000,000 hectares), laid down in the resolution of the Central Committee of January 5, 1930, was more than fulfilled. The five-year program of collective farm development had been fulfilled more than one and a half times in the space of two years.

In three years the amount of produce marketed by the collective farms had increased more than forty-fold. Already in 1930 more than half the marketed grain in the country came from the collective farms, quite apart from the grain produced by the state farms.

This meant that from now on the fortunes of agriculture would be decided not by the individual peasant farms, but by the collective and state farms.

While, before the mass influx of the peasantry into the collective farms, the Soviet power had leaned mainly on Socialist industry, now it began to lean also on the rapidly expanding Socialist sector of agriculture, the collective and state farms.

The collective farm peasantry, as the Sixteenth Party Congress stated in one of its resolutions, had become "a real and firm mainstay of the Soviet power."

3. POLICY OF RECONSTRUCTING ALL BRANCHES OF THE NA-
TIONAL ECONOMY. IMPORTANCE OF TECHNIQUE. FURTHER
SPREAD OF THE COLLECTIVE-FARM MOVEMENT. POLITICAL
DEPARTMENTS OF THE MACHINE AND TRACTOR STATIONS.
RESULTS OF THE FULFILMENT OF THE FIVE-YEAR PLAN IN
FOUR YEARS. VICTORY OF SOCIALISM ALONG THE WHOLE
FRONT. SEVENTEENTH PARTY CONGRESS

When heavy industry and especially the machine-building industry had been built up and placed securely on their feet, and it was moreover clear that they were developing at a fairly rapid pace, the next task that faced the Party was to reconstruct all branches of the national economy on modern, up-to-date lines. Modern technique, modern machinery had to be supplied to the fuel industry, the metallurgical industry, the light industries, the food industry, the timber industry, the armament industry, the transport system, and to agriculture. In view of the colossal increase in the demand for farm produce and manufactured goods, it was necessary to double and treble output in all branches of production. But this could not be done unless the factories and mills, the state farms and collective farms were adequately supplied with up-to-date equipment, since the requisite increase of output could not be secured with the old equipment.

Unless the major branches of the national economy were reconstructed, it would be impossible to satisfy the new and ever growing demands of the country and its economic system.

Without reconstruction, it would be impossible to complete the offensive of Socialism along the whole front, for the capitalist elements in town and country had to be fought and vanquished not only by a new organization of labour and property, but also by a new technique, by technical superiority.

Without reconstruction, it would be impossible to overtake and outstrip the technically and economically advanced capitalist countries, for although the U.S.S.R. had surpassed the capitalist countries in rate of industrial development, it still lagged a long way behind them in level of industrial development, in quantity of industrial output.

In order that we might catch up with them, every branch of production had to be equipped with new technique and reconstructed on the most up-to-date technical lines.

The question of technique had thus become of decisive importance.

The main impediment was not so much an insufficiency of modern machinery and machine-tools—for our machine-building industry was in a position to produce modern equipment—as the wrong attitude of our business executives to technique, their tendency to underrate the importance of technique in the period of reconstruction and to disdain it. In their opinion, technical matters were the affair of the "experts," something of second-rate importance, to be left in charge of the "bourgeois experts"; they considered that Communist business executives need not interfere in the technical side of production and should attend to something more important, namely, the "general" management of industry.

The bourgeois "experts" were therefore given a free hand in matters of production, while the Communist business executives reserved to themselves the function of "general" direction, the signing of papers.

It need scarcely be said that with such an attitude, "general" direction was bound to degenerate into a mere parody of direction, a sterile signing of papers, a futile fussing with papers.

It is clear that if Communist business executives had persisted in this disdainful attitude of technical matters, we would never have been able to overtake the advanced capitalist countries, let alone outstrip them. This attitude, especially in the reconstruction period, would have doomed our country to backwardness, and would have lowered our rates of development. As a matter of fact, this attitude to technical matters was a screen, a mask for the secret wish of a certain section of the Communist business executives to retard, to reduce the rate of industrial development, so as to be able to "take it easy" by shunting the responsibility for production on to the "experts."

It was necessary to get Communist business executives to turn their attention to technical matters, to acquire a taste for technique; they needed to be shown that it was vital for Bolshevik business executives to master modern technique, otherwise we would run the risk of condemning our country to backwardness and stagnation.

Unless this problem were solved further progress would be impossible.

Of utmost importance in this connection was the speech Comrade Stalin made at the First Conference of Industrial Managers in February 1931:

> "It is sometimes asked," said Comrade Stalin, "whether it is not possible to slow down the tempo a bit, to put a check on the movement. No, comrades, it is not possible! The tempo must not be reduced! ... To slacken the tempo would mean falling behind. And those who fall behind get beaten. But we do not want to be beaten. No, we refuse to be beaten!

> "Incidentally, the history of old Russia is one unbroken record of the beatings she suffered for falling behind, for her backwardness. She was beaten by the Mongol khans. She was beaten by the Turkish beys. She was beaten by the Swedish feudal lords. She was beaten by the Polish and Lithuanian gentry. She was beaten by the British and French capitalists. She was beaten by the Japanese barons. All beat her—for her backwardness. ...

> "We are fifty or a hundred years behind the advanced countries. We must make good this distance in ten years. Either we do it, or they crush us. ...

> "In ten years at most we must make good the distance we are lagging behind the advanced capitalist countries. We have all the 'objective' opportunities for this. The only thing lacking is the ability to make proper use of these opportunities. And that depends on us. *Only* on us! It is time we learned to use these opportunities. It is time to put an end to the rotten policy of non-interference in production. It is time to adopt a new policy, a policy adapted to the times—the policy of interfering in everything. If you are a factory manager, then interfere in all the affairs of the factory, look into everything, let nothing escape you, learn and learn again. Bolsheviks must master technique. It is time Bolsheviks themselves became experts. *In the period of reconstruction technique decides everything.*" (Stalin, *Leninism*, Vol. II, "The Tasks of Business Managers.")

The historic importance of Comrade Stalin's speech lay in the fact that it put an end to the disdainful attitude of Communist business executives to technique, made them face the question of technique, opened a new phase in the struggle for the mastery of technique by the Bolsheviks themselves, and thereby helped to promote the work of economic reconstruction.

From then on technical knowledge ceased to be a monopoly of the bourgeois "experts," and became a matter of vital concern to the Bolshevik business executives themselves, while the word "expert" ceased to be a term of disparagement and became the honourable title of Bolsheviks who had mastered technique.

From then on there were bound to appear—and there actually did appear—thousands upon thousands, whole battalions of Red experts, who had mastered technique and were able to direct industries.

This was a new, Soviet technical intelligentsia, an intelligentsia of the working class and the peasantry, and they now constitute the main force in the management of our industries.

All this was bound to promote, and actually did promote, the work of economic reconstruction.

Reconstruction was not confined to industry and transport. It developed even more rapidly in agriculture. The reason is not far to seek: agriculture was less mechanized than other branches, and here the need for modern machinery was felt more acutely than elsewhere. And it was urgently essential to increase the supply of modern agricultural machines now that the number of collective farms was growing from month to month and week to week, and with it the demand for thousands upon thousands of tractors and other agricultural machines.

The year 1931 witnessed a further advance in the collective-farm movement. In the principal grain-growing districts over 80 per cent of the peasant farms had already amalgamated to form collective farms. Here, solid collectivization had in the main already been achieved. In the less important grain-growing districts and in the districts growing industrial crops about 50 per cent of the peasant farms had joined the collective farms. By now there were 200,000 collective farms and 4,000 state farms, which together cultivated two-thirds of the total crop area of the country, the individual peasants cultivating only one-third.

This was a tremendous victory for Socialism in the countryside.

But the progress of the collective-farm movement was so far to be measured in breadth rather than in depth: the collective farms were increasing in number and were spreading to district after district, but there was no commensurate improvement in the work of the collective farms or in the skill of their personnel. This was due to the fact that the growth of the leading cadres and trained personnel of the collective farms was not keeping pace with the numerical growth of the collective farms themselves. The consequence was that the work of the new collective farms was not always satisfactory, and the collective farms themselves were still weak. They were also held back by the shortage in the countryside of literate people indispensable to the collective farms (bookkeepers, stores managers, secretaries, etc.), and by the inexperience of the peasants in the management of large-scale collective enterprises. The collective farmers were the individual peasants of yesterday; they had experience in farming small plots of land, but none in managing big, collective farms. This experience could not be acquired in a day.

The first stages of collective farm work were consequently marred by serious defects. It was found that work was still badly organized in the collective farms; labour discipline was slack. In many collective farms the income was distributed not by the number of work-day-units, but by the number of mouths to feed in the family. It often happened that slackers got a bigger return than conscientious hard-working collective farmers. These defects in the management of collective farms lowered the incentive of their members. There were many cases of members absenting themselves from work even at the height of the season, leaving part of the crops unharvested until the winter snows, while the reaping was done so carelessly that large quantities of grain were lost. The absence of individual responsibility for machines and horses, and for work generally, weakened the collective farms and reduced their revenues.

The situation was particularly bad wherever former kulaks and their toadies had managed to worm their way into collective farms and to secure positions of trust in them. Not infrequently former kulaks would betake themselves to districts where they were unknown, and there make their way into the collective farms with the deliberate intention of sabotaging and doing mischief. Sometimes, owing to lack of vigilance on the part of Party workers and Soviet officials, kulaks managed to get into collective farms even in their own districts. What made it easier for former kulaks to penetrate into the collective farms was that they had radically changed their tactics. Formerly the kulaks had fought the collective farms openly, had savagely persecuted collective farm leading cadres and foremost collective farmers, nefariously murdering them, burning down their houses and barns. By these methods they had thought to intimidate the peasantry and to deter them from joining the collective farms. Now that their open struggle against the collective farms had failed, they changed their tactics. They laid aside their sawn-off shotguns and posed as innocent, unoffending folk who would not hurt a fly. They pretended to be loyal Soviet supporters. Once inside the collective farms they stealthily carried on their sabotage. They strove to disorganize the collective farms from within, to undermine labour discipline and to muddle the harvest accounts and the records of work performed. It was part of their sinister scheme to destroy the horses of the collective farms by deliberately infecting them with glanders, mange and other diseases, or disabling them by neglect or other methods, in which they were often successful. They did damage to tractors and farm machinery.

The kulaks were often able to deceive the collective farmers and commit sabotage with impunity because the collective farms were still weak and their personnel still inexperienced.

To put an end to the sabotage of the kulaks and to expedite the work of strengthening the collective farms, the latter had to be given urgent and effective assistance in men, advice and leadership.

This assistance was forthcoming from the Bolshevik Party. In January 1933, the Central Committee of the Party adopted a decision to organize *political departments* in the machine and tractor stations serving the collective farms. Some 17,000 Party members were sent into the countryside to work in these political departments and to aid the collective farms.

This assistance was highly effective.

In two years (1933 and 1934) the political departments of the machine and tractor stations did a great deal to build up an active body of collective farmers, to eliminate the defects in the work of the collective farms, to consolidate them, and to rid them of kulak enemies and wreckers.

The political departments performed their task with credit: they strengthened the collective farms both in regard to organization and efficiency, trained skilled personnel for them, improved their management and raised the political level of the collective farm members.

Of great importance in stimulating the collective farmers to strive for the strengthening of the collective farms was the First All-Union Congress of Collective Farm Shock Workers (February 1933) and the speech made by Comrade Stalin at this congress.

Contrasting the old, pre-collective farm system in the countryside with the new, collective farm system, Comrade Stalin said:

"Under the old system the peasants each worked in isolation, following the ancient methods of their forefathers and using antiquated implements of labour; they worked for the landlords and capitalists, the kulaks and profiteers; they lived in penury while they

enriched others.   Under the new, collective farm system, the peasants
work in common, co-operatively, with the help of modern implements—tractors and agricultural machinery; they work for themselves and their collective farms; they live without capitalists and
landlords, without kulaks and profiteers; they work with the object
of raising their standard of welfare and culture from day to day."
(Stalin, *Problems of Leninism*, Russ. ed., p. 528.)

Comrade Stalin showed in this speech what the peasants had achieved
by adopting the collective farm way.   The Bolshevik Party had helped
millions of poor peasants to join the collective farms and to escape from
servitude to the kulaks.   By joining the collective farms, and having
the best lands and the finest instruments of production at their disposal,
millions of poor peasants who had formerly lived in penury had now
as collective farmers risen to the level of middle peasants, and had attained material security.

This was the first step in the development of collective farms, the
first achievement.

The next step, Comrade Stalin said, was to raise the collective farmers—both former poor peasants and former middle peasants—to an even
higher level, to make all the collective farmers prosperous and all the
collective farms Bolshevik.

"Only one thing is now needed for the collective farmers to
become prosperous," Comrade Stalin said, "and that is for them to
work in the collective farms conscientiously, to make efficient use of
the tractors and machines, to make efficient use of the draught
cattle, to cultivate the land efficiently, and to cherish collective farm
property."   (*Ibid.*, pp. 532-3.)

Comrade Stalin's speech made a profound impression on the millions
of collective farmers and became a practical program of action for the
collective farms.

By the end of 1934 the collective farms had become a strong and
invincible force.   They already embraced about three-quarters of all the
peasant households in the Soviet Union and about 90 per cent of the
total crop area.

In 1934 there were already 281,000 tractors and 32,000 harvester
combines at work in the Soviet countryside.   The spring sowing in that
year was completed fifteen to twenty days earlier than in 1933, and
thirty to forty days earlier than in 1932, while the plan of grain deliveries
to the state was fulfilled three months earlier than in 1932.

This showed how firmly established the collective farms had become in two years, thanks to the tremendous assistance given them by the Party and the workers' and peasants' state.

This solid victory of the collective farm system and the attendant improvement of agriculture enabled the Soviet Government to abolish the rationing of bread and all other products and to introduce the unrestricted sale of foodstuffs.

Since the political departments of the machine and tractor stations had served the purpose for which they had been temporarily created, the Central Committee decided to convert them into ordinary Party bodies by merging them with the district Party Committees in their localities.

All these achievements, both in agriculture and in industry, were made possible by the successful fulfilment of the Five-Year Plan.

By the beginning of 1933 it was evident that the First Five-Year Plan had already been fulfilled ahead of time, fulfilled in four years and three months.

This was a tremendous, epoch-making victory of the working class and peasantry of the U.S.S.R.

Reporting to a plenary meeting of the Central Committee and the Central Control Commission of the Party, held in January 1933, Comrade Stalin reviewed the results of the First Five-Year Plan. The report made it clear that in the period which it took to fulfil the First Five-Year Plan, the Party and the Soviet Government had achieved the following major results.

a) The U.S.S.R. had been converted from an agrarian country into an industrial country, for the proportion of industrial output to the total production of the country had risen to 70 per cent.

b) The Socialist economic system had eliminated the capitalist elements in the sphere of industry and had become the sole economic system in industry.

c) The Socialist economic system had eliminated the kulaks as a class in the sphere of agriculture, and had become the predominant force in agriculture.

d) The collective farm system had put an end to poverty and want in the countryside, and tens of millions of poor peasants had risen to a level of material security.

e) The Socialist system in industry had abolished unemployment, and while retaining the 8-hour day in a number of branches, had introduced the 7-hour day in the vast majority of enterprises and the 6-hour day in unhealthy occupations.

f) The victory of Socialism in all branches of the national economy had abolished the exploitation of man by man.

The sum and substance of the achievements of the First Five-Year Plan was that they had completely emancipated the workers and peasants from exploitation and had opened the way to a prosperous and cultured life for *ALL* working people in the U.S.S.R.

In January 1934 the Party held its Seventeenth Congress. It was attended by 1,225 delegates with vote and 736 delegates with voice but no vote, representing 1,874,488 Party members and 935,298 candidate members.

The congress reviewed the work of the Party since the last congress. It noted the decisive results achieved by Socialism in all branches of economic and cultural life and placed on record that the general line of the Party had triumphed along the whole front.

The Seventeenth Party Congress is known in history as the "Congress of Victors."

Reporting on the work of the Central Committee, Comrade Stalin pointed to the fundamental changes that had taken place in the U.S.S.R. during the period under review.

> "During this period, the U.S.S.R. has become radically transformed and has cast off the integument of backwardness and mediævalism. From an agrarian country it has become an industrial country. From a country of small individual agriculture it has become a country of collective, large-scale mechanized agriculture. From an ignorant, illiterate and uncultured country it has become—or rather it is becoming—a literate and cultured country covered by a vast network of higher, intermediate and elementary schools teaching in the languages of the nationalities of the U.S.S.R. (Stalin, *Seventeenth Congress of the C.P.S.U.*, "Report on the Work of the Central Committee of the *C.P.S.U.*[*B.*]," p. 30.)

By this time 99 per cent of the industry of the country was Socialist industry. Socialist agriculture—the collective farms and state farms—embraced about 90 per cent of the total crop area of the country. As to trade, the capitalist elements had been completely ousted from this domain.

When the New Economic Policy was being introduced, Lenin said that there were the elements of five social-economic formations in our country. The first was patriarchal economy, which was largely a natural form of economy, *i.e.*, which practically carried on no trade. The second formation was small commodity production, as represented by the majority of the peasant farms, those which sold agricultural produce, and by the artisans. In the first years of NEP this economic formation embraced the majority of the population. The third formation was private capital-ism, which had begun to revive in the early period of NEP. The fourth formation was state capitalism, chiefly in the form of concessions, which had not developed to any considerable extent. The fifth formation was Socialism: Socialist industry, which was still weak, state farms and col-lective farms, which were economically insignificant at the beginning of NEP, state trade and co-operative societies, which were also weak at that time.

Of all these formations, Lenin said, the Socialist formation must gain the upper hand.

The New Economic Policy was designed to bring about the com-plete victory of Socialist forms of economy.

And by the time of the Seventeenth Party Congress this aim had already been achieved.

"We can now say," said Comrade Stalin, "that the first, the third and the fourth social-economic formations no longer exist; the second social-economic formation has been forced into a secondary position, while the fifth social-economic formation—the Socialist for-mation—now holds unchallenged sway and is the sole commanding force in the whole national economy." (*Ibid.*, p. 33.)

An important place in Comrade Stalin's report was given to the question of ideological-political leadership. He warned the Party that although its enemies, the opportunists and nationalist deviators of all shades and complexions, had been defeated, remnants of their ideology still lingered in the minds of some Party members and often asserted themselves. The survivals of capitalism in economic life and particularly in the minds of men provided a favourable soil for the revival of the ideology of the defeated anti-Leninist groups. The development of peo-ple's mentality does not keep pace with their economic position. As a consequence, survivals of bourgeois ideas still remained in men's minds and would continue to do so even though capitalism had been abolished in economic life. It should also be borne in mind that the surrounding capitalist world, against which we had to keep our powder dry, was working to revive and foster these survivals.

Comrade Stalin also dwelt on the survivals of capitalism in men's minds on the national question, where they were particularly tenacious. The Bolshevik Party was fighting on two fronts, both against the devia-tion to Great-Russian chauvinism and against the deviation to local nationalism. In a number of republics (the Ukraine, Byelorussia, and others) the Party organizations had relaxed the struggle against local nationalism, and had allowed it to grow to such an extent that it had allied itself with hostile forces, the forces of intervention, and had become a danger to the state. In reply to the question, which deviation in the national question was the major danger, Comrade Stalin said:

"The major danger is the deviation against which we have ceased to fight, thereby allowing it to grow into a danger to the state." (*Ibid.*, p. 81.)

Comrade Stalin called upon the Party to be more active in ideological-political work, systematically to expose the ideology and the remnants of the ideology of the hostile classes and of the trends hostile to Leninism.

He further pointed out in his report that the adoption of correct decisions does not in itself guarantee the success of a measure. In order to guarantee success, it was necessary to *put the right people in the right place,* people able to give effect to the decisions of the leading organs and to *keep a check on the fulfilment* of decisions. Without these organizational measures there was a risk of decisions remaining scraps of paper, divorced from practical life. Comrade Stalin referred in support of this to Lenin's famous maximum that the chief thing in organizational work was the *choice of personnel and the keeping of a check on the fulfilment of decisions.* Comrade Stalin said that the disparity between adopted decisions and the organizational work of putting these decisions into effect and of keeping a check on their fulfilment was the chief evil in our practical work.

In order to keep a better check on the fulfilment of Party and Government decisions, the Seventeenth Party Congress set up a Party Control Commission under the Central Committee of the C.P.S.U.(B.) and a Soviet Control Commission under the Council of People's Commissars of the U.S.S.R. in place of the combined Central Control Commission and Workers' and Peasants' Inspection, this body having completed the tasks for which it had been set up by the Twelfth Party Congress.

Comrade Stalin formulated the organizational tasks of the Party in the new stage as follows:

1) Our organizational work must be adapted to the requirements of the political line of the Party;

2) Organizational leadership must be raised to the level of political leadership.

3) Organizational leadership must be made fully equal to the task of ensuring the realization of the political slogans and decisions of the Party.

In conclusion, Comrade Stalin warned the Party that although

Socialism had achieved great successes, successes of which we could be justly proud, we must not allow ourselves to be carried away, to get "swelled head," to be lulled by success.

"...We must not lull the Party, but sharpen its vigilance; we must not lull it to sleep, but keep it ready for action; not disarm it, but arm it; not demobilize it, but hold it in a state of mobilization for the fulfilment of the Second Five-Year Plan," said Comrade Stalin. (*Ibid.*, p. 96.)

The Seventeenth Congress heard reports from Comrades Molotov and Kuibyshev on the Second Five-Year Plan for the development of the national economy. The program of the Second Five-Year Plan was even vaster than that of the First Five-Year Plan. By the end of the Second Five-Year Plan period, in 1937, industrial output was to be increased approximately eightfold in comparison with pre-war. Capital development investments in all branches in the period of the Second Five-Year Plan were to amount to 133,000,000,000 rubles, as against a little over 64,000,000,000 rubles in the period of the First Five-Year Plan.

This immense scope of new capital construction work would ensure the complete technical re-equipment of all branches of the national economy.

The Second Five-Year Plan was to complete in the main the mechanization of agriculture. Aggregate tractor power was to increase from 2,250,000 hp. in 1932 to over 8,000,000 hp. in 1937. The plan provided for the extensive employment of scientific agricultural methods (correct crop rotation, use of selected seed, autumn ploughing, etc.).

A tremendous plan for the technical reconstruction of the means of transport and communication was outlined.

The Second Five-Year Plan contained an extensive program for the further improvement of the material and cultural standards of the workers and peasants.

The Seventeenth Congress paid great attention to matters of organization and adopted decisions on the work of the Party and the Soviets in connection with a report made by Comrade Kaganovich. The question of organization had acquired even greater importance now that the general line of the Party had won and the Party policy had been tried and tested by the experience of millions of workers and peasants. The new and complex tasks of the Second Five-Year Plan called for a higher standard of work in all spheres.

"The major tasks of the Second Five-Year Plan, *viz.*, to completely eliminate the capitalist elements, to overcome the survivals of capitalism in economic life and in the minds of men, to complete the reconstruction of the whole national economy on modern technical lines, to learn to use the new technical equipment and the new enterprises, to mechanize agriculture and increase its productivity—insistently and urgently confront us with the problem of *improving work in all spheres, first and foremost in practical organizational leadership*," it was stated in the decisions of the congress on organizational questions. (*Resolutions of the C.P.S.U.[B.]*, Russ. ed., Part II, p. 591.)

The Seventeenth Congress adopted new Party Rules, which differ from the old ones firstly by the addition of a preamble. This preamble gives a brief definition of the Communist Party, and a definition of its role in the struggle of the proletariat and its place in the organism of the dictatorship of the proletariat. The new rules enumerate in detail the duties of Party members. Stricter regulations governing the admission of new members and a clause concerning sympathizers' groups were introduced. The new rules give a more detailed exposition of the organizational structure of the Party, and formulate anew the clauses dealing with the Party nuclei, or primary organizations, as they have been called since the Seventeenth Party Congress. The clauses dealing with inner-Party democracy and Party discipline were also formulated anew.

4. DEGENERATION OF THE BUKHARINITES INTO POLITICAL DOUBLE-DEALERS. DEGENERATION OF THE TROTSKYITE DOUBLE-DEALERS INTO A WHITEGUARD GANG OF ASSASSINS AND SPIES. FOUL MURDER OF S. M. KIROV. MEASURES OF THE PARTY TO HEIGHTEN BOLSHEVIK VIGILANCE

The achievements of Socialism in our country were a cause of rejoicing not only to the Party, and not only to the workers and collective farmers, but also to our Soviet intelligentsia, and to all honest citizens of the Soviet Union.

But they were no cause of rejoicing to the remnants of the defeated exploiting classes; on the contrary, they only enraged them the more as time went on.

They infuriated the lickspittles of the defeated classes—the puny remnants of the following of Bukharin and Trotsky.

These gentry were guided in their evaluation of the achievements of the workers and collective farmers not by the interests of the people, who applauded every such achievement, but by the interests of their own wretched and putrid faction, which had lost all contact with the realities of life. Since the achievements of Socialism in our country meant the victory of the policy of the Party and the utter bankruptcy of their own policy, these gentry, instead of admitting the obvious facts and joining the common cause, began to revenge themselves on the Party and the people for their own failure, for their own bankruptcy; they began to resort to foul play and sabotage against the cause of the workers and collective farmers, to blow up pits, set fire to factories, and commit acts of wrecking in collective and state farms, with the object of undoing the achievements of the workers and collective farmers and evoking popular discontent against the Soviet Government. And in order, while doing so, to shield their puny group from exposure and destruction, they simulated loyalty to the Party, fawned upon it, eulogized it, cringed before it more and more, while in reality continuing their underhand, subversive activities against the workers and peasants.

At the Seventeenth Party Congress, Bukharin, Rykov and Tomsky made repentant speeches, praising the Party and extolling its achievements to the skies. But the congress detected a ring of insincerity and duplicity in their speeches; for what the Party expects from its members is not eulogies and rhapsodies over its achievements, but conscientious work on the Socialist front. And this was what the Bukharinites had showed no signs of for a long time. The Party saw that the hollow speeches of these gentry were in reality meant for their supporters outside the congress, to serve as a lesson to them in duplicity, and a call to them not to lay down their arms.

Speeches were also made at the Seventeenth Congress by the Trotskyites Zinoviev and Kamenev, who lashed themselves extravagantly for their mistakes, and eulogized the Party no less extravagantly for its achievements. But the congress could not help seeing that both their nauseating self-castigation and their fulsome praise of the Party were only meant to hide an uneasy and unclean conscience. However, the Party did not yet know or suspect that while these gentry were making their cloying speeches at the congress they were hatching a villainous plot against the life of S. M. Kirov.

On December 1, 1934, S. M. Kirov was foully murdered in the Smolny, in Leningrad, by a shot from a revolver.

The assassin was caught red-handed and turned out to be a member of a secret counter-revolutionary group made up of members of an anti-Soviet group of Zinovievites in Leningrad.

S. M. Kirov was loved by the Party and the working class, and his murder stirred the people profoundly, sending a wave of wrath and deep sorrow through the country.

The investigation established that in 1933 and 1934 an underground counter-revolutionary terrorist group had been formed in Leningrad consisting of former members of the Zinoviev opposition and headed by a so-called "Leningrad Centre." The purpose of this group was to murder leaders of the Communist Party. S. M. Kirov was chosen as the first victim. The testimony of the members of this counter-revolutionary group showed that they were connected with representatives of foreign capitalist states and were receiving funds from them.

The exposed members of this organization were sentenced by the Military Collegium of the Supreme Court of the U.S.S.R. to the supreme penalty—to be shot.

Soon afterwards the existence of an underground counter-revolutionary organization called the "Moscow Centre" was discovered. The preliminary investigation and the trial revealed the villainous part played by Zinoviev, Kamenev, Yevdokimov and other leaders of this organization in cultivating the terrorist mentality among their followers, and in plotting the murder of members of the Party Central Committee and of the Soviet Government.

To such depths of duplicity and villainy had these people sunk that Zinoviev, who was one of the organizers and instigators of the assassination of S. M. Kirov, and who had urged the murderer to hasten the crime, wrote an obituary of Kirov speaking of him in terms of eulogy, and demanded that it be published.

The Zinovievites simulated remorse in court; but they persisted in their duplicity even in the dock. They concealed their connection with Trotsky. They concealed the fact that together with the Trotskyites they had sold themselves to fascist espionage services. They concealed their spying and wrecking activities. They concealed from the court their connections with the Bukharinites, and the existence of a united Trotsky-Bukharin gang of fascist hirelings.

As it later transpired, the murder of Comrade Kirov was the work of this united Trotsky-Bukharin gang.

Even then, in 1935, it had become clear that the Zinoviev group was a camouflaged Whiteguard organization whose members fully deserved to be treated as Whiteguards.

A year later it became known that the actual, real and direct organizers of the murder of Kirov were Trotsky, Zinoviev, Kamenev and their accomplices, and that they had also made preparations for the assassination of other members of the Central Committee. Zinoviev, Kamenev, Bakayev, Yevdokimov, Pikel, I. N. Smirnov, Mrachkovsky, Ter-Vaganyan, Reingold and others were committed for trial. Confronted by direct evidence, they had to admit publicly, in open court, that they had not only organized the assassination of Kirov, but had been planning to murder all the other leaders of the Party and the Government. Later investigation established the fact that these villains had been engaged in espionage and in organizing acts of diversion. The full extent of the monstrous moral and political depravity of these men, their despicable villainy and treachery, concealed by hypocritical professions of loyalty to the Party, were revealed at a trial in Moscow, 1936.

The chief instigator and ringleader of this gang of assassins and spies was Judas Trotsky. Trotsky's assistants and agents in carrying out his counter-revolutionary instructions were Zinoviev, Kamenev and their Trotskyite underlings. They were preparing to bring about the defeat of the U.S.S.R. in the event of attack by imperialist countries; they had become defeatists with regard to the workers' and peasants' state; they had become despicable tools and agents of the German and Japanese fascists.

The main lesson which the Party organizations had to draw from the trials of the persons implicated in the foul murder of S. M. Kirov was that they must put an end to their own political blindness and political heedlessness, and must increase their vigilance and the vigilance of all Party members.

In a circular letter to Party organizations on the subject of the foul murder of S. M. Kirov, the Central Committee of the Party stated:

"a) We must put an end to the opportunist complacency engendered by the enormous assumption that as we grow stronger the enemy will become tamer and more inoffensive. This assumption is an utter fallacy. It is a recrudescence of the Right deviation, which assured all and sundry that our enemies would little by little creep into Socialism and in the end become real Socialists. The Bolsheviks have no business to rest on their laurels; they have no business to sleep at their posts. What we need is not complacency, but vigilance, real Bolshevik revolutionary vigilance. It should be remembered that the more hopeless the position of the enemies, the more eagerly will they clutch at 'extreme measures' as the only recourse of the doomed in their struggle against the Soviet power. We must remember this, and be vigilant.

"b) We must properly organize the teaching of the history of the Party to Party members, the study of all and sundry anti-Party groups in the history of our Party, their methods of combating the Party line, their tactics and—still more—the tactics and methods of our Party in combating anti-Party groups, the tactics and methods which have enabled our Party to vanquish and demolish these groups. Party members should not only know how the Party combated and vanquished the Constitutional-Democrats, Socialist-Revolutionaries, Mensheviks and Anarchists, but also how it combated and vanquished the Trotskyites, the 'Democratic-Centralists,' the 'Workers' Opposition,' the Zinovievites, the Right deviators, the Right-Leftist freaks and the like. It should never be forgotten that a knowledge and understanding of the history of our Party is a most important and essential means of fully ensuring the revolutionary vigilance of the Party members."

Of enormous importance in this period was the purge of the Party ranks from adventitious and alien elements, begun in 1933, and especially the careful verification of the records of Party members and the exchange of old Party cards for new ones undertaken after the foul murder of S. M. Kirov.

Prior to the verification of the records of Party members, irresponsibility and negligence in the handling of Party cards had prevailed in many Party organizations. In a number of the organizations utterly intolerable *chaos in the registration of Communists* was revealed, a state of affairs which enemies had been turning to their nefarious ends, using the possession of a Party card as a screen for espionage, wrecking, etc. Many leaders of Party organizations had entrusted the enrolment of new members and the issuance of Party cards to persons in minor positions, and often even to Party members of untested reliability.

In a circular letter to all organizations dated May 13, 1935, on the subject of the registration, safekeeping and issuance of Party cards, the Central Committee instructed all organizations to make a careful verification of the records of Party members and "to establish Bolshevik order in our own Party home."

The verification of the records of Party members was of great political value. In connection with the report of Comrade Yezhov, Secretary of the Central Committee, on the results of the verification of the records of Party members, a plenary meeting of the Central Committee of the Party adopted a resolution on December 25, 1935, declaring that this verification was an organizational and political measure of enormous importance in strengthening the ranks of the C.P.S.U.(B.)

After the verification of the records of Party members and the exchange of Party cards, the admission of new members into the Party was resumed. In this connection the Central Committee of the C.P.S.U.(B.) demanded that new members should not be admitted into the Party wholesale, but on the basis of a strictly individual enrolment of "people really advanced and really devoted to the cause of the working class, the finest people of our country, drawn above all from among the workers, and also from among peasants and active intelligentsia, who had been tried and tested in various sectors of the struggle for Socialism."

In resuming the admission of new members to the Party, the Central Committee instructed Party organizations to bear in mind that hostile elements would persist in their attempts to worm their way into the ranks of the C.P.S.U.(B.). Consequently:

> "It is the task of every Party organization to increase Bolshevik vigilance to the utmost, to hold aloft the banner of the Leninist Party, and to safeguard the ranks of the Party from the penetration of alien, hostile and adventitious elements." (Resolution of the Central Committee of the C.P.S.U.[B.], September 29, 1936, published in *Pravda* No. 270, 1936.)

Purging and consolidating its ranks, destroying the enemies of the Party and relentlessly combating distortions of the Party line, the Bolshevik Party rallied closer than ever around its Central Committee, under whose leadership the Party and the Soviet land now passed to a new stage—the completion of the construction of a classless, Socialist society.

BRIEF SUMMARY

In the period 1930-34 the Bolshevik Party solved what was, after the winning of power, the most difficult historical problem of the proletarian revolution, namely, to get the millions of small peasant owners to adopt the path of collective farming, the path of Socialism.

The elimination of the kulaks, the most numerous of the exploiting classes, and the adoption of collective farming by the bulk of the peasants led to the destruction of the last roots of capitalism in the country, to the final victory of Socialism in agriculture, and to the complete consolidation of the Soviet power in the countryside.

After overcoming a number of difficulties of an organizational character, the collective farms became firmly established and entered upon the path of prosperity.

The effect of the First Five-Year Plan was to lay an unshakable foundation of a Socialist economic system in our country in the shape of a first-class Socialist heavy industry and collective mechanized agriculture, to put an end to unemployment, to abolish the exploitation of man by man, and to create the conditions for the steady improvement of the material and cultural standards of our working people.

These colossal achievements were attained by the working class, the collective farmers, and the working people of our country generally, thanks to the bold, revolutionary and wise policy of the Party and the Government.

The surrounding capitalist world, striving to undermine and disrupt the might of the U.S.S.R., worked with redoubled energy to organize gangs of assassins, wreckers and spies within the U.S.S.R. This hostile activity of the capitalist encirclement became particularly marked with the advent of fascism to power in Germany and Japan. In the Trotskyites and Zinovievites, fascism found faithful servants who were ready to spy, sabotage, commit acts of terrorism and diversion, and to work for the defeat of the U.S.S.R. in order to restore capitalism.

The Soviet Government punished these degenerates with an iron hand, dealing ruthlessly with these enemies of the people and traitors to the country.

CHAPTER TWELVE

THE BOLSHEVIK PARTY IN THE STRUGGLE TO COMPLETE THE BUILDING OF THE SOCIALIST SOCIETY. INTRODUCTION OF THE NEW CONSTITUTION

(1935-1937)

1. INTERNATIONAL SITUATION IN 1935-37. TEMPORARY MITI-GATION OF THE ECONOMIC CRISIS. BEGINNING OF A NEW ECO-NOMIC CRISIS. SEIZURE OF ETHIOPIA BY ITALY. GERMAN AND ITALIAN INTERVENTION IN SPAIN. JAPANESE INVASION OF CENTRAL CHINA. BEGINNING OF SECOND IMPERIALIST WAR.

The economic crisis that had broken out in the capitalist countries in the latter half of 1929 lasted until the end of 1933. After that industry ceased to decline, the crisis was succeeded by a period of stagnation, and was then followed by a certain revival, a certain upward trend. But this upward trend was not of the kind that ushers in an industrial boom on a new and higher basis. World capitalist industry was unable even to reach the level of 1929, attaining by the middle of 1937 only 95-96 per cent of that level. And already in the second half of 1937 a new economic crisis began, affecting first of all the United States. By the end of 1937 the number of unemployed in the U.S.A. had again risen to ten million. In Great Britain, too, unemployment was rapidly increasing.

The capitalist countries thus found themselves faced with a new economic crisis before they had even recovered from the ravages of the preceding one.

The result was that the contradictions between the imperialist countries, as likewise between the bourgeoisie and the proletariat, grew still more acute. As a consequence, the aggressor states redoubled their efforts to recoup themselves for the losses caused by the economic crisis at home at the expense of other, poorly defended, countries. The two notorious aggressor states, Germany and Japan, were this time joined by a third—Italy.

In 1935, fascist Italy attacked Ethiopia and subjugated her. She did so without any reason or justification in "international law"; she

attacked her like a robber, without declaring war, as is now the vogue
with the fascists. This was a blow not only at Ethiopia, but also at
Great Britain, at her sea routes from Europe to India and to Asia
generally. Great Britain vainly attempted to prevent Italy from establishing herself in Ethiopia. Italy later withdrew from the League of Nations
so as to leave her hands free, and began to arm on an intensive scale.

Thus, on the shortest sea routes between Europe and Asia, a new
war knot was tied.

Fascist Germany tore up the Versailles Peace Treaty by a unilateral
act, and adopted a scheme for the *forcible* revision of the map of Europe.
The German fascists made no secret of the fact that they were seeking
to subjugate the neighbouring states, or, at least, to seize such of their
territories as were peopled by Germans. Accordingly, they planned first
to seize Austria, then to strike at Czechoslovakia, then, maybe, at Poland—which also has a compact territory peopled by Germans and
bordering on Germany—and then . . . well, then "we shall see."

In the summer of 1936, Germany and Italy started military intervention against the Spanish Republic. Under the guise of supporting
the Spanish fascists, they secured the opportunity of surreptitiously land-
ing troops on Spanish territory, in the rear of France, and stationing
their fleets in Spanish waters—in the zones of the Balearic Islands and
Gibraltar in the south, the Atlantic Ocean in the west, and the Bay of
Biscay in the north. At the beginning of 1938 the German fascists
seized Austria, thus establishing themselves in the middle reaches of the
Danube and expanding in the south of Europe, towards the Adriatic
Sea.

The German and Italian fascists extended their intervention in Spain,
at the same time assuring the world that they were fighting the Spanish
"Reds" and harboured no other designs. But this was a crude and
shallow camouflage designed to deceive simpletons. As a matter of fact,
they were striking at Great Britain and France, by bestriding the sea
communications of these countries with their vast African and Asiatic
colonial possessions.

As to the seizure of Austria, this at any rate could not be passed
off as a struggle against the Versailles Treaty, as part of Germany's
effort to protect her "national" interests by recovering territory lost in
the first Imperialist War. Austria had not formed part of Germany,
either before or after the war. The *forcible* annexation of Austria was
a glaring imperialist seizure of foreign territory. It left no doubt as to
fascist Germany's designs to gain a dominant position on the West
European continent.

This was above all a blow at the interests of France and Great Britain.

Thus, in the south of Europe, in the zone of Austria and the Adriatic, and in the extreme west of Europe, in the zone of Spain and the waters washing her shores, new war knots were tied.

In 1937, the Japanese fascist militarists seized Peiping, invaded Central China and occupied Shanghai. Like the Japanese invasion of Manchuria several years earlier, the invasion of Central China was effected by the customary Japanese method, in robber fashion, by the dishonest exploitation of various "local incidents" engineered by the Japanese themselves, and in violation of all "international standards," treaties, agreements, etc. The seizure of Tientsin and Shanghai placed the keys of the immense China market in the hands of Japan. As long as Japan holds Shanghai and Tientsin, she can at any moment oust Great Britain and the U.S.A. from Central China, where they have huge investments.

Of course, the heroic struggle of the Chinese people and their army against the Japanese invaders, the tremendous national revival in China, her huge resources of man-power and territory, and, lastly, the determination of the Chinese National Government to fight the struggle for emancipation to a finish, until the invaders are completely driven out from Chinese territory, all go to show beyond a doubt that there is no future for the Japanese imperialists in China, and never will be.

But it is nevertheless true that for the time being Japan holds the keys of China's trade, and that her war on China is in effect a most serious blow at the interests of Great Britain and the U.S.A.

Thus, in the Pacific, in the zone of China, one more war knot was tied.

All these facts show that a second imperialist war has actually begun. It began stealthily, without any declaration of war. States and nations have, almost imperceptibly, slipped into the orbit of a second imperialist war. It was the three aggressor states, the fascist ruling circles of Germany, Italy and Japan, that began the war in various parts of the world. It is being waged over a huge expanse of territory, stretching from Gibraltar to Shanghai. It has already drawn over five hundred million people into its orbit. In the final analysis, it is being waged against the capitalist interests of Great Britain, France and the U.S.A., since its object is a redivision of the world and of the spheres of influence in favour of the aggressor countries and at the expense of the so-called democratic states.

A distinguishing feature of the second imperialist war is that so far it is being waged and extended by the aggressor powers, while the other powers, the "democratic" powers, against whom in fact the war is directed, pretend that it does not concern them, wash their hands of it, draw back, boast of their love of peace, scold the fascist aggressors, and . . . surrender their positions to the aggressors bit by bit, at the same time asserting that they are preparing to resist.

This war, it will be seen, is of a rather strange and one-sided character. But that does not prevent it from being a brutal war of unmitigated conquest waged at the expense of the poorly defended peoples of Ethiopia, Spain and China.

It would be wrong to attribute this one-sided character of the war to the military or economic weakness of the "democratic" states. The "democratic" states are, of course, stronger than the fascist states. The one-sided character of the developing world war is due to the absence of a united front of the "democratic" states against the fascist powers. The so-called democratic states, of course, do not approve of the "excesses" of the fascist states and fear any accession of strength to the latter. But they fear even more the working-class movement in Europe and the movement of national emancipation in Asia, and regard fascism as an "excellent antidote" to these "dangerous" movements. For this reason the ruling circles of the "democratic" states, especially the ruling Conservative circles of Great Britain, confine themselves to a policy of pleading with the overweening fascist rulers "not to go to extremes," at the same time giving them to understand that they "fully comprehend" and on the whole sympathize with their reactionary police policy towards the working-class movement and the national emancipation movement. In this respect, the ruling circles of Britain are roughly pursuing the same policy as was pursued under tsardom by the Russian liberal-monarchist bourgeois, who, while fearing the "excesses" of tsarist policy, feared the people even more, and therefore resorted to a policy of pleading with the tsar and, consequently, of *conspiring* with the tsar against the people. As we know, the liberal-monarchist bourgeoisie of Russia paid dearly for this dual policy. It may be presumed that history will exact retribution also from the ruling circles of Britain, and of their friends in France and the U.S.A.

Clearly, the U.S.S.R. could not shut its eyes to such a turn in the international situation and ignore the ominous events. Any war, however small, started by the aggressors, constitutes a menace to the peaceable countries. The second imperialist war, which has so "imperceptibly" stolen upon the nations and has involved over five hundred million people, is bound all the more to represent a most serious danger to all nations,

and to the U.S.S.R in the first place.   This is eloquently borne out by
the formation of the "Anti-Communist Bloc" by Germany, Italy and
Japan.   Therefore, our country, while pursuing its policy of peace, set
to work to further strengthen its frontier defences and the fighting efficiency of its Red Army and Navy.   Towards the end of 1934 the U.S.S.R.
joined the League of Nations. It did so in the knowledge that the League,
in spite of its weakness, might nevertheless serve as a place where aggressors can be exposed, and as a certain instrument of peace, however feeble,
that might hinder the outbreak of war.   The Soviet Union considered
that in times like these even so weak an international organization as the
League of Nations should not be ignored.   In May 1935 a treaty of
mutual assistance against possible attack by aggressors was signed between
France and the U.S.S.R.   A similar treaty was simultaneously concluded
between the Soviet Union and Czechoslovakia.   In March 1936 the
U.S.S.R. signed a treaty of mutual assistance with the Mongolian People's
Republic, and in August 1937 a pact of non-aggression with the Republic of China.

2.   FURTHER PROGRESS OF INDUSTRY AND AGRICULTURE IN THE
     U.S.S.R. SECOND FIVE-YEAR PLAN FULFILLED AHEAD OF TIME.
     RECONSTRUCTION OF AGRICULTURE AND COMPLETION OF
     COLLECTIVIZATION. IMPORTANCE OF CADRES. STAKHANOV
     MOVEMENT. RISING STANDARD OF WELFARE. RISING CUL-
     TURAL STANDARD. STRENGTH OF THE SOVIET REVOLUTION

Whereas, three years after the economic crisis of 1930-33, a new
economic crisis began in the capitalist countries, in the U.S.S.R. industry
continued to make steady progress *during the whole of this period.*
Whereas by the middle of 1937 world capitalist industry, as a whole,
had barely attained 95-96 per cent of the level of production of 1929,
only to be caught in the throes of a new crisis in the second half of 1937,
the industry of the U.S.S.R. in its steady cumulative progress, had by
the end of 1937 attained 428 per cent of the output of 1929, or over
700 per cent of the pre-war output.
    These achievements were a direct result of the policy of reconstruc-
tion so persistently pursued by the Party and the Government.
    The result of these achievements was that the Second Five-Year
Plan of industry was fulfilled ahead of time.   It was completed by
April 1, 1937, that is, in four years and three months.
    This was a most important victory for Socialism.
    Progress in agriculture presented very much the same picture.   The

total area under all crops increased from 105,000,000 hectares in 1913 (pre-war) to 135,000,000 hectares in 1937. The grain harvest increased from 4,800,000,000 poods in 1913, to 6,800,000,000 poods in 1937, the raw cotton crop from 44,000,000 poods to 154,000,000 poods, the flax crop (fibre) from 19,000,000 poods to 31,000,000 poods, the sugar-beet crop from 654,000,000 poods to 1,311,000,000 poods, and the oil-seed crop from 129,000,000 poods to 306,000,000 poods.

It should be mentioned that in 1937 the collective farms alone (without the state farms) produced a marketable surplus of over 1,700,000,000 poods of grain, which was at least 400,000,000 poods more than the landlords, kulaks and peasants together marketed in 1913.

Only one branch of agriculture—livestock farming—still lagged behind the pre-war level and continued to progress at a slower rate.

As to collectivization in agriculture, it might be considered completed. The number of peasant households that had joined the collective farms by 1937 was 18,500,000 or 93 per cent of the total number of peasant households, while the grain crop area of the collective farms amounted to 99 per cent of the total grain crop area of the peasants.

The fruits of the reconstruction of agriculture and of the extensive supply of tractors and machinery for agricultural purposes were now manifest.

As a result of the completion of the reconstruction of industry and agriculture the national economy was now abundantly supplied with first-class technique. Industry, agriculture, the transport system and the army had received huge quantities of modern technique—machinery and machine tools, tractors and agricultural machines, locomotives and steamships, artillery and tanks, aeroplanes and warships. Tens and hundreds of thousands of trained people were required, people capable of harnessing all this technique and getting the most out of it. Without this, without a sufficient number of people who had mastered technique, there was a risk of technique becoming so much dead and unused metal. This was a serious danger, a result of the fact that the growth in the number of trained people, cadres, capable of harnessing, making full use of technique *was not keeping pace with,* and even *lagging far behind,* the spread of technique. Matters were further complicated by the fact that a considerable number of our industrial executives did not realize this danger and believed that technique would just "do the job by itself." Whereas, formerly, they had underrated the importance of technique and treated it with disdain, now they began to overrate it and turn it into a fetish. They did not realize that without people who had mastered technique, technique was a dead thing. They did not realize that to make technique highly productive, people who had mastered technique were required.

Thus the problem of cadres who had mastered technique became one of prime importance.

The executives who displayed an excessive zeal for technique and a consequent underestimation of the importance of trained people, cadres, had to have their attention turned to the study and mastery of technique, and to the necessity of doing everything to train numerous cadres capable of harnessing technique and getting the most out of it.

Whereas formerly, at the beginning of the reconstruction period, when the country suffered from a dearth of technique, the Party had issued the slogan, "technique in the period of reconstruction decides everything," now, when there was an abundance of technique, when the reconstruction had in the main been completed, and when the country was experiencing an acute dearth of cadres, it became incumbent on the Party to issue a new slogan, one that would focus attention, not so much on technique, as on people, on cadres capable of utilizing technique to the full.

Of great importance in this respect was the speech made by Comrade Stalin to the graduates from the Red Army Academies in May 1935.

"Formerly," said Comrade Stalin, "we used to say that 'technique decides everything.' This slogan helped us to put an end to the dearth in technique and to create a vast technical base in every branch of activity for the equipment of our people with first-class technique. That is very good. But it is not enough, it is not enough by far. In order to set technique going and to utilize it to the full, we need people who have mastered technique, we need cadres capable of mastering and utilizing this technique according to all the rules of the art. Without people who have mastered technique, technique is dead. In the charge of people who have mastered technique, technique can and should perform miracles. If in our first-class mills and factories, in our state farms and collective farms and in our Red Army we had sufficient cadres capable of harnessing this technique, our country would secure results three times and four times as great as at present. That is why emphasis must now be laid on people, on cadres, on workers who have mastered technique. That is why the old slogan, 'technique decides everything,' which is a reflection of a period already passed, a period in which we suffered from a dearth of technique, must now be replaced by a new slogan, the slogan *cadres decide everything.* That is the main thing now...."

"It is time to realize that of all the valuable capital the world possesses, the most valuable and most decisive is people, cadres. It must be realized that under our present conditions *cadres decide everything.* If we have good and numerous cadres in industry, agriculture, transport and the army—our country will be invincible. If we do not have such cadres—we shall be lame on both legs."

Thus the prime task now was to accelerate the training of technical cadres and rapidly to master the new technique with the object of securing a continued rise in productivity of labour.

The most striking example of the growth of such cadres, of the mastering of the new technique by our people, and of the continued rise in productivity of labour was the Stakhanov movement. It originated and developed in the Donetz Basin, in the coal industry, and spread to other branches of industry, to the railways, and then to agriculture. It was called the Stakhanov movement after its originator, Alexei Stakhanov, a coal-hewer in the Central Irmino Colliery (Donetz Basin). Stakhanov had been preceded by Nikita Izotov, who had broken all previous records in coal hewing. On August 31, 1935, Stakhanov hewed 102 tons of coal in one shift and thus fulfilled the standard output fourteen times over. This inaugurated a mass movement of workers and collective farmers for raising the standards of output, for a new advance in productivity of labour. Busygin in the automobile industry, Smetanin in the shoe industry, Krivonoss on the railways, Musinsky in the timber industry, Evdokia Vinogradova and Maria Vinogradova in the textile industry, Maria Demchenko, Maria Gnatenko, P. Angelina, Polagutin, Kolesov, Borin and Kovardak in agriculture—these were the first pioneers of the Stakhanov movement.

They were followed by other pioneers, whole battalions of them, who surpassed the productivity of labour of the earlier pioneers.

Tremendous stimulus was given to the Stakhanov movement by the First All-Union Conference of Stakhanovites held in the Kremlin in November 1935, and by the speech Comrade Stalin made there.

"The Stakhanov movement," Comrade Stalin said in this speech, "is the expression of a new wave of Socialist emulation, a new and higher stage of Socialist emulation. . . . In the past, some three years ago, in the period of the first stage of Socialist emulation, Socialist emulation was not necessarily associated with modern technique. At that time, in fact, we had hardly any modern technique. The present stage of Socialist emulation, the Stakhanov movement, on the other hand, is necessarily associated with modern technique. The Stakhanov movement would be inconceivable without a new and higher technique. We have before us people like Comrade Stakhanov, Busygin, Smetanin, Krivonoss, the Vinogradovas and many others, new people, working men and women, who have completely mastered the technique of their jobs, have harnessed it and driven ahead. We had no such people, or hardly any such people, some three years ago.... The significance of the Stakhanov movement lies in the fact that it is a movement which is smashing the old technical standards, because they are inadequate, which in a number of cases is surpassing the productivity of labour of the foremost capitalist countries, and is thus creating the practical possibility of further consolidating Socialism in our country, of converting our country into the most prosperous of all countries."

Describing the methods of work of the Stakhanovites, and bringing out the tremendous significance of the Stakhanov movement for the future of our country, Comrade Stalin went on to say:

"Look at our comrades, the Stakhanovites, more closely. What type of people are they? They are mostly young or middle-aged working men and women, people with culture and technical knowledge, who show examples of precision and accuracy in work, who are able to appreciate the time factor in work and who have learned to count not only the minutes, but also the seconds. The majority of them have taken the technical minimum courses and are continuing their technical education. They are free of the conservatism and stagnation of certain engineers, technicians and business executives; they are marching boldly forward, smashing the antiquated technical standards and creating new and higher standards; they are introducing amendments into the designed capacities and economic plans drawn up by the leaders of our industry; they often supplement and correct what the engineers and technicians have to say, they often teach them and impel them forward, for they are people who have completely mastered the technique of their job and who are able to squeeze out of technique the maximum that can be squeezed out of it. Today the Stakhanovites are still few in number, but who can doubt that tomorrow there will be ten times more of them? Is it not clear that the Stakhanovites are innovators in our industry, that the Stakhanov movement represents the future of our industry, that it contains the seed of the future rise in the cultural and technical level of the working class, that it opens to us the path by which alone can be achieved those high indices of productivity of labour which are essential for the transition from Socialism to Communism and for the elimination of the distinction between mental labour and manual labour."

The spread of the Stakhanov movement and the fulfillment of the Second Five-Year Plan ahead of time created the conditions for a new rise in the standard of welfare and culture of the working people.

During the period of the Second Five-Year Plan real wages of workers and office employees had more than doubled. The total payroll increased from 34,000,000,000 rubles in 1933 to 81,000,000,000 rubles in 1937. The state social insurance fund increased from 4,600,000,000 rubles to 5,600,000,000 rubles in the same period. In 1937 alone, about 10,000,000,000 rubles were expended on the state insurance of workers and employees, on improving living conditions and on meeting cultural requirements, on sanatoria, health resorts, rest homes and on medical service.

In the countryside, the collective farm system had been definitely consolidated. This was greatly assisted by the *Rules of the Agricultural Artel*, adopted by the Second Congress of Collective Farm Shock Workers in February 1935, and the assignment to the collective farms of the land cultivated by them *in perpetual tenure*. The consolidation of the collective farm system put an end to poverty and insecurity among the rural population. Whereas formerly, some three years earlier, the collective farmers had received one or two kilograms of grain per work-day-unit, now the majority of the collective farmers in the grain-growing regions were receiving from five to twelve kilograms, and many as much as twenty kilograms per work-day-unit, besides other kinds of produce and money income. There were millions of collective farm households in the grain-growing regions who now received as their yearly returns from 500 to 1,500 poods of grain, and in the cotton, sugar beet, flax, livestock, grape growing, citrus fruit growing and fruit and vegetable growing regions, tens of thousands of rubles in annual income. The collective farms had become prosperous. It was now the chief concern of the household of a collective farmer to build new granaries and storehouses, inasmuch as the old storage places, which were designed for a meagre annual supply, no longer met even one-tenth of the household's requirements.

In 1936, in view of the rising standard of welfare of the people, the government passed a law prohibiting abortion, at the same time adopting an extensive program for the building of maternity homes, nurseries, milk centres and kindergartens. In 1936, 2,174,000,000 rubles were assigned for these measures, as compared with 875,000,000 rubles in 1935. A law was passed providing for considerable grants to large families. Grants to a total of over 1,000,000,000 rubles were made in 1937 under this law.

The introduction of universal compulsory education and the building of new schools led to the rapid cultural progress of the people. Schools were built in large numbers all over the country. The number of pupils in elementary and intermediate schools increased from 8,000,000 in 1914 to 28,000,000 in the school year 1936-37. The number of university students increased from 112,000 to 542,000 in the same period.

This was a veritable cultural revolution.

The rise in the standard of welfare and culture of the masses was a reflection of the strength, might and invincibility of our Soviet revolution. Revolutions in the past perished because, while giving the people freedom, they were unable to bring about any serious improvement in their material and cultural conditions. Therein lay their chief weakness. Our revolution differs from all other revolutions in that it not only freed the people from tsardom and capitalism, but also brought about a radical improvement in the welfare and cultural condition of the people. Therein lies its strength and invincibility.

"Our proletarian revolution," said Comrade Stalin at the First All-Union Conference of Stakhanovites, "is the only revolution in the world which had the opportunity of showing the people not only political results but also material results. Of all workers' revolutions we know only one which managed to achieve power. That was the Paris Commune. But it did not last long. True, it endeavoured to smash the fetters of capitalism, but it did not have time enough to smash them, and still less to show the people the beneficial material results of revolution. Our revolution is the only one which not only smashed the fetters of capitalism and brought the people freedom, but also succeeded in creating the material conditions of a prosperous life for the people. Therein lies the strength and invincibility of our revolution."

3. EIGHTH CONGRESS OF SOVIETS. ADOPTION OF THE NEW CONSTITUTION OF THE U.S.S.R.

In February 1935, the Seventh Congress of Soviets of the Union of Soviet Socialist Republics passed a decision to change the Constitution of the U.S.S.R. which had been adopted in 1924. The change of the Constitution was necessitated by the vast changes that had taken place in the life of the U.S.S.R. since the first Constitution of the Soviet Union had been adopted in 1924. During this period the relation of class forces within the country had completely changed; a new Socialist industry had been created, the kulaks had been smashed, the collective farm system had triumphed, and the Socialist ownership of the means of production had been established in every branch of national economy as the basis of Soviet society. The victory of Socialism made possible the further democratization of the electoral system and the introduction of universal, equal and direct suffrage with secret ballot.

The new Constitution of the U.S.S.R. was drafted by a Constitution Commission set up for the purpose, under the chairmanship of Comrade Stalin. The draft was thrown open to nationwide discussion, which lasted five and a half months. It was then submitted to the Extraordinary Eighth Congress of Soviets.

The Eighth Congress of Soviets, specially convened to approve or reject the draft of the new Constitution of the U.S.S.R., met in November 1936.

Reporting to the congress on the draft of the new Constitution, Comrade Stalin enumerated the principal changes that had taken place in the Soviet Union since the adoption of the 1924 Constitution.

The 1924 Constitution had been drawn up in the early period of NEP. At that time the Soviet Government still permitted the development of capitalism alongside of the development of Socialism. The Soviet Government planned in the course of competition between the two systems—the capitalist system and the Socialist system—to organize and ensure the victory of Socialism over capitalism in the economic field. The question, "Who will win?" had not yet been settled. Industry, with its old and inadequate technical equipment, had not attained even the pre-war level. Even less enviable was the picture presented by agriculture. The state farms and collective farms were mere islands in a boundless ocean of individual peasant farms. The question then was not of eliminating the kulaks, but merely of restricting them. The Socialist sector accounted for only about 50 per cent of the country's trade.

Entirely different was the picture presented by the U.S.S.R. in 1936. By that time the economic life of the country had undergone a complete change. The capitalist elements had been entirely eliminated and the Socialist system had triumphed in all spheres of economic life. There was now a powerful Socialist industry which had increased output seven times compared with the pre-war output and had completely ousted private industry. Mechanized Socialist farming in the form of collective farms and state farms, equipped with up-to-date machinery and run on the largest scale in the world, had triumphed in agriculture. By 1936, the kulaks had been completely eliminated as a class, and the individual peasants no longer played any important role in the economic life of the country. Trade was entirely concentrated in the hands of the state and the co-operatives. The exploitation of man by man had been abolished forever. Public, Socialist ownership of the means of production had been firmly established as the unshakable foundation of the new, Socialist system in all branches of economic life. In the new, Socialist society, crises, poverty, unemployment and destitution had disappeared forever. The conditions had been created for a prosperous and cultured life for all members of Soviet society.

The class composition of the population of the Soviet Union, said Comrade Stalin in his report, had changed correspondingly. The landlord class and the old big imperialist bourgeoisie had already been eliminated in the period of the Civil War. During the years of Socialist construction all the exploiting elements—capitalists, merchants, kulaks and profiteers—had been eliminated. Only insignificant remnants of the eliminated exploiting classes persisted, and their complete elimination was a matter of the very near future.

The working people of the U.S.S.R.—workers, peasants and intellectuals—had undergone profound change in the period of Socialist construction.

The working class had ceased to be an exploited class bereft of means of production, as it is under capitalism. It had abolished capitalism, taken away the means of production from the capitalists and turned them into public property. It had ceased to be a proletariat in the proper, the old meaning of the term. The proletariat of the U.S.S.R., possessing the state power, had been transformed into an entirely new class. It had become a working class emancipated from exploitation, a working class which had abolished the capitalist economic system and had established Socialist ownership of the means of production. Hence, it was a working class the like of which the history of mankind had never known before.

No less profound were the changes that had taken place in the condition of the peasantry of the U.S.S.R. In the old days, over twenty million scattered individual peasant households, small and middle, had delved away in isolation on their small plots, using backward technical equipment. They were exploited by landlords, kulaks, merchants, profiteers, usurers, etc. Now an entirely new peasantry had grown up in the U.S.S.R. There were no longer any landlords, kulaks, merchants and usurers to exploit the peasants. The overwhelming majority of the peasant households had joined the collective farms, which were based not on private ownership, but on collective ownership of the means of production, collective ownership which had grown from collective labour. This was a new type of peasantry, a peasantry emancipated from all exploitation. It was a peasantry the like of which the history of mankind had never known before.

The intelligentsia in the U.S.S.R. had also undergone a change. It had for the most part become an entirely new intelligentsia. The majority of its members came from the ranks of the workers and peasants. It no longer served capitalism, as the old intelligentsia did; it served Socialism. It had become an equal member of the Socialist society. Together with the workers and peasants, it was building a new Socialist society. This was a new type of intelligentsia, which served the people and was emancipated from all exploitation. It was an intelligentsia the like of which the history of mankind had never known before.

Thus the old class dividing lines between the working people of the U.S.S.R. were being obliterated, the old class exclusiveness was disappearing. The economic and political contradictions between the workers, the peasants and the intellectuals were declining and becoming obliterated. The foundation for the moral and political unity of society had been created.

These profound changes in the life of the U.S.S.R., these decisive achievements of Socialism in the U.S.S.R., were reflected in the new Constitution.

According to the new Constitution, Soviet society consists of two friendly classes—the workers and peasants—class distinctions between the two still remaining. The Union of Soviet Socialist Republics is a Socialist state of workers and peasants.

The political foundation of the U.S.S.R. is formed by the Soviets of Deputies of the Working People, which developed and grew strong as a result of the overthrow of the power of the landlords and capitalists and the achievement of the dictatorship of the proletariat.

All power in the U.S.S.R. belongs to the working people of town and country as represented by the Soviets of Deputies of the Working People.

The highest organ of state power in the U.S.S.R. is the Supreme Soviet of the U.S.S.R.

The Supreme Soviet of the U.S.S.R., consisting of two Chambers with equal rights, the Soviet of the Union and the Soviet of Nationalities, is elected by the citizens of the U.S.S.R. for a term of four years on the basis of universal, equal and direct suffrage by secret ballot.

Elections to the Supreme Soviet of the U.S.S.R., as to all Soviets of Deputies of the Working People, are *universal*. This means that all citizens of the U.S.S.R. who have reached the age of eighteen, irrespective of race or nationality, religion, standard of education, domicile, social origin, property status or past activities, have the right to vote in the election of deputies and to be elected, with the exception of the insane and persons convicted by court of law to sentences including deprivation of electoral rights.

Elections of deputies are *equal*. This means that each citizen is entitled to one vote and that all citizens participate in the elections on an equal footing.

Elections of deputies are *direct*. This means that all Soviets of Deputies of the Working People, from rural and city Soviets of Deputies of the Working People up to and including the Supreme Soviet of the U.S.S.R., are elected by the citizens by direct vote.

The Supreme Soviet of the U.S.S.R. at a joint sitting of both Chambers elects the Presidium of the Supreme Soviet and the Council of People's Commissars of the U.S.S.R.

The economic foundation of the U.S.S.R. is the Socialist system of economy and the Socialist ownership of the means of production. In the U.S.S.R. is realized the Socialist principle: "From each according to his ability, to each according to his work."

All citizens of the U.S.S.R. are guaranteed the right to work, the right to rest and leisure, the right to education, the right to maintenance in old age and in case of sickness or disability.

Women are accorded equal rights with men in all spheres of life.

The equality of the citizens of the U.S.S.R., irrespective of their nationality or race, is an indefeasible law.

Freedom of conscience and freedom of anti-religious propaganda is recognized for all citizens.

In order to strengthen Socialist society, the Constitution guarantees freedom of speech, press, assembly and meeting, the right to unite in public organizations, inviolability of person, inviolability of domicile and privacy of correspondence, the right of asylum for foreign citizens persecuted for defending the interests of the working people or for their scientific activities, or for their struggle for national liberation.

The new Constitution also imposes serious duties on all citizens of the U.S.S.R.: the duty of observing the laws, maintaining labour discipline, honestly performing public duties, respecting the rules of the

Socialist community, safeguarding and strengthening public, Socialist property, and defending the Socialist fatherland.

> "To defend the fatherland is the sacred duty of every citizen of the U.S.S.R."

Dealing with the right of citizens to unite in various societies, one of the articles of the Constitution states:

> "The most active and politically conscious citizens in the ranks of the working class and other strata of the working people unite in the Communist Party of the Soviet Union (Bolsheviks), which is the vanguard of the working people in their struggle to strengthen and develop the Socialist system and which represents the leading core of all organizations of the working people, both public and state."

The Eighth Congress of Soviets unanimously approved and adopted the draft of the new Constitution of the U.S.S.R.

The Soviet country thus acquired a new Constitution, a Constitution embodying the victory of Socialism and workers' and peasants' democracy.

In this way the Constitution gave legislative embodiment to the epoch-making fact that the U.S.S.R. had entered a new stage of development, the stage of the completion of the building of a Socialist society and the gradual transition to Communist society, where the guiding principle of social life will be the Communist principle: "From each according to his abilities, to each according to his needs."

4. LIQUIDATION OF THE REMNANTS OF THE BUKHARIN-TROTSKY GANG OF SPIES, WRECKERS AND TRAITORS TO THE COUNTRY. PREPARATIONS FOR THE ELECTION OF THE SUPREME SOVIET OF THE U.S.S.R. BROAD INNER-PARTY DEMOCRACY AS THE PARTY'S COURSE. ELECTION OF SUPREME SOVIET OF U.S.S.R.

In 1937, new facts came to light regarding the fiendish crimes of the Bukharin-Trotsky gang. The trial of Pyatakov, Radek and others, the trial of Tukhachevsky, Yakir and others, and, lastly, the trial of Bukharin, Rykov, Krestinsky, Rosengoltz and others, all showed that the Bukharinites and Trotskyites had long ago joined to form a common band of enemies of the people, operating as the "Bloc of Rights and Trotskyites."

The trials showed that these dregs of humanity, in conjunction with the enemies of the people, Trotsky, Zinoviev and Kamenev, had been in conspiracy against Lenin, the Party and the Soviet state ever since the early days of the October Socialist Revolution. The insidious attempts to thwart the Peace of Brest-Litovsk at the beginning of 1918, the plot against Lenin and the conspiracy with the "Left" Socialist-Revolutionaries for the arrest and murder of Lenin, Stalin and Sverdlov in the spring of 1918, the villainous shot that wounded Lenin in the summer of 1918, the revolt of the "Left" Socialist-Revolutionaries in the summer of 1918, the deliberate aggravation of differences in the Party in 1921 with the object of undermining and overthrowing Lenin's leadership from within, the attempts to overthrow the Party leadership during Lenin's illness and after his death, the betrayal of state secrets and the supply of information of an espionage character to foreign espionage services, the vile assassination of Kirov, the acts of wrecking, diversion and explosions, the dastardly murder of Menzhinsky, Kuibyshev and Gorky—all these and similar villainies over a period of twenty years were committed, it transpired, with the participation or under the direction of Trotsky, Zinoviev, Kamenev, Bukharin, Rykov and their henchmen, at the behest of espionage services of bourgeois states.

The trials brought to light the fact that the Trotsky-Bukharin fiends, in obedience to the wishes of their masters—the espionage services of foreign states—had set out to destroy the Party and the Soviet state, to undermine the defensive power of the country, to assist foreign military intervention, to prepare the way for the defeat of the Red Army, to bring about the dismemberment of the U.S.S.R., to hand over the Soviet Maritime Region to the Japanese, Soviet Byelorussia to the Poles, and the Soviet Ukraine to the Germans, to destroy the gains of the workers and collective farmers, and to restore capitalist slavery in the U.S.S.R.

These Whiteguard pigmies, whose strength was no more than that of a gnat, apparently flattered themselves that they were the masters of the country, and imagined that it was really in their power to sell or give away the Ukraine, Byelorussia and the Maritime Region.

These Whiteguard insects forgot that the real masters of the Soviet country were the Soviet people, and that the Rykovs, Bukharins, Zinovievs and Kamenevs were only temporary employees of the state, which could at any moment sweep them out from its offices as so much useless rubbish.

These contemptible lackeys of the fascists forgot that the Soviet people had only to move a finger, and not a trace of them would be left.

The Soviet court sentenced the Bukharin-Trotsky fiends to be shot. The People's Commissariat of Internal Affairs carried out the sentence.

The Soviet people approved the annihilation of the Bukharin-Trotsky gang and passed on to next business.

And the next business was to prepare for the election of the Supreme Soviet of the U.S.S.R. and to carry it out in an organized way.

The Party threw all its strength into the preparations for the elections. It held that the putting into effect of the new Constitution of the U.S.S.R. signified a turn in the political life of the country. This turn meant the complete democratization of the electoral system, the substitution of universal suffrage for restricted suffrage, equal suffrage for not entirely equal suffrage, direct elections for indirect elections, and secret ballot for open ballot.

Before the introduction of the new Constitution there were restrictions of the franchise in the case of priests, former Whiteguards, former kulaks, and persons not engaged in useful labour. The new Constitution abolished all franchise restrictions for these categories of citizens by making the election of deputies universal.

Formerly, the election of deputies had been unequal, inasmuch as the bases of representation for the urban and rural populations differed. Now, however, all necessity for restrictions of equality of the suffrage had disappeared and all citizens were given the right to take part in the elections on an equal footing.

Formerly, the elections of the intermediate and higher organs of Soviet power were indirect. Now, however, under the new Constitution, all Soviets, from rural and urban up to and including the Supreme Soviet, were to be elected by the citizens directly.

Formerly, deputies to the Soviets were elected by open ballot and the voting was for lists of candidates. Now, however, the voting for deputies was to be by secret ballot, and not by lists, but for individual candidates nominated in each electoral area.

This was a definite turning point in the political life of the country.

The new electoral system was bound to result, and actually did result, in an enhancement of the political activity of the people, in greater control by the masses over the organs of Soviet power, and in the increased responsibility of the organs of Soviet power to the people.

In order to be fully prepared for this turn, the Party had to be its moving spirit, and the leading role of the Party in the forthcoming elections had to be fully ensured. But this could be done only if the Party organizations themselves became thoroughly democratic in their everyday work, only if they fully observed the principles of democratic centralism in their inner-Party life, as the Party Rules demanded, only if all organs of the Party were elected, only if criticism and self-criticism in the Party were developed to the full, only if the responsibility of the Party bodies to the members of the Party were complete, and if the members of the Party themselves became thoroughly active.

A report made by Comrade Zhdanov at the plenum of the Central Committee at the end of February 1937 on the subject of preparing the Party organizations for the elections to the Supreme Soviet of the U.S.S.R. revealed the fact that a number of Party organizations were systematically violating the Party Rules and the principles of democratic centralism in their everyday work, substituting co-option for election, voting by lists for the voting for individual candidates, open ballot for secret ballot, etc. It was obvious that organizations in which such practices prevailed could not properly fulfil their tasks in the elections to the Supreme Soviet. It was therefore first of all necessary to put a stop to such anti-democratic practices in the Party organizations and to reorganize Party work on broad democratic lines.

Accordingly, after hearing the report of Comrade Zhdanov, the Plenum of the Central Committee resolved:

"a) To reorganize Party work on the basis of complete and unqualified observance of the principles of inner-Party democracy as prescribed by the Party Rules.

"b) To put an end to the practice of co-opting members of Party Committees and to restore the principle of election of directing bodies of Party organizations as prescribed by the Party Rules.

"c) To forbid voting by lists in the election of Party bodies; voting should be for individual candidates, all members of the Party being guaranteed the unlimited right to challenge candidates and to criticize them.

"d) To introduce the secret ballot in the election of Party bodies.

"e) To hold elections of Party bodies in all Party organizations, from the Party Committees of primary Party organizations to the territorial and regional committees and the Central Committees of the national Communist Parties, the elections to be completed not later than May 20.

"f) To charge all Party organizations strictly to observe the provisions of the Party Rules with respect to the terms of office of Party bodies, namely: to hold elections in primary Party organizations once a year; in district and city organizations—once a year;

in regional, territorial and republican organizations—every eighteen months.

"g) To ensure that Party organizations strictly adhere to the system of electing Party Committees at general factory meetings, and not to allow the latter to be replaced by delegate conferences.

"h) To put a stop to the practice prevalent in a number of primary Party organizations whereby general meetings are virtually abolished and replaced by shop meetings and delegate conferences."

In this way the Party began its preparations for the forthcoming elections.

This decision of the Central Committee was of tremendous political importance. Its significance lay not only in the fact that it inaugurated the Party's campaign in the election of the Supreme Soviet of the U.S.S.R., but also, and primarily, in the fact that it helped the Party organizations to reorganize their work, to apply the principles of inner-Party democracy, and to meet the elections to the Supreme Soviet fully prepared.

The Party decided to make the idea of an election bloc of Communists and the non-Party masses the keynote of its policy in developing the election campaign. The Party entered the elections in a bloc, an alliance with the non-Party masses, by deciding to put up in the electoral areas joint candidates with the non-Party masses. This was something unprecedented and absolutely impossible in elections in bourgeois countries. But a bloc of Communists and the non-Party masses was something quite natural in our country, where hostile classes no longer exist and where the moral and political unity of all sections of the population is an incontestable fact.

On December 7, 1937, the Central Committee of the Party issued an Address to the electors, which stated:

"On December 12, 1937, the working people of the Soviet Union will, on the basis of our Socialist Constitution, elect their deputies to the Supreme Soviet of the U.S.S.R. The Bolshevik Party enters the elections in a *bloc*, an *alliance* with the non-Party workers, peasants, office employees and intellectuals. ... The Bolshevik Party does not fence itself off from non-Party people, but, on the contrary, enters the elections in a bloc, an alliance, with the non-Party masses, in a bloc with the trade unions of the workers and office employees, with the Young Communist League and other non-Party organizations and societies. Consequently, the candidates will be the joint candidates of the Communists and the non-Party masses, every non-Party deputy will also be the deputy of the Communists, just as every Communist deputy will be the deputy of the non-Party masses."

The Address of the Central Committee concluded with the following appeal to the electors:

"The Central Committee of the Communist Party of the Soviet Union (Bolsheviks) calls upon all Communists and sympathizers to vote for the non-Party candidates with the same unanimity as they should vote for the Communist candidates.

"The Central Committee of the Communist Party of the Soviet Union (Bolsheviks) calls upon all non-Party electors to vote for the Communist candidates with the same unanimity as they will vote for the non-Party candidates.

"The Central Committee of the Communist Party of the Soviet Union (Bolsheviks) calls upon all electors to appear at the polling stations on December 12, 1937, as one man, to elect the deputies to the Soviet of the Union and the Soviet of Nationalities.

"There must not be a single elector who does not exercise his honourable right of electing deputies to the Supreme organ of the Soviet state.

"There must not be a single active citizen who does not consider it his civic duty to assist in ensuring that all electors without exception take part in the elections of the Supreme Soviet.

"December 12, 1937, should be a great holiday celebrating the union of the working people of all the nations of the U.S.S.R. around the victorious banner of Lenin and Stalin."

On December 11, 1937, the eve of the elections, Comrade Stalin addressed the voters of the area in which he was nominated and described what type of public figures those whom the people choose, the deputies to the Supreme Soviet of the U.S.S.R., should be. Comrade Stalin said:

"The electors, the people, must demand that their deputies should remain equal to their tasks; that in their work they should not sink to the level of political philistines; that in their posts they should remain political figures of the Lenin type; that as public figures they should be as clear and definite as Lenin was; that they should be as fearless in battle and as merciless towards the enemies of the people as Lenin was; that they should be free from all panic, from any semblance of panic, when things begin to get complicated and some danger or other looms on the horizon, that they should be as free from all semblance of panic as Lenin was; that they should be as wise and deliberate in deciding complex problems requiring a comprehensive orientation and a comprehensive weighing of all pros and cons as Lenin was; that they should be as upright and honest as Lenin was; that they should love their people as Lenin did."

The elections to the Supreme Soviet of the U.S.S.R. took place on December 12 amidst great enthusiasm. They were something more than elections; they were a great holiday celebrating the triumph of the Soviet people, a demonstration of the great friendship of the peoples of the U.S.S.R.

Of a total of 94,000,000 electors, over 91,000,000, or 96.8 per cent, voted. Of this number 89,844,000, or 98.6 per cent, voted for the candidates of the bloc of the Communists and the non-Party masses. Only 632,000 persons, or less than one per cent, voted against the candidates of the bloc of the Communists and the non-Party masses. All the candidates of the bloc were elected without exception.

Thus, 90,000,000 persons, by their unanimous vote, confirmed the victory of Socialism in the U.S.S.R.

This was a remarkable victory for the bloc of the Communists and the non-Party masses.

It was a triumph for the Bolshevik Party.

It was a brilliant confirmation of the moral and political unity of the Soviet people, to which Comrade Molotov had referred in a historic speech he delivered on the occasion of the Twentieth Anniversary of the October Revolution.

CONCLUSION

What are the chief conclusions to be drawn from the historical path traversed by the Bolshevik Party?

What does the history of the C.P.S.U.(B.) teach us?

1) The history of the Party teaches us, first of all, that the victory of the proletarian revolution, the victory of the dictatorship of the proletariat, is impossible without a revolutionary party of the proletariat, a party free from opportunism, irreconcilable towards compromisers and capitulators, and revolutionary in its attitude towards the bourgeoisie and its state power.

The history of the Party teaches us that to leave the proletariat without such a party means to leave it without revolutionary leadership; and to leave it without revolutionary leadership means to ruin the cause of the proletarian revolution.

The history of the Party teaches us that the ordinary Social-Democratic Party of the West-European type, brought up under conditions of civil peace, trailing in the wake of the opportunists, dreaming of "social reforms," and dreading social revolution, cannot be such a party.

The history of the Party teaches us that only a party of the new type, a Marxist-Leninist party, a party of social revolution, a party capable of preparing the proletariat for decisive battles against the bourgeoisie and of organizing the victory of the proletarian revolution, can be such a party.

The Bolshevik Party in the U.S.S.R. is such a party.

"In the pre-revolutionary period," Comrade Stalin says, "in the period of more or less peaceful development, when the parties of the Second International were the predominant force in the working-class movement and parliamentary forms of struggle were regarded as the principal forms, the party neither had nor could have had that great and decisive importance which it acquired afterwards, under conditions of open revolutionary battle. Defending the Second International against attacks made upon it, Kautsky says that the parties of the Second International are instruments of peace and not of war, and that for this very reason they were powerless to take any

353

important steps during the war, during the period of revolutionary action by the proletariat. That is quite true. But what does it mean? It means that the parties of the Second International are unfit for the revolutionary struggle of the proletariat, that they are not militant parties of the proletariat, leading the workers to power, but election machines adapted for parliamentary elections and parliamentary struggle. This, in fact, explains why, in the days when the opportunists of the Second International were in the ascendancy, it was not the party but its parliamentary group that was the chief political organization of the proletariat. It is well known that the party at that time was really an appendage and subsidiary of the parliamentary group. It goes without saying that under such circumstances and with such a party at the helm there could be no question of preparing the proletariat for revolution.

"But matters have changed radically with the dawn of the new period. The new period is one of open class collisions, of revolutionary action by the proletariat, of proletarian revolution, a period when forces are being directly mustered for the overthrow of imperialism and the seizure of power by the proletariat. In this period the proletariat is confronted with new tasks, the tasks of reorganizing all party work on new, revolutionary lines; of educating the workers in the spirit of revolutionary struggle for power; of preparing and moving up reserves; of establishing an alliance with the proletarians of neighbouring countries; of establishing firm ties with the liberation movement in the colonies and dependent countries, etc., etc. To think that these new tasks can be performed by the old Social-Democratic parties, brought up as they were in the peaceful conditions of parliamentarism, is to doom oneself to hopeless despair and inevitable defeat. If, with such tasks to shoulder, the proletariat remained under the leadership of the old parties it would be completely unarmed and defenceless. It goes without saying that the proletariat could not consent to such a state of affairs.

"Hence the necessity for a new party, a militant party, a revolutionary party, one bold enough to lead the proletarians in the struggle for power, sufficiently experienced to find its bearings amidst the complex conditions of a revolutionary situation, and sufficiently flexible to steer clear of all submerged rocks in the path to its goal.

"Without such a party it is useless even to think of overthrowing imperialism and achieving the dictatorship of the proletariat.

"This new party is the party of Leninism." (Joseph Stalin, *Leninism*, Vol. I, pp. 87-8.)

2) The history of the Party further teaches us that a party of the working class cannot perform the role of leader of its class, cannot perform the role of organizer and leader of the proletarian revolution, unless it has mastered the advanced theory of the working-class movement, the Marxist-Leninist theory.

The power of the Marxist-Leninist theory lies in the fact that it enables the Party to find the right orientation in any situation, to understand the inner connection of current events, to foresee their course and to perceive not only how and in what direction they are developing in the present, but how and in what direction they are bound to develop in the future.

Only a party which has mastered the Marxist-Leninist theory can confidently advance and lead the working class forward.

On the other hand, a party which has not mastered the Marxist-Leninist theory is compelled to grope its way, loses confidence in its actions and is unable to lead the working class forward.

It may seem that all that is required for mastering the Marxist-Leninist theory is diligently to learn by heart isolated conclusions and propositions from the works of Marx, Engels and Lenin, learn to quote them at opportune times and rest at that, in the hope that the conclusions and propositions thus memorized will suit each and every situation and occasion. But such an approach to the Marxist-Leninist theory is altogether wrong. The Marxist-Leninist theory must not be regarded as a collection of dogmas, as a catechism, as a symbol of faith, and the Marxists themselves as pedants and dogmatists. The Marxist-Leninist theory is the science of the development of society, the science of the working-class movement, the science of the proletarian revolution, the science of the building of the Communist society. And as a science it does not and cannot stand still, but develops and perfects itself. Clearly, in its development it is bound to become enriched by new experience and new knowledge, and some of its propositions and conclusions are bound to change in the course of time, are bound to be replaced by new conclusions and propositions corresponding to the new historical conditions.

Mastering the Marxist-Leninist theory does not at all mean learning all its formulas and conclusions by heart and clinging to their every letter. To master the Marxist-Leninist theory we must first of all learn to distinguish between its letter and substance.

Mastering the Marxist-Leninist theory means assimilating *the substance* of this theory and learning to use it in the solution of the practical problems of the revolutionary movement under the varying conditions of the class struggle of the proletariat.

Mastering the Marxist-Leninist theory means being able to enrich this theory with the new experience of the revolutionary movement, with new propositions and conclusions, it means being able to *develop it and advance it* without hesitating to replace—in accordance with the substance of the theory—such of its propositions and conclusions as have become antiquated by new ones corresponding to the new historical situation.

The Marxist-Leninist theory is not a dogma but a guide to action.

Before the Second Russian Revolution (February 1917), the Marxists of all countries assumed that the parliamentary democratic republic was the most suitable form of political organization of society in the period of transition from capitalism to Socialism. It is true that in the seventies Marx stated that the most suitable form for the dictatorship of the proletariat was a political organization of the type of the Paris Commune, and not the parliamentary republic. But, unfortunately, Marx did not develop this proposition any further in his writings and it was committed to oblivion. Moreover, Engels' authoritative statement in his criticism of the draft of the Erfurt Program in 1891, namely, that "the democratic republic...is...the specific form for the dictatorship of the proletariat" left no doubt that the Marxists continued to regard the democratic republic as the political form for the dictatorship of the proletariat. Engels' proposition later became a guiding principle for all Marxists, including Lenin. However, the Russian Revolution of 1905, and especially the Revolution of February 1917, advanced a new form of political organization of society—the Soviets of Workers' and Peasants' Deputies. As a result of a study of the experience of the two Russian revolutions, Lenin, on the basis of the theory of Marxism, arrived at the conclusion that the best political form for the dictatorship of the proletariat was not a parliamentary democratic republic, but a republic of Soviets. Proceeding from this, Lenin, in April 1917, during the period of transition from the bourgeois to the Socialist revolution, issued the slogan of a republic of Soviets as the best political form for the dictatorship of the proletariat. The opportunists of all countries clung to the parliamentary republic and accused Lenin of departing from Marxism and destroying democracy. But it was Lenin, of course, who was the real Marxist who had mastered the theory of Marxism, and not the opportunists, for Lenin was advancing the Marxist theory by enriching it with new experience, whereas the opportunists were dragging it back and transforming one of its propositions into a dogma.

What would have happened to the Party, to our revolution, to Marxism, if Lenin had been overawed by the letter of Marxism and had not had the courage to replace one of the old propositions of Marxism, formulated by Engels, by the new proposition regarding the republic of Soviets, a proposition that corresponded to the new historical conditions? The Party would have groped in the dark, the Soviets would have been disorganized, we should not have had a Soviet power, and the Marxist theory would have suffered a severe setback. The proletariat would have lost, and the enemies of the proletariat would have won.

As a result of a study of pre-imperialist capitalism Engels and Marx arrived at the conclusion that the Socialist revolution could not be victorious in one country, taken singly, that it could be victorious only by a simultaneous stroke in all, or the majority of the civilized countries. That was in the middle of the nineteenth century. This conclusion later became a guiding principle for all Marxists. However, by the beginning of the twentieth century, pre-imperialist capitalism had grown into imperialist capitalism, ascendant capitalism had turned into moribund capitalism. As a result of a study of imperialist capitalism, Lenin, on the basis of the Marxist theory, arrived at the conclusion that the old formula of Engels and Marx no longer corresponded to the new historical conditions, and that the victory of the Socialist revolution was quite possible in one country, taken singly. The opportunists of all countries clung to the old formula of Engels and Marx and accused Lenin of departing from Marxism. But it was Lenin, of course, who was the real Marxist who had mastered the theory of Marxism, and not the opportunists, for Lenin was advancing the Marxist theory by enriching it with new experience, whereas the opportunists were dragging it back, mummifying it.

What would have happened to the Party, to our revolution, to Marxism, if Lenin had been overawed by the letter of Marxism and had not had the courage of theoretical conviction to discard one of the old conclusions of Marxism and to replace it by a new conclusion affirming that the victory of Socialism in one country, taken singly, was possible, a conclusion which corresponded to the new historical conditions? The Party would have groped in the dark, the proletarian revolution would have been deprived of leadership, and the Marxist theory would have begun to decay. The proletariat would have lost, and the enemies of the proletariat would have won.

Opportunism does not always mean a direct denial of the Marxist theory or of any of its propositions and conclusions. Opportunism is sometimes expressed in the attempt to cling to certain of the propositions of Marxism that have already become antiquated and to convert them into a dogma, so as to retard the further development of Marxism, and, consequently, to retard the development of the revolutionary movement of the proletariat.

It may be said without fear of exaggeration that since the death of Engels the master theoretician Lenin, and after Lenin, Stalin and the other disciples of Lenin, have been the only Marxists who have advanced the Marxist theory and who have enriched it with new experience in the new conditions of the class struggle of the proletariat.

And just because Lenin and the Leninists have advanced the Marxist theory, Leninism is a further development of Marxism; it is Marxism in the new conditions of the class struggle of the proletariat, Marxism of the epoch of imperialism and proletarian revolutions, Marxism of the epoch of the victory of Socialism on one-sixth of the earth's surface.

The Bolshevik Party could not have won in October 1917 if its foremost men had not mastered the theory of Marxism, if they had not learned to regard this theory as a guide to action, if they had not learned to advance the Marxist theory by enriching it with the new experience of the class struggle of the proletariat.

Criticizing the German Marxists in America who had undertaken to lead the American working-class movement, Engels wrote:

"The Germans have not understood how to use their theory as a lever which could set the American masses in motion; they do not understand the theory themselves for the most part and treat it in a doctrinaire and dogmatic way, as something which has got to be learned off by heart and which will then supply all needs without more ado. To them it is a dogma and not a guide to action." (Marx and Engels, *Selected Correspondence*, pp. 449-450.)

Criticizing Kamenev and some of the old Bolsheviks who in April 1917 clung to the old formula of a revolutionary democratic dictatorship of the proletariat and the peasantry at a time when the revolutionary movement had gone on ahead and was demanding a transition to the Socialist revolution, Lenin wrote:

"Our teaching is not a dogma, but a guide to action, Marx and Engels always used to say, rightly ridiculing the learning and repetition by rote of 'formulas' which at best are only capable of outlining *general* tasks that are necessarily liable to be modified by the *concrete* economic and political conditions of each separate *phase* of the historical process. . . . It is essential to realize the incontestable truth that a Marxist must take cognizance of real life, of the concrete *realities*, and must not continue to cling to a theory of yesterday. . . ." (Lenin, *Collected Works*, Russ. ed., Vol. XX, pp. 100-101.)

3) The history of the Party further teaches us that unless the petty-bourgeois parties which are active within the ranks of the working class and which push the backward sections of the working class into the arms of the bourgeoisie, thus splitting the unity of the working class, are smashed, the victory of the proletarian revolution is impossible.

The history of our Party is the history of the struggle against the petty-bourgeois parties—the Socialist-Revolutionaries, Mensheviks, Anarchists and nationalists—and of the utter defeat of these parties. If these parties had not been vanquished and driven out of the ranks of the working class, the unity of the working class could not have been achieved; and if the working class had not been united, it would have been impossible to achieve the victory of the proletarian revolution.

If these parties, which at first stood for the preservation of capitalism, and later, after the October Revolution, for the restoration of capitalism, had not been utterly defeated, it would have been impossible to preserve the dictatorship of the proletariat, to defeat the foreign armed intervention, and to build up Socialism.

It cannot be regarded as an accident that all the petty-bourgeois parties, which styled themselves "revolutionary" and "socialist" parties in order to deceive the people—the Socialist-Revolutionaries, Mensheviks, Anarchists and nationalists—became counter-revolutionary parties even before the October Socialist Revolution, and later turned into agents of foreign bourgeois espionage services, into a gang of spies, wreckers, diversionists, assassins and traitors to the country.

"The unity of the proletariat in the epoch of social revolution," Lenin says, "can be achieved only by the extreme revolutionary party of Marxism, and only by a relentless struggle against all other parties." (Lenin, *Collected Works*, Russ. ed., Vol. XXVI, p. 50.)

4) The history of the Party further teaches us that unless the Party of the working class wages an uncompromising struggle against the opportunists within its own ranks, unless it smashes the capitulators in its own midst, it cannot preserve unity and discipline within its ranks, it cannot perform its role of organizer and leader of the proletarian revolution, nor its role as the builder of the new, Socialist society.

The history of the development of the internal life of our Party is the history of the struggle against the opportunist groups within the Party—the "Economists," Mensheviks, Trotskyites, Bukharinites and nationalist deviators—and of the utter defeat of these groups.

The history of our Party teaches us that all these groups of capitulators were in point of fact agents of Menshevism within our Party, the lees and dregs of Menshevism, the continuers of Menshevism. Like the Mensheviks, they acted as vehicles of bourgeois influence among the working class and in the Party. The struggle for the liquidation of these groups within the Party was therefore a continuation of the struggle for the liquidation of Menshevism.

If we had not defeated the "Economists" and the Mensheviks, we could not have built the Party and led the working class to the proletarian revolution.

If we had not defeated the Trotskyites and Bukharinites, we could not have brought about the conditions that are essential for the building of Socialism.

If we had not defeated the nationalist deviators of all shades and colours, we could not have educated the people in the spirit of internationalism, we could not have safeguarded the banner of the great amity of the nations of the U.S.S.R., and we could not have built up the Union of Soviet Socialist Republics.

It may seem to some that the Bolsheviks devoted far too much time to this struggle against the opportunist elements within the Party, that they overrated their importance. But that is altogether wrong. Opportunism in our midst is like an ulcer in a healthy organism, and must not be tolerated. The Party is the leading detachment of the working class, its advanced fortress, its general staff. Sceptics, opportunists, capitulators and traitors cannot be tolerated on the directing staff of the working class. If, while it is carrying on a life and death fight against the bourgeoisie, there are capitulators and traitors on its own staff, within its own fortress, the working class will be caught between two fires, from the front and the rear. Clearly, such a struggle can only end in defeat. The easiest way to capture a fortress is from within. To attain victory, the Party of the working class, its directing staff, its advanced fortress, must first be purged of capitulators, deserters, scabs and traitors.

It cannot be regarded as an accident that the Trotskyites, Bukharinites and nationalist deviators who fought Lenin and the Party ended just as the Menshevik and Socialist-Revolutionary parties did, namely, by becoming agents of fascist espionage services, by turning spies, wreckers, assassins, diversionists and traitors to the country.

"With reformists, Mensheviks, in our ranks," Lenin said, "it is *impossible* to achieve victory in the proletarian revolution, it is *impossible* to retain it. That is obvious in principle, and it has been strikingly confirmed by the experience both of Russia and Hungary. ... In Russia, difficult situations have arisen *many times*, when the Soviet regime would *most certainly* have been overthrown had Mensheviks, reformists and petty-bourgeois democrats remained in our Party...." (Lenin, *Collected Works*, Russ. ed., Vol. XXV, pp. 462-63.)

"Our Party," Comrade Stalin says, "succeeded in creating internal unity and unexampled cohesion of its ranks primarily because it was able in good time to purge itself of the opportunist pollution, because it was able to rid its ranks of the Liquidators, the Mensheviks. Proletarian parties develop and become strong by purging themselves of opportunists and reformists, social-imperialists and social-chauvinists, social-patriots and social-pacifists. The Party becomes strong by purging itself of opportunist elements." (Joseph Stalin, *Leninism*.)

5) The history of the Party further teaches us that a party cannot perform its role as leader of the working class if, carried away by success, it begins to grow conceited, ceases to observe the defects in its work, and fears to acknowledge its mistakes and frankly and honestly to correct them in good time.

A party is invincible if it does not fear criticism and self-criticism, if it does not gloss over the mistakes and defects in its work, if it teaches and educates its cadres by drawing the lessons from the mistakes in Party work, and if it knows how to correct its mistakes in time.

A party perishes if it conceals its mistakes, if it glosses over sore problems, if it covers up its shortcomings by pretending that all is well, if it is intolerant of criticism and self-criticism, if it gives way to self-complacency and vainglory and if it rests on its laurels.

"The attitude of a political party towards its own mistakes," Lenin says, "is one of the most important and surest ways of judging how earnest the party is and how it *in practice* fulfils its obligations towards its *class* and the toiling *masses*. Frankly admitting a mistake, ascertaining the reasons for it, analysing the conditions which led to it, and thoroughly discussing the means of correcting it—that is the earmark of a serious party; that is the way it should perform its duties, that is the way it should educate and train the *class*, and then the *masses*." (Lenin, *Collected Works*, Russ. ed., Vol. XXV, p. 200.) And further:

"All revolutionary parties, which have hitherto perished, did so because they *grew conceited*, failed to see where their strength lay, *and feared to speak of their weaknesses*. But we shall not perish, for we do not fear to speak of our weaknesses and will learn to overcome them." (Lenin, *Collected Works*, Russ. ed., Vol. XXVII, pp. 260-61.)

6) Lastly, the history of the Party teaches us that unless it has wide connections with the masses, unless it constantly strengthens these connections, unless it knows how to hearken to the voice of the masses and understand their urgent needs, unless it is prepared not only to teach the masses, but to learn from the masses, a party of the working class cannot be a real mass party capable of leading the working class millions and all the labouring people.

A party is invincible if it is able, as Lenin says, "to link itself with, to keep in close touch with, and, to a certain extent if you like, to merge with the broadest masses of the toilers—primarily with the proletariat, but also with the non-proletarian toiling masses." (Lenin, *Collected Works*, Russ. ed., Vol. XXV, p. 174.)

A party perishes if it shuts itself up in its narrow party shell, if it severs itself from the masses, if it allows itself to be covered with bureaucratic rust.

"We may take it as the rule," Comrade Stalin says, "that as long as the Bolsheviks maintain connection with the broad masses of the people they will be invincible. And, on the contrary, as soon as the Bolsheviks sever themselves from the masses and lose their connection with them, as soon as they become covered with bureaucratic rust, they will lose all their strength and become a mere cipher.

"In the mythology of the ancient Greeks there was a celebrated hero, Antæus, who, so the legend goes, was the son of Poseidon, god of the seas, and Gæa, goddess of the earth. Antæus was very much attached to the mother who had given birth to him, suckled him and reared him. There was not a hero whom this Antæus did not vanquish. He was regarded as an invincible hero. Wherein lay his strength? It lay in the fact that every time he was hard pressed in a fight with an adversary he would touch the earth, the mother who had given birth to him and suckled him, and that gave him new strength. Yet he had a vulnerable spot—the danger of being detached from the earth in some way or other. His enemies were aware of this weakness and watched for him. One day an enemy appeared who took advantage of this vulnerable spot and vanquished Antæus. This was Hercules. How did Hercules vanquish Antaeus? He lifted him from the earth, kept him suspended in the air, prevented him from touching the earth, and throttled him.

"I think that the Bolsheviks remind us of the hero of Greek

mythology, Antæus. They, like Antæus, are strong because they maintain connection with their mother, the masses, who gave birth to them, suckled them and reared them. And as long as they maintain connection with their mother, with the people, they have every chance of remaining invincible.

"That is the key to the invincibility of Bolshevik leadership." (J. Stalin, *Mastering Bolshevism*, pp. 58-60.)

Such are the chief lessons to be drawn from the historical path traversed by the Bolshevik Party.

GLOSSARY

Decembrists—Revolutionaries of the nobility who were opposed to the autocratic monarchy and serfdom. They organised an unsuccessful revolt in December 1825.

Manilovism—Smug complacency, inactivity, futile daydreaming; from Manilov, a character in Gogol's *Dead Souls*.

Okhrana—Secret political police department in tsarist Russia, formed to combat the revolutionary movement.

Nepman—A private manufacturer, trader, or profiteer in the early period of the New Economic Policy (NEP).

Technical minimum—Minimum level of technical knowledge required of workers in Socialist industry.

Trudoviki—A petty-bourgeois group formed in 1906 consisting of part of the peasant members of the First State Duma headed by Socialist-Revolutionary intellectuals.

Borotbists—Left wing of the Ukrainian Social-Revolutionaries, a chauvinist nationalist party; until 1918 they published a central organ known as *Borotba*.

Zemsky Nachalnik—An official with police, magisterial and administrative functions appointed from the nobility.

Zemsky Sobor—An assembly of representatives of the estates convened in Russia in the sixteenth and seventeenth centuries to deliberate with the government.